MW00780706

THE HORN

THE YALE MUSICAL INSTRUMENT SERIES

Books in this series trace the history and development of a particular instrument or family of instruments from its origins to the present day, with an explicit emphasis on performance practice. Authors are at once leading scholars and acknowledged performers.

Jeremy Montagu TIMPANI AND PERCUSSION
Ardal Powell THE FLUTE
Geoffrey Burgess and Bruce Haynes THE OBOE
Trevor Herbert THE TROMBONE
Eric Hoeprich THE CLARINET
John Wallace and Alexander McGrattan THE TRUMPET
James B. Kopp THE BASSOON
Stephen Cottrell THE SAXOPHONE
David Lasocki and Robert Ehrlich THE RECORDER
Renato Meucci and Gabriele Rocchetti THE HORN

THE YALE MUSICAL INSTRUMENT SERIES

THE HORN

RENATO MEUCCI AND GABRIELE ROCCHETTI

YALE UNIVERSITY PRESS
NEW HAVEN AND LONDON

For information about this and other Yale University Press publications, please contact:
U.S. Office: sales.press@yale.edu   yalebooks.com
Europe Office: sales@yaleup.co.uk   yalebooks.co.uk

Set in Fournier MT by IDSUK (DataConnection) Ltd
Printed in Great Britain by TJ Books, Padstow, Cornwall

Library of Congress Control Number: 2023946547

ISBN 978-0-300-11893-3

A catalogue record for this book is available from the British Library.

10 9 8 7 6 5 4 3 2 1

In memory of William "Bill" Waterhouse
London, 1931–Florence, 2007

CONTENTS

List of Figures ix
List of Musical Examples xviii
List of Tables xxiii
Abbreviations xxiv
Acknowledgments xxvi
Foreword xxvii

PART I

1	Preliminary Note on Roman Military Instruments	3
2	Early Horns and Calls	5
3	The Coiled *Trompe*	8
4	Spiral Instruments	13
5	Early French Hunting Fanfares	19
6	Hooped Models	22
7	Preserved Instruments	30
8	Von Sporck and the *Trompe de Chasse*	42
9	The Natural Hunting Horn (*Jagdwaldhorn*)	49
10	Trumpet and Horn Players	80
11	The Natural Horn at its Zenith (*Orchesterwaldhorn*)	88
12	Duets	109
13	Four Case Studies: Vivaldi, Bach, Handel, Telemann	111
14	Instruments' Names in the Baroque Era	112

PART II

15	The Classic Era	119
16	New Crook Systems	140

CONTENTS

17   The Classical Repertoire   171
18   The Heyday of the Hand Horn   183
19   Transitional Systems   212

PART III

20   Valve Horns   227
21   Further Valve Systems   237
22   Reports by Contemporaries   257
23   Early Music Literature   266
24   Valve Dissemination: A Regional Overview   281
25   A Few Leading Composers   307
26   Double Horn   308
27   The Horn in the Second Half of the Twentieth Century   324
28   The Repertoire of the Second Half of the   331
      Twentieth Century
29   The Present-Day Horn   337

      Bibliography   *340*
      Index   *363*

Readers will find the following online
at http://yalebooks.co.uk/book/9780300118933/
the-horn/
Appendix I. Notation
Appendix II. High vs. Low Horn in Haydn's Symphonies
Appendix III. Two Letters by Blühmel

FIGURES

1. Etruscan *cornu* and *lituus* on a first-century BC funeral relief. L'Aquila, Museo Nazionale inv. OPS 222.

2. Trajan's column in Rome, 113 AD, hindered bucina (left), two *tubae* (center), three *cornua* (below). Cast in Rome, Museo della Civiltà Romana.

3. Mahillon Co., flugelhorn in G-shape ("*buccina*"). Brussels, Musée des instruments de musique, inv. LD0242. ImageStudio © Royal Museums of Art and History, Brussels.

4. Paduan Bible, *ca.* 1400. London, British Library, Ms. Add. 15277, fol. 34r.

5. Anonymous fresco, *Hunting Scene, ca.* 1470. Vigevano, Castle.

6. J. Du Fouilloux, *La Vénerie*, 1561, fol. 32v.

7. M. Praetorius, *Syntagma Musicum*, 1619/20, pl. XXII.

8. J. Fyt and T. Rombouts, *L'ouïe*, before 1637.

9. P. Boel (attrib.), *Trophée de la chasse*, mid-seventeenth century.

10. G. B. Bracelli, *Istrumenti musicali e boscarecci*, 1640s.

11. Coiled *trompe*, seventeenth century. Dresden, Kunstsammlungen, inv. X.179. Staatliche Kunstsammlungen Dresden, Rüstkammer. Photo: Carola Finkenwirth.

12. I. Le Chein, coiled *trompe*, 1604. Museum Hof van Busleyden, Mechelen, inv. VO139, on loan to Antwerp, Museum Vleeshuis.

13. "Villedieu" coiled *trompe*, mid-seventeenth century. Paris, Musée de la Musique, inv. E.132. Photo: Renato Meucci.

14. Jac. Crétien, half-moon horn, second half of the seventeenth century. Paris, Musée de la Musique, inv. E.364. Photo: Thierry Ollivier.

15. C. Dröschel/M. Nagel, small hooped *trompe*, 1647. Graz, Universalmuseum Joanneum GmbH, Kulturhistorische Sammlung, inv. 14.921.

16. H. van Balen, *Diana Having Her Bath*, early seventeenth century, detail. Vercelli, Museo Borgogna.

17. *Ballet de la délivrance de Renaud*, 1617, from *Discours au vray du ballet dansé par le Roy*, Paris, Ballard 1617, table 3.

18. *Neuer . . . abgefertigter Freud- und Friedenbringender Postreuter im Jahr 1648* (New Postal Courier, bringing joy and peace, despatched . . . in 1648), mid-seventeenth century.

19. J. W. Haas, miniature horn, 1681. Vermillion, National Music Museum, inv. 7213. National Music Museum, University of South Dakota. Photo: Mark Olencki.

20. H. Geyer, miniature "parade" horn, 1698. Linz, Oberösterreichisches Landesmuseum, inv. Go 186. OÖ. landes-Kultur GmbH (Oö. Landesmuseum), Musiksammlung. Photo: Alexandra Bruckböck.

21. D. Breitschneider, *Ensemble of Six Hunters Blowing Together*, 1591. Ms. in D-Dl, Mscr.J.9, fol. 86.

22. M. Mersenne 1637, lib. V, 245: *grand cor (AB), cor à plusieurs tours (CD), trompe (EF), huchet (NO), cornet de poste (PO)*.

23. J. Miel, *La curée*, 1659–1661, detail. Venaria Reale, Palace.

24. J. Miel, *Laisser courre*, 1659–1661, detail. Venaria Reale, Palace.

25. M. Sweerts, *Young Hunting Horn Player*, mid-seventeenth century. Private ownership, formerly Galerie Canesso, Paris.

26. A. F. Boudewyns, *Le roy à la chasse au cerf*, engraving after a painting by van der Meulen, *ca.* 1680, detail. Amsterdam, Rijksmuseum inv. RP-P-1907-4962.

27. J. Cotelle le jeune, *Vue du labyrinthe avec Diane et ses nymphes*, ca. 1690, detail. Versailles, Palace, as of pre-1998. From Bouëssée 1979, 88, 89.

28. J. Cotelle le jeune, *Vue du labyrinthe avec Diane et ses nymphes*, ca. 1690, detail. Versailles, Palace, as of pre-1998. From Bouëssée 1979, 88, 89.

29. N. Bonnart, *Gentilhomme sonnant du cor*, 1680–1690. Paris, Bibliothèque nationale de France, VM PHOT MIRI-14.

30. J.-B. Martin, *Vue de l'Orangerie et du Château de Versailles depuis les hauteurs de Satory*, 1696, detail. Versailles, Palace inv. MV750.

31. Hooped *trompe* in Senlis. Musée de la Vénerie, inv. H32.

32. Hooped *trompe*, formerly in Paris, pictured in Morley-Pegge.

33. J. Crétien, hooped *trompe*, Vernon, end of the seventeenth century (?). Private ownership.

34. H. Starck, "French horn," 1667. Copenhagen, Musikhistorisk Museum, inv. F99.

35. G. Fr. Steinmetz, "French horns," after 1693. Berlin, Musikinstrumenten-Museum, inv. 4187, 4188.

36. G. Fr. Steinmetz, "French horn," before 1694. Vermillion, National Music Museum, inv. 4013. National Music Museum, University of South Dakota. Photo: Mark Olencki.

37. C. N. Gijsbrechts, 1671; Jean Raon-Pierre Granier, Versailles, Trianon, 1688; David Téniers le jeune, before 1690.

38. C. Weigel, *Der Trompetenmacher*, 1698.

39. M. Engelbrecht, *Der Trompeten- Posaun- und Waldhornmacher*, 1730–1740.

40. G. B. Curlando, *Hunting Scene, ca.* 1689. Oberschleißheim, Lustheim Palace.

41. *Waldhornisten des sächsischen Hofjägercorps*, February 9, 1697. Dresden, Kupferstichkabinett Dresden, Ca 192, F 43.

42. D. W. Baumgart, Hanover, *ca.* 1690. Hanover, Historisches Museum, inv. VM 048012.

43. H. F. von Fleming 1724, table XXIII, between pp. 160 and 161.

44. "Weigel's widow," *Austrian hautboy Corp*, after 1725.

45. F. Bonanni, *Corno raddoppiato*, 1722, table XVII.

46. J.-B. Oudry, *Louis XV chassant le cerf dans la forêt de Saint Germain.* Toulouse, Musée des Augustins. Photo: Daniel Martin.

47. H. Rigaud (attrib.), M. A. Marquis de Dampierre. Unknown private ownership, formerly the De Brosses collection.

48. J. C. Kirchner, *Statue of Hunting Servant*, 1727–1732. Moritzburg Castle, balustrade.

49. Le Brun, *Trompe "Dauphine,"* 1721. Edinburgh, Music Instruments Museum, inv. no. 2161. Photo: Antonia Reeve.

50. Pettex-Muffat, *Trompe "d'Orleans"* with silver leadpipe and silvered garland, late nineteenth century. Formerly Flachs collection.

51. F. A. de Garsault, *Notionaire, ou mémorial raisonné*, 1761, pl. xxxi.

52. Racines, Bozen, Wolfsthurn Castle, tapestry, 1740 (detail); Palazzo Torri, Nigoline (Brescia, Italy), living room fresco, 1741 (detail).

53. Dresden revels for the wedding of the electoral prince, 1719. Dresden, Kupferstichkabinet, Ca 200, Bd. II, fol. 64 d.

54. L. M. van Loo, *The Family of Philip V*, 1743, detail. Madrid, Prado.

55. Duet players from *New Instructions for the French-Horn*, ca. 1780.

56. Mozart's *Musikalischer Spass*, first edition, 1797.

57. Hampel–Punto, *Méthode, ca.* 1794, 1, range of first and second horns.

58. J. C. Nabholz, *Johann Mareš*, posthumous portrait, St. Petersburg, 1796. After Findeizen 1929, II, 99.

59. O. J. Vandenbroek, *Méthode*, ca. 1797, 14.

60. Vandenbroek, *Méthode*, ca. 1797, first "*main*" (hand).

61. Vandenbroek, *Méthode*, ca. 1797, second "*main*" (hand).

62. Vandenbroek, *Traité général*, after 1803, 3 (*Traité*).

63. The position of the hand in Duvernoy's handbook.

64. J. C. Hofmaster, *ca.* 1750. Edinburgh, Music Instruments Museum; inv. 3297. Photo: Antonia Reeve.

65. Anonymous horn with a set of two master crooks and four crooks, late eighteenth century. Formerly Flachs collection (Flachs 1994, 138, fig. 128).

66. J. G. Haltenhof horn, 1761. Bochum, Musikinstrumentensammlung Grumbt, coll. Grumbt, inv. SG 809. Photo: Renato Meucci.

67. Hampel–Punto, *Seule et Vrai Méthode*, ca. 1794, title page.

68. L. B. Coclers, portrait of horn player Pelting (?) with an *Inventionshorn* similar to the 1776 Haltenhof model. Amsterdam, Rijksmuseum, inv. RP-P-1883-A-7109.

69. J. F. Cormery, *Inventionshorn* with set of crooks. Paris, Musée d'arts et métiers, inv. 01613. © Musée des arts et métiers, Cnam / Photo: Laurence Reibel.

70. Horn by A. Kerner. Florence, Galleria dell'Accademia, inv. 195.

71. J. Kerner, *Inventionshorn*. Musikinstrumentenmuseum der Universität Leipzig, inv. 1686. By kind permission of Musikinstrumentenmuseum der Universität Leipzig.

72. M.-A. Raoux, *Cor solo* with G, F, E, E-flat (on instrument), D crooks, 1826–1827. Formerly the property of Giovanni Puzzi (on loan to Horniman Museum, London, W.83 to E-1926).

73. Schott catalog from 1827, horn section. *Cäcilia* 1827, supplement.

74. Horn by M. Saurle. Privately owned. Photo: G. Rocchetti.

75. Horn by M. Saurle. Nuremberg, MIR 85. Photo: G. Kühnel (Nuremberg).

76. L.-G. Blanchet, alleged portrait of Rodolphe, signed "Rome 1759."

77. L. Gatti, *Nitteti*, libretto. Bologna, Museo internazionale e biblioteca della Musica, Lo.9049, 8.

78. F. A. Rosetti, *Concerto per il Corno Primo e Secondo*, cat. C.61, title page. Harburg, Swabia, Öttingen-Wallersteinsche Bibliothek, RISM 450025477.

79. J. Nagel and F. Zwierzina, silhouette. From "Rosetti-Forum", Heft 14, 2013, 10.

80. Horn mute, eighteenth century. Edinburgh, Music Instruments Museum, inv. 3298. Photo: Raymond Park.

81. Mute for natural horn. From Wirth ca. 1876, 6, fig. iii.

82. "Comma" device by B. Millgrove, *The Monthly Magazine*, November 1797.

83. F. Duvernoy, *Méthode* (1799, 2), mouthpiece models for first and second horns.

84. L. F. Dauprat, *Méthode* (1824, I, 12), proportions of the mouthpieces for *cor alto* and *cor basse*.

85. Vandenbroek, *Méthode*, ca. 1797, 2, range of the *cor du milieu*.

86. Playbill for *Don Juan* in Paris, 1805. From *Le Figaro*, January 8, 1922.

87. Dauprat, *Méthode*, 1824, III, title page.

88. W. Sandbach, invention horn with terminal crooks, Edinburgh, 1810–1830. Edinburgh, Music Instruments Museum, inv. 0203. Photo: Antonia Reeve.

89. P. Toschi, *Portrait of Puzzi*. Fontanellato, Rocca Sanvitale, Sala dei cimeli.

90. Sketches from Porfiryeva–Stepanov art. Kyoò'bel' (Kölbel), Ferdinand (1998).

91. Russian horns, from F. J. Bertuch, *Bildbuch für Kinder*, vol. 6, Weimar, Landes Industrie Comptoir, 1807, 589.

92. Anonymous keyed invention horn, first quarter of the nineteenth century. Basel, Historisches Museum, inv, 1980.2057. © Historisches Museum Basel. Photo: Peter Portner.

93. Fingering table of Bergonzi's horn, after the manuscript table by the same author, by Dick Martz.

94. J.-B. Dupont, omnitonic horn, *ca.* 1818. Paris, Musée de la Musique, inv. E.1017. Photo Claude Germain, 2020.

95. J.-C. Labbaye, omnitonic horn, *ca.* 1820. Paris, Musée de la Musique, inv. E.1016. Photo Thierry Ollivier, 1997.

96. C. Sax, omnitonic horn, 1833. Boston, Museum of Fine Arts, inv. 17.2004.

97. J. Callcott, omnitonic horn, *ca.* 1851. Oxford, Bate Collection, inv. 98.

98. Drawing from the *Repertory of Patent Inventions*, vol. 36, 1820, pl. XVI.

99. *Allgemeine Musikalische Zeitung*, May 3, 1815, cols. 309–310.

100. Tubular and box valves. From Heyde 1987a, 16, 18. Herbert Heyde, *Das Ventilblasinstrument*, BV 225 © 1987 by Breitkopf & Härtel, Wiesbaden.

101. Fingering table. From Heyde 1987a, 19. Herbert Heyde, *Das Ventilblasinstrument*, BV 225 © 1987 by Breitkopf & Härtel, Wiesbaden.

102. F. G. A. Dauverné, *Méthode pour la trompette*, 1857, xxv.

103. Stölzel's price list, from Sundelin 1828b, 48.

104. L. Dall'Asta, horn with two rotary valves, 1822. Bologna, Museo internazionale e biblioteca della Musica, inv. 1847.

105. J. F. Anderst, horn, *ca.* 1820, and butterfly valve

106. Sattler's trumpet, illustration from *AMZ*, 1821, 411.

107. A. Nemetz, *Hornschule*, Vienna, Diabelli, 1829.

108. J. Kail, *Scala für das chromatische Tasten-Waldhorn in F und E*, Prague, Berra, 1831. From Heyde 1987a, 262. Herbert Heyde, *Das Ventilblasinstrument*, BV 225 © 1987 by Breitkopf & Härtel, Wiesbaden.

109. Horn by Uhlmann, 1830, patent, detail. From Heyde 1987a, 298, tab. 44. Herbert Heyde, *Das Ventilblasinstrument*, BV 225 © 1987 by Breitkopf & Härtel, Wiesbaden.

110. Diagram of the Viennese valve from Vermillion, National Music Museum website

111. Erste Wiener Produktive Genossenschaft, Viennese horn with duplicated shanks (B-flat), crooks (A), two sets of valve slides (B-flat or A size), and F crook with original mouthpiece, first quarter of the twentieth century. Photo: G. Rocchetti. http://collections.nmmusd.org/UtleyPages/ Utleyfaq/brassfaqDoublepiston.html

112. Müller's (?) horn with early *Mainzer* machine, 1828–1830. Weber 1835, fig. D, 76.

113. *Neumainzer* machine horn by C. A. Müller. Private ownership.

114. F. Červený, Viennese horn in C alto, 1850–1857. Private ownership. Photo: G. Rocchetti.

115. Trombone, *système belge*. Private ownership. Photo: G. Rocchetti.

116. Rotary valve attributed to Blühmel. From Heyde 1987a, 29. Herbert Heyde, *Das Ventilblasinstrument*, BV 225 © 1987 by Breitkopf & Härtel, Wiesbaden.

117. Diagram of rotary valves from Vermillion, National Music Museum website (http://collections.nmmusd.org/UtleyPages/Utleyfaq/brassfaqRotary. html#stringrotary).

118. Drawing of a non-operating/operating Berlin valve from Vermillion, National Music Museum website (http://collections.nmmusd.org/ UtleyPages/Utleyfaq/brassfaqBerlin.html).

119. Drawing of Périnet valve, top sprung model from Vermillion, National Music Museum website.

120. J. G. Kastner, *Méthode, Fingering scale for the 2-valve horn.* From a rare 1845 Italian edition of his tutor.

121. Goudot jeune, two-valve horn, 1842. Paris, Musée de la Musique inv. E.1251. Photo: Thierry Ollivier, 1998.

122. Two-valve horn, from a rare English version of Gounod's *Méthode* (after Humphries 2000).

123. Ch. Roth, Strasbourg, two-valve horn with E-flat crook, *ca.* 1881. Private ownership. Photo: G. Rocchetti.

124. The horn by Labbaye and the Stölzel box valves imitated by Schuster. Fétis 1827, table between 158–159.

125. F. W. Schuster, horn with square valves, Karlsruhe, *ca.* 1850. Private ownership. Photo: U. Hübner.

126. Dauprat, *Du cor à Pistons*, 1828, title page and p. 5.

127. J. E. Meifred, *Notice sur la fabrication . . .*, 1851, table, partial reproduction.

128. *Valvules* of A. Deshays. From *Description des machine et procédés . . .*, 1834.

129. W. Červený, *Tonwechselmaschine.* From Heyde 1987a, 299, fig. 46. Herbert Heyde, *Das Ventilblasinstrument*, BV 225 © 1987 by Breitkopf & Härtel, Wiesbaden.

130. Meifred, *Première étude raisonnée*, 1829, title page detail. From Mürner 2016.

131. J.-B. Mengal, *Méthode de cor et Cor à pistons*, *ca.* 1840, 50.

132. B. Asioli, *Transunto . . . corno a macchina*, 1840, n.n. plate.

133. Meifred, *Méthode*, 1840, Ii, Halary horn, mechanism detail.

134. Detail of the Halary horn in Historisches Museum Basel, Inv. Nr. 1962.64. Mürner 2016, 232.

135. L. Frontori, *Metodo . . .*, 1849: title page, and p. 4.

136. *Cor sauterelle* by M. A. Raoux, descending third valve, *ca.* 1850. Private ownership. Photo: G. Rocchetti.

137. *Cor sauterelle* by Raoux Millereau, from the *Grande Méthode* by H.-J. Garigue, *ca.* 1888.

138. Uhlmann horn with rotary valves, *ca.* 1874. Private ownership. Photo: G. Rocchetti.

139. Couesnon, "French" horn of 1912 with alternative piston and slide for normal third valve. After Baines.

140. Couesnon, *cor sauterelle*, ascending system, Paris, *ca.* 1900. Private ownership. Photo: G. Rocchetti.

141. Comparative fingering chart for the two "French" horn systems. From Dick Martz's website (http://www.rjmartz.com/horns/Millereau_047/).

142. *Cor d'harmonie, à 3 gros pistons*, from the 1878 Gautrot catalog, No. 309.

143. Fingering chart of Chaussier horn. From Chaussier 1889, ix.

144. C. Mahillon, piston horn, *ca.* 1850. Paris, Musée de la Musique, inv. E.980.2.273. Photo: Thierry Ollivier.

145. Mahillon catalog, 1911, showing that the model was still in production in that year, no. 122.

146. L.-H. Merck, *Méthode pour le cor à 6 pistons indépendants* (*ca.* 1874), fingering table for the horn with six independent piston valves.

147. C. Pace, two Stölzel valve horns. London, Royal College of Music, inv. RCM0164.

148. Raoux-type horns, made by Buffet and retailed by Hays, London, 1912. Courtesy of Dirk Arzig.

149. A. Apparuti, horn with two Stölzel valves, with detail of the valves and added crook. Modena, Museo civico di arte, Inv. SM.52.

150. Riedl horn, from Tosoroni's *Metodo*, 1846.

151. Horn player, from F. Paoli, *Idea del Corno a macchina*, 1849.

152. Horns for right or left hand, from Canti's *Metodo*, 1878.

153. G. B. Cazzani, horn with a semitone valve applied on the tuning slide, before 1912. Private ownership. Photo: G. Rocchetti.

154. A. Romero, *Método de trompa de pistones o cilindros con nociones de la mano*, 1871, title page and introduction on the hand horn.

155. A. Dodworth, *Brass Band School*, 1853, 22.

156. I. Fiske catalog, 1868, new and old rotary valves.

157. Fingering table for a three-valve horn. From Langey 1890.

158. Double horn by E. Kruspe. *Zeitschrift für Instrumentenbau*, 1899–1900, 98.

159. A compensating Raoux horn with a mechanism added in *ca* 1925. Private ownership. Photo: G. Rocchetti.

160. É. Vuillermoz portrayed with a Selmer compensating double horn. Photo: Studio Piaz Paris.

161. Kruspe catalog, 1929, "Horner" model. Courtesy of Dirk Arzig.

162. Kruspe catalog, 1929, "Fritz Kruspe" model. Courtesy of Dirk Arzig.

163. Kruspe catalog, 1935, no. 10 "Walter Kruspe" model. Courtesy of Dirk Arzig.

164. D. Ceccarossi presents his Rampone & Cazzani horn and some LPs to the Museo Nazionale degli Strumenti Musicali in Rome, 1986.

165. Geyer's model horn. From John Ericson's website.

166. O. Tied's patent (Germana Patent 222527). From Dick Martz's website.

167. Knopf compensating horn, from Knopf catalog, *ca.* 1934. From Dick Martz's website.

168. De Prins, "Radio Wonder Hoorn." From Dick Martz's website.

169. G. B. Cazzani, compensating double horn, *ca.* 1920. Private ownership. Photo: G. Rocchetti.

170. L. Sansone five-valve single B-flat horn, *ca.* 1950. From Dick Martz's website.

171. Hand position in the bell, from G. Mariani, *Metodo popolare per corno da caccia, ca.* 1890.

172. F. Schediwy, B-flat/F high double horn, before 1944. Private ownership. Photo: G. Rocchetti.

173. Kalison, Milan, horn mod. L 22 B-flat/F alto. From the firm's catalog of *ca.* 2001.

174. E. Schmid B-flat/E-flat alto horn with additional valve for stopped notes.

175. Schmid, fingering for the B-flat/E-flat alto horn. From *Brass Bulletin*, 1996.

176. Paxman, London, dual-bore compensating triple-descant horn in F/B-flat (and A for stopped notes)/F alto.

177. Alexander, full triple horn, detail of the three-way valve mechanism. From Heyde 1987a, 135. Herbert Heyde, *Das Ventilblasinstrument*, BV 225 © 1987 by Breitkopf & Härtel, Wiesbaden.

178. Schematic of the same instrument's tubing. From Heyde 1987a, 304. Herbert Heyde, *Das Ventilblasinstrument*, BV 225 © 1987 by Breitkopf & Härtel, Wiesbaden.

MUSICAL EXAMPLES

1. C. Caresana, *La Caccia del toro a 5 voci*, 1674 bars 1–6. Napoli, Biblioteca dei Girolamini, Musica manoscritta 164.
2. J. de Cambefort and Jean-Baptiste Boësset, *Le Ballet de la nuit*, 1653, 4th entrée. Paris, Bibliothèque nationale de France, Rés. F.501.
3. Lully, *La Princesse d'Elide*, ms. score. Paris, Bibliothèque nationale de France, Rés.F.531.
4. Lully, *Isis*, Act III, Sc. VI. Paris, Bibliothèque nationale de France, Rés. F.1708, fol. 127v.
5. *Recueil de pièces de viole en musique et en tablature, Relance*, and *Fanfare de veüe*, ca. 1666, c.82r. Washington, Library of Congress, Ms M2.1 T2.17C. Case.
6. J. Kuhnau, *Welt adieu ich bin dein müde*, bars 1–4. Leipzig, Leipziger Stadtbibliothek—Musikbibliothek, RISM 225005061.
7. F. W. Zachow, *Nun aber gibst du, Gott, einen gnädigen Regen*, no. 20, *Corno grosso* in F. Dresden, Sächsische Landesbibliothek, Staats- und Universitätsbibliothek, RISM 211005428.
8. G. Torelli, *Sinfonia*, before 1709, I horn in "Ffaut" (F). Bologna, Archivio musicale della Basilica di San Petronio, Lib.T.2.
9. G. Bononcini, *Sacrificio a Venere*, aria of Timeta "E' un bel contento al cor." Wien, Österreichische Nationalbibliothek, Musiksammlung, Mus.Hs. 18285.
10 & 11. A. D. Philidor, first and second notation, 1705. Versailles, Bibliothèque Municipal, Ms. Mus. 168.
12. J.-B. Morin, *La chasse du cerf*, p. 2.
13. A. Lotti, *Teofane*, Act II, Aria "Sciolgasi, movasi," solo horns in low C, from the full score. Dresden, Sächsische Landesbibliothek—Staats- und Universitätsbibliothek, RISM 212006085.

14. Lotti, *Teofane*, contemporary keyboard transcription of the same aria, with horns transcribed at concert pitch. Dresden, Sächsische Landesbibliothek—Staats- und Universitätsbibliothek, RISM 212006090.

15. J. D. Zelenka, *Capriccio* ZWV 185, first horn (in A). Dresden, Sächsische Landesbibliothek—Staats- und Universitätsbibliothek, RISM 212002994.

16. Handel, *Giulio Cesare*, aria "Va tacito e nascosto," bars 1–5, scoring: hn, I vn, II vn, va, Cesare, bc. London, British Library, fol. 63v., RISM 804002164.

17. G. A. Ristori, *Don Chisciotte*, II mov., *Corno di caccia in F*, bars 8–21. Dresden, Sächsische Landesbibliothek—Staats- und Universitätsbibliothek, RISM 212007651.

18. B. A. Petri, *In diem Johannis Baptistae*. Darmstadt, Universitäts- und Landesbibliothek, Musikabteilung, RISM 450002627.

19. Hasse, *Cleofide*, aria "Cervo al bosco." Dresden, Sächsische Landesbibliothek—Staats- und Universitätsbibliothek, RISM 270000632.

20. Pergolesi, *Salustia*, aria "Odio di figlia altera." Naples, Biblioteca del Conservatorio di Musica San Pietro a Majella, RISM 850008894.

21. Lotti, *Polidoro*, Act III, Choir "Giove ascolta," bars 19–27. Naples, Biblioteca del Conservatorio di Musica San Pietro a Majella, RISM 850008748.

22. L. Vinci, *La caduta dei decemviri*, Act I, Aria "Spietata gelosia," bars 47–53. Naples, Biblioteca del Conservatorio di Musica San Pietro a Majella, 32.4.10.

23. F. Durante, *Abigaile*, excerpt of horn part. From Fröhlich 1834, 6.

24. L. Mozart, *Concerto in Dis à 2 Corni Principali*, I mov. (horns in E-flat). Harburg, Swabia, Öttingen-Wallersteinsche Bibliothek, III 4 1/2 4° 421).

25. Hampel (attr.), *Concerto ex D dur*, Lund J:13, excerpt (horn in D); Pokorny, *Concerto per corno secondo*, excerpt (horn in E-flat). Regensburg, Fürst Thurn und Taxis Hofbibliothek, RISM 450010520.

26. M. Corrette, *La Choisy* XIV, I mov., horn in low C.

27. Rameau, *Les Fêtes de Polymnie*, Act II, Chorus, first horn in G, bars 44ff.

28. F. Barsanti, *Concerto Grosso*, op. 3, no. 4 in D, I mov., bars 21–32.

29. S. Noguera, *Villancico*. València, Archivo del Real Colegio-Seminario del Corpus Christi, Z 2/16.

30. Hampel–Punto, *Méthode*, ca. 1794, 83.

31. J. Mysliveček, *Bellerofonte*, Act II, Sc. 11, Aria "Palesar vorrei col pianto," bars 14–20. Lübeck, Stadtbibliothek, Musikabteilung, RISM 452012196.

32. From V. Roeser, *Essai d'instruction à l'usage de ceux qui composent pour la clarinette et le cor, ca.* 1764, 15.

33. From F. Francoeur, *Diapason général de tous les instruments à vent*, 1772, 44.

34. Gehra/Gehring, *Concerto ex D-Dur*, I mov., bars 82–96. Lund, Universitetsbiblioteket, RISM 190002487.

35. J. C. Trial's "*Ariette.*" From Francoeur 1772, 47.

36. T. Traetta, *Solimano*, aria "Disperata invan mi affanno," solo horn. Mantua, Biblioteca dell'Accademia nazionale virgiliana di scienze lettere e arti, filza VIII, n. 23.

37. N. Jommelli, *Olimpiade*, Act III, Sc. III, scoring: I vn, II vn, I ob, II ob, solo hn (in F), Megacle, bc.

38. Jommelli, *Demofoonte*, Act III, Sc. VI, aria "Odo il suon de' queruli accenti," solo horn in E-flat. Milan, Biblioteca del Conservatorio di Musica G. Verdi, Fondo Noseda.

39. E. R. Duni, *La fée Urgèle*, aria "Ah! Que l'amour."

40. P. Pételard le jeune, *Le plaisir de la campagne*, solo horn (first section).

41. L. Gatti, *Nitteti*, Act II, Sc. 5, aria "Puoi vantar le tue ritorte." Bologna, Museo internazionale e biblioteca della musica di Bologna, FF.99.

42. Mysliveček, *Demetrio*, in comparison with Mozart's Horn Concerto.

43. Mozart, Horn Concerto KV. 412 (386B) / 514 (autograph PL-Kj). Kraków, Biblioteka Jagiellońska, Berol. Mus. ms. autogr. Mozart 412, 417. Used with permission.

44. F. Devienne, *Les Visitandines*, Act II, Sc. II, aria "O toi dont ma mémoire," obbligato horn introduction.

45. F. A. Rosetti, *Concerto Corno Secondo Principale in F*, cat. C.53, solo horn in F, II mov. Harburg, Swabia, Öttingen-Wallersteinsche Bibliothek, RISM 450025474. Used with permission.

46. E. Nappi, *Concerto a corno da caccia*, c. 5r, scoring: solo hn, I vn, II vn, basso. Ancona, Biblioteca comunale Luciano Benincasa, RISM 850012768. Used with permission.

47. Böck brothers, *10 Pièces pour Deux Cors et Basse*, Trio no. 2 two horns in E-flat and bass.

48. Mozart, Duet no. 3 KV. 487 / 496a, autograph in Wien, Gesellschaft der Musikfreunde in Wien, A. 164.

49. Paisiello, *Messe . . . 1804*, "Et incarnatus", full score. Paris, Bibliothèque nationale de France, Rés. *Vma Ms. 867.*

50. J.-F. Lesueur, *Le Triomphe de Trajan*, beginning of the solo for Duvernoy.

51. G. Spontini, *Milton*, horn in F and in E-flat compared. Aafter Delpriori 2007/8, 43–44. Used with permission.

52. Beethoven, Ninth Symphony, III mov., bars 95–97, fourth horn part; the same passage described as a hand horn solo by Berlioz (1843–1844, 174); open sounds marked with circles in Gevaert (1863, 73).

53. Beethoven, *Fidelio*, Leonora's aria. From Gevaert 1885, 209.

54. Beethoven, *Die Ruinen von Athen*, Breitkopf score, 1864, 90.

55. Weber, *Freischütz*, Overture, horns in F and C. Berlin, Staatsbibliothek zu Berlin - Preußischer Kulturbesitz, Musikabteilung, Mus.ms.autogr. Weber, C. M. v. 7. Used with permission.

56. H. Marschner, *Hans Heiling*, Overture.

57. Schubert, Symphony no. 9, beginning of horn solo.

58. Cimarosa, *Li due baroni di rocca azzurra*, first horn solo. Dresden, Sächsische Landesbibliothek—Staats- und Universitätsbibliothek, RISM 270001297.

59. F. Paer, *Agnese*, Uberto's aria, second horn part, Dresden, Sächsische Landesbibliothek—Staats- und Universitätsbibliothek, RISM 270001569.

60. Rossini, *Matilde di Shabran*, solo horn (excerpt).

61. J. S. Mayr, *Né l'un né l'altro*, Milan 1807, horn solo in F, written for Belloli.

62. L. Belloli, *Il labirinto*, Horn Duet no. 18. Milan, Biblioteca del Conservatorio di musica G. Verdi A.36.6.4. Used with permission.

63. Rossini, *Aureliano in Palmira*, horn solo in low C, written for Belloli.

64. Paer, aria and choir with obbligato horn for Mozart's *Clemenza di Tito*, "Se all'Impero amici Dei," Act II, Sc. VIII. Milan, Biblioteca del Conservatorio di musica G. Verdi, PTRMS 26.

65. Mareš's system of alternating two horns pitched in C and E-flat. After Stählin 1770, 190.

66. A. C. Adam, Andante from the Overture of *Die Hamadryaden*, 1840, excerpt. Berlin, Staatsbibliothek zu Berlin - Preußischer Kulturbesitz, Musikabteilung, RISM 452001987.

67. J. F. Halévy, *La Juive*. From Gevaert 1890, 239.

68. J. W. Kalliwoda, *Introduction et Rondo*, excerpt from the solo introduction.

69. Mendelssohn, Symphony no. 3 "Scottish." From Gevaert 1890, 178.

70. Mendelssohn, Symphony no. 3 "Scottish," bars 439ff., horns in (high) A and D.

71. P. Dukas, *Villanelle pour Cor avec accomp.t d'Orchestre ou de Piano*, 1906, horn in F, opening section *"sans les Pistons"* (without valves).

72. R. Vaughan Williams, Symphony no. 3, first horn solo.

73. B. Britten, *Serenade* op 31, "Prologue."

74. O. Messiaen, *Des Canyons aux Étoiles*, VI. "Appel Interstellaire," solo horn.

75. H. Baumann, *Elegia for Naturalhorn*, excerpt.

TABLES

1. Hunting treatises of the sixteenth and seventeenth centuries.
2. High-pitched early "French horns" (up to 1710).
3. A provisional list of early artistic use of the horn, 1700–1715.
4. The Leichamschneiders' known horns.
5. Wenster manuscript.
6. French early editions to 1770.
7. British early editions to 1770.
8. Provisional list of names for the natural horn in baroque times.
9. English system of crooks and couplers.
10. Crooks and couplers of Saurle's horns in Florence.
11. Terminal crooks of a Couturier horn, Lyon, *ca.* 1840.
12. Compositions with solo horn by Mozart.
13. Provisional list of solo compositions written for, or by, Duvernoy.
14. Provisional list of obbligato horn arias, ensemble pieces, and so on in Italian operas.
15. Provisional list of the earliest solo performances with chromatic horn.
16. Handbooks for the valve horn prior to 1850.
17. Remarkable wind quintets up to the 1960s.
18. Some concertos for solo horn and orchestra from 1960 to today.

ABBREVIATIONS

art.	article
b.	born; bar (measure)
ca.	circa
cf.	Lat. *confer*, compare
chap.	chapter
d.	death, died
ed.	edition, -or, -ed
ex.	example, extended
f., ff.	following
fl.	Lat. *floruit*, florished
fn.	footnote
fol., fols.	folio, -s
mod.	model
mov.	movement
ms.	manuscript
n.d.	no date
n.n.	not numbered
no., nos.	number, -s
p., pp.	page, pages
Pl.	Plate number
r.	Lat. *recto*; reigned
repr.	reprint, -ed
sc.	scene
st	semitone
s.v.	Lat. *sub voce*
t	tone

trans.	translated, -tion
v.	Lat. *verso*
vol., vols	volume, -s

MUSICAL INSTRUMENTS (AFTER GROVE)

bc	basso continuo
bn	bassoon
db	double bass
hn	horn
hp	harp
ob	oboe
rec	recorder
va	viola
vc	cello
vn	violin

INSTITUTIONS

BNM	Munich, Bayerisches Nationalmuseum
KHM	Vienna, Kunsthistorisches Museum
MdM	Paris, Musée de la musique
MfA	Boston, Museum of Fine Arts
MiM	Brussels, Musée d'instruments de musique
NMM	Vermillion, National Music Museum

The Appendices and Notes to Parts I, II and III (online) are considered integral to the text. Cross-references 'above', 'below', 'aforementioned', etc. are used accordingly.

ACKNOWLEDGMENTS

During the long preparation of this book, we have incurred debts of gratitude to many people. Among them are: Josep Antoni Alberola Verdú (Valencia), Dirk Arzig (brasstacks.de), Patrizio Barbieri (Rome), Helen Barsby (Berlin), Javier Bonet (Madrid), Cristian Bosc (Chambave, Aosta), Pamela Bromley (Warwick Castle), Stewart Carter (Winston-Salem, NC), Beatrix Darmstädter (Vienna), Giovanni Paolo Di Stefano (Amsterdam), Rainer Egger (Bern), John Ericson (Tempe, AZ), Laura Facchin (Verona), Malcolm Gerrat (London), Brunello Gorla (Milan), Marcel Güntert (Landshut Castle Museum, former director), Win Hüsken (Mechelen), Andreas Jungwirth (Plank am Kamp, Austria), Thomas Kiefer (Germany/Vienna), Douglas Koeppe, Jindřich Kolda (Kuks), Firma Meinl (Munich), Massimo Monti (Rome), Claudio Paradiso (Latina), Francesco Passadore (Vicenza), Paxman Musical Instruments Ltd. (London), Markus Raquet (Nuremberg), Gabriele Rossi Rognoni (London), Richard Seraphinoff (Bloomington, IN), Arian Sheets (Vermillion, SD), Edward Tarr (†), Gaspare Nello Vetro (†), John Wallace (London), and Tereza Žůrková (Prague).

We also emphasize the help given by the following colleagues and advisors: Christian Ahrens (Bochum, Berlin), Luca Alziati (Milan), Allyn Budka (Gattico-Veruno, Italy), Sabine Klaus (Vermillion), Thierry Maniguet (Paris), Richard J. Martz (www.rjmartz.com), Arnold Myers (Edinburgh), and Anneke Scott (London).

Special thanks also go to the colleagues who read part or all of the manuscript and submitted detailed expert comments: Herbert Heyde (New York), Ulrich Hübner (Darmstadt), John Humphries (Epsom, Surrey), Thomas Hiebert (Fresno), and Giorgio Marinello (Turin).

Finally, for their patience, availability, and support, an affectionate thank you goes to those who have been closest to us during the last two decades: Ilaria Pavarani (Parma) e Silvia Bertoletti (Brescia).

Renato Meucci & Gabriele Rocchetti
October 2023

FOREWORD

The authors of this book are a historian, also a hornist in his youth, and a horn professional active as a freelance both in traditional orchestras and in historically informed performance practice. The book is focused on topics that are often out of reach when consulting the web, and concentrates instead on original research and patient analysis of sources. Thus, the space dedicated to the current instrument and to the most recent models is comparatively slim, since the internet allows one today not only to discover almost everything about the contemporary horn and its production (see the online sources listed in the Bibliography as a starting point), but also to debate all the main issues concerning the active practice of the instrument (the website *The Horn Call* would suffice as an example).

The same reasoning prompted us to reject the usual scheme that presents today's instrument first, followed by the historical development of the instrument. After a brief description of the instruments of classical antiquity (*tuba*, *cornu*, *bucina*, *lituus*), the names of which have been reintroduced with different meanings in more recent times, the text focuses on the invention of the horn and on the main stages in the subsequent history of the instrument. It mostly covers major new developments, generally skipping over minor experiments and variations and taking into consideration the fact that in past centuries choices and preferences could vary significantly between different locations, even those very close to one another geographically. In some instances, we summarize information already covered in the most authoritative previous texts, such as Gregory (1961), Fitzpatrick (1970), Morley-Pegge (1973), and Baines (1976), and we direct the reader to those works for more details. In other cases, we distance ourselves from credited opinions by the most respected authors, discussing our position with detailed argumentation.

After the earliest appearances of hooped horns with tapered tubing in 1659–1661 in Turin, Italy (*Musica a corte* 2023), and soon after in Versailles, French sources from 1680 to 1700 consistently show circular instruments with lengths, cylindrical bores, and terminal yards much like a "circular trumpet" (mostly built in Nuremberg, then the main center of trumpet making). In order to avoid the previous term, which may raise some eyebrows, we call all these models "hooped *trompe*," which hopefully effectively renders the concept just as well. Whatever the name, the horn became an instrument in its own right only when, in addition to the hooped body, a new manufacturing process allowed for the introduction of the large flared bell, a feature that gave the instrument a dramatically different sound. This revolutionary innovation may have been the invention of a weapon maker from Hanover, D. W. Baumgart, who most probably devised the so-called gusset. This latter was a structural feature of the new *lieblich-pompeusen Waldhörner*, as Mattheson called them in 1713, a definition that leaves no doubt as to the originality of the instrument's sound after the adoption of the gusset.

A critical decision was our rejection of a notable assertion made by Gerber in 1792. According to Gerber, the *Inventionshorn*, that is, the horn with sliding crooks, was invented by Johann Werner of Dresden in 1755. After a time-consuming investigation and a long debate, we eventually decided to strongly contradict this assumption (while also suggesting a possible reason for this decision). Instead, we attribute this crucial discovery to Johann Gottfried Haltenhof of Hanau some twenty years later.

Another important point where we challenge what has hitherto been taken as fact is that the first inventor of the valves was Friedrich Blühmel and not Heinrich Stölzel. Furthermore, the names of the so-called Stölzel and Blühmel valves should be switched around, although we will continue to use the established terminology because of its accredited and widespread (though mistaken) acceptance.

The decision to leave aside any detailed discussion of acoustics was also difficult. Much progress has been made in this field during recent decades, including some remarkable contributions based on digital engineering research. It seems more prudent to direct expert readers to reference books such as those by Fletcher-Rossing (1998) or Benade (1990), and less expert students to the concise explanations found in all major books on brass instruments and to the many resources available on the internet.

Furthermore, to avoid weighing down the text with information on players who lived in the last century whose biographies and discographies are easily available online, biographical details are limited to a few major figures on whom we concentrated our research and generally contain new information about their respective lives.

We ask readers to forgive a certain focus on Italian topics. The motivation to do so is in no way attributable to our personal backgrounds. Rather, it is that the horn in Italy has never been thoroughly studied, despite the crucial role played by the country in the history of music and, as will be shown, in that of our instrument at various stages too.

The word "falsetto" is also used in this book instead of "factitious" tones (or notes) because it had been used by Praetorius and because it seems to lend itself to a wider meaning than "lipped down notes." The note names generally refer to written pitch and include the appropriate transposing key (however, written pitches are in roman while concert pitches are in italics). We have not included a chapter dedicated to performance practice; rather, plenty of information is scattered throughout the book, according to the development of the instrument.

Further research that, for reasons of space, could not be included in this volume, can be accessed online at http://yalebooks.co.uk/book/9780300118933/ the-horn/. The online repository features comments with insights and curiosities, suggestions for further research and future studies, three appendices, many in-depth case studies on selected composers, as well as figures, tables, and musical examples. To be clear: the figures, musical examples, and tables referenced in the text are consecutively numbered, regardless of their location, either in the book itself or online.

Finally, this book is gratefully dedicated to the memory of a distinguished gentleman whose many talents, both as a musician and as a human being, were accompanied by an in-depth knowledge of musical instruments, as well as by an enlightened and passionate cosmopolitan attitude.

PART I

PART I

1
PRELIMINARY NOTE ON ROMAN MILITARY INSTRUMENTS

Even though the history of the horn properly begins with the appearance of a new instrument used in the royal hunt in the mid-sixteenth century, a quick look backward is needed to clarify the horn's background and the etymology of some Latin words found in the treatises and scores discussed in this book—namely *tuba*, *cornu*, *bucina*, and *lituus*, the names of Roman military instruments.

The *tuba* was straight and made of a brass-like metal. The same material was also used for the *cornu* (horn), which was first made of melted metal bent in a "C" shape and later, beginning with the first century BC, of sheet metal bent in a "G" shape, in both cases with a horizontal brace. The *bucina* was a simple animal horn used primarily to perform signals within the camp. The *lituus*, also made of sheet

Figure 1. Etruscan *cornu* and *lituus* on a first-century BC funeral relief.

Figure 2. Trajan's column in Rome, 113 AD, hindered bucina (left), two *tubae* (center), three *cornua* (below; the third, in the middle of the scene, is hardly distinguishable).

metal and shaped like a long "J," was decommissioned by the military after having been used for centuries in Etruria and Rome. Since the first century AD, the term was only used in poetic language.

However, a late medieval misinterpretation of a passage from *De re militari* by Vegetius (fourth–fifth century AD) in which Roman military instruments are carefully described, led to the reversal of the meanings of the two terms *cornu* and *bucina* (spelled *buccina* in medieval sources), thus paving the way for a long-term misunderstanding (Meucci 1989).[1] (See online, "Buccina—a critical term," and Figure 3 online).

---

[1] Another terminological misuse was made by Friedrich Behn, a pioneer of musical archeology, who, in the early twentieth century, called some metal instruments found in archeological excavations in Central Europe *lituus* (Behn 1912–1913); they were in fact medieval signaling instruments (Tamboer–van Vilsteren 2006).

2
EARLY HORNS AND CALLS

The use of small curved animal horns and their metal counterparts is a remarkable ancient tradition well documented during the Middle Ages (Ebitz 1986). Examples include the "oliphant," said to be used by Roland at Roncesvalles (eighth century),[1] and the horn belonging to St. Francis (1181/2–1226), which he used to gather devotees and can now found in the Assisi monastery. This same function was also documented by Salimbene of Parma (1221–*ca.* 1288), who described a certain friar Benedict "of the *cornetta*" in his *Chronicle*. The latter used a small brass horn that he could play very loudly as well as softly for the same purpose.[2]

Far more precious specimens, which fetch exorbitant prices in the antiquarian market today, were made of finely carved ivory or engraved silver. Examples of the latter include the precious horns received by Francis I of France from manufacturers of Verona and Venice in 1532 and 1537 respectively.[3] Another item, two feet and two inches long, decorated in Rome in 1598 by a celebrated engraver, Filippo Tommasini, was formerly located in Warwick Castle (Hall 1845, 4). An exceptional example is that of the two medieval golden horns found in Gallehus, Southern Jutland, Denmark, in 1639 and in 1734. They were stolen and recast in 1802, but accurate drawings of the horns had previously been made (Brüchle-Janetzky 1976, 61) that allowed for the production of the copies, which are on display at the National Museum in Copenhagen today.

In Britain, a curved model that was small in size (about 25cm) was used—as depicted, for instance, in Michael Drayton's *Poly-olbion* (1612)—until a straight model was introduced for the hunt in the late seventeenth century (Cameron 1905, 6). The

---

[1] A description of the royal hunt during the time of Roland is contained in Kling 1911, 97–98; see also Karstädt 1964, 30–35.

[2] De Adam 1966, 100: "The small horn in copper or brass which he blew with terrifying as well as gentle sounds."

[3] Prunières 1911, 233; see also Laborde 1877/1880, II, 235.

latter was said to emit sounds that were more recognizable of various hunting positions (Baines 1976, 147).

Horns up to about 60cm in length can easily produce a single sound, so for centuries, hunting signals were in fact limited to a single note with rhythmic variation (true "Morse signals," as Karstädt 1964, 39, calls them). However, many experiments to increase the 60cm length by creating an additional loop in the tubing were documented. This allowed for more sounds without increasing the overall size of the instrument.

Before the end of the fourteenth century, the technique of metal tube bending, already known in classical antiquity, had been rediscovered or (re)imported from the Middle East. The metallurgical procedure was promptly applied to trumpet making, thus allowing for S-shaped and folded tubes, which made the instrument easier to handle and carry, and, of course, enhanced the number of notes obtainable (see Figure 4).[4]

Bending tubes of internal conical shapes, such as those necessary for the horns used in the hunt, was much more difficult. An early attempt to that effect is documented on a tapestry made after 1450 (Saumur, Church of Notre-Dame de Nantilly),[5] and in a fresco discovered decades ago in the castle in Vigevano, near Milan (see Figure 5). In both cases, the instruments have strange central helical

Figure 4. Paduan Bible, *ca*. 1400.

[4] In addition to the Padua Bible illuminations, see also Cellesi 1906 on the construction of trumpets in Siena by goldsmiths in the fourteenth and fifteenth centuries.

[5] Reproduction in Lesure 1968, tables 54–55 (drawing in Baines 1976, 149, fig. 26a).

Figure 5. Anonymous fresco, *Hunting Scene*, *ca.* 1470.

coils. Perhaps they are made of a wound metal strip, but they may also be protective coatings made of leather or other materials. At any rate, given the conical profile of the bore, they are the result of a particularly laborious process.

Starting from the mid-sixteenth century, hunting horns were in fact commonly built long enough to produce at least two notes (a number that later increased owing to a proportional lengthening of the tube), thus giving way to the modern tradition of hunting signals first documented by Du Fouilloux in 1561. His seminal book, as well as many subsequent hunting treatises written in French (see Table 1 online), seems to reflect the numerous innovations in hunt signaling and in the use of the horns that took place in France thenceforward.

3
THE COILED *TROMPE*

In Du Fouilloux's book, the new coiled model, the *trompe*, is depicted and described for the first time (see Figure 6), and the author comments on its capacity for producing two different sounds, the higher (*grêle*) used in deer hunting and the lower (*gros*) in that of the boar.[1] This coiled model was mostly used in France,

Figure 6. J. Du Fouilloux, *La Vénerie*, 1561, fol. 32v.

---

[1] Du Fouilloux 1561, chap. 42: "One must play the *gresle*, since it is not appropriate to play the *gros* with the *trompe* in any deer hunting situations"; the term is defined as follows in Serré de Rieux 1734, 284: "*Gresle* is the clear tone of the trompe [. . .], *gros-ton* is its low sound."

where it was probably invented, but also appeared elsewhere—certainly in Turin where it was portrayed by Melchior Hamers (1638–1709/10), a lesser-known Flemish painter active at the Savoy court (*Musica a corte 2023*, tab. 55). It is likely referred to in an inventory of the Medici court in Florence (1587) that mentions "twisted trumpets, French style" (Ferrari 1993, 18). Another probable reference is the entry "trombette da Paris" (trumpets from Paris) in a list of musical instruments belonging to the Milanese collector Ardemanio in 1619 (Toffetti 2004, 55). The coiled model is also depicted, along with other signal instruments, in the *Syntagma Musicum* of Praetorius under the heading *Jägerhörner* (see Figure 7 online).

A different model with a larger coil and rather wide bore is portrayed, for example, in the painting *L'ouïe*, attributed to the Dutch artists Jan Fyt and Theodoor Rombouts (before 1637) (see Figure 8). A similar instrument played in

Figure 8. J. Fyt and T. Rombouts, *L'ouïe*, before 1637.

the same position was depicted some years later by another Dutch painter active in Paris, Jacques Fouquières (1580–1659) (illustrated in Bouëssée 1979, 70). An additional one can be seen in a drawing by Stefano Magnasco (*ca.* 1635–1672/3) located in Florence (illustrated in Brüchle-Janetzky 1976, fig. 33), and again in the *Plan des forêts*, an illuminated manuscript from 1668 by Étienne Compardelle (illustrated in Gétreau 2006, 45, fig. 3). Finally, Pieter Boel (1622–1674), or even his teacher, the same Jan Fyt, painted soon after 1650 an instrument (see Figure 9) quite similar to a specimen preserved in the Musée de la musique in Paris, which we will discuss presently.

A totally different specimen is pictured among a group of etchings from the 1640s, *Figure con strumenti musicali e boscarecci* (Pictures with musical and forest instruments) by Giovan Battista Bracelli, an artist active in Florence and Rome between 1624 and *ca.* 1649 (see Figure 10 online).[2] Although some artistic license has been taken, the horn featured here shows an unusually wide central hoop, which is most likely the reason for the downward grip. Although we treated this etching with marked skepticism for a long time, especially because of its early

Figure 9. P. Boel (attrib.), *Trophée de la chasse*, mid-seventeenth century.

---

[2] Reproduction in Heinitz 1929, table III/1; see also Baines 1976, fig 26b. For a complete reproduction of Bracelli's etchings, with musicological commentary, see Meucci–Ghirardini 2019.

date, we now view this picture as evidence that this type of body had already been experimented with just before the middle of the seventeenth century (see online, "Eclectic representations").

Despite numerous iconographic representations, we have only found a few examples of existing coiled *trompe*. The first, which has a very small coil and a total length of about 50cm, which was probably built in France in the first half of the seventeenth century, is now held in the Kunstsammlungen in Dresden (Heyde 1986, pl. 82) (see Figure 11 online). A second, from 1604 and now in Antwerp, somewhat resembles the instrument portrayed by Fyt and Rombouts (see Figure 12 online).[3] A third, with narrower bore and wider loop, is in turn in the Musée de la musique in Paris (inv. E.132) (see Figure 13). It has a length of about 126cm, a loop that is 22cm in diameter, an overall size of 45cm, and an entirely tapered tube. Although it is not dated, it is likely from the mid-seventeenth century. The "Villedieu" mark and the lilies of France, engraved on both bell and mouthpiece, do, moreover, suggest that this specimen was the result of a royal commission,

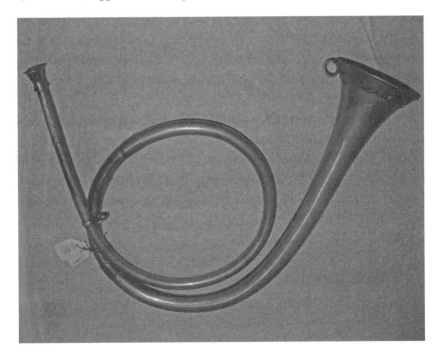

Figure 13. "Villedieu" coiled *trompe*, mid-seventeenth century.

[3] Scale models of these coiled instruments, such as the one from Ambras Castle, which is 7cm long, have also been documented (Schlosser 1920, 100, inv. A.320, table L).

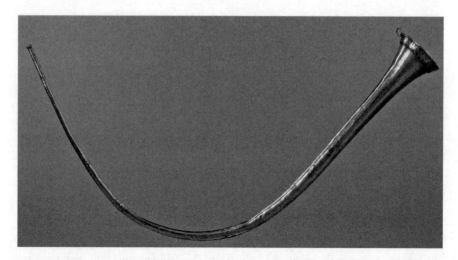

Figure 14. Jac. Crétien, half-moon horn, second half of the seventeenth century.

probably built in the famous foundries of Villedieu-les-poêles in Normandy (see Dupâquier 1969, 984). This item, with its wide, circular, less cumbersome shape, may constitute an elaboration of the half-moon model also built in Villedieu (Flachs 1994, 152, fig. 143; Egger 2006, 365, fig. 2) and also by various members of the Crétien family, originally active in Vernon, Normandy, and later for a long time in Paris (see Figure 14).

Finally, there is the old small-scale instrument (19cm in diameter) built in 1647 in Nuremberg (see Figure 15 online). It bears the mark of Conrad Dröschel, but as Dröschel was already dead by 1644, it was evidently made by his journeyman and successor Nagel (Körner 1969; Stradner 1986, 41). Owing to the lack of evidence that it was conceived for hunting purposes, we conjecture other possible uses for this small item whose complete reliability has, moreover, recently been called into question (Klaus 2012, 154–155).

4
SPIRAL INSTRUMENTS

It is well documented that during the early seventeenth century, while the coiled *trompe* was being developed, a spiral model existed as well. This model was sometimes called a horn (Virdung 1511: *Jeger-horn*), other times a trumpet (Praetorius 1619/20: *Jägertrommet*), and sometimes both names were used interchangeably in the same text (Mersenne 1637, although normally using *cor* for the spiral model and *trompe* for the coiled one, does not avoid a promiscuous use of the two terms).[1] However, this nominal uncertainty seems excusable since a clear distinction between horn and trumpet would become possible only after the eventual differentiation of the two instruments, documented—as we shall see—only toward the late seventeenth century (cf. Klaus 2012, 156).

The first evidence of the spiral model appears in Mantua, Italy, in 1486—therefore much earlier than that of the coiled one. "Two short trumpets made like a snake, to be hung around the neck" were recorded (Canal 1881, 5), a description that could fit an object with concentric circles of metal tubing. In nearby Brescia, a craftsman named Fayta was renowned in the early sixteenth century for several types of instruments that he built, some of which were "snake-like" horns and therefore probably spiral instruments.[2]

---

[1] He seems to assign the term *cor* a more generic value than *trompe*. He refers to the folded trumpet using the name it is called today *trompette*. A discussion of both the terms *cor* and *trompe* is found in Eppelsheim 1961, 140–149.

[2] An obituary written by Pandolfo Nassino (Fayta died during a plague epidemic, on August 27, 1529) states that "he made plenty of instruments for playing, but most of all he made horns in the shape of snakes which in fact lacked nothing but movement" (Brescia, Biblioteca Queriniana, C.1, f. 352).

This model, after rapidly spreading throughout Europe, was promptly abandoned in Italy and France,[3] but remained in use in German-speaking countries for a long time. This is confirmed by numerous written and iconographic sources and preserved specimens from the area between Germany and Bohemia. In Prussia, on the other hand, an instrument of this type was still in use during the mid-eighteenth century (Heyde 1994, 50) (see online, "*Welsche Trompete*").

Of the iconographic evidence of spiral instruments, some paintings are worth mentioning: the famous *Allegory of Hearing* by Jan Brueghel from 1615–1618, and the *Education of Achilles* by Peter Paul Rubens from 1630 (both in the Prado Museum, Madrid), as well as the latter's other paintings related to hunting contexts (Balis 1986). The engravings by Wenzeslaus Hollar (1607–1677) are also noteworthy (Morley-Pegge 1973, 2, pl. I),[4] as well as a little-known painting by Hendrick van Balen (1575–1632), reported by Carlone (1995, 89–90, fig. 153) (see Figure 16).

Figure 16. H. van Balen, *Diana Having Her Bath*, early seventeenth century, detail.

[3] Maricourt 1627 (1858, 135): "In the past there were *trompes* folded five or six times, which were dismissed because they cannot be heard at a great distance in the woods and because they are difficult to play"; cf. Furetière 1690, I, s.v. "Cor," which states that the *cors tortillez*, with eight or nine loops of tubing, are "practically no longer in use."

[4] See also the iconographic examples mentioned by Dahlqvist 1993b, 175–177.

Of the surviving specimens, the oldest is attributed to Valentin Springer of Dresden, *ca.* 1570 (Heyde 1986, pl. 86); another, built in Dresden as well, was made before 1668 (Heyde 1986, pl. 87); a third, built by Johann Wilhelm Haas of Nuremberg in 1688 is in the Trompetenmuseum, Bad Säckingen (Tarr 1986); finally, the one built by Pfeifer of Leipzig in 1697 disappeared during World War II (Menke 1934, 200; Heyde 1985, 116–117, pl. 1; Dahlqvist 1993b, 178).[5]

This same spiral model, which Mersenne called a *cor à plusieurs tours* and stated was already in decline in France in his time (1637), made at least one appearance in the French ballet repertoire of the early seventeenth century. It was carried onto the stage by the "*démon de la chasse*" in the *Ballet de la délivrance de Renaud*, 1617 (Christout 1967, 158) (see Figure 17 online).

IMPERIAL TRUMPETERS' PRIVILEGES

The spiral trumpet survived in German countries far longer than elsewhere. This is most likely because, in a large Germanic area, the group of people who were permitted to use the folded trumpet was strictly limited to members of the guild of court and field trumpeters. Municipal and other players were forbidden to play the instrument, so many tried to replace it with alternative models.

The prohibition was established by an imperial privilege of 1623 in favor of the aforementioned brotherhood of trumpeters. The measure was revived with some modifications in 1630, 1653, and 1706, and was reaffirmed by the Kings of Saxony and Poland with edicts (*Mandaten*) issued with slight variations on at least three occasions (1661, 1711, 1736), thus documenting, it seems, how common breaches of these rigid rules were.[6] The Saxon decree of 1661 stated that military use of the court trumpet was reserved to members of the brotherhood of art (*Kunstverwandte*) and that the instrument could not be replaced using "trombones in the manner of trumpets," a transgression that occurred, for example, in 1673 and 1702 in the cities of Altenburg and Meiningen respectively (Michel 1975, 139). The Edict of 1711 also forbade the replacement of trumpets with "horns in the manner of trumpets," as well as with the so-called invention trumpets, that is, the many

---

[5] An appealing variant is the "Allgäuische Waldhorn" (natural horn of the Allgäu region), a sort of wooden alphorn folded in a spiral shape, which dates back to the sixteenth century (Vienna, KHM A.281).

[6] For careful consideration of these rules, see Altenburg 1973, 38–85, as well as Tarr 2001 with the English translation of the *Mandat* of 1736; an English version of the imperial Edict of 1653 is found in Smithers 1971.

fancy forms encountered with these instruments (probably including the famous item built for Cesare Bendinelli in 1595 by Anton Schnitzer, which is preserved in Verona).[7]

That the spiral model was considered to be a true substitute of the trumpet is confirmed by its description in the entry "Trumpeter" of the monumental encyclopedia published in Saxony around the mid-century under the editorship of Johann Heinrich Zedler (1745, 1105). Furthermore, spiral instruments, both preserved or documented, turn out to be pitched in D or C, that is, the traditional keys of the trumpet (for the item portrayed in the hands of Gottfried Reiche, see Heyde 1987c, and Dahlqvist 1993b, 175).

The aforementioned Edict of 1711 may also have been the result of a lively dispute between two trumpeters of the Weimar court over a student who had first agreed an apprenticeship with one of them and then switched to another (Ahrens 2015, 57–76). To settle the dispute, a judgment was requested from no less than the prorector of the University of Jena (Michel 1975, 140; cf. Ahrens 2015, 90–96). The petition is related, as it seems, to an unusual dissertation discussed at that university by candidate lawyer Christian Gantzland, which was also published in 1711. In this study, written in Latin with many phrases and words in German, unique consideration is given to the rights and role of Saxon trumpeters and the use of trumpet substitutes was strongly discouraged (see online, "Gantzland or Wildvogel?").

THE POST HORN

In 1494, Emperor Maximilian I made the decision to entrust the management of the imperial mail to the nobleman Francesco de Tassis (1459–1517), whose family came from an Italian village not far from Bergamo, now called Camerata Cornello. Tassis was the founder of the modern postal service, and his name has become famous worldwide through the word "taxi."

The imperial privilege was the source of a centuries-long conflict between the Tassis family (which later became Thurn und Taxis) and various authorities, municipalities, and guilds that claimed similar rights, but in 1614, the Tassis family prevailed (Kalmus 1937, 178–179). Tassis equipped its postilions with a simple animal horn or a metal copy of the same, which was necessary to announce the mailmen's arrival. By the end of the sixteenth century, however, a new miniature

---

[7] On "invention trumpets" (*Inventionstrompeten*), see Klaus 2012, 84–85.

coiled model was adopted, at least in German countries. Praetorius probably refers to an imitation of the latter shape, and to the spiral trumpet as well, in the following passage (1619, II, 33): "Some have trumpets built like post horns or wound around like a snake" (*etliche lassen die Trummeten / gleich einem Posthorn / oder wie eine Schlange zusammen gewunden / fertigen*).

Before the mid-seventeenth century, the use of this small model by mail carriers was also documented in iconographic sources, including an illustration from just after the Thirty Years War (1648), when many European routes were eventually reopened (see Figure 18 online). Another illustration of these tiny instruments is also found in Weigel's famous book, published in 1698, in which a *Trompetenmacher* (trumpet maker) is portrayed with the results of his work, including post horns. According to the accompanying text, the post horns were "too well-known everywhere for there to be a need to describe them" (see Figure 38, p. 36).

A miniature horn from 1681, an artifact of wonderful workmanship, bears a remarkable resemblance to these items. It was created by the founder of the most famous Nuremberg workshop, Johann Wilhelm Haas, 1649–1723 (Vermillion, NMM, inv. 7213) (see Figure 19 online). It was probably a gift commemorating the birth of his son and future successor Wolf Wilhelm and, like similar small items, was probably intended more for decoration than for practical use (cf. Klaus 2012, 147–153).

A specimen with a somewhat larger coil, lavishly decorated but also quite small, dates back to 1698 and was made by the Viennese maker Hans Geyer, demonstrating that this appealing "parade" model had successfully made its way to Vienna (Heinzl 1976, 244, fig. 15) (see Figure 20 online).[8] Some twenty years later, an interesting report related to the pomp and pageantry surrounding the wedding of Frederick Augustus II (Dresden, 1719), heir to the throne of Saxony, to the daughter of the Emperor Joseph I, Maria Josefa, likely also refers to a small object of this type: "Viennese silver horns were given particular prominence, and the superintendent of the mail service, the chamber nobleman Baron von Mordaxt, who from 1709 also served as 'Director of Pleasures,' was commended for having exhibited a post horn of solid gold decorated with precious stones" (Becker-Glauch 1951, 101).

---

[8] For the subsequent history of the post horn, we refer readers to Hiller 2000, who also deals with the use of this instrument in art music.

For a long time, the usual features of the post horn, at least in German countries, were the minimal ones just described. Only later, when the hooped horn was invented, was the latter's shape reproduced in smaller dimensions for the mailmen's convenience. This novel format, destined to become the symbol of the postal service almost everywhere, dates back therefore merely to the early eighteenth century, the period of the oldest known surviving specimens. An experimental forerunner, however, may possibly be the 1647 miniature hooped *trompe* by Dröschel/Nagel (see Chapter 3).

5

EARLY FRENCH HUNTING FANFARES

Signals played by several small horns in unison have been documented since the end of the sixteenth century (see D. Bretschneider's engraving from 1591, reproduced in Blaut 1999, fig. 12 (see Figure 21 online), and the painting *The Animal Baiting*, from 1609, in Brüchle-Janetzky 1976, 72). They could hardly go beyond a thunderous roar in unison. A few decades later, however, we find the first evidence of a multiphonic piece performed in hunting ceremonies by a horn ensemble (see Figure 22 online). In 1637, after describing the models in use in France at his time, Mersenne refers to fanfares played by a consort of hunting horns of different sizes and models, which were of course in the same key (lib. V, 247):

> If hunters wish to have the pleasure of giving concerts in four or more parts with their horns, it is fairly easy, provided they know how to produce the right tones and how to properly proportion the length and width of their horns so that they maintain the same relations as the organ pipes. For example, if the largest *cor* is six feet long, it will sound a fifth lower than the one which is four feet long (I will explain later whether their width should also be in the ratio of 3/2); and if one adds a third *cor* three feet long, it will sound a fourth higher than the second one, so that the three instruments will form a perfect trio and will play the three main tones of the first mode. To these, it will be easy to add three or four more to play the other chords.

Given the measurements reported,[1] these instruments were pitched in 6' F, in 4' C, and in 3' F, and therefore were all short and capable of producing very few sounds. They gave way, however, to the adoption of hunting signals with more elaborated

---

[1] Here and henceforth, the reference is not strictly to the modern value (30.48cm). The foot unit once varied considerably from city to city, although not deviating too far from the one mentioned.

melodic lines than those previously heard. This was obviously obtained by using longer tubes, which allowed additional pitches from the harmonic series— particularly those that make up the major triad. So, if the ancient French signals for the sighting of the deer reported by Du Fouilloux (1561, Chap. 42, p. 115) and Mersenne (1637, 270) consisted of three long notes, three short notes, and one long note, the introduction of new models allowed for the transformation of such rhythmic sounds in a true, though simple, melody.

The earliest notated evidence of this repertoire of hunting signals is in *Recueil de pièces de viole en musique et en tablature*, a manuscript from around 1666 that contains music for viol and also twenty-five hunting signals covering the range from the third to the eighth harmonics.[2] They are written with syllables put on a staff in place of the notes, while another staff shows the transcription into measured notation (see Appendix I online). It is probably the exercise of a student who, for personal practice, wrote down these signals and their embellishments. These included the breath vibrato (notes linked with a slur), *Bebung* or *Schwebung* in German (Altenburg 1795, 94), which was typical of the eighteenth century and has remained in use in the *trompe* tradition up until the present day.

The appropriate time for these elaborated performances was the *curée*, the hounds' meal during the break of the hunt, which was usually accompanied by cheerful polyphonic fanfares intended to entertain. A vivid description is found in Salnove (1655, 166–168), as summarized by Dunoyer (1868, II, 399):

> The *curée* was always done with great solemnity. The King or the chief hunter attended and played the *trompe* as well as all the assistants, and every one had to take off their gloves or risk seeing them confiscated by the *valets de chiens* (dogs' stewards).

The first known horn virtuoso, Livet or Olivet, was also active during this period. La Borde (1780, III, 517) talked about him in connection with the French hunt during the reign of Louis XIII (1610–1643): "Livet played the horn under the reign of Louis XIII better than anyone else before him. He particularly excelled at fanfare performances." In more or less the same period, there was also an equally spectacular *trompe* virtuoso, the Marshal of France, François de Bassompierre

---

[2] Washington Library, Ms. M2.1.T2 17C (case); published in Cheney 1998 (see also Cheney 2008). The manuscript also mentions the Parisian address of the maker Jacques Crétien.

(1579–1646). A friend of the same Louis XIII, he was evidently not inferior to Livet in the performance of hunting calls, and also in the performance of other stunts, such as drinking from his boot filled with wine (*Encyclopediana* 1791, 164).

It was likely from ensemble performances, in which the royal highnesses personally participated, that the fanfare repertoire for two or more horns, which would become the typical repertoire for these instruments during hunting expeditions, was derived.

6
HOOPED MODELS

It is now time to introduce in detail the design that gave way to the modern history of the instrument, the "hooped" *trompe* proper. Almost the entire length of the instrument's tubing was bent into a wide circle (say, at least 30cm in diameter), which made up the body of the instrument, leaving only the mouthpipe and the end of the bell-yard outside.

The first appearance of this model is documented in Turin, which is located in the northwestern part of Italy, but in a context strongly influenced by France and by French hunting traditions. Because of this, it is also possible that the specimens used there were made by local artisans of the Vicco family (Meucci 2023, 187). This new model was promptly introduced also in the French hunt, and then its main center of production was moved, as it seems, to Nuremberg.

HORNS AT VENARIA REALE (TURIN)

That the hooped horn was promptly adopted in the mounted hunt is made clear by a series of iconographic sources related to the Italian court with the closest ties to France: the Savoy court in their capital, Turin, where the palace and hunting ground of Venaria Reale is located. Designed and described by the architect Amedeo Cognengo of Castellamonte (1613–1683), the manor house was commissioned by the Duke Charles Emmanuel II (1634–1675), and construction began in 1658 (Castellamonte 1674). Here, the earliest evidence of a circular *trompe* is constituted by a series of paintings from 1659–1661 by Jan Miel (1599–1663), one of which portrays the *curée* (the hounds' meal) accompanied by the sound of the instruments. These instruments were also called *"gran trombe ritorte"* (large twisted trumpets; see also p. 44), a term that is also encountered in a ballet performed in Turin in 1660 on the occasion of the wedding of Margaret Yolande, Charles Emmanuel's sister, to the duke of Parma (*L'unione per la peregrina Margherita reale e celeste*, Turin, 1660, 8).

Figures 23 & 24. J. Miel, *La curée*, detail (above); *Laisser courre*, detail (below), 1659–1661.

The powerful mother of Charles Emmanuel and Margaret Yolande, Christine of France (1606–1663) was the sister of the French king Louis XIII. This relationship explains the close connection between the two courts of Turin and Paris as well as the practice of horseback hunting in the Savoy realm, a tradition otherwise uncustomary in Italy. From Venaria Reale, the new fashion for hooped horns soon traveled back in the opposite direction (toward France), since these novel instruments certainly proved to be of utmost effectiveness in the mounted hunt while also allowing for a larger number of different sounds than the coiled ones.

There is no conclusive evidence to indicate that the horns were supplied to Venaria by local artisans. However, at least one member of a dynasty of *pajuolai* or *chaudronniers* (caldron makers and coppersmiths) that later in the century would supply horns to the hunting crew of Venaria Reale was already in service of the court of Savoy at the beginning of the seventeenth century. The coppersmith Carlo Pantaleone Vicco (1610?–1678) was working in this craft during the very years in which Miel portrayed the new model of the instrument (1659–1663) (see Odling-Girodo 1999–2000, repr. 2023). In addition, there is no evidence of any contemporary production abroad of horns with the aforementioned characteristics (neither in France, nor in Nuremberg, where this type was never built).

Whatever the case, the wide circular shape seen in Venaria was soon adopted in Versailles as well. Cardinal Flavio Chigi, papal legate to the court of France, provided evidence that likely indicates this. In his diary, he recorded that he attended a *curée* of the hounds in Versailles in 1664 during which some twisted trumpets ("*alcune trombe ritorte*") attracted his attention (Lionnet 1996, 147) (see also online, "A typical Italian performance technique?" and Figure 25 online).

HOOPED "*TROMPE*" IN VERSAILLES

The usefulness of a hooped instrument in the hunt was promptly recognized at the French court. Here, some substantial innovation took place: An even wider circular shape was developed and the instruments in Versailles, apart from some transitional instances, soon assumed features similar to Nuremberg trumpets bent in a circular shape.

An engraving from circa 1680 by Adriaen Frans Boudewyns (Bouëssée 1979, 36, who attributed it to R. Bonnart) is the oldest known iconographic evidence that documents the use of a hooped horn in France similar to those in Turin, with the later customary posture of using one arm for support (see Figure 26 online). A slightly later painting (1688–1691) by Jean Cotelle le jeune, *Vue du labyrinthe avec Diane et ses nymphes* (see Figure 28), in addition to portraying a small hooped instrument of this kind and the old crescent model (the former was replaced with a second half-moon item in a restoration of 1998), also shows a new type of horn with a larger central body suggesting an approximate pitch of high F (6 feet) (see Figure 27). Incidentally, all three items show a similarly flaring bell.

Figures 27 & 28. J. Cotelle le jeune, *Vue du labyrinthe avec Diane et ses nymphes*, *ca.* 1690, two details.

Another instrument is clearly depicted in a portrait engraved by Nicolas Bonnart, entitled *Gentilhomme sonnant du cor*, which dates back to 1680–1690 and shows what may be a high C (8-feet) instrument that is very similar to a trumpet folded in a circular shape (see Figure 29). A similar specimen is depicted in a high relief on the facade of the Versailles Palace dated 1687 (Bouëssée 1979, 80), as well as in a painting by Jean-Baptiste Martin (1659–1735) titled *Vue perspective du château de Versailles sur la place d'armes et les écuries* circa 1688 (reproduced in Bouëssée 1979, 37). The *Vue de l'Orangerie et du Château de Versailles depuis les hauteurs de Satory*, also by Martin, is slightly later and speaks for itself. Dating back to 1696, it shows a hooped instrument with its harness, in this case played by a rider on horseback (see Figure 30).

In conclusion, while mounted hunting was imported to the Savoy court under the influence of the customs and traditions of the French court, once the utility and convenience of the hooped instrument seen at Venaria Reale (Turin) had been demonstrated, it was promptly adopted in the French royal hunt. But, given the massive number of instruments needed for the sportsmen in Versailles, some orders were probably sent to Nuremberg, giving way to the manufacture of a sort of circular trumpet) (see online, "Looking for instruments in Nuremberg?").

THE GERMAN PATH

Modern researchers had previously taken it for granted that the circular model was not only common, but was also invented and developed in the French capital. This thesis was first proposed by Gerber (1792, 547), although some authors writing shortly after him did raise doubts about this.[1]

Recently, new evidence has been presented that explains how, in order to avoid the vexations imposed by the Saxon trumpeters, a hooped instrument may also have been devised in Germany (most likely in Thuringia).[2] In addition to the

---

[1] Cf. Koch 1802, col. 766: "According to some opinions, the horn was invented in Paris in around 1680, but this invention could not be anything other than a mere improvement"; Lipowsky 1811, 26: "The Horn (Corno di caccia) is said to have been invented about the year 1680 in Paris"; Schilling 1835–1838, III, 634: "Someone in Paris (who?) first came to the idea of bending the long tube of the horn in 1680."

[2] Confirmation also comes from Domnich's 1807 method, p. ii, according to which the large hooped instrument appeared for the first time in Germany in the middle of the seventeenth century. Cf. Fröhlich 1834, 5.

Figure 29. N. Bonnart, *Gentilhomme sonnant du cor*, 1680–1690.

Figure 30. J.-B. Martin, *Vue de l'Orangerie et du Château de Versailles depuis les hauteurs de Satory*, 1696, detail.

discussion found in Meucci (2006), the following testimony is also relevant (Schneider, 1834, 34, fn.):

> As for the origin of the horn, another story has also been handed down, which may be partially rooted in imagination. The peasants of Thuringia frequently used the trumpets for entertainment, a fact that their sovereign expressly forbade because the trumpets were to be played only in the presence of highly ranked individuals. The farmers therefore brought the trumpets to each other and bent them in circular shape, thus creating horns—if the *fabula* is true. However, the cause of this prohibition certainly corresponds to the spirit of the time: until not long prior, kettledrums could only be played in the presence

of the upper class, when a "doctor" or a person of rank was attending, as it was then said. Nowadays, anyone who wishes can play the timpani for pleasure or passion.

This testimony – quoted also in Rossmann 1866, 3 – is far from fanciful, as demonstrated by the aforementioned articles of the Saxon *Mandaten* prohibiting the use of the trumpet by non-members of the guild—particularly the 1711 article that explicitly forbade *Waldhörner* and "other instruments arranged in the manner of trumpets."

It therefore does not seem overly bold to consider these circular instruments (or "horns in the manner of trumpets") to be replacements for the prohibited folded ones, which nevertheless preserved the main sounding features of the trumpet proper. This is confirmed in the text by Gantzland quoted above (Chapter 4, p. 16). He states that the *cornu sylvestre*, or *Waldhorn*, "equals the trumpet in sonority, so that, if not a skilled professional, one can hardly distinguish the former from the latter" (Gantzland 1711, 12).

The circular model, once demonstrated efficiently in French royal hunting parties, may, in fact, have given way to a massive demand for refined items, a demand that could be met by the Nuremberg makers. Weigel (1698, 232), referring to the craftsmen of this city, says, "*Die heut zu Tag gewöhnliche Arbeit der Trompeter-Macher sind meistens Trumpets / Trombones / Wald- und Posthörner*" (The instruments produced by today's trumpet makers are mainly trumpets, trombones, natural and post horns).

As the Crétiens seemed to be the sole Parisian manufacturers by the close of the seventeenth century,[3] while they could have partially met the enormous demand for new hunting horns at the turn of the century, it would have been likely some instruments were also produced by the multitude of makers in Nuremberg. A clue regarding this twofold production is a difference in shape between a more conical and tapered profile on the one hand and a more cylindrical one on the other (not to mention the higher workmanship of the Nuremberg production). Instrument manufacture in Villedieu, on the contrary, likely did not play any significant role after its inspiring beginning.

---

[3] Two Raoux horns cited in Rühlmann 1870, now located in Munich, are more recent than the date reported by the writer, 1703, which—incidentally—does not appear on the instruments themselves.

7

PRESERVED INSTRUMENTS

The oldest surviving examples agree with that which has been described thus far; dating back to the second half of the seventeenth century and the first years of the following one, they are mostly pitched in a size matching that of the trumpets, and as far as we know, they were almost all made in Nuremberg, with few exceptions.

In fact, one of the oldest specimens is an instrument by an anonymous maker, currently held at the Musée de la Vénerie of Senlis, not far from Chantilly, which may not come from Nuremberg; it has a total length of 227cm, a 12mm bore, a body that is 48cm in diameter, and a 14.5cm-wide bell reinforced by a decorative garland, and most likely pitched between high C and D (Bouëssée 1979, 35, 84 with figure) (see Figure 31). This instrument, presented to the museum by the commander Gaston De Marolles, is, in our opinion, the same one reproduced in Morley-Pegge (1973, table II/1), and which Marolles reported to have been the property of Mlle Stéphanie Frilloux in Paris (Marolles 1930, 39, fig. 11) (see Figure 32).

One specimen that certainly came from France is a Crétien hooped *trompe*. The instrument has two and a half loops and is the only known such model made by one of the Crétien family members. The horn recently passed through the antiquarian market (Vichy, April 7, 2018) and comes from the Samovault collection. It bears a circular inscription on the garland with the name JEHAN CHRESTIEN a Vernon around a deer and a fleur-de-lys that suggests that it may have been the result of a royal commission (see Figure 33 online). According to the family tree reconstructed by Corinne Vaast (2015, 183), only two members of the family bore this name. The first Jean is the son of the founder of the dynasty (Raulin Chrestian I) of whom no further biographical information is known but who may have worked, like his brother Jacques I, who settled in Paris, until the end of the seventeenth century. We know just as little about the second Jean Crétien, but he likely lived in Paris until the early eighteenth century. The place reported on the mark, Vernon, suggests that it was the former Jean who built the instrument) (see online, "New research on the Crétiens").

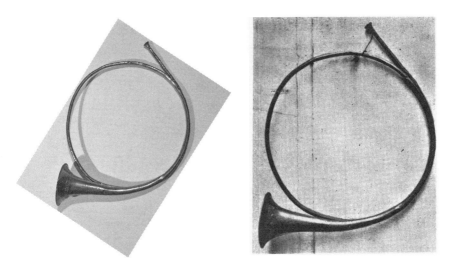

Figures 31 & 32. Hooped *trompe* in Senlis, Musée de la Vénerie, inv. H32 (left) and the one formerly in Paris (right), pictured in Morley-Pegge (note the small dent where mouthpipe and hoop overlap and the embossed scallop shells all around the bell's garland, barely visible from the photo).

The oldest hooped *trompe* surely built in Nuremberg is instead a 1667 instrument by Hieronimus Starck (Copenhagen, Musikhistorisk Museum, inv. F99) (see Figure 34 online). This type may be called *"französisches Waldhorn,"* or "French horn" (!), according to the sources reported below (see Chapter 8, p. 45). Equipped with rings for the belt, it is still entirely in its original condition, apart from a leadpipe that might originally have been a little longer; the tubing, 190cm long, forms a hoop that is 33cm in diameter with a 9mm initial bore, a cylindrical shape, and a final 10cm-wide bell, matching that of contemporary trumpets. Its length is about the 6 feet mentioned by Mersenne for *le plus grand cor*, to which this hooped model could be a convenient alternative. A circular instrument by Johann Carl Kodisch from 1684 in the Utley collection is of a similar high pitch (6' F), as is another by Wolf W. Haas in the same collection (Klaus 2012, 153–154).

Other specimens in D (7'), C (8'), or B-flat (9')—the most usual pitches of the trumpet (the difference could depend also on pitch standards)—are listed in Table 2 (online). Most of them have a receiver allowing for the insertion of a trumpet mouthpiece, while tubing is wrapped in one or, more often, in two loops. This is the case for two pairs built in Nuremberg, by Fr. G. Steinmetz after 1693 (Berlin, Musical Instrument Museum, inv. 4187 and 4188) (see Figure 35) and by J. F. Ehe,

Figure 35. G. Fr. Steinmetz, "French horns," after 1693.

after 1707 respectively (Salzburg, Museum Carolino-Augusteum, inv. 24.1 and 24.2). A similar instrument, undated and marked by W. W. Haas, is located in Basel (Historisches Museum, inv. 1980.2118); another by J. L. Ehe is privately owned in Munich, Bavaria (http://www.ewaldmeinl.de/bhornen.htm).

Additional Nuremberg specimens have a body formed up by as much as three and a half loops of tubing. They include one from 1694, not in its original condition, by Johann Wilhelm Haas (1649–1723), which is held in Paris (MdM, inv. E.1454); another, to be restored, is held in Milan (Castello Sforzesco, inv. 878) and has a mark and bell dimensions that imply that it was made by the son of the former, Wolf Wilhelm, or even his nephew, Ernst Johann Conrad Haas. The aforementioned pair of hooped *trompes* by F. Ehe (Museum Carolino-Augusteum, Salzburg) also have two crooks, like those that were used to tune trumpets and trombones since at least Praetorius's time (1619/20, pl. VIII) (see Table 2 online).

Such a long list was necessary in order to emphasize the central role played by Nuremberg in producing high-pitched instruments with trumpet-like tubing and to corroborate another assertion by Gantzland. Indeed, while remarking that one could hardly distinguish the sound of horn and trumpet from each other, he adds that in those days, the horn was already being built with one, two, or three loops (Gantzland 1711, 12), as demonstrated by Table 2 (online) (see also Weigel 1698, 233) (see online, "A crucial passage by Gantzland"). On the coeval ambiguity between the terms "horn" and "trumpet," and the use of "horns in the manner of trumpets," see Ahrens (2023) and Rocchetti (2023a) (the latter mostly dedicated to the circulation of the opening hunting signal of Bach's first Brandenburg concert).

UNUSUAL WRAPS

Attempts to build hooped *trompes* with a different arrangements of the tubing are documented, for example, by an engraving by Sébastien Leclerc (1670) after a drawing by Charles Le Brun (1664) entitled *Allégorie de l'air* (Gétreau 2006, 47, fig. 4e); here, amidst many other models, one is depicted with two intertwined loops, not unlike the rings of the Olympic flag; a similar wrap is pictured by Weigel (1698, "Der Trompentenmacher"), in this case with inner loops that are not interlocking (see Figure 38, p. 36).

Another shape with loops on the same plane, possibly inspired by the spiral trumpet, is depicted by Cornelius Gijsbrechts (*ca.* 1630–*ca.* 1675) in his still life *Hunting Equipment on a Wall* from 1671 (Copenhagen, Statens Museum for Kunst, inv. 3065). It is also reproduced in Versailles in two high reliefs on the external walls of the buildings, the entrance courtyard of the Grandes Ecuries (1681) and a window of the Trianon (1688) (Bouëssée 1979, 81), as well as in a hunting scene painted by David Téniers le jeune, who died in 1690 (Brüchle-Janetzky 1988, 42) (see Figure 37 online). One such instrument was made before 1694 by Fr. G. Steinmetz in Nuremberg (see Figure 36).

MANUFACTURING PROCEDURES

Today, it is common knowledge that brass is an alloy of copper and zinc. This awareness dates back, however, only to the end of the seventeenth century; it was then that zinc was recognized as a chemical element, and only after its commercialization in around 1740 was it used to produce brass (Hachenberg 1992, 229). A similar brass-like metal had previously been obtained, and it was known for millennia as a "colored" variety of copper, not an alloy of two elements. To obtain that variety, copper was added with "calamine," a mineral that, during a casting process called "cementification," made the copper much more suitable and

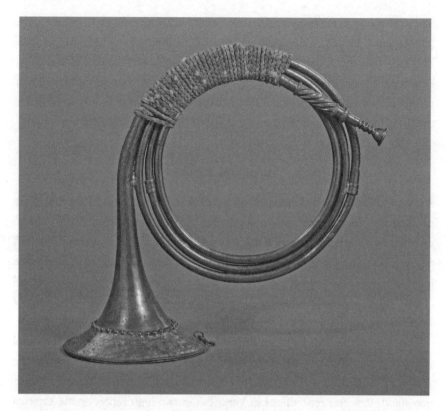

Figure 36. G. Fr. Steinmetz, "French horn," before 1694.

easier to melt, to work, and to weld. The mineral also turned it yellow. The quality or the purity of the metal available to the artisans could vary according to the quantity of scraps it contained, and in some cases this caused serious problems in the manufacturing of musical instruments (Hachenberg 1992, 240).

According to a description in Halle (1764, 372), instrument makers made use of sheets of brass (*Latunmessing*) that were numbered 8 or 9 (contemporary trade numbering). These were 6 feet long, 18 inches wide (approx. 180 x 45cm), and "the thickness of music paper." The sheets were obtained after a long and demanding procedure reported in detail in a manuscript written by the master smelter Marcus Fulda (1689–1734), who inspected and described three German foundries in 1715, one of which was located in Nuremberg (Hachenberg 2006).[1]

---

[1] A further biographical study on Fulda was published by Hachenberg and Helmut Ullwer in 2005, while both edited the complete edition of the manuscript (Hachenberg–Ullwer 2013).

According to this valuable description, melting 250 pounds of yellow copper produced four plates that each weighed 62.5 pounds and had a thickness of 6.6mm and a surface area of about 550cm^2. From each of the aforementioned plates, strips with a width of 3.3–10.6cm, depending on what they were to be used for (rolling or drawing), were cut. These strips were then annealed and stretched lengthwise by hammering them on an anvil adapted for the purpose. This invariably took four or five processing cycles (each cycle consisted of hammering, annealing, and smearing the metal with tallow or linseed oil). They were eventually flattened with a water-powered hammer, and the cycle was repeated until an even plain sheet was created. Flattening was also performed in several cycles. Some fifteen to twenty cycles were required from the initial cast plate to the strip of maximum width (i.e. the one with minimum thickness). During flattening, much care was taken to prevent impurities in the metal. For this reason, each anvil had bellows emitting a jet of air to keep out dust and debris.

According to Fulda, from the thickness of 6.6mm cited previously, twenty-one different widths of sheet were obtained, from 21.2cm to a maximum of 34.5cm. The actual thickness is not reported by Fulda, but from his data we could estimate a minimum value of about 1.2mm, even though for some uses (e.g. instrument making), further thinning was evidently possible (see Hachenberg 2006, 438, fn. 8). This case is confirmed by Halle, who makes reference to sheets of 45cm in width and of "music paper thickness" (i.e. about 0.4–0.5mm).

Metal sheets were sold in rolls (in wrapped bundles) or folded into packages. Half a ton of "long and wide metal plate, Vienna standard, without impurities" cost 59 thalers in Salzburg in 1715; half a ton of "pure and fine metal wire" 70 thalers. For comparison's sake, the annual salary of a master smelter rose to about 70 thalers in Salzburg at the time. This shows how costly the metal was with respect to the work involved (Hachenberg 2006, 437–438).

In order to create the main tubes of the instrument, the metal sheet was cut longitudinally and wrapped around a cast iron rod of the required size, with the two flaps pulled close together. Then, the longitudinal seam was brazed with hard solder, usually silver, beaten with a wood hammer in order to even out the surface, and eventually polished.

The main concern for the makers was, however, the construction of the bell. In order to obtain the required flare, they cut the metal sheet in the form of an upside-down goblet (hanging from the belt in Engelbrecht's engraving: see Figure 39) and then wrapped it on a mold of wood or iron corresponding to the desired shape. In this case, one of the two flaps was teethed and the other inserted between the indents in order to make the joint more solid. On the anvil or on another appropriate tool, the junction was then soldered and hammered until the teeth almost disappeared (the operation shown in Weigel's picture: see Figure 38) (see online, "The limitations of brass sheets").

Another challenging operation for the builders was the bending of the tube in order to give the desired shape to the instrument. For this operation, molten lead was poured into the tubing and left to consolidate. Then the piece was folded around a wooden shape corresponding to the desired curve. Any possible wrinkle

Figure 38. C. Weigel, *Der Trompetenmacher*, 1698.

C. P. Maÿ.   Mart Engelbrecht excud. A.V.

Faiseur de Trompettes, etc. **Trompeten Posaun u. Waldhornmacher.**
*1. Cor de chasse. 1. Waldhorn. 2. Trompettes. 2. Trompeten. 3. planche de laiton. 3. Messinges Blech. 4. devidoir 4. der Haspel. 5. et
ceaux à courte coupe. 5. eine kleine Scher. 6. maillet. 6. hölzerner Hamer. 7. force. 7. eine grosse Scher. 8. chef d'oeuvre de trompete. 8. ein Haupt-
stuk vo der Trompete. 9. un pot de fer blanc. 9. ein Blech Kanlen. 10. les ailes du devidoir. 10. die wellen vo. Haspel. 11. rasinoir pour fer. 11. Zieh-
eisen. 12. montant du fer blanc. 12. Betrag blech. 13. cuillere à jetter en moule. 13. giesslöffel. 14. les pinces. 14. Zangen. 15. chaudiere à fondre.
15. der schmelz Kessel. 16. barre de fer. 16. Eiserne stange. 17. pot pour la fonte. 17. giesstiegel. 18. Etcau. 18. schrausstoble. 19. pincettes. 19. Zanglein.
20. Enclume. 20. Anbos. 21. pied de l'enclume. 21. Anb. suss. 22. coin a former les tromp. 22. Keil wo die Trom. darüber geschl. werd. 23. trompet. 23. Po-
saune. 24. cornet de poste. 24. Posthorn.*

Figure 39. M. Engelbrecht, *Der Trompeten- Posaun- und Waldhornmacher*, 1730–1740.

created during the folding process was gently beaten with a hammer, and the piece was eventually warmed at a low temperature so that the lead on the inside would drip out (Barclay 1992, 140–145). Other procedures (joining individual parts, decoration, garnishes, engravings, etc.) did not pose any technical problems, except of course that of the desired quality of the final piece of work, which in Nuremberg was frequently very high.[2]

A hundred years later, when the main European production center had moved to Vienna, a similar manufacturing process, although with more elaborate procedures and new processing systems (including the one invented in 1820 by Labbaye Jr. for bending tubes without using lead), is reported by Keeß 1830, II, 3–4.

EARLY USE IN THE ORCHESTRA

Hunting signals may have been included in the oldest works of the Italian musical theater, such as in the "Hunters' Chorus" in the comedy *Il rapimento di Cefalo* (Florence, 1600); in the "musical play" *La caccia* (The hunt), which was written for a feast in Turin on September 27, 1620 (Solerti 1904, III, 24, and I, 140 respectively); possibly in *Bacco trionfante dell'Indie*, an "eclogue and pastoral hunt" performed on the occasion of the birthday of Charles Emmanuel I of Savoy in Rome on January 22, 1624; or in a *Caccia teatrale* (Theatrical hunt) performed in 1632 in Turin (Ménestrier 1681, 322 and 325). However, the music of these plays has been irretrievably lost, and one cannot be sure, from a musical point of view, how the hunting calls may have been reproduced.

Another example could be the opera *Erminia sul Giordano* by Michelangelo Rossi (Rome, 1633), which is considered to be the earliest work requiring the instrument in the orchestra (Karstädt in MGG1, vol. III, col. 745). However, even though a scene in the libretto is headed "Hunters' Chorus" (Goldschmidt 1901, I, 67; Fitzpatrick 1970, 5, fn. 1), the printed score (Rome 1637) does not include hunting signals identifiable as such.

The well-known "hunting call" in *Le nozze di Teti e di Peleo* by Francesco Cavalli (1639) is a piece that was supposed to imitate the sound of a horn band like the one described by Mersenne (Morley-Pegge 1973, 79–80). However, it should

---

[2] For a general description of the materials and ancient methods used for building musical instruments, see Heide 1991; a practical handbook on baroque trumpet construction is contained in Barclay 1992.

be remarked that this music is written for a string quintet (cf. Baines 1976, 150), with parts modified or transposed by an octave in order to keep them within the staff, as was common in music notation in order to avoid ledger lines.

We would also draw readers' attention to the autograph score of *La Caccia del toro a 5 voci con violini per la nascita di Nostro Signore* (1674) by Cristoforo Caresana (1640–1709), in which the hunting signals, with voices in addition to strings, show considerable similarities to those by Cavalli (see Musical example 1 online).

In short, the hypothesis that Italy was the first country to adopt the use of the horn as an orchestral instrument must be rejected. At most, Italy was the first to depict hunting signals and fanfares using string instruments. It would instead be more fruitful to direct our attention toward France, and to the Paris court in particular, where, according to Prunières (1914, 185):

> In the *Fées des forests de Saint-Germain* (The fairies of the forests of St. Germain), rustic hunters arrive "dancing a ballet to the song of their horns (*cors*)" and, approaching the model representing music, "take the lutes hang around their farthingale . . . dancing another ballet to the sweet songs of their voices and lutes." Other times, musicians settle for going around the room while playing their instruments.

The ballet *Fées des forests de Saint-Germain* was performed on February 11, 1625, and this description could thus document one of the first actual appearances of the horn on the French theatrical scene, at that date a half-moon horn in all probability.

HORNS ON THE STAGE

Of much greater importance to our narration is, however, the presence of the instrument in *Le Ballet de la nuit*, composed by Jean de Cambefort and Jean-Baptiste Boësset, perhaps with a contribution by Jean-Baptiste Lully. The ballet was staged on February 23, 1653 (Ménestrier 1682, 258) and is cited by Castil-Blaze (1856, 72) with the title *La Cour de miracles*.[3] The libretto (F-Pn, Rés. Yf-1212, p. 8) reads, "Six Hunters tired and fatigued, and that the Night calls to the rest, arrive sounding their horns," thus also documenting the number of players. The music, preserved in a collection by Philidor aîné (F-Pn, Rés.F.501), contains

---

[3] On court ballets during the time of Louis XIV, see Christout 1967.

Musical example 2. J. de Cambefort and Jean-Baptiste Boësset, *Le Ballet de la nuit*, 1653, 4th entrée.

a short signal entrusted to the "premier dessus" and based on harmonics four to ten (bars 1–6). Though scored for a string instrument, using French notation (see Appendix I online), it is also an early example of a call entirely playable on a large hooped horn (the key is G, requiring an instrument of around 157cm) (see Musical example 2).

The initial appearance of the instrument on stage, in dance performances at the French royal court, does remind us of the relevance of the hunting tradition to the highest French aristocracy. Several kings of France (e.g. Louis XI, Francis I, Charles IX, Louis XIII), besides being experienced hunters, were also horn players and dancers,[4] which explains the timely admission of the instrument, the symbol of the hunt, into the French royal ballet and operatic tradition.

The first occurrence of hooped horns proper was long considered to have occurred in this same context, in a comédie-ballet by Lully entitled *La Princesse d'Elide*, which was performed in Versailles in 1664 at the inauguration of the renovated palace. The score, preserved in the same collection (F-Pn, Rés.F.531, see Musical example 3 online), contains the *Air des valets des chiens et des chasseurs avec Cors de chasse*, and the libretto (p. 29) explicitly mentions both *cors* (at that

---

[4] See Bassompierre 1703, II, 90–91. Of the modern studies, see Carré 1937, 12, 15, 23.

time probably half-moon-shaped models) and *trompes de chasse* (most probably hooped horns):

> Lyciscas rose with all the effort in the world and started shouting with all his might, several *cors* and *trompes de chasse* were heard, and concerting with the violins began the air of an entrée, to which six valets danced with great accuracy and style, resuming at certain cadenzas the sound of their horns and trompes.

The instruments are still only used on stage where, according to the libretto, dancers playing the valets alternate dancing and playing the instruments "at certain cadenzas." What is unique here is that, for the first time, they are "concerting with the violins," certainly playing by heart. Several scholars have instead considered the fanfare-like parts of the orchestra to be genuine writing for horns, thus introducing far-fetched explanations of their unusually large compass, but this is another imitation of hunting instruments by a string ensemble (Baines 1976, 150–151).[5]

A similar imitation of hunting instruments by the string section is found in Lully's *Isis* (Paris, 1677). In Act III, Scene VI, the "Courons à la chasse" chorus is punctuated several times by an intervention of string instruments that imitate a fanfare in five parts (F-Pn, Rés. F.1708, fols. 124v–128v) (see Musical example 4 online).

One may also observe that these signals are particularly similar to the eighth and ninth calls ("*relance*" and "*fanfare de veüe*") from the *Recueil de pièces de viole en musique et en tablature*, the manuscript mentioned in Chapter 5 from circa 1666 (see Musical example 5 online).

---

[5] In this regard, we must rectify what we wrote in *Grove* 2001, s.v. "Horn," where it is stated that the earliest documentation of the hooped horn is provided by an engraving by Israël Silvestre (*Les plaisirs de l'Isle enchantée, ca.* 1676). This engraving in fact dates back to a later German publication.

8

VON SPORCK AND THE *TROMPE DE CHASSE*

Beyond the Rhine, hunting was traditionally practiced on foot and at fixed positions. It was only with Count von Sporck's famous trip to Paris and his sudden infatuation with the French royal chase, played on horseback, that this type of hunting was introduced in the German countries.[1]

Count Franz Anton von Sporck (1662–1738) was the son of an imperial cavalry commander who accumulated a fortune with his victories in the Thirty Years War and against the Turks. After the commander's death, his still seventeen-year-old son took over the administration of the immense family estate. Before beginning, however, he had to conclude his cultural training with the "grand tour," a journey throughout European capitals, like every highborn young man from Germany. He began the trip in 1680 and, after a return to home, resumed it in 1682. While visiting Italy, France, England, Holland, and Germany, von Sporck increased his knowledge of every field of art history and literature, as well as theater, music, and opera (Nettl 1953). The young nobleman also pursued religious ideals, as made apparent by his affiliation with the Jansenist movement—a decision that later resulted in a heresy charge and an overwhelming amount of trouble (Benedikt 1923, 29–31, 190–216).

One very important stop in his journey was Versailles, which had been recently transformed, under the orders of the "Sun King" Louis XIV, into the most lavish royal residence in Europe. There, von Sporck was especially struck by the ceremony of the deer hunt and the use of the *trompes*, and left behind two of his servants to learn the instrument (Gerber 1792, 547). On their return, these men became the founders of the Bohemian horn school, destined to play a key role in the development of the European horn-playing tradition. According to various

[1] Some discontentment with the new hunting customs was documented, among others, by Fleming (1719) and still later by Döbel (1746, III, 105), who both speak with regret of the good old days when metal hunting horns were ignored (cf. Paul 1976, 47).

sources, they were Wenzel Sweda (Svída) (*ca.* 1638–*ca.* 1710) and Peter Röllig (*ca.* 1650–1723) (see online, "For Czech researchers . . .").

Von Sporck also deserves credit, it seems, for the beginning of the instrument-making tradition in Bohemia: circa 1720, he commissioned horns "like the ones used in France" from a certain Wiesczeck (Vischek) of Prague (Quoika 1956, 71, fn. 161).

HUNTSMEN AND "VIRTUOUS" BEHAVIOR

Hunting and hunting ceremonies constituted an unavoidable commitment in the life of the most prominent personalities of the time. This activity was in fact used as a way to promote the ideas of courage, chivalry, and nobility, which had been exalted by the aristocracy since the Middle Ages, as summarized in the German concept of *Tugend* (virtue and bravery).

After von Sporck's eventual return, Bohemia, Austria, and the entire empire were soon acquainted with the French hunting practice. This sport assumed such a high status that the starting signal was usually given by a "lord," and every participant had to have his own *Waldhorn* around his shoulder, under penalty of exclusion from the ceremony. Thus, the ability to play the instrument became at least as important to those men as their hunting skills.

The same count founded a new order of chivalry dedicated to St. Hubert, the patron saint of hunters, in 1695. Many years later, on November 3, 1723, he had the honor of awarding this distinction to the Emperor Charles VI, when the latter visited Bohemia in order to be crowned king of that nation. Later on, von Sporck also gave the same qualification to various other people, and the Order of St. Hubert lasted until 1938, when it was forcibly abolished by the Nazis. It was re-established on an international scale in 1950 (http://www.iosh-usa.com/about-us/history-of-the-order).

The nobleman not only introduced the instrument in the hunt, however. He encouraged its acceptance in Bohemian music venues as well.

This, and much more information on the early dissemination of the horn in the East German countries, is thoroughly discussed in Horace Fitzpatrick's *The Horn and Horn-Playing and the Austro-Bohemian Tradition from 1680 to 1830*. We cite this text countless times in this book, and it is also relevant owing to its ability to evoke the aristocratic environment in which the horn took its first and decisive steps in music history. Aside from this incomparable merit, however, we should nevertheless warn the reader about several exaggerations and many misprints in the text, which have also been pointed out by various reviewers.[2]

As for the musical side of the instrument, however, we believe that the role of the count has been overestimated in the past and should actually be reconsidered and scaled down, as will become apparent next.

THE *TROMPE DE CHASSE* AT MUNICH

The French mounted hunt and the *trompe de chasse* were soon also adopted at the court of Bavaria in Munich. This may be explained by the fact that the Elector of Bavaria, Ferdinand Maria, had married Henriette Adelaide of Savoy (1636–1676), a member of the reigning house of Turin and Venaria Reale and the sister of Charles Emmanuel II and Margaret Yolande of Savoy (see also Chapter 6, p. 22).

The presence of an ensemble of *trompes* at the Munich court is documented as early as 1662, the year that Crown Prince Maximilian Emanuel II was born (Ménestrier 1669, 47):

> At the Carrousel of Bavaria of the year 1662, as the procession started parading from a huge tower, it began with an awful harmony of extraordinary *trompes*, similar to those given to the Furies of Hell (. . .).

Sei trombe ritorte (six twisted trumpets) are also mentioned in the libretto (p. 17) of the *Antiopa giustificata* by di P. P. Bissari, music (lost) by J. C. Kerll, represented in 1662 on same occasion. Further evidence of *trompes* in Munich is found in the diaries of the ambassador of Parma, Federico Pallavicino, who also visited the court in 1662. In the royal cabinet he saw "three *olicorni*, two about three '*braccia*' (arms) and one four '*piedi*' (feet) long."[3]

The term *olicorni*—which is unlike any other used in this period—refers to the Greek ὅλος (entirely in itself), thus possibly alluding to a hooped or a spiral shape. It is the measurements that interest us, however, since the synonymous *braccia* and *piedi* used in Parma at the time were about 55cm (Martini 1883, 507). Thus, the first two *olicorni* (three "*braccia*") would measure more than 165cm, corresponding to

---

[2] For example, see reviews of the book by A. Baines, "Music and Letters," 52/4 (1971), 438–441; K. Polk, "Notes," 2nd ser., 28/2 (1971), 226–227; and J. H. Wheeler, *GSJ*, 25 (1972), 139–141.

[3] Parma, State Archives, *Carteggio Farnesiano Estero*, Busta 3, Baviera, fol. 5r.

the surviving Starck horn in Copenhagen from 1667 (6½ ft), or the Kodisch in Basel from 1684 (6 ft); the third instrument (four "*piedi*") was in turn a bit less than 220cm (*ca.* 7 ft), like the two Steinmetz horns now located in Berlin (*ca.* 1693).

The close dynastic ties between Munich and Turin were prolonged during the reign of the aforementioned Maximilian Emanuel II (r. 1679–1726). This explains the presence of the Turinese painter Giovanni Battista Curlando (*ca.* 1650–1710) at the Bavarian court. In circa 1689, Curlando decorated the Lustheim palace in Oberschleißheim. There, he portrayed Maximilian with some hunters, three of whom are holding large hooped instruments whose bells are unfortunately hidden from view (http://www.pizka.de/gansp.html) (see Figure 40 online). In the painting, the Elector's brother, Joseph Clemens, also appears, dressed in red, with a hunting horn next to the Ganspöck brothers—Johann Caspar (died 1741) and Matthias (died 1730)—who, according to information in Pizka (1986, 140–141), would have been in the service of the prince since at least 1706/7. In 1717, they were sent to Paris, presumably to increase their repertoire of hunting signals.

"FRANZÖSISCHE WALDHÖRNER"

What has been said on the early emergence of the horn in Munich (Bavaria) may also apply to other European courts, where the presence of the instrument seems to depend on the direct relationships with Paris more than on von Sporck's disseminating role. Apart from the compositions discussed in the next section, "Early scores," which include parts for *trombae breves* that were "also called French" (see Janowka 1701), we can observe that in German and East European sources this geographical appellation is found even before the memorable date of 1682, thus unveiling other possible routes through which the instrument may have spread.

At least two occurrences have been noted by Ahrens (2005), the first in a hunting textbook from 1670, whose author, Johann Christoph Lorber, makes a neat distinction between the simple signal horn ("*Hifthorn*") and the *Waldhorn*, much probably a hooped *trompe*. The second and more significant report, by Gabriel Tzschimmer, describes an official meeting in 1678 between the Elector of Saxony, Johann Georg II, and his brother in Dresden; here, during the banquet that followed the hunt, "the hunters performed with their French and other horns" (*mit Französischen Wald- und anderen Hörnern*) (see also Ahrens 2014, 91, fns. 29 and 30).

The existence of this difference seems further supported by a 1702 inventory found in Moravia at the court of Leopold Ernst Gellhorn, Count of Blansko, which mentions "3 französische Waldhörner," making a clear difference between these instruments and the model that was called "Waldhorn" elsewhere (Freemanová 2006, 216). Moreover, four large "französische Waldhörner" built by "Trompetenmacher" Jan Gayer (Geier) of Vienna (fl. *ca.* 1659–1698) were purchased by Prince Leopold Ignaz von Dietrichstein in 1700 (Žůrková 2023, 66).

The "French" descriptor found in German sources prior to 1682 thus questions the idea, often found in previous literature, that von Sporck was the only patron of the horn in Bohemian and German countries.

EARLY SCORES

In some cases—independently, as it seems, from von Sporck's two servants sent (or left) to learn the instrument in Versailles—the hooped *trompe* made its entry into art music in the not too distant Moravian country.

The first occurrence is in an anonymous *Sonata da caccia con un cornu* (RISM 550265365),[4] preserved in Kroměříž (Moravia) and copied after 1670 by Pavel Vejvanovský (*ca.* 1640–1693), a composer and trumpeter who was active there for more than thirty years (Meyer 1956, 394). It was formerly attributed to Johann Heinrich Schmeltzer (1620/3–1680), as noted by Baines (1976, 143), who also reports a short excerpt; here an 8-foot C instrument is used in a solo role, performing signal tunes with the accompaniment of two violins, two violas, and continuo. Brewer (2011, 178–179), neglecting the attribution to Schmeltzer (and thus the dating before 1680, year of the latter's death), drew attention instead to two alternative versions of the horn part: one lower (and easier) written in alto clef (fol. 2r), and one higher notated in French treble clef (with *g'* as bottom line and lowest note of the horn as well) (fol. 2v).[5] He also remarks that the way both versions were notated, rather than the traditional staff notation, exploits the lines to indicate the different harmonic sounds, as in a sort of tablature (see also Appendix I online, "Preorchestral notation"). However, Schmeltzer deserves to be cited also for composing a ballet dedicated to Diana—included in the comedy

[4] An identification number is used for each RISM catalog item.
[5] The French violin clef was commonly used by French composers during the seventeenth and eighteenth centuries in order to keep alto register instruments within the staff as much as possible (see online, Appendix I).

Die vermeinte Brueder- und Schwesterlibe (1680, Ms. in A-Wn Mus.Hs. 16588)—performed by a violin band and a hunting horn (Marcaletti 2023, 24–26). Lacking a music part explicitly written for the latter, this probably doubled the strings, which play a melody mostly made out of the harmonic series, with autonomous interventions. An imitation of the horn by the violin band, as in ballet music at Versailles, is also encountered in the aria "Diana nim gschwind," in the short opera *Die ßiben Alter stimben ʒu ßamben* (Prague, 1680) once again with music by Schmeltzer (Marcaletti 2023, 25–27).

Another early example also comes from Vejvanovský, whose *Sonata venatoria* (Hunting sonata) from 1684 calls for *2 Clarini seu Trombae breves* (RISM 550264961). The latter term, meaning "short" trumpets, has been cautiously interpreted as a spiral trumpet (Baines 1976, 143; see also Smithers 1971, 189), also because Vejvanovský calls the ordinary trumpet *tuba campestris* (Latin for *Feldtrompete*) (see online, "A source on *'trombae breves'"*). However, the name *trombae breves*, which is also found with some alternative spellings (Dahlqvist 1993a, 32–33), could fit the early hooped *trompe* too. Actually, the oldest surviving items of the latter model (the mentioned Starck 1667 and Kodisch 1684) are very short in length (barely over 6 ft) and date back to the period when Vejvanovský was active.[6] They could therefore constitute an example of the "French" trumpet mentioned in both Weigel (1698, 232) and Janowka (1701, 315) (see also Altenburg 1795, 11). Identifying this instrument as the hooped *trompe* is a tentative assumption indeed, but one that seems nevertheless worth evaluating, given the increasing contemporary vogue of French *trompes*.

In addition, we should mention *I trionfi del fato* by Agostino Steffani (Hanover 1695), which, according to Carse (1925, 109, mus. ex. 35), contains a march that requires a group of *"trompes"*: the preserved scores (GB-Lbl and D-Hs), however, clearly point to a trumpet ensemble with accompanying timpani.

Another score that was for many years thought to be written for early horns is the Concerto à 4. Corne de Casse [*sic*], Posthorn, 2 violini and basso continuo by a certain Ursinus (RISM 240005186). It was attributed to the German writer and composer Johann Beer (1655–1700), whose name was often Latinized as "Ursinus" (bear) (Kade 1893, I, 130–131). However, Reine Dahlqvist demonstrated that the

---

[6] Two *trombae breves* are also called for in his *Offertorio pro omni tempore* (1687, RISM 550264936) and in two *Sonata à 5*: The first, undated but written after 1680 (RISM 550264951), calls for "*2 Clarini Trombae breves*"; the other, dated 1689 (RISM 550264953), calls for *2 Trombae breves* even though the separate parts are for two "clarino in D."

preserved parts (Schwerin, Landesbibliothek) were created much later by a copyist, Johann Peter Fick, who died in 1743. Thus, the author is probably Andreas Friedrich Ursinus (1694–1781), the organist at Tønder in Denmark (Dahlqvist 1994, 145–154). In this composition, both horn and post horn are written alternately on the same staff (an excerpt is found in Baines 1976, 155), therefore possibly indicating that a single performer had to switch from one instrument to another. The presence of another concerto for two horns and two post horns in the same library (RISM 240001532) with an opening melody that matches the previous piece and a staff with the same double writing strongly confirms Dahlqvist's theory. Finally, a further consideration in favor of a later dating (1725–1730) is the use of the "classical" notation, a system devised well after the death of Johann Beer (see Appendix 1 online, "Classical notation").

All in all, these early scores are of meager significance as far as both authenticity and musical originality is concerned. We must wait a few years before encountering the beginning of the unequivocal artistic involvement of the new instrument.

9

THE NATURAL HUNTING
HORN (*JAGDWALDHORN*)

If, up until the 1680s, the horn could be defined, with few initial exceptions, as "a trumpet folded in another way," during the last decade of the eighteenth century, the adoption of a large bell gave it a totally new appearance and its well-known "mellow" timbre. This was paralleled by the abandonment of the high tonalities of the trumpet in favor of lower ones and by the gradual dismissal of the clarino register. The new models were mostly pitched in (or around) 12-ft F and 14-ft D and could be further lowered by one to three semitones by means of shanks or crooks, as had long since been usual with trumpets and trombones.

From this point forward, a growing repertoire emerged for the new instrument, and it began to be accepted in the orchestra and in sacred, chamber, and military music. Solo fanfares for one or more horns also began to be written. In the meantime, the first uses of notes out of the harmonic series are encountered, most probably obtained with a clever use of the "falsetto" technique discussed below.

This rapid evolution gave way to a number of names (see Chapter 9, p. 78, and Chapter 14) that were well justified during the initial period of the instrument's use but are nowadays rather misleading. To reduce this nominal multiplicity, four comprehensive definitions were proposed by Birsak in a stimulating 1976 essay, all related to the most common German name, *Waldhorn* (pl. *Waldhörner*): the first two, "hunters' horns" and "hunting horns" (*Jägerhörner* and *Jagdhörner*) apply to models already discussed, while the "natural hunting horns" (*Jagdwaldhörner*) are discussed in this chapter, and the "natural orchestral horns" (*Orchesterwaldhörner*), will be covered in Chapter 11.[1]

---

[1] We have not followed the detailed distinctions between models proposed by Birsak faithfully. Although useful, they seem too constrained with respect to present-day information.

THE LARGE FLARED BELL

The overall features of early hooped models imply a tone similar to that of the trumpet, but the large flared bell allowed for the production of an unprecedented and appealing sound. To achieve this goal, it was necessary, however, to overcome the metallurgical limit faced when making a bell more than 15–17cm in diameter.

The problem can easily be understood by taking into account both the materials and manufacturing procedures of those days (see Chapter 7, p. 33). As already reported, metal sheets available at the time measured approximately 180 x 45cm with a thickness of approximately 0.5mm, which allowed for a maximum bell diameter of about 15cm (45 divided by 3.14 – the Greek π value – gives a diameter of 14.33cm).

It was also possible, as sometimes happened, to begin with a thicker sheet, for example approximately 0.7mm, and then patiently hammer the sheet or rub it with a spatula in order to spread the metal over the mandrel, but this involved an exhausting quantity of work and a greater risk of damaging the metal.

To easily obtain a bell larger than 15cm, a trick was developed that, as far as we know, was used for the first time in two different instruments. The first is a horn from 1689 attributed to the famous maker Michael Koch of Dresden (fl. 1674– ca. 1715), who adopted a solution that was so expensive it was prohibitive for other makers. A more practical solution was devised by an amateur musical instrument maker from Hanover, Dietrich Wilhelm Baumgart (fl. 1689–1692), who was probably the inventor of the humble "gusset," which was used by all makers up to modern times.

The attractive and unique sound of the new instrument immediately found acceptance in Saxony, a country where the rules and privileges of the court trumpeters were more rigid, constituting an entirely new entity that no longer could be confused with trumpets and their tone.

It is this feature of the sound that Johann Mattheson described in 1713 in *Das neu-eröffnete Orchestre*: he clearly describes the change in sonority of the "*lieblich-pompeuse Waldhörner*" (the lovable and pompous natural horns), emphasizing the radical difference from the "rude" and "jarring" trumpet. He also states that it was promptly adopted in church, theater, and chamber music, and even declares that, while other sizes were also in use, the F horn was the "most fascinating of all" (Mattheson 1713, 267–268) (see Figure 41 online).

RADICAL ATTEMPTS BY KOCH AND BAUMGART

The 1689 horn attributed to Michael Koch of Dresden (Leipzig, MIM, inv. 1661) has one and a half loops and is 264cm in length (less than 9 feet, still a trumpet pitch). The leadpipe projects out from the body of the instrument, which is left-handed and solidly reinforced by a supporting brace; another brace is located between the body and the bell in order to make the instrument sturdier and suited to the mounted hunt. However, the more substantial novelty is that while the initial bore is only 7.9mm, the bell, with a garland decorated by chased shells, is a good 21cm in diameter (Heyde 1982, 124–126, pl. 12). With such tapered tubing, a deep conical mouthpiece with wide rim can be used—like the one preserved with the instrument—thus reinforcing the dark and characteristic tone of the instrument (illustrated in Heyde 1982, pl. 77).

To obtain the wide flare of the bell, Koch took advantage of a very expensive trick: Instead of using the brass sheet vertically in order to fit both the main tube sections and the bell, he designed the latter on a horizontal sheet so as to exploit the entire width for the reversed goblet profile. The process was likely exceptional, given the prohibitive cost of materials, since the discarded metal had to be lost or recast—an enormous waste of material and time (in fact, since he worked for the king of Saxony, he had a quantity of resources at his disposal that was unusual with respect to other makers).

An entirely different process was adopted by Dietrich Wilhelm Baumgart of Hanover. In around 1690, this craftsman, a weaponsmith by profession, created a large bell using a much less expensive technique: He drew the profile on the same sheet used for the main tube, as was customary apart the experiment by Koch, but in order to achieve the desired bell shape, he added a large triangular "gusset," which in one preserved instrument constitutes a good half of the bell (Lustig 2006, 301–304). It was indeed a rough manufacturing process that resulted in an instrument of overall poor appearance, probably for hunting purposes and pitched in 14-ft D (about 420cm, with a short initial yard missing), a size that was found in art music at least twenty years later (see Figure 42).

The appearance of a hooped horn with wide bell in German-speaking countries must have been observed with some attention in Nuremberg, as an instrument with a bell larger than was usual is portrayed by Weigel in the workshop of a local maker (see Figure 38). Weigel (1698, 233) also provides the first detailed description of the different models then on the market: "The *Waldhörner* are large and small

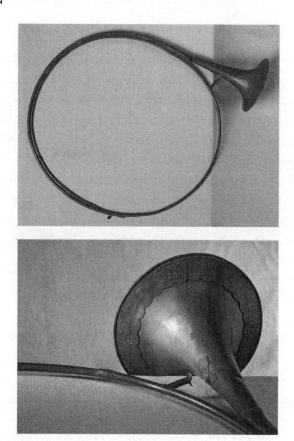

Figure 42. D. W. Baumgart, Hanover, *ca.* 1690.

and folded in various ways, some with a body as large as a wide bowl, which gives a very strong and resonant sound; others called 'coupled' are bent folded over twice, three and even four times."

It is likely that the famous Nuremberg artisans initially showed some interest in the new instrument, maybe after orders from France and other communities in Germany. However, they remained on the margins of the history of the horn. This is probably because, unlike trumpets, the new instrument's construction appeared mostly rudimentary to them, since it was dictated by affordability—a concept that had never been the concern of the masterful Nuremberg craftsmen.

The prompt admission of the new model in the French *chasse* led to a change in horn production in France. The Crétiens, who had been associated with the traditional half-moon shape of the instrument up to this point, became involved with the new hooped model (Vaast 2015, 183). At about the same time, the leadership in German instrument manufacturing moved to Vienna, where the refined production of the Leichamschneiders, of Adam Ferber, and of many other subsequent skilled manufacturers took place.

CAMMERTON AND CHORTON

Given the crucial importance of German-speaking countries in the early history of the horn, we must mention the two main tuning pitches in use there: the chamber and the choir (or church) pitch, *Cammerton* and *Chorton* respectively. Neither one can be identified in terms of absolute frequencies, but rather in a "range" of frequencies about a whole tone apart. Chamber pitch was between 409 and 427 Hz and chapel pitch was between 453 and 479 Hz. These are approximately one semitone below and one above the frequency area centered around modern pitch, a' = 440 Hz (Haynes 2002, lii).

In addition, a "musical revolution" occurred in Paris in the 1670s, with Hotteterres and Philidors's invention of new woodwind instruments made from detachable parts. They were tuned to an even lower pitch, between 384 and 397 Hz (approximately one semitone below *Cammerton* and a minor third below the *Chorton*), as was common in France. They were readily introduced in German countries, where chamber music was rapidly influenced by the novelty. This lower pitch was then named *A-Cammerton* (i.e. A-chamber pitch) or even *tief-Cammerton* (low-chamber pitch). Starting in the 1730s, chamber instruments gradually went back to the previous *Cammerton* (now called "Italian pitch"), eventually restoring the previous distance of about one tone between the two main tuning pitches (Fürstenau 1862, II, 51–52, fn.; Haynes 2002, 208).

To match the required intonation, the pitch of brass instruments could be lowered using one or more "shanks," that is, a short extension of the tube. If this was not enough, the appropriate "crook" could be used to lower the instrument one semitone or more; other accompanying instruments, usually keyboards, instead used transposition to play in unison. A third option, well documented in period music, was to notate the woodwind instruments in one key while the rest of the ensemble played in another, usually at a distance of one tone (Dahlqvist 1993a, 33–34; Haynes 2002, 183–184).

According to German sources, the new *Waldhorn* had been conceived in *Cammerton* since its adoption in art music, so if a horn sounded in F, the organ—

which was usually tuned on *Chorton*—should play in E-flat (see Mattheson cited below).

We cannot dwell further on this subject here, but we might add that the volume published by Haynes in 2002, despite not dealing specifically with our instrument, certainly unveils perspectives that can lead to further knowledge and insights to this regard (see online, "An apparent incongruity of tonalities", and Musical example 6 online).

SIZES OF NATURAL HORNS

The beginning of the artistic performance in German countries is mirrored by the differentiation of horn sizes—something that would have been of little use in the hunt. We might add that trumpets had never been made in such a variety of pitches and were instead confined to the usual sizes of C and D (Koch 1980, 195) and high F, which was called for by some German composers (Dahlqvist 1993a) and later by those of the Neapolitan school.[2] An early documentation of the horn's tonalities comes from the manuscript of James Talbot, written toward the end of the seventeenth century (see Baines 1948), where in addition to the B-flat size (around 9 ft), all other pitches "from 8 ft to 16 ft" are also recorded. This is indeed quite early documentation, since written music in lower keys would emerge only some twenty years later. Mattheson (1713, 267–268) refers, in turn, to horns tuned in church pitch G and in chamber pitch F, apparently disregarding the higher pitches. This was most likely because these were similar in sound to the trumpet proper, which he hardly appreciated.

THE 14-FOOT D SIZE

The Baumgart horn (*ca.* 1690), with one and a half hoops, is probably the oldest known instrument pitched to such a low key. Considering that part of the tube is missing, it could well have been tuned one octave lower than the horns used in the hunt up to this point—a size that would soon constitute the new standard for the activity. It was likely this model, with a very large hoop, that was first called *Parforcehorn* or even *Perforcehorn* (see "Early terminology," pp. 78–79), a term

---

[2] On the latter use, see Hell 1971, 56–57. For the F trumpet outside of Italy, see Proksch 2011.

regularly found in German sources since the end of the seventeenth century and closely related to hunting. The items depicted by Curlando in the painting of Oberschleißheim Lustheim castle (1689) might also belong in this category, but as their bells are concealed in the picture, a precise identification is difficult.

Horns in low D were usually made with only one and a half hoops—a favorite format for the hunt, but bulky and inconvenient for art music performance. Horns in D intended for artistic purposes would in fact only come somewhat later: The oldest preserved specimen is probably one with three loops and a half by Leichamschneider, Vienna 1709 (Lustig 2006, 296–297), while one with two and a half hoops by Le Brun, Paris 1721, is in the Edinburgh museum (see Figure 49); another Le Brun, dated 1729, was formerly part of a private collection in Paris (see Morley-Pegge 1973, 4, pl. II).

THE 12-FOOT F SIZE

Those who played the horn for artistic purposes soon grew to prefer the size of F, which also had a unique and particularly attractive sound. Mattheson (1713, 267), in the passage quoted above, in addition to stating his absolute preference for this key,[3] also argues that the "sound of the horn is darker and fuller with respect to the rude and strident one of trumpets or *clarinen* (when they are not in good hands) since it is tuned a fifth lower."

To obtain a key lower than the high ones of the trumpets, the simplest idea was obviously increasing the diameter of the circle, as was done by Baumgart. A similar principle was applied by Johann Leichamschneider (1679–1742) for an F horn from 1710 (Vienna, KHM, inv. 118 511), an instrument that, together with a 14-ft D horn with three and a half hoops made by his older brother Michael (1676–1751), represent the oldest surviving products by these distinguished Viennese makers.

However, here Koch of Dresden was once again a true innovator: In 1710, he built an instrument with a body diameter like that of his C horn from 1689 but with doubled tubing—a useful solution for getting from the key of C to that of F and also increasing the instrument's sturdiness (cf. Baines 1976, 153). This item (Leipzig, MFM, inv. 1663; Heyde 1982, 127–129, pl. 13) also has a bell made without concern for the price (i.e. without the gusset) and is richly decorated with

[3] An almost identical description is found in Barnickel 1737, 420–421.

the insignia of Frederick Augustus "the Strong," Elector of Saxony (see Marolles 1930, 42). Its importance is all the more apparent if one remembers that, the following year, the horn was officially admitted to the court of Dresden (Fürstenau 1862, II, 58).

Probably owing to the close relationships between Dresden and Vienna (see again Fürstenau 1862, II, 59), this new design was immediately copied in the latter city by the Leichamschneiders, namely with one horn by Michael dated 1711 (Vienna, Technischesmuseum), a pair by Michael dated 1712 that are now in Milan (Museo del Castello Sforzesco, inv. 543, 544), and a pair from 1718, both in Basel (Historisches Museum, inv. 1878.22 and 1980.2013). The same constructive principle was soon endorsed by other manufacturers, among them Eichentopf of Leipzig (an item from 1722 by him is in Munich, BNM, inv. 1976/856).

The wrap with two and a half loops was largely preferred for F horns, while the one with three and a half was soon mostly adopted for D horns (F horns in three loops seem to be a specialty of the Haas family; e.g. Nuremberg, GNM, inv. MIR 75).

These models with two and a half or three and a half loops may even have found their way into the hunt (some specimens have cords, useful for such a purpose), but their small and handy size was likely conceived for indoor music performances (Keeß 1824, 167).

THE APPEARANCE IN ART MUSIC

It is uncertain whether at the time Count von Sporck became fascinated by the Parisian horns they were already commonly played in pairs, but the fact that he left (or sent) two servants to learn the instrument at Versailles may have been down to such a custom. Even though the oldest hunting signals handed down in written sources consist of solo tunes—such as those reported by Philidor aîné or his grandson Pierre Danican, as well as those contained in Morin's *La chasse du cerf* (1708) and in subsequent compositions—the possibility that a second voice was added extemporaneously is not out of the question.

The first certain evidence of a requirement for a pair of horns is nevertheless found in the operatic repertoire, with the "musical entertainment" *Diana rappacificata con Venere e Amore* by Carlo Agostino Badia (*ca.* 1672–1738) performed in Vienna in 1700; here, two horns in F perform fanfare-like idiomatic tunes in triple time (Haller 1970, 175–176). Then, two horns in E-flat are requested in a *Requiem* by Bernard Reinold performed at the Hradisko Cloister on September 12, 1702 (Sehnal 2008, 116). *La monarchia stabilita* by Hugo von Wilderer, which calls for two horns in D, dates from 1703 (Koch 1980, 145). In other cases, the presence of the horns is only known through librettos or chronicles of the time, since the music has been lost forever. The score of *Octavia* by Reinhard Keiser (1674–1739), however, remains. The opera was performed in Hamburg on August 5, 1705, where the paired horns were used in both concertante and orchestral roles (Haller 1970, 176); here, *corne de chasse* in the key of high C (8 ft) are called for, with a range from *c'* to *c'''* (fourth–sixteenth harmonic).

From this time on, compositions with horns in one of these two tonalities (high C or F) constantly increased in number, including the wedding music by Klingenberg and pieces such as *Die von Cupid aufgelöste Licentiaten-Frage* by Michael Rohde (1708). Here the horns are notated in (high) B-flat in church pitch (thus high C in chamber pitch), a difference in tonality not unlike that in Mattheson's example (see above) and in surviving works by Klingenberg and Boxberg (see Table 3 online).

At almost the same time, "Corne de chasse major" in the key of low D are eloquently called for in the music of Zachow (died 1712), and he also uses two higher tonalities, F and A ("corne de chasse") (Thomas 1966, 237–248). Then, in 1714, Gunther W. Jacob (1685–1734) asked for the keys of E-flat, G, A, and B-flat in the same score, thus paving the way for the alternating use of different tonalities in one and the same composition (see Musical example 7 online).[4]

SMALL ENSEMBLES

Table 3 (online), although not exhaustive, lists many of the most ancient artistic uses of the horn, some of which are in small ensembles. Chamber groups are also documented in literary sources, such as in Leipzig on May 31, 1698, on the occasion of Tsar Peter the Great's visit to the city. There, an ensemble conducted by Christoph Stephan Scheinhardt, musician and leader of a local music company, accompanied the official meal with "violins, oboes, natural horns [*Waldhörner*], trumpets, timpani and French shawms [*Schalmeien*]" (Schering 1921, 47).

---

[4] Christian Ahrens (2014, 87–89) recently expressed his conviction that the pitches of D and low C were used earlier. However, we have not found confirmation over the course of our research, at least prior to the use of low D by Zachow.

Furthermore, at the court of Duke Christian of Sachsen-Weissenfels, a "hunting band" consisting of two oboes, two horns, and two bassoons existed since 1704. A similar but larger set of instruments is pictured by Fleming in a 1724 hunting scene, probably moments just before the *curée* (see Figure 43 online). Another example comes from Zeitz, also in Saxony, where in 1715 a local band was constituted by oboes and "*Waldhörner*" (Werner 1911, 96). A famous piece of iconographic evidence, dating back to just after 1725 and signed by the widow of the engraver Johann Ch. Weigel (who had died in that year), also shows two horn players in a civil or military band consisting of a trumpet, two horns, three oboes, and a bassoon (see Figure 44 online). The same ensemble was used for a music performance in Nuremberg in 1731; here three groups all used this same set of instruments (Whitwell 1983, III, 10). Although, in 1722, Bavarian military bands were still made up of six oboes and two horns, similar ensembles with mainly double reed instruments, previously very common, underwent a progressive decline and eventually fell out of use (see again Whitwell 1983, III, 10).

Apart from these pieces of literary and iconographic evidence, the first known composition for a small chamber ensemble is by Friedrich Gottfried Klingenberg (1670?–1720), organist at Szczecin and pupil of Buxtehude (Snyder 2007, 130). There are in fact more than ten wedding cantatas by him (one is lost) for the unusual ensemble of voice, two horns, two oboes, bassoon, and harpsichord. The oldest is *Die unbekandte Straussen-Liebe ward am hochzeitlichen Freuden-Fest* (1704), but he wrote other similar cantatas until at least 1711. The horn parts are usually pitched in C (alto) and are difficult to perform, owing both to the high register and the constant use of the eleventh harmonic, which requires "falsetto" (a topic we will cover in Chapter 10). The first of the pair reaches the sixteenth harmonic and the second never steps down below the fifth. Another remarkable feature of these compositions is that the singer and harpsichord play in B-flat, while the horns are in C. They are therefore tuned in choir pitch and in chamber pitch respectively, which implies the difference of one tone.

J. G. C. Störl (1675–1719) from Stuttgart (Owens 1995, 344) wrote a *Marche* using only wind instruments—two oboes, two horns, and a bassoon—in circa 1711 (D-ROu), although some doubts have been raised about its dating (Hofer 2006, 38). The scanty survival of similar music from the early eighteenth century, with or without a marked military feel—a repertoire certainly relevant to the initial use of the horn—is in all likelihood because of both the mnemonic performance of the instrumentalists and the lack of care given to the preservation of these everyday compositions. Gerber's general commentary (1792, 548) provides, with certainty, valuable information about the entire matter:

> The first attempt to introduce [the horn] in an ensemble with other instruments was encountered in military music; and we have a notion of this kind of compositions thanks to the everyday marching of regiments. The intervention of band players in dance music ensembles, as well, was in turn the probable reason for adopting the instrument in the latter genre of music; this created the opportunity to demonstrate its usefulness in conjunction with stringed instruments, thus ultimately favoring its adoption in concert halls.

HORNS IN SACRED MUSIC

That the horn quickly also made its entry into instrumental ensembles in monasteries and churches is documented by a 1703 payment for horns and crooks supplied by the Leichamschneiders to the Kremsmünster Benedictine monastery in Upper Austria (Fitzpatrick 1970, 33). The previous year, 1702, the monastery in Hradisko, near Olomouc (northern Moravia), had bought "two horns of a new type, folded in two large circles," likely made by the same craftsmen in Vienna, and had sent a young man to the city to learn how to play them (Freemanová 2006, 216, quoting Sehnal).

In this same period, the ancient Latin word *lituus* was reintroduced as an erudite translation of the name *Waldhorn* to refer to the instrument in the Slavic Catholic regions and sometimes in southern Germany. Among other sources, there is a document from 1706 from the Bohemian monastery in Ossegg (Osek) that mentions "Litui vulgo Waldhörner duo ex Tono G," or "Two Litui, commonly known as Waldhörner, in G" (Nettl 1921–1922, 357). In a very instructive paper, Hans Oscar Koch (1980, 149–155) has amply illustrated this meaning, citing examples from sacred compositions from this area with scores requiring two *litui* and parts that are simply labeled "horn."

The oldest example of such terminology comes from the city of Prague in circa 1700 in compositions by Nikolas Franz Xaver Wentzely (*ca.* 1643–1722) (see Koch 1980, 151). This is followed by the *Anathema Gratiarum* published in Prague in 1714 by the Benedictine Gunther Wenzel Jacob (1685–1734). Another occurrence is found in *Requiem à 12* of 1719 (RISM 300511016) by Johann Martin Prandel (fl. 1706–1709), choirmaster of Breslau Cathedral. There is in addition a well-known motet by Bach (BWV 118, see below), and many other pieces—mostly by Catholic authors—up to at least circa 1780 (Koch 1980, 153).[5] A relevant reference to the use of the horn in sacred repertoire can also be found in the 1712 inventory of the Nuremberg Frauenkirche, which mentions "two natural horns that Mr. Captain Nüztel donated to the choir" (Nickel 1971, 346). In the same inventory, four clarinets that had recently been purchased are also listed, so it appears that the musical organization there was very modern for the time.

Although it comes much later, it may prove enlightening here to mention a comment by Christian Fr. D. Schubart, written in 1784 but published some twenty years later (Schubart 1806, 314): "The hunter with the horn (*Jagdhornist*) sounds and awakens the companions and the forest with his staccato style, always leaping with an unequal rhythm. The horn player (*Hornist*) groans in church, producing notes with a heavy heart, a blowing that immediately revives the entire instrumental accompaniment. In the concert hall and the opera, the natural horn player (*Waldhornist*) can still add an 'infinite array of feelings.'" When Schubart wrote this passage, the differences between these genres were quite obvious, but it is likely that they had existed from the very beginning of the artistic history of the horn.

DISSEMINATION IN EUROPE

An observation that immediately arises from reading the list of early compositions for horn reported in Table 3 (online) is that almost all were created by German or Slavic composers, and even when Italians began to use the horn, their pieces were mainly intended for venues and circumstances related to the Habsburg Empire, to which Italy largely belonged. An isolated instance is found in a symphony by Giuseppe Torelli (1658–1709), which employs a pair of horns (see Musical example 8 online). The piece was probably written during his stay in Germany or in Vienna, between 1698 and 1700, or even upon his return to Bologna, where the autograph score is preserved (Passadore 2007, 328–329). Some doubts about this composition remain, however, as the horns are used here in a *ripieno* (harmonic) role, a function adopted much later by the Neapolitan masters, and are notated in bass clef, sounding one octave higher—another later tradition of the Neapolitan school (see Appendix I online, "Neapolitan and Italian notation").

---

[5] Numerous other scores including this instrument's name are cataloged in the RISM archives, including compositions by Hasse (RISM 454000172) and even by Johann Stamitz (RISM 240004237).

Aside from this early case, the use of the horn in Italy properly began in Naples, where some performances are reported, starting with a serenade by Scarlatti from 1713 (see Table 3 online). The next place of admission is Venice, with the first version of *Orlando furioso* by Ristori and Vivaldi (see Chapter 13 online, "Vivaldi"), which was staged with great success in 1713 and contains the chorus "Al fragor de' corni audaci" (At the clamor of brave horns) (Act II, Sc. 13). This chorus was then slightly modified and reused by Vivaldi in *Orlando* (1714) and in *Orlando furioso* (1727). Antonio Lotti was also interested to the horn, which he promptly used in *Polidoro* (Venice, February 4, 1715), the same year that Alessandro Scarlatti wrote the opera *Tigrane* (1715), with which a steady and seminal tradition of the horn began in Naples.

A pair of horns is also used in a concertante role in *Oracolo del fato* by Francesco Gasparini, a composition of which two scores are preserved in Vienna (A-Wn); one is related to a performance that took place in Barcelona before 1711 (Biagi Ravenni 1986 [ii]) for the visit of the future emperors (Charles and Elizabeth Cristina) and another to a performance that took place in Vienna on October 1, 1719. Here two *trombe da caccia* in F are required, a literal translation into Italian of the French *trompe de chasse*. The Barcelona performance of this "great cantata" is also the earliest known occurrence of the horn on Spanish soil; nonetheless, the first example of genuine Spanish music for the instrument is the *Dixit Dominus* by Josep Prades (1689–1757) from 1726 (Verdú 2000, 44). The instrument was permanently adopted in Valencian chapels after 1729/30 (Verdú 2000, 47).

In England, the "French horn" is mentioned for the first time in an advertisement for the maker William Bull published in *The Loyal Protestant & True Domestick Intelligence* in 1681/2 (Morley-Pegge 1973, 17) and in the James Talbot's treatise manuscript from the close of the seventeenth century (Oxford, Christ Church; see Baines 1948). The same definition is found again in the well-known list of Bull instruments from 1699 (reproduced in various publications, among which see Bacon 2000). The only known horn by Bull dates back to the same year. The instrument is discussed in an unfamiliar article by Anthony Baines in which he asserts (Baines 1982, 157), "The Bull bell is genuine. But [. . .] we do not know what William Bull's 1699 horn was like—how many coils, how much tapered, how wide the mouthpiece socket, and what key it was in." One of the first known performances using the instrument took place in London in 1704 with the help of German musicians (Fitzpatrick 1970, 51). The oldest printed editions with horns are from circa 1712: *Lost is My Love*, op. VII by William Corbett, which has an unusual orchestration using voice, two recorders, two horns, two violins, two violas, and continuo. The first use by Handel dates back in turn to around 1715. He called for the instrument in the Concerto HWV 331-1 in two movements then used in the first version of *Water Music*, and adopted it permanently only after 1720 with *Radamisto* (see Chapter 13 online, "Handel"). The presence of horns in the first version of *Pan and Syrinx* (1717) by Johann Ernst Galliard (1687–1749) is documented by Blandford (1922, 545).

In 1720, two "French Hunting Horns made by J. Leichamschneider" were included in an inventory drawn up by J. C. Pepusch for James Brydges, duke of Chandos (Baker 1949, 139–140), even though no music for horn by Pepusch has been found. An unusual horn type of English make is also worth mentioning. Its description is found in *Critica Musica* by Mattheson (1723, I, 254): "Engelländische Cors de Chasse,"—that is, English hunting horns—"that can be kept in hat cases (*in Hüten*) so that you can store and transport them." It was interpreted as such an instrument with a demountable bell (Carse collection no. 254 at the Horniman Museum in London),[6] while a similar one is in the Museum Carolino-Augusteum (Fitzpatrick 1976). For more information on the horn in Britain outside the concert hall during the eighteenth century see Humphries (2023).

THE FIRST PROFESSIONAL ORCHESTRA MEMBERS

After what has been said so far, it is not surprising that many courts were trying to hire performers able to play the instrument that had become so fashionable. The oldest known example is that of Count Lamberg, lord of Upper Austria, who in 1703 asked Count von Sporck to find him a horn player. The latter replied that he would not be able to meet the demand because one of his was already advanced in age (Piersig 1927, 82, fn. 2; Fitzpatrick, 1970, 91).

Starting in 1706, many princely courts of Germany began to hire horn players for their orchestras on a permanent basis. In this regard, Fitzpatrick (1970, 50) stated that the first two generations of professionals were of Bohemian origin and training, and that some of them would have had previous training as trumpet or trombone players, often at the music schools of convents and monasteries. The same author has identified Hermoläus Smeykal (*ca.* 1685–1758), who was born in

---

[6] We suppose that, in Mattheson's text, the German *in Hüten* should be loosely understood as hat cases, rather than (literally) "in hats." For the latter interpretation see Morley-Pegge 1973, 13, and table II/3.

Kutná Hora (Kuttenberg) in Bohemia and trained at the Jesuit monastery in the city, as the first professional horn teacher. He later settled in Prague, where he played in the orchestra of the Jesuit seminary of St. Wenceslas (Dlabacž 1815, III, 123). His pupils were Joseph Matiegka (1728–1804), who in turn became one of the main Bohemian horn instructors and, in all probability, also the famous Hampel. In addition, since Austrian imperial diplomats maintained orchestras in their service even outside their home country (Quoika 1956, 67–71), some horn players emigrated and moved to various other European cities, from Brussels to St. Petersburg to Constantinople (Fitzpatrick 1970, 63), and to Naples, as we will see presently.

In 1706, Johann Theodor Zeddelmayer (*ca.* 1675–after 1736) was hired permanently by the court of the Duke Christian of Sachsen-Weissenfels, the same nobleman who maintained a band consisting of two oboes, two horns, and two bassoons from 1704. In 1710, Duke Anton Ulrich von Brauschweig-Wolfenbüttel recruited another horn player, Laurenz Georg Reichel (fl. *ca.* 1710–1731), whose virtuosity can be inferred from the obbligato appearing in the opera *Clelia* (1730) by Georg Caspar Schürmann (1672/3–1751) (Fitzpatrick 1970, 57, quoting Schmidt 1933, 123ff.).

According to Köchel (1869, 80) in the Hofkapelle of the imperial court of Vienna, little changed during the final years of Joseph I's tenure, but when Charles VI, who was passionate about music and hunting, took the throne in 1711, the horn was used ever more frequently in the court chapel with the 1712 hire—after Wenzel Rossi (*ca.* 1685–1740), already enrolled as oboe and horn player (Marcaletti 2023, 28–38)—of Friedrich Otto (1686–1718).

Not surprisingly, on November 3, 1723, von Sporck was able to admit the Emperor Charles VI, his wife Elisabeth Christine, the king of Poland Frederick Augustus I, the king of Prussia Frederick William, and other aristocrats of the most celebrated European nobility to the order of St. Hubert, the prestigious association of enthusiastic hunters that he had founded (Benedikt 1923, 112).

An unflattering judgment as to the frequent use of the horn in Vienna was, conversely, expressed a few years later, in 1717, by Lady Mary Wortley Montagu (1763, I, 108), who, with regard to the local musical life, observed: "[The ballrooms of the great houses] are very magnificently furnished, and the music good, if they had not that detestable custom of mixing hunting horns with it, that almost deafen the company. But that noise is so agreeable here, that they never make a concert without them."

In Dresden, meanwhile, horn players had been employed in a stable manner since 1711, such as Johann Adalbert Fischer (*ca.* 1677–after 1722) and Franz Adam Samm (*ca.* 1678–1723) (Fürstenau 1862, II, 58), and from the same year in Düsseldorf, Pangratz and Hoffmann (Fitzpatrick 1970, 95). Of particular interest is the hire of Johann Wilhelm Lumpe at the Stuttgart court chapel in June 1713 and that of the second horn, Johann Christoph Biener (died 1748), who were said to "play very well, providing proof every day, and are very diligent in their service" (Owens 1995, 188–189). From that point on, all the pieces written for the court chapel were characterized by the presence of horns, which were also used in *concerti grossi*. A little later, in 1714, the horn was permanently added to the orchestra in Darmstadt with the hiring of Johann Philipp Mahler (Noack 1967, 187), and also to the orchestra in Mainz in 1717, with the hiring of Johann Ondratscheck (Fitzpatrick 1970, 98).

Another significant occurrence can be found at the Munich court, where in 1715 the brothers Johann Caspar and Mathias Ganspöck were hired (Nösselt 1980, 72). Their subsequent educational trip to Paris was probably aimed at learning the use of the instrument in the hunt, as at that date no leading artistic use of the horn was documented in the French capital.

The first stable employment of horn players in Italy also dates back to this period: In Lucca in 1716, two horn players, Wenceslao Fideler and Josepho Hartosch, were referred to as "Virtuosi of His Royal Highness." They were joined by Giovanni Amadio Hachr and John Strengel in 1719, and finally, in 1720, by John Michael Raich. All of them were Germans or foreigners, at least according to their surnames.[7] Giuseppe Grandi, Francesco Antonio Bondioli, Giuseppe Maria Bondioli, and Gaetano Tossi (Cataldi 1985, 107–108), on the other hand, were certainly Italian. The four *trombetta*, or trumpet players (see online, "*Tromba da caccia, tromba, trombetta*"), were hired for the performance of *Tito Manlio* by Vivaldi (Mantova, January 1719), which calls for two trumpet and two horn players.

These are just examples, chosen almost randomly, but they make the phenomenon and the speed of the instrument's dissemination apparent. It had spread throughout European courts even before a radical novelty arrived from

---

[7] In Livorno, Tuscany, two other German hornists—Joanni Knüttel and Joanni Beck—were active in 1729, while in nearby Lucca, for the celebration day of Santa Croce in 1727, a large ensemble included the horn players David Klingmann, Giovanni Strengel, and a certain Finopasi in the "concerto grosso" (Fanelli 1997, 441–442).

Naples, the training place for generations of composers, who exploited the horn in a manner very differently from how it had been used up until this point.

ADOPTION IN THE ITALIAN OPERA

The earliest use of the horn in the orchestra was to evoke hunting scenes on the stage (a tradition that lasted a very long time at the French court); in German countries, in addition, a growing artistic function was developed in the various musical genres mentioned. However, it was left to Italian opera composers to contribute the harmonic and tonal function that became a distinctive feature of the instrument in the pit, which also fostered the replacement of thorough bass with a new kind of orchestral accompaniment. In this period, in fact, composers of "Neapolitan" birth, adoption, or training were responsible for the dissemination of a new use of the horn in all major European chapels. Let's see, however, how the horn arrived in Naples.

NAPLES

At the beginning of the eighteenth century, Italy was divided into a number of separate states that, with the exception of the Kingdom of Sardinia (Savoy, Piedmont, and Sardinia isle proper) and the Papal States (which included most of central Italy), were ruled by the Habsburg Empire. The Kingdom of Naples, passed by the Spaniards to the Austrians in 1707 after the War of Spanish Succession, was briefly led by Count Wirich von Daun between 1707 and 1708, who returned permanently to Naples as viceroy from 1713 to 1719.

As well as the adoption of the mounted hunt in Piedmont and that of the hooped *trompe* in Versailles owing to the close dynastic relationships between Turin and Paris, the musical customs of the Viennese aristocracy spread elsewhere, and owing to dynastic reasons, first of all to Naples. This is proved by the appearance of the instrument in the capital of Southern Italy, in the music chapel of the Austrian rulers. It is revealing that a serenade by Alessandro Scarlatti, *Amore, pace e provvidenza* (Love, peace and providence), performed at the royal palace in 1711 calls for trumpets (RISM 452507603).

Just three months after the appointment of von Daun in Naples (1713–1719), however, during the celebrations for the birthday of Empress Elisabeth Christine on August 28, 1713, the horn made its official entry in the Neapolitan musical tradition. Among other sources, the *Gazzetta di Napoli* (35, August 29, 1713) mentions the performance of the serenade *Il Genio austriaco, Zefiro, Flora, il Sole, Partenope e il Sebeto* (The Austrian genius, Zephyr, Flora, Sun, Partenope and Sebeto) by the same author, in which "the harmonious instruments were innumerable: timpani, trumpets, horns, and also flutes, all sort of strings, and organ, and a great number of musicians for the choir" (Prota-Giurleo 1952, 89).

Another possible occasion when horns were present was a few months later during the celebrations held for the name day of Empress Elisabeth (November 17, 1713): At the Teatro S. Bartolomeo, an opera by Antonio Lotti, the *Porsenna*, was "arranged and directed" by Alessandro Scarlatti, which possibly implies the addition of horns. In fact, the latter, who was an undisputed musical leader in Naples, made constant use of the instrument in his later operas, paving the way to its constant presence—with a new role—in the operatic orchestra (Dent 1905, 159). And his example was followed by all the composers of the Neapolitan school, who were hired by the dozens by the major European chapels.

These circumstances literally confirm what was asserted by Heinrich Domnich in his *Méthode* (1807)—namely that it was Scarlatti and Lotti who introduced the horn to the Italian orchestra, importing it from the German countries.[8] Domnich's text continues to refer to the use of the instrument in the later music by Hasse and Alberti, when the Neapolitan school was already using it on a regular basis. In fact, it had been exploited since at least 1718 in the scores of Sarro, Porpora, Vinci, Feo, Leo, Pergolesi, and many others.

A NEW MUSICAL IDIOM

Beyond its capacity to evoke the hunt and the march, the horn mostly aroused the interest of the Neapolitan composers for its tonal characteristics and its harmonic function, which supported the texture of the entire orchestra. Another feature of Neapolitan writing was to limit the technical requirements, giving every average instrumentalist the opportunity to play their respective part, and thus making

---

[8] Domnich 1807, p. III, fn. 1: "The horn had arrived to this point when two Italian composers that flourished at the end of the seventeenth century and at the beginning of the eighteenth, Lotti and Alessandro Scarlatti, brought him from Germany to their homeland, and used it in their compositions. The example of these two great masters was soon followed by Hasse 'the Saxon' and Alberti, their disciples. From this moment the horn was, so to speak, naturalized in Italy; and everybody knows what good use of it was made by Leo, Vinci, Porpora, Durante, Pergolese, etc., and then by Jomelli, Guglielmi, Sarti, Piccinni, Sacchini, etc., both in theater and in church [music]."

the circulation of their music easier. This compositional principle held firm for the horn in this repertoire for more than a century—up to the point when valves were finally introduced, even if from time to time solos in the opera's symphony or concertante parts together with singers were entrusted to clever orchestral players.

Although surprising, given the intensity of the Neapolitan musical scene, there are no surviving horns that were made in Naples or known to have come from there that date back to the first half of the eighteenth century (or even much later). However, archival evidence about their makers is not lacking. For instance, one Cristoforo Antonio D'Aula was active from 1732 to 1743 (Nocerino 2009a, 48), while Gaetano Albano is documented to have worked from 1768 to 1784 (Nocerino 2009b, 795).

ROME

Another center to be mentioned is Rome, where, in the years between 1704 and 1719, Count Johann Wenzel von Gallas was imperial ambassador (1669–1719). He came from a family who were members of the highest level of Bohemian aristocracy and had a strong musical tradition, and had an orchestra in his service, with some members that he likely brought with him from Austria to Rome.[9]

An early example of the use of horns in Rome was on August 28, 1714, also during the birthday celebration of Empress Elisabeth Christine. Owing to the interest of von Gallas, a serenade by Giovanni Bononcini, *Sacrificio a Venere* (Sacrifice to Venus), was performed (Chirico 2014) (see Musical example 9). According to a contemporary report on the *Serenata*, four horns were in service (probably in two pairs), and to our knowledge, this was the first time this had ever occurred.[10] In January 1715, an opera by Bononcini that requires two horns, *Astarto*, was staged at the Teatro Capranica. Also in Rome, on April 21 of that year, *trombe da caccia* were called for in the oratorio *La ribellione di Assalonne* (The uprising of Absalom) by Antonio Caldara, as well as in a cantata from the same time period, *Amor senza amore* (Love without love). It is worth noting that in the payment rolls for the performance of the oratorio in 1715, the two players of

[9] Fitzpatrick 1970, 63, assumed that he settled in Naples, a statement that we replicated in *Grove* 2001, s.v. "Horn." In fact, Gallas remained in Rome for a good fifteen years, moving to Naples only in 1719, where he died after a few months.

[10] Libretto in I-Rc (Sartori 1990–1994, no. 19752). See also Fitzpatrick 1970, 64, referring to Benedikt 1927, 624–627.

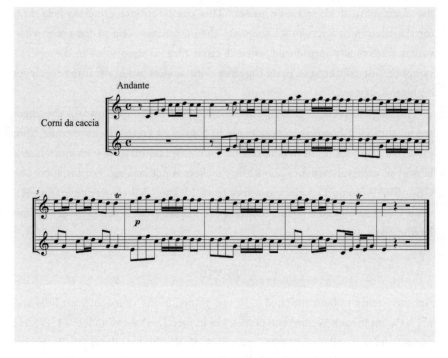

Musical example 9. G. Bononcini, *Sacrificio a Venere*, aria of Timeta "E' un bel contento al cor."

the *trombe da caccia* "are listed as *le due corni da caccia,* thus hornists" (Dahlqvist 1993b, 181, citing U. Kirkendale). The first Roman opera with horns by Alessandro Scarlatti, *Telemaco*, dates back to 1718, and it was followed by *Marco Attilio Regolo* in 1719 and *La Griselda* in 1721.

Shortly after, three pieces of iconographic evidence of the horn can be found in the well-known *Il Gabinetto armonico* by Filippo Bonanni, published in Rome in 1722. In addition to the illustration of a simple curved horn ("Corno per la Caccia") and one with a central coil ("Altro Corno da Caccia"), there is also that of a "Corno raddoppiato [. . .] molto più grande, e sonoro" ("Doubled horn [. . .] much bigger, and louder")—that is, the common horn, which "produces an amazing sound, exceeding that of other instruments" (see Figure 45 online).

ANOTHER PATH: VENICE

Finally, we must mention at least one other Italian wellspring, Venice, in particular for the musical relationships that linked this city and the Dresden court. In the lagoon capital, the horn appeared, in all likelihood, in 1713, or at the latest in 1714 (Rocchetti 2023b, 176–182), in the music of Vivaldi, and subsequently in that by Lotti, in 1715 (see Table 3 online). Its use was at the beginning purely virtuosic, in full consonance with the German tradition, instead of as harmonic support for the orchestra in the vein of the Neapolitan school. Initially, only the key of F was requested—that in which the *trombon da caccia*, the Venetian name for the new instruments (see Chapter 13 online, "Vivaldi"), were pitched. The subsequent arrival in Venice of German composers and instrumentalists in order to study there—including Stölzel (1713–1714), Heinichen (1713–1716), and Pisendel (1716–1717)—as well as Lotti's journey to Dresden (1717–1719) for the production of some of his works, were the basis for new experiences relating to the use of the instrument.[11]

LARGE HOOPED HORNS IN THE FRENCH HUNT

During the early history of the hooped horn, specimens used in the French royal hunt probably had to be made in Paris, mostly by the Crétiens,[12] and also imported from Nuremberg, and later perhaps even from Vienna.[13] However, domestic production, already seen in Paris at the turn of the century, greatly increased in the 1710s. Specimens with a very large body, with one and a half loops of tubing and a wider bell, began to be made by the Crétiens, who were later followed by Le Brun, Raoux, Carlin, and many others.

The most reliable research on the French *trompe de chasse* (Marolles 1930; Bouëssée 1979; Flachs 1994) contends that this new model was pitched in D (14 ft). However, aside from some iconographic and literary evidence, at least one French horn of this type with a length of 16 ft has survived: the monumental item made by Crétien at the beginning of the 1710s, with a body of about 93cm in diameter

---

[11] The use of horns in Lotti's works written for Dresden—the D key, for instance, which had not yet been employed in Venice—clearly reflects the virtuosity of the local musicians.

[12] This statement is in contrast with what previously wrote on the subject (Meucci 2006, 18–19), as it takes into account the results of fresh research on the Crétien family by Corinne Vaast (2015). See in particular the inventory compiled in 1691 after the death of Jacques I (p. 183): "124 one-hooped and 31 large two-hooped *trompes*; 15 small one-hooped, and 60 both in one, two and three loops."

[13] The unusual term "*coranthorn*," probably derived from the French *chasse courante* (or *chasse à courre*), appears in a payment receipt signed by the famous Viennese maker Michael Leichamschneider in 1708 (Haupt 1983, 346) and may point to the idea that at least some of his instruments were sent to Paris.

(Paris, MdM, E.890).[14] A *trompe* of this size, extremely delicate, would likely have been held with both hands, which would make it quite difficult, if not impossible, to play on horseback (Bouëssée 1979, 39). Nevertheless, it is this model that appears in the hands of Marc-Antoine Marquis de Dampierre (1678–1756)[15], and of two other noblemen portrayed with realism by Jean-Baptiste Oudry (1686–1755) in a painting of 1730 entitled *Louis XV chassant le cerf dans la forêt de Saint Germain* (Bouëssée 1979, 96–97) (see Figure 46).

The repertoire of hunting fanfares, which was expanded and made famous by the Marquis Dampierre, was written for a horn of this size with one and a half loops. Dampierre played this model his entire life, and in France it was later called "a la Dampierre" (*Grove* 2001, s.v.) (see online, "A gigantic *trompe*," and Figure 47 online).

As the French mounted hunt was passionately imitated east of the Rhine, it is not surprising that this new model was also introduced in Saxony. An example is found at the entrance balustrade of the hunting castle of Moritzburg, near Dresden:

Figure 46. J.-B. Oudry, *Louis XV chassant le cerf dans la forêt de Saint Germain*; detail, the Marquis Dampierre.

[14] In August 1713 a large hooped horn by Nicholas Crétien (not in the family tree reported in Vaast 2015, 183) was purchased with some other specimens by Marquis Dampierre and other buyers (Dufourcq – Benoît 1969, 225; see also Gétreau 2009, 185).

[15] French huntsman and musician in the service of the duke of Maine. He acquired his musical training at the court at Sceaux and remained faithful to the friends he made there for the rest of his life. These friends included Campra, Bernier, Mouret, Lalande, and Collin de Blamont, many of whom, like Dampierre himself, also played the viol.

here two sandstone statues, the work of Johann Christian Kirchner in 1727–1732,[16] portray pageboys with such a model, which had, in the meantime, come to be known as a *Parforcehorn* in the German countries (see Figure 48).

The inconvenience and delicacy of these large specimens probably convinced French manufacturers to switch to a more convenient and durable format. Apparently, it was the Parisian maker Le Brun who was the first to produce a hunting horn in D with two and a half loops in France. The instrument had a total

Figure 48. J. C. Kirchner, *Statue of Hunting Servant*, 1727–1732.

---

[16] The dating to around 1660 and the attribution of these sculptures to Wolf Ernst Brohn (*ca.* 1600–1664) is pure fiction. However, it turns up repeatedly in various texts and, surprisingly enough, on the official website of the castle: https://www.dresden-und-sachsen.de/dresdner_umland/moritzburg.htm.

length of approximately 454cm, and the diameter of the body was less than 60cm, like the 1721 item preserved in the Edinburgh Museum.[17] Since previous texts (e.g. Marolles 1930, 43) argue that this model was devised for the 1729 birth of the Dauphin of France, Louis, it can be assumed that the event simply provided the occasion for giving this horn the epithet *à la Dauphine*, which was later commonly used for this model (see Figure 49).

The "Dauphine" type, which remained in use until at least the mid-nineteenth century, was in turn superseded by the *trompe d'Orleans*, a model devised by the Périnet company, with tubing wrapped in three loops and a body diameter of about 35cm (see Figure 50). This is the final form of the French hunting horn, designed in around 1831 for an order made by the duke of Orleans, son of Louis-Philippe II. It is still preferred by players of the *trompe de chasse* today and is used in two variants, a lighter one (840 g) played by the *maître* (principal), and another more robust one (940 g) used by the *piquers*, or valets (Bouëssée 1979, 116).

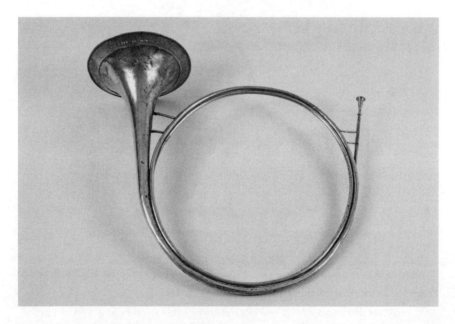

Figure 49. Le Brun, *Trompe "Dauphine,"* 1721.

[17] Another horn by Le Brun, from 1729, mentioned in Marolles 1930, 43, as the property of Mlle Frilloux, was still in a Parisian private collection during the 1960s (Morley Pegge 1973, 4, pl. II).

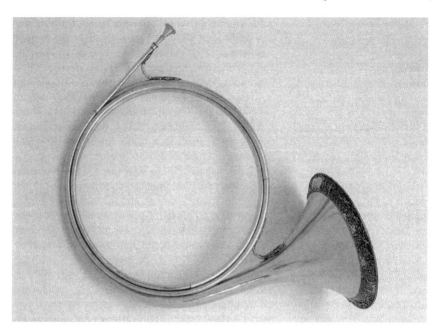

Figure 50. Pettex-Muffat, *Trompe "d'Orleans"* with silver leadpipe and silvered garland, late nineteenth century.

FRENCH SIGNALS AND FANFARES

After the 1666 manuscript collection published by Cheney in 1998, the next documentation of French hunting calls is by André Danican Philidor l'aîné (*ca.* 1652–1730). It dates back to 1705: The first part is titled "Tous les appels de trompe pour la chasse" and the second "Autres appels de chasse fait par Philidor l'aîné" (both in Versailles, Municipal Library, Ms. Mus. 168). These two groups of signals are of crucial relevance for demonstrating the transition from one *trompe* to another. In fact, Philidor writes for two different instruments, using two different types of notation, but strictly maintaining the same pattern and style of music. The first group is written in French treble clef (the same notation found, for example, in the aforementioned *Ballet de la nuit*; see also Appendix I online), with the use of all harmonics from the third (g) to the twelfth (g"); the second group, written in alto clef, employs the same sounds one octave lower (thus from G to g'). Had Philidor been thinking of the same instrument, he would probably have used the same notation. It is instead much more probable that in the first case he referred to an old high-pitched circular *trompe* and in the second to the new instrument pitched an octave lower (cf. Dahlqvist 1994, 2, fn. 7) (see Musical examples 10 and 11).

His nephew Pierre Danican Philidor (1681–1731) is responsible for a further set of signals, placed at the end of the *Troisième Œuvre contenant une suitte à deux flûtes traversieres seules et une autre suitte, dessus et basse pour les hautbois, flûtes violons etc. avec une réduction de la Chasse*, published in Paris in 1718 (it is pitched in D, but "the bassoon has to read in G").

Musical examples 10 and 11. A. D. Philidor, first (above) and second (below) notation, 1705.

This collection is unique owing to the introduction of some effects, the most important—later named *tayauté*—being the execution of a kind of tremolo on all downbeats of the triadic rhythm typical of hunting calls.[18] It is paralleled by the

[18] The *tayauté* would also become part of the artistic repertoire for horn through the compositions of Hofmann, Beer-Fick, Telemann, Handel, and others.

"breath vibrato," also found in the Washington manuscript from 1666 (Cheney 1998) and in Philidor's signals, consisting in a slow vibrato obtained by the movement of the throat when emitting certain syllables (da, ha, has, etc.).

Meanwhile, the number and variety of fanfares had increased thanks to Dampierre, who seems also to have been the first to put a collection of fanfares in two parts, the *Récueil de fanfares pour la chasse*, down on paper. Although published posthumously in around 1775, it had been completed by 1723 (Gétreau 2006, 66). Another set of pieces attributed to Dampierre (*Tons de chasse et fanfares*) is found in Serré de Rieux 1734 (cf. Dampierre 2001), while a collection of two-part *Fanfares nouvelles* published in 1738 is signed with his initial ("par Mr. D.").[19] As for the admission of the instrument in the orchestra, the first evidence of a hooped *trompe* in this role is encountered in the divertissement *La chasse du cerf* by Jean-Baptiste Morin, performed in Fontainebleau in 1708 (see Musical example 12). In the *Avis* (Morin 1708, 1), the author indicated "the places where the *trompe* or the *trompette* can play, but since it is rare that such instruments take part in the concert, oboes or violins may also be used for the same purpose." A "*trompe ou trompette*" pitched in 8-ft C, with fanfare-like tunes that again might have been written by Marquis de Dampierre (*Grove* 2001, s.v.), is called for.

Apart from the few examples cited in Table 3 (online) and the numerous subsequent ones listed by Gétreau 2006 in her appendix 2, in 1718 horns were included

Musical example 12. J.-B. Morin, *La chasse du cerf*, p. 2.

---

[19] For the sake of completeness, we should also mention Servais Bertin (fl. 1730–1740), *Airs sérieux et à boire à une et deux voix, ronde de table, vaudevilles, tons de chasse et fanfare . . .* 2nd ed., Paris, l'auteur, s.d. (*ca.* 1737).

in the comedy by Antoine Coypel, *Les amours à la Chasse*,[20] in 1719 in *Les plaisirs de la Campagne* by Toussaint Bertin de La Doué (with *cor de chasse* in low D and C), in 1721 in *Les élémens by* Lalande and Destouches, in 1725 in *La reine des Péris* by Jean-Baptiste-Maurice Quinault (with a huge hunting scene), in 1726 in *Les festes de l'été* (2nd edition as *Bruit de chasse*) by Michel Pignolet de Montéclair, in the *Suite de symphonies et de fanfares* by Jean-Joseph Mouret in 1729,[21] and in the divertissement *La Chasse du Cerf* (1731) by Quinault; these many pieces for *cors de chasse* demonstrate a growing interest in the adoption of the instrument.

In the same year in which Toussaint Bertin de La Doué called for the horn in low C, Lotti used a pair of horns in low C in his *Teofane* (Dresden 1719). The comparison between the orchestral score and a contemporary keyboard transcription leaves no doubt about the absolute pitch of the horns (see Musical examples 13 and 14). However, had the horn stuck to this imitation of the hunting repertoire, it would hardly have earned the lasting success that marked its glorious subsequent history.

Musical example 13. A. Lotti, *Teofane*, Act II, Aria "Sciolgasi, movasi," solo horns in low C, from the full score (octave notation, see online, Appendix I).

Musical example 14. Contemporary keyboard transcription of the same aria, with horns transcribed at concert pitch.

---

[20] According to d'Origny 1788, I, 50, "L'Amours à la Chasse [. . .] was composed, it is said, to give the public the pleasure of listening two German hunting horn players, then in Paris."

[21] Performed at the Hôtel de la Ville on the occasion of a visit by the king in October 1729 (*Mercure de France* 2525, October 1729) and again "by the hunting horns of the Count of Charolais at Concert Spirituel" in December of that year (Pierre 2000, 132).

MUNICH AGAIN

The aforementioned familial relationships between the rulers of Bavaria, France, and Savoy lasted well beyond the beginning of the eighteenth century, which explains the similar interests in the hunt and the *trompe*, as well the spin-offs of hunting repertoire in the art music of their respective chapels. Prince Maximilian Emanuel II, after having hired the two hornist brothers Johann Caspar and Mathias Ganspöck for his private orchestra in 1715, sent them to Paris, imitating the example of von Sporck thirty-five years earlier. Also at the court of Munich, in honor of the patron saint of hunting, Hubertus, a mass by Pietro Torri was performed in 1722 and was a remarkable success (Nösselt 1980, 77).

EARLY TERMINOLOGY

When the French mounted hunt was introduced for the first time beyond the Rhine, the instrument was immediately called *Waldhorn* in German regions and *Jägerhorn* in Austria (Ahrens 2014, 90). Several decades later, however, after the appearance of the new large model with one and a half loops, the latter assumed the hybrid, half-French, half-German name *Parforcehorn* (or *Perforcehorn*), with a series of variants, such as *cornu* (*corne*) *par force*.[22]

The earliest occurrence of the likely use of the word *Waldhorn* to reference the hooped *trompe* is contained in the 1670 hunting treatise by Johann Christoph Lorber (Ahrens 2014, 91, fn. 29). In addition, there is a chronicle from the same period (Wicquefort 1682, 357) that tells of an ambassador from Guinea, Matthaeus Lopez, who traversed Paris, also in 1670, with a cortege of Moors, one of whom played a "Waldhorn instead of the trumpet." With short delay, the name *Waldhorn* is also found in a French–German dictionary (*Dictionnaire 1689*, II, 130), and in many others later on, as, for example, in the first edition of Johann Rädlein's trilingual dictionary (1711, vol. 1, 650, 1027).

The oldest mention of the *Parforce-jagd* can be, in turn, traced back to a hunting treaty from 1689 (Täntzer 1689, III, 56). The instrument's name appears in the variant "corni parforce" in a cantata by Römhild of 1714, followed by compositions by Bach, Telemann, Stölzel, and others (see Table 8, p. 112). Further examples are found in the account books of the Gotha court from 1719 (Ahrens

---

[22] A further variant, "*coranthorn*," mentioned previously, appears only once in 1708 (Haupt 1983, 346).

2006, 136) and in literary sources such as Fleming (1719, 297) and, about ten years later, in Gross (1730, 470).

As to the French terminology, both *trompe de chasse* and *cor de chasse* were used interchangeably until the mid-eighteenth century (see Figure 51 online). However, after the horn was finally accepted in the opera orchestra, with the hiring of two hornists, Mozer and Sieber, in 1767 (Castil-Blaze, 1855, II, 345), *cor de chasse* had become the usual name for their instruments. This latter term had in the meantime disappeared from the vocabulary of the hunt and was definitively replaced with the term *trompe de chasse* (D'Yauville 1788, 413, s.v. "trompe").

In England, the geographical background was used as a reference, so "French horn" came into use early and lasted permanently (it had already appeared in the aforementioned advertisement by Bull, 1699), whilst the use of the instrument in hunting was eventually abandoned. When, however, a certain Gottfried Pepusch visited London in 1704 with a Hautboisten band from Berlin, the group performed on "Hautbois, Flute and German Horns," and a month later with "Hunting horns" (Dart 1960, 339). This seems to indicate—in comparison with the definition "French horn"—that a new model was exhibited, probably the new larger one that was not yet used in England.

In Italy, two terms were traditionally used: the name "corno da caccia" and its cousin "tromba da caccia," which was more commonly used by composers belonging to and influenced by the Neapolitan school. The term is found in countless scores and is clearly derived from the corresponding French name "trompe de chasse."

It may also be noted that in Iberian languages (Spanish and Portuguese) the horn is still today called a *trompa*, a name derived from *trompa da caça*.

10
TRUMPET AND HORN PLAYERS

Until the end of the seventeenth century, theorists valued the trumpet and deemed it an essential part of the music scene, as stated, for instance, by the organist, composer, and scholar Andreas Werckmeister: "The trumpet possesses in itself the correct order of all consonances and an entire book could therefore be written about it" (Werckmeister 1691, chap. VIII, 22).

Starting in the beginning of the following century and with the entrance of the horn into art music, however, there was an increasing lack of interest in this noble and respected instrument, and many trumpeters progressively began to practice the horn, which eventually became the more important instrument (Dahlqvist 1991, 56–58).

An eloquent proof of this seems to be offered by the growing interest in the latter instrument from the aristocracy of the time and the parallel preference for hornists to the detriment of trumpet players, a trend that first emerged in Bohemian and Slavic countries, in which a massive diffusion of the horn had taken place. In the castle of Dobříš in Bohemia, lackey Martin Konvička was described in 1718 as the "trumpeter of the prince," while in 1724, he was cited as "hornist" (Volek 1983, 44).[1] In Silesia, trumpeters capable of doubling on trumpet and horn ("tubicen et lituista") were documented in the Piarist seminary of Stará Voda, where in 1721 new horns were purchased for the music in service of the institute (Sehnal 1983, 37). In the monastery of Zdar nad Sázavou in Moravia, two trumpeters enrolled in 1727 often played the horn, and in 1732, Count Lažanský replaced the two trumpet players of his chapel in Manětín with two hornists (Sehnal 1978, 135).

---

[1] Fitzpatrick 1970, 51, emphasizes that the earliest horn players had previously been trained on the trumpet or trombone, but that in the first two decades of the century, it was necessary to create "a sound idiomatic training at some stage" for the horn.

As for Saxony, where a strict guild protocol protected trumpet playing, a similar replacement was documented in Leipzig, where the *Stadtpfeifer* (municipal players), including the "trumpeter of Bach," Gottfried Reiche, were allowed to play various instruments. Further evidence is supplied by an audition judged by Bach himself in 1745 where the candidate Pfaffe successfully played violin, oboe, flute, horn, and trumpet (Schering 1921, 44).

In Dresden, where an even more rigid guild regulation had been in force for a long time, the growing success of the Italian melodrama involved the marginalization of the trumpet, a tendency definitely demonstrated by Hasse's complete lack of interest in this instrument (Fürstenau 1862, II, 176, fn.).

CLARINO TECHNIQUE

It is conceivable that instrumentalists able to switch from trumpet to horn favored the adoption of the "clarino" technique on the latter instrument. This allowed trumpeters to perform melodies in the high register (over the eighth harmonic), and, once applied to the horn, it allowed the new instrument, given its greater length of tubing, to perform diatonic and partially chromatic scales up to the twenty-seventh harmonic (Baines 1976, 31).[2]

In Dresden, the various pairs of musicians hired after 1711 (the first being the aforementioned Bohemians Fischer and Samm) were expected to play the horn in "clarino" style; this is demonstrated by the virtuoso passages found in music by composers active there since the 1710s, including Lotti, Heinichen, and Hasse. The same technique was also requested by composers elsewhere (Vivaldi in Venice, Zelenka in Vienna, Telemann in Hamburg, etc.).

The exploitation of the trumpet technique meant that the horn's hunting idiom, with its characteristic melodies in triadic rhythm covering only few harmonics, usually from the fourth to the twelfth, was progressively set aside.

THE EARLY SOLOISTIC STYLE

After some vocal compositions that required horns pitched in different keys, instrumental music also began to call for a variety of tonalities. At least in solo and

---

[2] A wide range of clarino passages can be found in Dahlqvist 1991, 58ff.

clarino writing, this should be interpreted as a request for different sizes of the instrument, as in these cases the use of crooks would be an obstacle to the performer.

One example is a composition by the Bohemian Jan D. Zelenka (1649–1745), the *Capricci* for 2 hn, 2 ob, bn, 2 vn, va, bc, which was presumably written in Vienna between 1717 and 1719; here, a pair of horns in D are used for the first *Capriccio* ZWV 182 (RISM 212002991), in G for the second ZWV 183 (RISM 212002998, dated January 24, 1718), in F for third ZWV 184 (RISM 212002993, *ca*. 1718), and in A for the fourth ZWV 185 (RISM 212002994, October 20, 1718) (see Musical example 15 online).[3] The parts are extremely high, repeatedly requiring the horn in D to climb up to the twenty-fourth harmonic (*a*", *concert pitch*), and the horn in A to the eighteenth harmonic (*b*", *concert pitch*). On the other hand, these same parts, especially in the two pieces in G and A, rarely go below the fourth harmonic, which is again an appropriate range for the clarino and eliminates any resemblance to hunting music.

Meanwhile, some composers started to entrust the instrument with an "obbligato" role in the accompaniment of vocal parts, such as in the *Serenata nel Giardino cinese* written by Heinichen in 1719. In this composition, the solo part for *corno da caccia* in F in Saturn's aria (T, hn, theorbo and bc) was probably written for the Bohemian hornist Fischer, together with the famous lutenist Sylvius Weiß (Hiebert 1992, 114, fn. 20). It is markedly virtuosic, and once again has a melodic pattern very close to the style of the clarino trumpet and a range extending from the fifth to the eighteenth harmonic.

Another example is the aria "Va tacito e nascosto" (see Musical example 16 online) from *Giulio Cesare in Egitto* by Handel, staged in London on February 20, 1724 (in the revised version from 1732 the Coro "Viva viva il nostro Alcide" in the first act with horns in A and D was added). The challenging part of the obbligato horn, again in F, allows us to assume that among the many skills of the instrumentalist for whom the part was conceived—possibly an otherwise unknown Mr. China (see Beakes 2007, 176)—there was likely the ability to balance the sound with the singer's voice, with whom they share a remarkable virtuosity.

Two other examples are found not much later in compositions by Giovanni Alberto Ristori (1692–1753). The first is a short aria with E-flat-horn obbligato ("Parmi udir") sung by the character Alceste in the opera *Calandro* (Pilnitz, 1726);

---

[3] A fifth Capriccio dated 1729 (RISM 212002985) is preserved in D-Dl Mus.2358-N-2.

the second is the central movement of the three-part Ouverture ("*Apertura*") in the melodrama *Un pazzo ne fa' cento, ovvero Don Chisciotte* (Dresden, 1727).[4] In the latter, the author writes a demanding part for F horn (Rühlmann 1872, 413), perhaps the oldest example of a solo in the slow movement of an orchestral piece, and the horns also play various showy passages during the reminder of the opera. The soloist was likely Johann Adam Schindler, who was the principal horn and performed with his brother Andreas in the Dresden court chapel between 1723 and 1733 (Hiebert 1992, 119) (see Musical example 17 online).

It is apparent from these examples that orchestral horn players were becoming increasingly more acquainted with demanding performances on their instrument and learning how to blend their sounds with those of the voice. This is also the case for Balthasar Abraham Petri's (1704–1793) cantata *In diem Johannis Baptistae* (1730) for T., hn (in F), and organ (D-DS = RISM 450002627) (see Musical example 18 online) (see also online, "An eccentric German soloist").

The most representative soloistic case in point is probably, however, that of Hasse's *Cleofide* (1731, RISM 270000632), in which the aria "Cervo al bosco" (Act III, Sc. 6) contains a memorable D-horn obbligato (see Musical example 19 online). Requiring masterful virtuosity, and including one of the earliest cadenzas written for the instrument (only the horn solo in the overture of Ristori's *Don Chisciotte* had included one prior to this point), it was probably inspired once more by the exceptional skillfulness of one of the Schindler brothers, presumably Johann Adam.

In 1732, Pergolesi staged *Salustia*, in which the aria "Odio di figlia altera" (see Musical example 20) includes two horns in D who interact with the main character with extreme virtuosity, including awkward broken arpeggios and fast sixteenth note triplets that, apart from a slightly less exaggerated use of the high register, are as demanding as those from *Cleofide*.

This example parallels several others in music written by composers from Vivaldi to Handel, in which a pair of horns, rather than only one instrument, play a soloistic role—a confirmation that the two instruments had assumed a function as a unit, later documented by the vast idiomatic repertoire of duets dedicated to them.

---

[4] In Act II of his *Don Chisciotte*, Ristori also calls for two "post horns," the first in B-flat and the second in F, in the courier's aria titled "Buon corrier sempr'è affrettato."

Musical example 20. Pergolesi, *Salustia*, Aria "Odio di figlia altera."

THE "FALSETTO"

Initially developed by cornett players and thus already named by Praetorius (1619/20, II, 36), the falsetto was adopted by trumpeters both to produce notes not part of the harmonic series and to refine the tuning of some harmonics, such as the eleventh. Keeping in mind that the falsetto had been used by trumpet players since at least Girolamo Fantini's 1638 treatise (cf. Conforzi 1994, 37); that horns had long been considered "trumpets built in a circular shape"; and that several trumpeters doubled on the horn, or left the trumpet for the horn, it is not surprising that this technique was also applied to the new instrument. An enlightening clue in this regard is found in Eisel (1738, 75): "On the horn the semitones cannot be obtained at all, with the exception of B-flat and F sharp, and only these." Using the falsetto, it was in fact possible for the player to lower the eighth harmonic in order to obtain the leading tone and to bend the intonation of the eleventh. In addition, some skilled players were apparently also able—contrary to what Eisel claimed— to produce other passing notes and several in the low register as well (see online, "Falsetto and *trompe de chasse*").

The two main centers in which this novelty was first encountered were Venice and Dresden, cities with a close musical relationship and in which the horn made a very early appearance.

Musical example 21. Lotti, *Polidoro*, Act III, Choir "Giove ascolta," bars 19–27.

For Venice, an example of non-harmonic notes is found in Vivaldi's Concerto RV 574, circa 1714, with the use of the E (a minor third below the third harmonic for F horn). In Antonio Lotti's *Polidoro* (February 1715), b' is repeatedly encountered as lowered eight harmonic (again for F horn), either attacked directly by the second horn, as a passing note, or even in arpeggios (see Musical example 21, and Rocchetti 2006, 269). The same non-harmonic pitch is also used in other compositions by Vivaldi (RV 538 and RV 97, Mantua, *ca.* 1719; see also Chapter 13 online, "Vivaldi").

In Dresden, non-harmonic notes were used by Heinichen, who may have attended the Venice performance of Lotti's *Polidoro* (he spent a long time in that city between 1710 and 1716 before being hired as Kapellmeister in Dresden).[5] In his *Sonata à 2 violini, violetta, 2 corni da caccia e corno da posta* (undated autograph in D-Dl = RISM 212002992), several non-harmonic sounds appear, especially in the second movement, where, unusually, the horns play in a minor key (F minor). Particularly rare is the use of the seventh harmonic, usually avoided owing to its low intonation, even though the non-harmonic notes are doubled by the strings, who provide reinforcement. Hiebert (1992, 116ff.) dates this composition to around 1719 and uses it as a case study on the early use of the hand technique.

Somewhat later, in 1724, Vivaldi staged his *Giustino* in Rome, in which f' is used as a passing note between the sixth and fifth harmonics by the horn in F (see the music example in Rocchetti 2006, 272). A more demanding example is in Vinci's *La caduta dei Decemviri*, performed in Naples at the Teatro San Bartolomeo in 1727, where b' and a' are required in a descending scale (bar 52), again doubled by the basses for support (see Musical example 22).

---

[5] In D-Dl there is a manuscript copy (RISM 212001258) of the *Sinfonia* from Lotti's *Polidoro*, in which the part originally written for the trumpets has been transcribed for the horns.

Musical example 22. L. Vinci, *La caduta dei decemviri*, Act I, "Spietata gelosia," bars 47–53.

Musical example 23. F. Durante, *Abigaile*, excerpt of horn part.

In 1736, Francesco Durante's oratorio *Abigaile* was performed in Rome. Only a short fragment of the horn part, published in 1834 by Fröhlich, seems to have survived (see Musical example 23).[6] Fröhlich's transcription is for horn in G, which implies an extensive use of non-harmonic notes obtained using "a change of embouchure," as he suggests. Nevertheless, the example is actually written in Neapolitan notation (see Appendix I online), which is also used elsewhere by Durante (e.g. in his *Messa per i defonti*, I-PAc). The key is D, which is clearly demonstrated by the two initial sharps (even though the first is misplaced), so the only artificial sound for the D turns out to be the leading note, C sharp.

[6] According to MGG2 1989, vol. 3, col. 988 (s.v. "Durante"), the scores of *Abigaille* and *S. Antonio da Padova* were once in the possession of Rev. Father Martini of Bologna.

We are inclined to regard all the aforementioned non-harmonic notes as examples of falsetto, rather than as an early use of the hand in the bell. The latter, however, remains a possible alternative, even though it is difficult to imagine an early, episodic acceptance of the hand technique in Dresden, namely in the same music chapel in which, a few decades later, it will be claimed to have been invented. The fact that these non-harmonic sounds made their appearance in Venice, Dresden, Rome, and Naples (since at least 1727 in the latter case), and even elsewhere,[7] testifies to a large dissemination of the practice, which seems to be a valid argument to confirm our assessment (see online, "An undervalued piece of evidence by Mattheson").

[7] A later piece of evidence of the falsetto is contained, inter alia, in the Handelian example in the *Complete Tutor* by Thompson and Simpson, published in London in 1746 (reproduction in Morley-Pegge 1973, appendix 3a), which also calls for the note b.

11

THE NATURAL HORN AT ITS ZENITH
(*ORCHESTERWALDHORN*)

According to Gerber (1792, 548), 1730 could be considered to be a watershed year in which the most extensive development of the natural horn took place, with the use of a greater number of keys and the affirmation of a distinguished solo repertoire to which the most famous composers of the time contributed. After the instrument's initial acceptance in theaters in Dresden, Vienna, Naples, and Venice, the horn progressively became a more regular presence in the orchestras of many other cities that were subject both to the influence of the imperial power and/or to that of Italian melodrama.

As for the variety of tonalities required and the use of crooks, we would draw attention to a unique manner of exploitation of the latter in the orchestra, which seems to have been overlooked until now. Three main sizes of the instrument were used—high, middle, and low—and up to three crooks were added to each size in order to obtain additional pitches. We will examine this ingenious system in detail, but we must promptly note that even in its heyday, attempts were made to create a single horn with a complete set of crooks in order to use a single instrument to produce the whole range of keys required for orchestral playing.

NATURAL HORN CROOKS

Crooks and shanks had been used since the sixteenth century in order to adapt trumpets and trombones to different tuning pitches, as was documented by Praetorius (1619/20, pl. VIII). The first known occurrence of the use of crooks for the horn is the set that Michael Leichamschneider supplied to the abbot of Kremsmünster (1703, see below). This provision predates the appearance of vocal compositions requiring different tonalities, at first in sacred music and later in the opera, by a few years (at least initially, key changes do not seem to be required in instrumental music). If the horns in C/ B-flat and F/ E-flat called for in sacred pieces discussed are plausibly due to differences in pitch among the instruments required (see Chapter 9, p. 53), the first known examples of music calling for different crooks may include a sacred cantata by F. W. Zachow (died 1712) that uses the keys of D, F, and A. The change of E-flat, G, A, and B-flat crooks is also called for by Gunther Wenzel Jacob (1685–1734) in *Anathema Gratiarum* of 1714.

In music treatises, crooks are documented for the first time by Joseph Fr. B. C. Majer (1732, 41), who points out that the horn—of which he also includes a rough illustration—can be tuned with shanks (*Setzstücke*) and crooks (*Krumbögen*), just as he described for the trumpet. Nevertheless, by that date the use of crooks had become customary in every type of repertoire, particularly in orchestral music.

Conversely, the adoption of crooks with hunting horns is quite unusual. An occurrence is seen, for example, on a 1740 tapestry depicting a large instrument with a small crook to lower the pitch by a semitone or so (Racines, near Bolzano (I), Wolfsthurn Castle, Museum of Hunting). The only reasonable explanation for the use of crooks in this context could be ensemble playing, such as that which took place during the *curée*, though it is not pictured here. Another example, not related to the hunt, is documented in Nigoline, Northern Italy (for both, see Figure 52 online).[1]

The adoption of crooks also led to a different way of holding the instrument, which now needed a more stable grip in order to prevent the accidental detachment of the crooks. Thus, it is probably no coincidence that even the hunter in Wolfsthurn's tapestry wields his great hunting horn with two hands—a less elegant position than was used previously, but certainly a more stable and balanced one. Incidentally, he also places, anachronistically, the mouthpiece on the side of the mouth, as it was when the horn first appeared at Venaria Reale.

FEW CROOKS FOR EACH SIZE

The newer sizes of 14ft-D and of 12ft-F horns, together with the earlier 8ft-C horn, constituted the three main sizes of the instrument (low, middle, and high respectively). The three of them, coupled with one to three terminal crooks, allowed for performance in all keys. This system was a convenient alternative to the initial practice of using a different horn for each key—a solution that, limited

---

[1] Another early example of a crook is found in an anonymous Italian painting from the early 1700s entitled *Allégorie musicale de Pan* (see https://gallica.bnf.fr/ark:/12148/btv1b8418862p. r=All%C3%A9gorie%20musicale%20de%20Pan?rk=21459;2).

to few sizes, remained the choice preferred by soloists. The three-size system constituted instead a cheaper and common option until the complete set of crooks for a single instrument came into use—a solution that was not devised, however, until well after the middle of the century.

The application of crooks to different sizes of the instrument is probably documented for the first time by Roeser in around 1764 and later by Francoeur in 1772. The former stated (Roeser 1764, 13) that to obtain "the tonality of E ('*Esimi naturel*'), a semitone extension should be added to the F-horn, and that C requires in turn a whole tone extension added to the D size." Francoeur (1772, 37), repeating almost verbatim the text of Roeser, adds that "B-fa-sib" (B-flat horn) may be obtained by adding a semitone extension to the higher-pitched instrument (horn in B natural). Neither one mentions the key of low B-flat, on the other hand. This is quite surprising, as it was very common in the second half of the eighteenth century. However, the gap is filled in by Vandenbroek in his *Méthode* (*ca.* 1797, 23), as he mentions it explicitly, also stating that the key of high C ("Ut en haut") had no longer been used for some years.

In addition, Roeser offers interesting comments on the character of the different tonalities, from low to high C (Roeser 1764, 13). Low C, even though less resonant, is the sweetest key, easier for high notes and less for low ones; D, E, and E-flat are louder and less difficult in the low register than low C; F and G are even louder, but in these keys one should use less of the high range of the instrument and more of the low range; and A, B-flat, and high C are the loudest and most difficult tonalities to play, and the high register is therefore used less. He also acknowledges (Roeser 1764, 17) the different roles of the first and second horns, arguing that composers should learn the range of each of them well. In this regard, he also mentions one Mr. Ebert in a footnote, a member of the Académie Royale de Musique and the only horn player in Paris capable of playing equally well in both registers.

Sir Samuel Hellier's description of two of his horns before they underwent some changes in 1767 to be modernized and adapted to a new system must also refer to the horn sizes with few crooks (Frew-Myers 2003, 10). In 1780, La Borde (I, 254–255) provides a more detailed description of this set-up, mentioning high C, G, and low B as master sizes and reporting that they were 8', 10'8", and 18'6" long respectively. The three sizes system is also documented in the *Art du faiseur d'instruments de musique, et lutherie* (in *Encyclopédie méthodique* 1785, 126), but six years later, the horn player Jean Brun (1759–1809) eliminated all mention of this three-part system while revising the text for the volume *Musique* of the same *Encyclopédie méthodique* (1791, I, 376–378), evidently considering it completely out of date.[2]

Gerber also refers (1792, 548) to old horns built in three sizes—E-flat, G, and B-flat—to which shanks and crooks could be added to lower the pitch by a semitone or more, although he specifies that this solution involves "new difficulties, partly in the choice of the size, partly owing to the different ways of producing sound and holding the instrument, and finally, since it makes tuning even more difficult." If Gerber is referring to church pitches (he was an organist by profession, after all), when transposed in chamber pitch, E-flat and G would coincide with the two keys mentioned by Mattheson some eighty years before. The latter left out high B-flat (in Gerber's terminology)—probably because at that early date, that key was still associated with the circular *trompe* used in the hunt, in which he was not interested. Another piece of evidence is found in Koch (1802, 884, art. "Krummbogen"), where a neat distinction between two crooks, a larger one that lowers the pitch by one tone and a smaller one that lowers it by a semitone, is made. In addition, there was, of course, the possibility of using both together in order to further lower the pitch.

At any rate, the clearest description of the system with a few terminal crooks on different-sized horns is mentioned in Fröhlich (1811, 2–3), who considers them to be a fallback option considering the other systems that had been introduced in the meantime:

> To lower a high horn, or to give it a lower pitch by elongating the tubing, one may use circular piece of tubes, alone or in pairs, and longer or shorter in length, which are inserted at the entrance of the instrument and are called crooks. The larger crook is normally long enough to lower the instrument by one step, while the smaller brings it down by a half step (occasionally two larger crooks are used together in order to lower of the pitch by two tones). If one wants to lower a horn from high B-flat to G, he must connect two crooks,

[2] Apart from being explicitly acknowledged by M. Framery who signed the text in question, this contribution by Brun is also mentioned by Fétis 1860–1865, V, 212, s.v. "Lebrun," who reminds readers about the suicide of this distinguished hornist. He was renowned to the point of being known to the future empress of France, Joséphine de Beauharnais (Ducrest 1828, 32–33) but was left without the means to support himself after his brilliant career ended.

the larger of which put the instrument a step lower, that is in Ab, and a smaller one that lowers the instrument another half step to G.

Finally, a later reference to this system is found in Keeß (1824, 167), who, while still commenting on this old system, also notes that the instruments previously intended for art music were smaller than those used in hunting: "Once there were only the so-called *Jagdwaldhörner* and the somewhat smaller ones used by the musicians. Three horns were used for all tonalities."

THE ROLE OF THE LEICHAMSCHNEIDERS

We have repeatedly mentioned the Leichamschneider brothers, Michael (1676–1751) and Johann (1679–1742), because of the importance and the quality of their craftsmanship.[3] Their work constituted, in fact, the beginning of a new and glorious horn-manufacturing tradition in Vienna, which was continued by Adam Ferber, Karl Starzer, Anton Kerner Sr., and others.[4]

The first evidence of the use of crooks with the horn, mentioned previously, dates back to 1703 and consists of a receipt Michael Leichamschneider sent to the abbot of Kremsmünster.[5] It lists "a couple of large Jägerhörner"—then the Austrian synonym for the German *Waldhorn* (Ahrens 2014, 90)—and "four new double crooks," "four new shanks," and "2 mouthpieces." Based on this document, Fitzpatrick (1970, 28–44) considered the Leichamschneiders to be the inventors of the natural orchestral horn, which was fitted with a complete set of crooks in order to obtain any tonality required by the score. In light of what has been said, however, it was instead a pair of the aforementioned horns with two crooks each, used to lower the pitch, and with two tuning shanks. In other words, they were

[3] The most recent and reliable biographical data on the builders of this dynasty is contained in Hopfner 2002. Further information can be found in *Grove* 2001, s.v. (H. Fitzpatrick/J. K. Page).

[4] Hermann 1782, 32: "Vienna has long been renowned for its fine musical instruments, and especially for hunting horns, which are built here with the utmost perfection." For the close relations of cohabitation and kinship between those famous builders, and also the Huschauers and the lesser known Michael Pecht, see Starzer 1998, 80–90.

[5] Kellner 1956, 296 (see also Ahrens 2014). Fitzpatrick 1970, 33: "List / what I have made as follows / Firstly 1 pair great *Jägerhorn* at 34 Gullden / Item 4 new double *Krumbögen* 7 Gulden/ Further 4 new *Stickel* / Further 2 new mouthpieces, each one 30 Kreuzer makes 1 Gulden / For each case thereto is 1 Gulden / Summa 43 Gulden 36 Kreuzer / Honorius Abbot / Michael Leichnemschneider/ Burgher, Trumpet and Horn-Maker."

likely one of the three sizes described above—in all probability, that of F, as surviving Leichamschneider horns are usually pitched in this tonality, which is frequently requested in the oldest extant pieces of art music (see Table 4 online).

According to some opinions, the Leichamschneiders may even have had a role in devising the F-model with two and a half loops, which was credited to Michael Koch of Dresden; at least, according to present knowledge, the latter's horn from 1710 was created a couple of years before Leichamschneiders' eventual preference for this particular shape and size.

A unique item built by Leichamschneider in 1721 (Schloß Wallerstein, at Harburg in Bavaria) is also in the same key. The instrument is characterized by a compact body that, contrary to Fitzpatrick's belief (1970, 35, fig. IVa), was not designed to accommodate a full set of different crooks; as emerged during the restoration, the large diameter of the mouthpiece socket is only due to the lack of a good piece of the leadpipe.[6]

The rare ability of the Leichamschneiders was emphasized many years ago by Jeremy Montagu, who examined two 1725 horns from Tredegar House in Duffryn near Cardiff with Johann's mark, which were subsequently sold at auction (Montagu 1986). Their construction surprisingly featured a main body made from a single piece of tubing, constructed over a mandrel about two meters long (a sort of lengthened knitting needle) and then cleverly folded in a circle with extreme skill.

Owing to the lack of a comprehensive list of Leichamschneiders' horns in previous literature, and to expand upon the list focused solely on Michael Leichamschneider, presented in Berdychová (2014), we have proposed in Table 4 (online) a tentative list that will certainly be extended in the future. It mostly contains instruments in F, built in Vienna, and usually marked Michael (those with Johann's mark are expressly indicated), even though it is likely that the two brothers also worked together.

Finally, we must make note of the aforementioned Hradisko monastery near Olomouc, which bought two "horns of a new type, folded in two large circles" from Vienna in 1702—possibly from the Leichamschneiders themselves (Freemanová 2006, 216, quoting Sehnal). As we know of no documents on horn

---

[6] See the restoration report by Ursula Menzel (1995). We would like to thank the Öttingen-Wallerstein archive staff for their helpful communications.

production in Vienna from the time before this provision, this could be the first evidence related to the skilled Viennese brothers.

CROOKS FOR ORCHESTRAL HORNS

From the 1720s, especially in the German countries and later in the Neapolitan operatic repertoire, an increasing number of tonalities, and therefore crooks, can be found. Once again, according to Gerber, they were primarily if not exclusively intended for orchestral use since they impede soloistic playing by requiring, as already noted, the use of a different grip.[7]

While the most usual and economical system remained the application of crooks of semitone or whole tone to three different sizes of the instrument, makers began to experiment with using a greater number of crooks for one and the same instrument (a complete set would only arrive, however, a few decades later)—even though, of course, it still remained possible to build a different horn for each key.[8]

In 1718, two *Waldhörner* of Viennese make (again probably by the Leichamschneiders) were bought in Dresden. They were equipped with six pairs of crooks and two silver mouthpieces and cost a good 50 thalers (Fürstenau 1862, II, 58). The inventory of the parish church of Stare Křečany from 1730 (Northern Bohemia) includes the following description of the crooks belonging to a pair of horns (Freemanová 2006, 217): "*Dis Crompogen 2, F: Bogen 2, Ganze Thons 3, Halbe Thons 3, Grossbogen 2.*" If our interpretation is correct, this refers to a body in high C or B-flat, with crooks that lowered the pitch by a semitone (*halb Thon*), a tone (*ganz Thon*), a tone and a half (*halb* plus *ganz Thon*), and two tones (*Grossbogen*), and in addition F (*Bogen*) and E-flat (*Dis Crompogen*), which implies a very large array of tonalities that could be obtained. Could this be a prime example of the inventive mind of Johann Werner of Dresden? Twenty years later, in 1749, an inventory from the Piarist monastery of Nitra (Slovakia) reports the acquisition of "new horns with 6 crooks and 6 attachments, or steclis" (*Litui novi cum 6 Circulis & 6 additamentis seu steclis*) (Szórádová 2006, 231, fn. 17).[9]

---

[7] Gerber 1792, col. 550: "In solo performance, or during duets, the virtuoso uses only a simple horn without any crooks."

[8] In 1753, for example, the duke of Aumont ordered seven pairs of horns in the keys of C, D, E, F, B, A, and G from the Parisian maker Carlin (Gétreau 2006, 37 and 68).

[9] The word "steclis" does not appear to have any possible meanings aside from "shank," or "tuning bit," but to our knowledge, it is not used by any other sources.

An early Italian document refers to a maker from Turin, Carlo Giuseppe Vicco (*ca.* 1697–*ca.* 1745), who delivered "two newly invented *corni da caccia*, supplied with seven removable crooks" to the Suardi brothers in 1735. These horns were built for brothers Matteo and Felice Suardi, who had been members of the Turin orchestra since at least 1734. Two further orders were processed in 1736 and in 1737, the latter with the provision for another "8 brass crooks" (Odling–Girodo 1999–2000) (see online, "Two German horn players in Turin").

The first Spanish documentation regarding the purchase of crooks (*tudeles*) dates back to 1738 and consists of a document from the Municipal Archive of Alzira: "A Mosén Gabriel Lázaro, kappelmeister, one pound for eight crooks bought for the horns of the villa" (Verdú 2000, 57). It is unclear, however, for how many instruments these eight crooks were intended.

No definitive information is available on the appearance of the crooks in England prior to the instruments made by Hofmaster, which will be discussed later and whose crooks likely date back to well after the middle of the eighteenth century. Equally uncertain is the situation in France, where "*le cor de Symphonie, avec ses tuyaux de rechange*" was only introduced in 1765 by Rodolphe (Castil-Blaze, 1855, II, 345). In both countries, instead, a remarkable development of the duet repertoire is reported, which required instruments without crooks (see below) (see also online, "The first crooks in America?").

SOLOISTIC CONCERTOS IN THE LATE BAROQUE PERIOD

In the solo repertoire developed in the meantime—the soloistic concertos for horn and orchestra being a leading representative—crooks were generally not used. The respective scores, in addition, rarely recorded the date of composition. Thus, only analysis of the music writing can help to narrow down their date. This implies comparison of harmonic-melodic structures and compositional techniques with the few dated manuscripts, but this type of analysis falls outside the scope of this book.[10]

In the earliest compositions, the instrument is either not used in the slow movement or, if present, remains in the major key imposed by the harmonic series. Only in a second stage would melodies also appear in minor keys. Many themes

---

[10] Such an approach is adopted, for instance, in a dissertation by Kearns 1980, who reviews all the solo horn concertos of the Thurn und Taxis chapel in Regensburg.

were initially inspired by the hunting repertoire, which was later abandoned in favor of a broader exploitation of the clarino technique and greater melodic and harmonic freedom. Meanwhile, an increasing differentiation between the roles of first and second horn was codified, as demonstrated by the double horn concertos and the emergence of soloistic concertos for first horn, which frequently made use of the clarino register, and for second horn, which mostly used the falsetto and, later on, the hand technique.

GERMANY

With the exception of the earliest examples (those by Beer, Vejvanovský, and the anonymous *Sonata da caccia*, discussed in Chapter 8, p. 46), the first appearance of a true soloistic horn repertoire has long been identified as the Concerto à 7 in E-flat by "Hoffmann," now preserved in Dresden (D-Dl = RISM 210044722). Here, the part of the obbligato horn uses a range from the fifth to the sixteenth harmonics, and the archaic structure of the composition (Adagio, Allegro, Adagio, Minuet) could provide confirmation of its old age and of the attribution to Melchior Hoffmann, an organist and composer who worked in the same city and died in 1715. On the other hand, the use of the E-flat key, which was uncommon at the time but later become much more frequent for solo concertos, suggests a later date and the attribution to another Hoffmann, perhaps Johann Georg (1700–1780). In any event, a decisive argument toward a later dating of this piece is its presence in the important collection of eighteen solo horn concertos preserved at the University of Lund, including pieces by various German composers and soloists: the aforementioned Hoffmann, Fischer, Graun, Quantz, and other less well-known or anonymous authors (for Hoffmann's concerto, see Dahlqvist 2006, with music example).

The date of compilation of this collection, according to Rasmussen (1961–1962), who first focused on it, is likely to have been between 1720 and 1745. Scharnberg (1978, 81), however, maintained that the same manuscripts were written somewhat later, in the years 1750–1770, with the possible exception of the concerto by Förster, who died in 1745.

A point in favor of Scharnberg's argument is that in 1763, the publishing house Breitkopf included a concerto for horn by J. J. Quantz (1697–1773), complete with the musical incipits, in one of its catalogs. This allows the ninth piece in the collection to be definitively identified.[11] A second catalog from 1764 also mentions the "I. Concerto, *a Corno di Caccia obligato, Oboe, Violino coll Basso*" by Graun, which is probably number seven in the collection. Finally, a third list from the same house, this time from 1783, allows for the identification of a concerto copied by Quantz and written by the famous oboist and composer Johann Christian Fischer (1733–1800), whose date of birth leaves no doubts as to the date of composition of at least this piece.[12]

Table 5. Wenster manuscript

Call no.	Author	Composition
J:1	Schulz	*Concerto ex Dis del. Sig: Schultz* (Concerto ex D sharp for horn, flauto traverso, violin, and basso) // RISM 190003300
J:2	Anonymous (but Hoffmann)	*Concerto ex Dis.* (Concerto ex D sharp for horn, two oboes, and strings) // RISM 190001717
		Cf.: Concerto Co VV.ni Oboi Corni obl: Viola Del Sigr Hoffmann (Concerto ex D sharp for horn, two oboes, and strings) // RISM 210044722
J:3	Quantz (but Johann Cristian Fischer)	*Concerto ex Dis del: Sig. Qwantz* (Concerto ex D sharp for horn and strings); copied by Quantz // RISM 190002435
J:4	anonymous	*Concerto ex Dis del: Sig* (Concerto ex D sharp for horn, two oboes, and basso) // RISM 190001716
J:5	Förster (Christoph Heinrich)	*Concerto ex Dis dur del: Sig. Förster* (Concerto ex D sharp for horn and strings) // RISM 190002453
J:6	Anonymous	*Concerto ex E dur* (Concerto for horn, oboe d'amore, and basso) // RISM 190001715

[11] See Robert Ostermayer's website http://www.corno.de/shop/Horn-Orchester/rom021.html.

[12] In the collection in Lund (Sammlung Wenster J:22), there is another horn concerto by H. F. Johnsen (see Table 5), dated 1751, which seems not to have been taken into consideration yet.

Call no.	Author	Composition
J:7	Graun (Carl Heinrich?)	*Concerto ex D dur del: Sig. Graue* (Concerto for horn, oboe d'amore, and basso) // RISM 190002530
J:8	Graun (Carl Heinrich?)	*Trio ex D dur del: Sig. Graun* (Trio for violin, horn, and b.c.) // RISM 190002545
J:9	J. J. Quantz	*Concerto ex Dis dur del: Sig. Quantz* (Concerto for horn, oboe, and strings) // RISM 190003089
J:10	Knechtel (Johann Georg)	*Concerto ex D dur del: Sig. Knechtel* (Concerto for horn and strings) // RISM 190002871
J:11	Anonymous (J. G. Knechtel)	*Concerto ex Dis dur.* (Concerto for horn and strings) // RISM 190001722
J:12	Förster (Christoph Heinrich)	*Concerto ex Dis dur del: Sig. Förster* (Concerto for horn and strings) // RISM 190002453
J:13	Anonymous (attrib. to Anton Hampel)	*Concerto ex D dur.* (Concerto for horn and strings) // RISM 190001686
J:14	Röllig (Johann Georg?)	*Concerto ex Dis dur del: Sig. Röllig* (Concerto ex D sharp for horn and strings) // RISM 190003121
J:15	Röllig (Johann Georg?)	*Concerto ex D dur del: Sig. Röllig* (Concerto ex D for horn and strings) // RISM 190003120
J:16	Graun (Carl Heinrich?)	*Concerto ex D dur del: Sig. Graun* (Concerto for horn and strings) // RISM 190002529
J:17	Reinhardt (Carl?)	*Concerto ex Dis dur del: Sig. Reinhardt* (Concerto ex D sharp for horn and strings) // RISM 190003108
J:17b	Gehra/Gehring	*Concerto ex D dur del: Sig. Gehra/Gehring* (Concerto ex D for horn and strings) // RISM 190002487
J:22	Henrik Philip Johnsen (1717–1779)	*Concerto per un Corno di H P Johnsen* (autograph, 1751) (Concerto ex D sharp for horn and strings) // RISM 190002838

Aside from the issues of dating, this relevant collection of baroque concertos (the one by Gehra is discussed in Part II online, "The concerto by Gehra/

Gehring") confirms the central role of instrumental music in the German-Bohemian area and the interest of musicians and composers in the concertante role of the horn. One may note, in particular, an affinity toward the musical tendencies prevalent in Dresden during the first half of the eighteenth century, on which some of these compositions apparently relied, as was also noted by Rasmussen (1961–1962). The clarino technique remains predominant (e.g. in the Knechtel concerto), but in some pieces—the more recent ones, as it seems—the mid-low register is also used (as in no. 13, attributed to Hampel). This is likely an indication of the increasing specialization of some players in this range and the instrument's new expressive possibilities.

DRESDEN

We should actively consider the musical and technical developments in the solo horn writing that occurred in Dresden, where several renowned horn players were active beginning in 1710: the aforementioned Fischer and Samm, followed by the brothers Johann Adam and Andreas Schindler,[13] Anton Hampel and Karl Haudek, and others. In 1719, the wedding of Prince Frederick Augustus II and Maria Josepha of Austria, during which music assumed a central role and the horn was reserved a special place within, provided a strong push for the development of horn music (see Figure 53 online). Several young composers attended the event and could have been inspired by the instrument while listening to compositions by Lotti and Heinichen.

In addition to these composers (and to Telemann, Handel, and others), Christoph Heinrich Förster (1693–1745) also participated in the celebration. He was then a pupil of Heinichen, who likely wrote two concertos for horn and strings that are now preserved in Lund. Both are in E-flat and written in a compositional style that likely dates back to the early 1740s. We can observe that the "second" of the two concertos (the Pizka edition) may have been written earlier than the other for stylistic reasons: the horn here climbs up to the twentieth harmonic, and pitches below the eighth harmonic are only used twice (in the *ripieno* section, on beats 1 and 16); there are no notes outside the harmonic series, and the simple compositional

---

[13] Johann Adam (fl. 1723–1733) and Andreas (fl. 1723–1737) became members of the Dresden court orchestra in 1723. J. A. Hasse's opera *Cleofide* (1731), the "Quoniam" of Bach's B minor Mass (1733), and the soloistic parts in ensemble concertos by J. F. Fasch, attest to Schindler's abilities. See Fitzpatrick 1970, 96 (Fischer and Adam) and 100–101 (Schindler).

structure, as well as the similarity to Vivaldi's style, all suggest a date of composition predating that of his "first" concerto (see also online, *"Für den Dresdener Kollegen . . ."*).

WALLERSTEIN

To the prestigious names of horn players active in Dresden, we might add those of their colleagues serving in the House of Oettingen-Wallerstein in Harburg, Bavaria: Christoph Fritsch and Andreas Eder, both active beginning in 1746, Friedrich Domnich (1729–1790), in service between 1747 and 1751, Joseph Fritsch from 1752 to 1766, Johann Türrschmidt (1725–1800) from 1752 to 1766, and again, from 1773 to after 1780, and Joseph Joseph (1727–1804).[14]

For this particular court, and likely for Türrschmidt and Fritsch, Leopold Mozart (1719–1787) wrote a double horn concerto in E-flat dated August 3, 1752 (see Musical example 24 online). The part of the first horn is written in pure clarino style (sixth to twentieth harmonics), while that of the second is analogous to the parts for second horn in some of the Lund concertos (including virtuosic leaps from the second to the twelfth harmonics).

Leopold Mozart also wrote another horn concerto in D major, preserved in the same archive,[15] which may also have been conceived for Johann Türrschmidt. In this piece, a distinguished command of the clarino technique (eighth to twenty-first harmonics) is also required, but the harmonic texture suggests a date of composition close to that of the double concerto.

Again for the House of Oettingen-Wallerstein, Leopold Mozart wrote in 1755 a *Sinfonia di caccia* with four obbligato horns (two in G, two in D) and strings (RISM 450025262), and he included this curious remark: "Firstly, the horns in G should be played quite raucously, as is customary during the hunt, and as loudly as possible. A *Hifthorn* may also be used. Secondly, there should be several barking dogs, and the other performers are to shout ho-ho etc. together, but only for six bars."[16] This rustic composition also calls for some gunshots (*"Kugel bix"*), which are usually entrusted to the timpani in indoor performances. During the Andante,

---

[14] On the latter, see Fitzpatrick 1970, 124, and Kearns 1980, 4, fn. 9. A complete list of the hornists of this court (based on Grünsteudel 2013) can be found in Chapter 17, "*Horn players at Wallerstein.*"

[15] *Sinfonia di camera ex D# / a 5 / Violino solo / Cornu Solo / 2 viole et / Basso per il violone / è Violoncello A.S. L: Mozart /* in D-HR III 1/2 4° 516, manuscript score from circa 1760 (published in DTB 9/2; RISM 450025242).

[16] Cited in the Doblinger edition by Dr. Helmut Riessemberger, 1969.

the horns in G are silent while the pair in D perform some solos and a series of echoes that, according to the surviving orchestral material, were originally played by two different groups, one of which was only used for these echoes.

Various compositions by Franz Xaver Thomas (František) Pokorny (1729–1794) were also written for the Wallerstein court. A student of Joseph Riepl (1709–1782) and a young violinist living in Wallerstein, Pokorny was particularly interested in the horn, and later, while living in Mannheim in order to study with Stamitz, he received a commission for six concertos that he wrote in 1754. Representative of the "*empfindsamer Stil*" (sensitive style) of the mid-eighteenth century, his writing for the instrument is definitely innovative (Kearns 1980, 75) and required marked virtuosity and an increased range as it explored new tonal possibilities through the use of low register and falsetto sounds, and released the instrument from the limits of tonic-dominant harmony.

These examples confirm that Dresden cannot boast an exclusive role in the beginning of the development of the solo horn repertoire, and other early examples show this as well (Vivaldi in Mantua, Zelenka in Vienna, and Handel in London). It is apparent that there are some similarities between the Lund concertos and those written in other places by other authors during the same period. Furthermore, a certain affinity between Pokorny's and Mozart father's writing for horn can be observed. It was surely a result of collaboration with the same performers, but was even more probably a derivative of the performance tradition that was already established in Bavaria and nearby areas (Mannheim), a tradition that may proudly stand separately from that of the Lund concertos (see also online, "A scale for two concerts," and Musical example 25 online).

Starting with the double horn concertos by Pokorny, soloists were required to face extensive concertante parts, which paved the way for the double concertos written later. On the other hand, the Concertos for Horn and Orchestra in D major by F. J. Haydn (extensively discussed in Chapter 17 online) were markedly conservative in terms of horn technique.

FRANCE

One of the earliest soloistic uses of the horn in France is found circa 1740 in *La Choisy XIV. Concerto comique pour les cors de chasse, musette, vièle, flûte, violon avec la basse* by Michel Corrette (1707–1795) (RISM 990011379) (see Musical example 26 online). The style is somewhat antiquated, and the horn, which is "tacet" in the second movement, as in the oldest concertos, mostly performs hunting calls and simple melodies.

The key of the piece, C, is clearly the "low" one, which was rare in horn solo repertoire but well documented in other settings and by several surviving instruments as well. Some of these include the horn with one huge hoop from Crétien (Paris MdM E.890, undated) and other items illustrated in Fitzpatrick (1970, pl. XIII): one (his fig. *c*) by Johann Georg Grinwolt (Grünwald) of 1735 and an anonymous pair (fig. *d*) dating back to 1750, all of which are found in the Prague National Music Museum (inv. 578 E, 581 E and 582 E, respectively).

Another piece was also performed on this or a similar model: a cantata for soprano titled *Actéon* by Joseph Bodin de Boismortier (1689–1755), published in 1737, which called for a *cor de chasse* in C in the air with continuo "*Que le son du cor.*"

Four horn players, Edouard, Capelle, Vibert, and Herbert, performed a *Quatuor de Cors-de-Chasse* on the day of Pentecost in 1750 (*Mercure de France*, June 1750, 199). The next solo concerto to our knowledge dates back to April 9, 1751, when the German horn player Ernst "*joua seul un Concerto à 2 Cors-de-chasse, de la composition de M. Schifer*" (*Mercure de France*, May 1751, 190).[17]

These are isolated solo performances, later to become increasingly frequent, but, returning to the French orchestral repertoire, we can observe that two horn players were a constant presence in the orchestra de la Pouplinière starting in late 1748, when "two new German hunting horns" performed a symphony by J. P. Guignon (*Mercure de France*, December 1748, 181). They were in all probability the two German players, Syryyneck (Širineck; see Fitzpatrick 1970, 113) and Steinmetz (Staimetz, Slamitz; see Fitzpatrick 1970, 118–119), although their names are only explicitly mentioned in 1753 (Cucuel 1913, 26). The same players also performed occasionally at the Concert Spirituel, where in 1754 Steinmetz played a concerto he wrote and a "new symphony with corni da caccia and oboe." The following year, he performed another with "clarinets and corni da caccia" (Brenet 1900, 223).

We have only dealt with instrumental music so far, but Cucuel (1913) also focuses on a passage from the *Memoirs* of the composer François-Joseph Gossec (1734–1829), who claimed to have introduced the horn into French operatic music

---

[17] Reported incorrectly (or documented by unknown sources) in Pierre 2000, 433. The *Mercure de France* (187, May 1751) also reports the following comment on the concerto played by Ernst: "Cette nouveauté a paru plus singulière qu'agréable."

in 1757 (Gossec 1829, 220). In spite of this primacy, Cucuel cites the use of horns in *Achille et Déidamie* by André Campra, 1735, and in some works of Rameau, and one might add the suite of dances *Les Élémens* by Jan-Féry Rebel père, printed in 1737, which included *cors de chasse* pitched in D.

Doubts as to Gossec's claim have already been raised by Adam Carse (1925, 113): "The parts in Rameau's *Hippolyte et Aricie* and in most of his succeeding operas supply sufficient evidence [. . .] that the credit given to Gossec for having introduced horns into French orchestras in 1757, as stated by several writers, is unmerited" (see online, "Rameau and the horn," and Musical example 27 online).

A peculiar use of the instrument in France, well before 1750, was, finally, represented by several compositions for horn duo, or for ensembles with two horns (see Chapter 12).

ENGLAND

The first known examples of British concertos for solo horn(s) after Handel's Concerto with Two Horns HWV 331,1 (*ca.* 1715) seems to be that by Francesco Barsanti (1690–1770), published in Edinburgh in 1742 as *Concerto Grosso*, op. 3, nos. 1–5 (see Musical example 28 online). Timpani, usually associated instead with fanfares of trumpets, are used as accompaniment for the two solo horns.

The Egerton music collection of the British Library (Add. 71539), recently studied by Thomas Hiebert, contains as many as fourteen compositions with two horns and six with only one, two of which are of particular interest owing to the use of the low C key (Hiebert 2006, 239–246). The first, entitled "Corno solo" (no. 27 in the collection), is a unique example, as it is written for horn and bc.; the second is the Concerto (no. 17) with Violino, Oboe, Cornu Solo, Basso, written by the otherwise unknown Carlo Vernsberg, which might, however, reveal the family name of the horn player and composer simply known as "Mr. Charles" (see Chapter 13 online, "Mr. Charles" section within "Handel").

Although there are no decisive arguments as to the dating of these manuscripts, Hiebert (2006, 240) points out that they were written in the mid-eighteenth century, certainly between 1746 and 1780, the year of Lady Egerton's death. In this concerto various sounds outside the series of natural harmonics are exploited, which implies the use of the hand technique, a believable occurrence given the respective dates. In addition, the key of low C in this and in other solo pieces could be the result of a British preference, already documented in 1746 by Christopher

Winch's *The Complete Tutor* (he, in any case, recommends beginners adopt that of D). Further confirmation of the use of the low C crook in Britain is found in the correspondence of Sir Samuel Hellier (see Frew-Myers 2003) and in another English handbook that follows the text of Winch exactly, mentioning the pitches of G, F, E, D, and of course C (*Apollo's Cabinet: or the Muse's Delight*, 1756, I, 25).

ITALY

One of the earliest Italian pieces of evidence on the eighteenth-century horn is the description of a singular mechanical invention reported in the *Giornale de' Letterati d'Italia* in 1712 (vol. X, art. XI, 489–493). It deals with a pneumatic machine devised by the Milanese Giovanni Baillioni for Countess Margherita Visconti and located at her villa in Lainate near Milan. It was a kind of water organ whose bellows "give air to many *trombe ritorte*, that is, twelve *corni da caccia*, which with a secret device play in concert two at once." The reviewer remarks (p. 490) that organ pipes and flutes produce the sound by a stream of air broken against an edge, while the horn needs "the lips pressed and closely matching each other, until the air is forced to fly out through a thin chink between them, so that they are put into vibration, thus substituting the function of the edge." He continues with a description of the horn that seems worth quoting at length (p. 491):

> besides a mouthpiece ("*imboccatura*") different from that of the trumpets (from which the sound, at least in this aspect, is more arduous to obtain), it is a more lacking instrument than the trumpet, producing no other sounds aside from the four scalar tones of D, E, F, and G, and those jumping from G [misprinted: Q], C, E, G, and C. And here another obstacle is the low G, a lot of wind and little force in the chest is required so that the sound does not make an upward jump. On the other hand, to go up to high G, and even more so to reach upper C, greater force in chest and less amount of breath is required; in fact, the latter must diminish in order to vibrate with greater energy, thus achieving more frequent vibrations, from which the uppermost sound springs out [. . .] with a *corno da caccia* made up by three loops, or circles.

A few years later, however, the horn had already fully entered into the instrumental and theatrical Italian repertoire, even though as a solo instrument it had made only occasional appearances. These include what seems to be the first ever composition for two horns and orchestra, Vivaldi's Concerto per due corni e archi (RV 538) from circa 1719. Otherwise, the horn in Italy remained mainly connected to the opera, the most relevant and most performed musical tradition in this country.

SPAIN AND PORTUGAL

After the aforementioned first appearance in Barcelona in the *Oracolo del fato* by Gasparini (1711), the permanent inclusion of the instrument in the orchestra happened some twenty years later. One of the first occurrences could have been *La Dorinda* (1730?) by the Italian composer Francesco Corradini (Coradigni), which calls for two *Trompas de caça* (in two arias in F and one in D),[18] which play both a timbral and harmonic role, in full conformity with the author's Neapolitan training. A few years later (1736) there is also a setting of *Dixit Dominus a 5 o a 8, con violines y bajones o trompas de caça* (RISM 100015417) of Manuel Paradís, chapel master at the Cathedral of Tuy until 1744.[19]

There is little information available on Spanish horn players. We can only mention Juan Martin Blumenstengel, a name that leaves little doubt as to his German origins. Although referred to as player of *clarín* and *trompa* in the Royal Chapel of Spain as late as 1741, he had in fact begun this double role when the court was moved to Andalusia, between 1729 and 1733 (Kenyon 2005, 74). His instrument may have been similar to those portrayed in a still life by the court painter Michel-Ange Houasse, who died in 1730; here, a pair of horns with one and a half loops is depicted (probably in the key of G, which was used along with that of F in the music played by Blumenstengel at this time). The instruments may even have been German-built, since "no Spanish horn is known to have survived from the early or mid-eighteenth century" (Kenyon 2005, 78).

Perhaps this same instrumentalist participated in a 1746 performance of the *Letania* with violins, oboes, "*trompas y clarines*" by Carlos Patiño (1600–1675), as revised by Francesco Corselli (Madrid, Archives of the Palacio Real, Leg. I.458 Cat.227). Similar adaptations of older music to the new style in the chapel in the Palacio Real in Madrid may be found in the *Oratorio al Santissimo* by Ramón

---

[18] The second act ends with the aria "Voy surcando el mar ayrado," which has music and lyrics that are identical to *Artaserse* by Leonardo Vinci (Rome, 1730, aria "Vo solcando un mar crudel"). The work also contains an aria from Feo's *Siface* (1723), thus confirming the suspicion that it is actually a *pasticcio* (Dietz, in *Grove* 2001, s.v. "Corradini").

[19] See Mariano Pérez Gutiérrez, *Diccionario de la música y los músicos*, Madrid, ISTMO, 1985, vol. III, 17, s.v.

Garay (1613–1673), with manuscript parts for *trompa* I and II, or in the *Salve Regina* by Lorenzo Penna (1613–1693), with two *corno*.

A name that is certainly Iberian is that of José Antonio Chicos, "*Profesor de trompa nacido in Jaén al año 1709*" (professor of horn born in Jaén in 1709), of whom we have no further information (Pedrell 1897, 353). He may have been a student of Blumenstengel, and his two sons Juan Martín and Juan José, both horn players, may have as well. In addition, in 1748, two more hornists belonging to the Spanish Royal Guard and recruited in the same chapel were documented: the Bohemian Juan José Birnkraut and the Neapolitan (of German descent) Antonio Scheffler. From that point on, and thanks to instruments owned by the two musicians, the tonalities used included G, F, E, E-flat, D, and B-flat.

Remaining in Spain, at this time concertante parts had already been introduced in operatic music and in *Villancicos* (popular songs)—an example of which is *Para Oirlas* (1739) by Salvator Noguera (? –1768) (see Musical example 29). It is not until 1788, however, that a piece with solo horn with a definite date of composition is found: the *Sonata de trompa* of Cabaza (see the music example in Verdú 2000, 67). A horn player is portrayed along with other musicians playing on raised alcove over the reigning family in a painting by Louis Michel van Loo, *The Family of Philip V*, from 1743 (Prado Museum, Madrid) (see Figure 54 online). Here, the instrument is held up in a showy position, which would be highly unlikely in a true performance.

As for Portugal, with the 1708 marriage of King João V to Maria Anna of Austria, the relationship with Vienna became very close, and music acquired a crucial importance in the life of the court. In fact, their daughter, Maria Barbara of Portugal, had Domenico Scarlatti as a teacher from 1718. Once she became the future queen of Spain (1729) by marriage, she brought him with her to the court of Madrid in 1733.

In addition, if the dating of circa 1734 of the cantata with three voices, violins, oboe, flutes, trumpets, and horns entitled *Gloria, Fama, Virtù* by António Teixeira

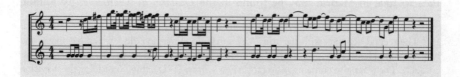

Musical example 29. S. Noguera, *Villancico*.

(1707–1774) is correct, a pair of horns in the keys of D and F must have taken part in its performance at the Real Seminário da Patriarcal in Lisbon, where the score is preserved (http://purl.pt/78).

AMERICA

If until recently, only few pioneers from the American horn-playing tradition were known, now Kathryn Eileen Bridwell-Briner's dissertation *The Horn in America from Colonial Society to 1842* (2014) presents a larger array of documentation, embracing a time span of almost one and a half centuries. Most of the dissertation deals with the players active during the period in question, but it also includes a comprehensive list of performances, purchases of instruments, advertisements, and last but not least, a number of domestic workers and servants also capable of playing the horn.

The instrument arrived in the New World with the many immigrant communities from the various countries of the Old Continent and was mainly used in the colonies' military bands and in civil bands. Only later would it be included in theatrical and itinerant orchestras.

The first occurrence of the word "hunting horn"—without details about models, pitches, and so on—is related to the Moravian community who emigrated to the new country. In 1735, religious refugees brought "two trumpets and two hunting horns" with them that were subsequently sold to the governor of Georgia when the colony was dissolved in 1739 (Bridwell-Briner 2014, 11). In 1736, an announcement by John Keen and Henry Makeroth appeared on *The South Carolina Gazette and General Advertiser* (Charleston) advertising them as teachers for "all gentlemen in town or county that are inclin'd to learn to blow the French horn." We must wait until 1752, however, to find the first documented "solo on the French horn," which occurred during a performance of *The Beggar's Opera* with instrumental accompaniment. Neither the author of the piece nor the player of the solo are mentioned in the notice contained in *The Maryland Gazette* (August 27, 1752). Jonas Green, editor of the journal and secretary of the Annapolis Masoni Society, is the most likely performer, being the only amateur horn player known in the area (Heintze 1978, 235, fn. 41). Snedeker (1997, 151) also suggests that the music was taken from the original version by Pepusch, whose setting, however, does not call for the presence of the instrument. Green may have contributed the performance by adapting some passages by Pepusch to his own skill. He also did something like this with the "Old Club Song of Robin and Jeck" (October 26, 1752), a song whose vocal part (see the music example in Snedeker 1997, 154) could be easily adapted to the natural harmonics of the horn. Even though an exact performance of the melody would require the adoption of the hand technique, there is no evidence that it was used at such an early date so far from Europe.

12
DUETS

In France and England, printed collections of duets were published during the eighteenth century, predominantly influenced by the characteristic style of hunting repertoire, but also showing the influence of dance and entertainment music. This repertoire gave way to a progressively consolidated tradition, so that the first comprehensive method ever published, that of Hampel–Punto, was mostly conceived for two parts.

With regard to France, where a stronger influence of the hunting repertoire is apparent, a series of duet collections was published beginning in the early 1730s (see also Cucuel 1913, 23) (see Table 6 online).

In England, a collection of horn duets had been published by John Walsh in 1733: *Forrest Harmony, Book the second: Being a Collection of the most Celebrated Aires, Minuets, and Marches [. . .] made on purpose for two French Horns by the greatest Masters* (see Humphries 2000, 14). Evidently, because of the editorial success, this "second" collection was followed by a third and a fourth in 1736 and 1744 respectively (both were reprinted several times). Although considered lost for decades, a copy of the first collection of these duets ("Book the First"), also from 1733, was eventually located in the library of the University of Birmingham, in the Shaw-Hellier collection (276) (Frew-Myers 2003, 9, fn. 15).

These early examples were soon followed by many others, demonstrating the keen interest aroused in England by this music. The list given in Table 7 (online) is very likely an incomplete one, but certainly gives a realistic idea of the editorial output.

Finally, we would like to mention the well-known *New Instructions for the French-Horn*, published in around 1780. It contains a small collection of duets as well as an eloquent and frequently reproduced illustration of two horn players with their instruments standing side by side mirroring each other (see Figure 55 online).

A similar posture must have inspired a unique prescription by Ch. W. Gluck, who asked two performers to play with their bells facing each other in the aria "Caron t'appelle" from *Alceste* (French version, 1776). They could therefore obtain the "dull and gloomy sounds" suitable for the hellish scene (De l'Aulnaye 1816, 519, fn. 2). The actual effect must have been unsatisfactory to the players, however, since the prescription does not appear in the first edition of the score (Paris, 1776, 230), and Dauprat deprecates that effect as "sourd, cuivré, désagréable" (Dauprat 1824, III, 20, fn. 1). A contrary opinion was expressed by Berlioz (1844, I, 306).

According to Gerber (1792, 550), at the end of the century virtuosos were still using instruments without crooks, mainly pitched in E-flat, which became the most frequently used tonality for solo concertos. It seems, therefore, no coincidence that the duet players depicted in the *New Instructions* are equipped with simple horns, or even that on the title page of the first edition of Mozart's *Musikalischer Spass* KV.522, published in 1797, a nice caricature appeared in which the two performers have simple horns, but now (twenty years after *New Instructions*) hold them with their right hand in the bells (see Figure 56 online).

13
FOUR CASE STUDIES: VIVALDI, BACH, HANDEL, TELEMANN

Before concluding Part I with a list of the many different names we have encountered in the scores and literary sources since the appearance of the hooped horn and until the second quarter of the eighteenth century, we would like to draw attention to the four most representative composers of the late baroque era. What has been narrated about the history of the instrument can thus be usefully compared with what was actually expected by the most distinguished artists of the period, who exploited an instrument still limited in its expressive possibilities, yet were able to bring out attractive and surprising musical results. See Chapter 13 online for Vivaldi, Bach, Handel, and Telemann.

14

INSTRUMENTS' NAMES IN THE BAROQUE ERA

Concluding our overview on the definitive affirmation of the horn as part of the orchestra, it seems practical to summarize the terminological variety encountered in the baroque period, in parallel with the increasingly widespread use of the instrument.

Table 8. Provisional list of names for the natural horn in baroque times (literary sources are in brackets)

Date	Name	Author/Composer	Place	Source/Bibliography
1660	*trombe ritorte*	(anonymous)	Turin	*L'unione per la peregrina*
1662	*olicorni*	(F. Pallavicino)	Munich	Parma, State Archives, *Carteggio Farnesiano Estero*, Busta 3, Baviera, fol. 5r
1664	*trombe ritorte*	(F. Chigi)	Italian author in Paris	Lionnet 1996, 147
1670	*Waldhorn*	(J. C. Lorber)	Weimar	Ahrens 2014, 91
1672	*trombe di metallo*	(A. Castellamonte)	Turin	Castellamonte 1674, 21, see fig. between 20–21
1678	*franƶösische Waldhörner*	(G. Tzschimmer 1680)	Dresden	Becker-Glauch 1951, 77
1680-	*Jägerhörner*	various sources	Austria	Ahrens 2014, 90
1698	*Waldhörner*	(J.C. Weigel)	Regensburg	Weigel 1698, 232
ca. 1700	*litui*	N. F. X. Wentzely	Prague	Koch 1980, 151
1702	*franƶösische Waldhorn*	(inventory)	Blansko (Czech Republic)	Freemanová 2006, 216

Date	Name	Author/Composer	Place	Source/Bibliography
1704– 1707	*Cornua sylvestria*	(inventory)	Rajhrad Benedictine monastery (Czech Republic)	Žůrková 2023, 66
1705	*corne de chasse*	R. Keiser	Hamburg	Haller 1970, 176
1706	*litui vulgo Waldhörner*	(inventory)	Osek (Czech Republic)	Koch 1980, 152, and Freemanová 2006, 217
1707	*tuba sylvatica*	J. F. Ryvola	Teplice (Czech Republic)	Freemanová 2006, 216
1707	*jakhorny*	(inventory)	Nová Paka (Czech Republic)	Žůrková 2023, 66
1708	*coranthorn*	(M. Leichamschneider)	Vienna	Haupt 1983, 346
1711	*tromba da caccia*	F. Gasparini	Barcelona	*Oracolo del fato*
1711	*cornu sylvestre (=Waldhorn)*	(C. Gantzland)	Jena	Gantzland 1711, 11
1711	*cornibus venatoriis concertantibus*	J. C. F. Fischer	Augsburg	D-OB = RISM 990018204
before 1712	*corne de chasse maggiore* (in D)	F. W. Zachow	Halle	Koch 1980, 149; DDT 1095, Band 21/22 (not in RISM)
before 1712	*corne de chasse* (in F and A)	F. W. Zachow	Halle	Koch 1980, 149; DDT 1905, Band 21/22 (not in RISM)
before 1712	*corno grosso* (in F)	F. W. Zachow	Halle	RISM 211005428
1712	*corni di selva*	C. Graupner	Darmstadt	RISM 450005793
1712	*lituos ex F cum temporatoriis / 1 Par ex A'*	(inventory)	Kosmonosy (Czech Republic)	Žůrková 2023, 66

Date	Name	Author/Composer	Place	Source/Bibliography
1713	*Cornetti di caccia / Cors de chasse / Waldhorn*	(J. Mattheson)	Hamburg	*Das neu-eröffnete Orchestre,* 267
1714	*trombon da caccia*	A. Vivaldi	Venice	*Orlando finto pazzo* (I-Tn Giordano 38.1)
1714	*corni parforce* (in F)	J. T. Römhild	Luckau (Niederlausitz)	RISM 220034259
1714	*cornetti da caccia*	R. Keiser	Hamburg	RISM 190002852
1714	*2 Corn. de Chass*	C. Graupner	Darmstadt	RISM 450005857
1714	*litui*	G. W. Jacob	Prague	RISM 990032279
ca. 1714	*3 corni da caccia*	J. S. Bach	Mühlhausen	RISM 450103576
1715	*trombe da caccia*	A. Caldara	Rome	RISM 451013023; Dahlqvist 1993, 181
1715	*2 Waldhörner*	M. Rohde		S-L, Wenster F:22; RISM 190003139
1719	*corne par force* (in C)	G. P. Telemann	Frankfurt	TWV 1:232 *Festo Micheli archang.;* RISM 450003827
1720	*Cornu del Caccia*	G. Klingenberg	Stettin	printed edition
1721	*cornu par force* (in D)	G. Lindemann	Stettin	RISM 190002927
1721	*cornibus Venaticis seu Sylvestribus*	–	Banskà Bystrica (Slovakia)	Szórádová 2006, 229, fn. 7
before 1722	*corno grande*	J. Kuhnau	Leipzig	Koch 1980, 149
1722	*corno raddoppiato*	(F. Bonanni)	Rome	*Gabinetto Armonico*

Date	Name	Author/Composer	Place	Source/Bibliography
1722	*Clarini*, [vel] *lituis, vel Cornua Venatoria ex D*	"Del Sig: Prendilo" (?)	Lambach	RISM 603001439
1722	*cornu del caccio*	G. Klingenberg	Stettin	PL-SA, 1086 | 895
1722	*corno di caccia surdinato*	G. P. Telemann	–	TWV 5:2 (RISM 225004588)
1722–1723	*corno di selva (= Waldhorn)*	C. Graupner	Darmstadt	RISM 450006014
ca. 1723	*corni de selve*	G. P. Telemann	–	TWV 1:1345 (RISM 210000114)
1723	*corno o tromba da tirarsi*	J. S. Bach	Leipzig	BWV 46
1723–1724	*corno da tirarsi*	J. S. Bach	Leipzig	BWV 67 and 162
1725	*tubis sylvestribus*	–	Banskà Bystrica (Slovakia)	Szórádová 2006, 229, fn. 7
1725	*tubae venatorie vulgo Jägerhorn*	–	Žilina (Slovakia)	Szórádová 2006, 229, fn. 8
1726	*valtorni*	(A. M. Lucchini)	Venice	libretto of *Dorilla in Tempe* by Vivaldi
1727	*Clarini vel Cornua Venatoria ex D*	A. Caldara	Lambach	RISM 603001803
1727	*litui in F*	F. S. Lechleitner	Poznań	RISM 300033300
ca. 1730	*corne de casse*	A. F. Ursino	Tønder (Denmark)	RISM 240005186
ca. 1733	*tromba selvatica*	G. P. Telemann	Hamburg	*Tafelmusik*

Date	Name	Author/Composer	Place	Source/Bibliography
1733–1734	*corno di selv. G*	C. Graupner	Darmstadt	RISM 45000638
1735	*corne par force*	J. S. Bach	Leipzig	Cantata BWV 14
ca. 1737	*lituus*	J. S. Bach	Leipzig	Cantata BWV 118
s.d.	*cornu grand* (in D)	G. P. Telemann	–	RISM 806042562
s.d.	*grand cornu du Chasse* (in D)	G. P. Telemann	–	Cantata TWV 1:677; Cantata TWV 1:1125
s.d.	*cornois*[1]	G. P. Telemann	–	TWV 1:284 (RISM 450008964); TWV 1:1454 (RISM 450008943)
s.d.	*tromba sylvest.*	J. Valentin Meder	–	Koch 1980, 148

[1] The term "cornois" is used in a dozen scores by different copyists, including Johann Heinrich Kromm (for Telemann's music) and Anton Mang Vilser.

PART II

PART II

15

THE CLASSIC ERA

The main innovation that characterizes the period after 1750 is represented by experiments aimed at exploiting the use of the hand in the bell, a practice traditionally attributed, not without exaggeration, to the famous second horn of the Dresden court, Anton Hampel.

In parallel, the features of the instrument underwent a series of experiments whose first result is represented by the invention of terminal crooks: a full set of additional tubing for all pitches consisting of the combination of one or two master crooks and corresponding couplers. It is not possible to determine who may have invented them, but this most probably occurred in England shortly after the middle of the century.

A demonstration of the vigorous research that began with the conception of a complete series of crooks is the appearance of "fork crooks," with two endpieces that were inserted into two receivers located inside the circle, in the early 1760s. It was a seminal idea that gave way to a new phase of experimentation and is documented by an unparalleled specimen built in 1761 by Johann Gottfried Haltenhof.

Fifteen years later, another crucial discovery took place: the invention of slide crooks—yards of tubing that slid into each other. Their invention is usually attributed to Johann Werner of Dresden, the craftsman who certainly worked alongside the great Hampel, but in this book it will be reassigned, for reasons explained below, to the aforementioned Haltenhof.

The same principle was modified a few years later, plausibly by Anton Kerner Sr. of Vienna, with the invention of a full series of slide crooks that were inserted into a forked receiver at the center of the instrument and therefore more comfortable to move and to tune. It was again the same maker who moved the next step forward: a complete set of conical terminal crooks for each tonality with a master slide to adjust the pitch.

If it is therefore conceivable that the duke of Aumont could still order seven horns, each in a different key, in 1753 (see Chapter 11, fn. 8), it may instead seem quite surprising that these models, bound to the old baroque tradition, were still built and employed at the end of the century.[1] However, one must remember that horns had multiple uses. Instruments pitched in a single key, in addition to being used in hunting, were preferred by virtuosos for solo repertoire (in these cases they were sometimes made with precious metals and therefore very expensive). In addition, horns with few crooks for each size were still produced, evidently for contexts (military, sacred, and dance) in which frequent changes of tonality, and therefore of crooks, were unnecessary (see online, "A prolific Munich maker").

The wide variety of models invented and built in the second half of the century means that there is no single description of the "classical horn," but we can point out some general tendencies of the newly developed models:

a) application of full sets of crooks (unlike those intended to vary the pitch of the main size by up to three semitones);
b) more and more widespread use of slide crooks and tuning slides;
c) increase in the diameter of the main section of the bore (from 9 to 11.5mm); and
d) increase in the size of the bell (outer diameter at the rim of up to 30cm), with a consequent increase in volume and change of timbre.

The latter transformation is certainly linked to the spread of the hand technique, long used exclusively by the greatest virtuosos, who made use of it almost fifty years prior to the general diffusion of the technique in the orchestra. It became common practice at almost the same time as the first experiments with valves were taking place.

ANTON HAMPEL

The invention of the hand technique is commonly attributed to a horn player of Moravian origin: Anton Joseph Hampel (or Hampl, 1710–1771), born in Bährn

---

[1] The inventory of the Cöthen chapel, for example, reports a long list of horns of different sizes in as late as 1773: "(No. 30) 2 G horns, J.H. Eichendopf [Eichentopf], 1733; (No. 31) 2 E-flat Horns, J.H. Eichendopf; (No. 33) 2 E Horns; (No. 34) 2 C Horns; (No. 35) 2 F Horns" (Fitzpatrick 1970, 35, fn. 1).

(today Beroun), the younger brother of a horn player named Johann Michael (1695–1732), both employed in 1722 in the music chapel of the prince of Liechtenstein.[2] Anton was appointed second horn of the Dresden Hofkapelle in 1737 and kept that position until about 1768; he was initially paired with J. G. Knechtel and later with Carl Haudek.

It may therefore seem surprising that in the first edition of Gerber's book (1792, s.v. "Spörcken"), Hampel is not mentioned at all, appearing in an article fully dedicated to him only in the second edition (1812), and, moreover, without being credited as a pioneer of the hand horn! In fact, in the aforementioned 1792 article (of which Fitzpatrick 1970 provides an English version on pp. 219–226 that is not entirely faithful to the original text), the use of the hand was documented circa 1750, with no reference to the Dresden area, by performers who specialized in the role of second horn, such as a certain Bachmann, who was able to play the entire low octave with the help of this technique.[3]

The role of Hampel as the sole inventor of the same technique, reported in every history of the horn, is actually credited only by sources after his death, and has reasonably been questioned by some scholars.[4] On the other hand, it may be indicative that in the *Seule et vraie méthode pour apprendre facilement les élémens des Premier et Second Cors* by the same Hampel and his pupil Punto (Paris, *ca.* 1794), the sounds obtained with the hand are only briefly illustrated on the first page and at the end of the volume (Hampel–Punto 1794, 83–86) (see Figure 57).[5] The remainder consists of a large number of exercises for two horns, a sort of long duet with variations, suited to the main purpose stated in the title, that is, "to easily learn the technique of first and second horn." It is reasonable to assume that most of the *Méthode* was written by Hampel prior to his introduction of the hand

---

[2] Fresh biographical information on both brothers is to be found in Ágústsson 2017, 25–26.

[3] The second horns "had already been able, in around 1750, to play the entire lower octave using the hand, as I heard done several times by the late Bachmann, the former second horn of Mr. Reinert" (Gerber 1792, 551). Bachmann, of whom little is known (Fitzpatrick 1970, 207 and 226), played in Sondershausen with Carl Reinert (1730–1801). The latter was probably the same Reinert (Reinhardt) who wrote a horn concerto now located in Lund (see Chapter 11, p. 97), and the first, again according to Gerber, to introduce the invention horn in Sondershausen.

[4] Fitzpatrick 1970, 86; Morley-Pegge 1973, 87; and especially, Heyde 1987b, quoted in the main text.

[5] Those for a *premier cor* are from g' to c''' chromatically, and for the *second* from b to g'', plus a few sounds in the lower register.

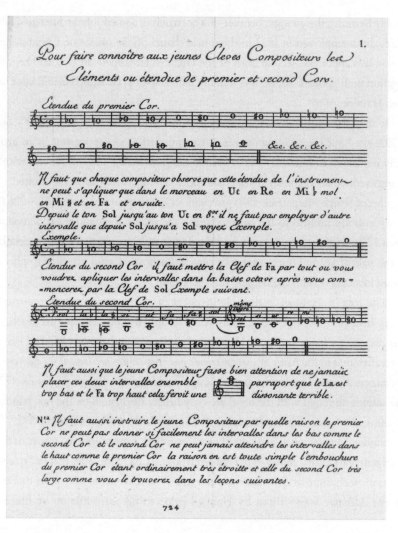

Figure 57. Hampel–Punto, *Méthode*, *ca.* 1794, 1, range of first and second horns.

technique, while the short initial scales and the final pages are additions made by Punto (see Musical example 30 online).[6]

[6] Another piece by Hampel that has been lost is a *Lection pro cornui* (1762), a manuscript whose detailed description is found in Schlesinger 1910, 705 (with music example). According to Schlesinger, the exercises contained "do not prove conclusively that they were intended to be played on hand-stopped horns, with the exception, perhaps, of the A, the 13th harmonic from C, which could be not easily obtained except by hand-stopping on the hand-horn" (see Morley-Pegge 1973, 202).

The information about the role played by Hampel in conceiving the hand technique mostly comes from Heinrich Domnich (1767–1844), a German horn player, composer, and teacher active in France, who commended the former in his own *Méthode* (Domnich 1807, iv). He had first-hand information from his teacher, the aforementioned Punto, who, together with his colleague Franz Wiesbach,[7] had gone to study in Dresden with Hampel, most probably in 1763 (Fitzpatrick 1970, 111). Although basically reliable, the narration by Domnich may nevertheless be somewhat exaggerated in a sort of tribute to the great pioneer of the school.

According to Domnich, Hampel was inspired by oboe players from the same time period who used cotton balls stuffed into the bell of their oboes to obtain a sweeter and muffled sound from their instruments. This solution may have been suggested by the need to balance their tone with that of other instruments, such as in an opera written by Giovanni Alberto Ristori for Naples (*Temistocle*, 1738, aria "Aspri rimorsi atroci"; D-Dl, Mus. 2455- F-6) that calls for oboes "*ser[r]ati*" ("closed", i.e. muted).

Domnich also states that Hampel was surprised to discover that using a stopper for the same purpose (we do not know exactly how this was made) could raise the sound of the horn by a half step.[8] From that point, he began new experiments that enabled him to produce the entire scale, and he later realized that the hand could effectively replace cotton balls, thus giving way to the hand-horn technique. In addition, he stated that the collaboration between Hampel and the Dresden maker Johann Werner led to a fundamental innovation, the *Inventionshorn* (cf. Gerber 1812, II, 493). We strongly doubt that this was the case, however, in the current meaning of the term, and we will discuss this matter more extensively below.

Apart from the experiments with stoppers, Hampel also devised a mute device that "does not raise or lower the pitch of the instrument" (Gerber 1812, II, 493). A mute device had been in fact used on the horn more widely than one might

---

[7] Franz Wiesbach, Matiegka's pupil, was sent to study in Mannheim and Dresden together with Punto by Count Johann von Thun, a man whose role in the history of the horn should be investigated further. When Wiesbach then returned to Prague, he gained a reputation as a fine virtuoso. See Dlabacž 1815, III, 209 and Fitzpatrick 1970, 198–199.

[8] These stoppers, regardless of their constructive features, would have had to be inserted deep into the bell to raise the pitch by a semitone. This could be Hampel's new discovery since the contemporary Roeser (*ca.* 1764) already refers to the partial occlusion, as occurs with the use of the hand in the same way, lowering the pitch by a semitone.

think.[9] The first certain example is in Vivaldi's Concerto with viola d'amore, RV 97, circa 1719, with "*2 Corni da Caccia sordini*"; then there is at least one request by Telemann in 1722 (*Corni da caccia surdinati* in TWV 5:2; see Aringer 2006, 121); and in 1725, for an oratorio by Alessandro Scarlatti to be performed in Rome, payments were made to "Ludovico for the *corni sordini*" (i.e. muted horns), and "Lorenzino for the *corni sordini*" (La Via 1995, 435). A further example is encountered in the *Requiem* written by Zelenka for the death of Frederick Augustus "the Strong" in 1733 (Heyde 1987b, 46). The metal mutes purchased in Sondershausen in 1738 (Ahrens 2007), some of which were equipped with a device for regulating the damping of the sound (Ahrens 2008), are particularly relevant. Finally, as far as the main period of Hampel's scholarship is concerned, muted horns were also called for in the opera *Parataio* (*La Pipée*) by Jommelli (Paris 1753) and in one aria of Traetta's *Buovo d'Antona* (Venice 1758).

Some documents of outstanding importance could also clarify the role of Hampel and, especially, the exact dates of his fundamental discoveries. However, they are mentioned in an essay by Volek (1983), who failed to cite the source of his information. In these 1767 documents, Haudek (Hampel's first horn) communicated to the Count Johann Joseph von Thun (1711–1788) that:

a) the new hand technique had not been discovered by Hampel alone, but by both of them;

b) the discovery shortly predated April 1767, therefore three years after Punto's stay in Dresden (1763–1764), so—according to Professor Volek—it is unlikely that Punto could have learned this technique while studying there;

c) the new technique was appreciated especially for the harmonic enrichment that it allowed, also proving useful in ensemble music; and

d) the exact dates of the experimentation with stoppers or "mutes" by Hampel were established.

According to the same documentation, Hampel and Haudek personally visited von Thun to explain and demonstrate the method they devised.[10] Unfortunately,

---

[9] Although the destination cannot be defined with certainty, some mutes are mentioned in the inventory of the workshop of Charles Crétien, on the date of his wife's death in 1714 (Vaast 2015, appendix),

[10] Volek's article was also published in a Czech edition of the same volume (*Minulost a přítomnost lesního rohu. 300 let lesního roku v Čechách*, Brno 1984, pp. 36–43) but again without referring to the archival sources.

Professor Volek failed to provide details on the locations of the aforementioned documents (see online, "Two lost letters by Hampel," and Figure 58 online).

If the dates are indeed those reported, Hampel's discovery was even later than that of the first treatise, which describes an (albeit rudimentary) hand technique: that by Valentin Roeser from *ca*. 1764, which we will discuss presently (see Musical example 32). In addition, in 1767, when such a technique would have been discovered in Dresden, the opera *Bellerofonte* by Josef Mysliveček was presented in Naples. Here, the horn, pitched in E-flat, is required to play an isolated e' (written c#", bar 16) while the orchestra rests, as if the composer wanted to emphasize the use of this unusual sound. This implies the use of the hand (see Musical example 31).

Musical example 31. J. Mysliveček, Bellerofonte, Act II, Sc. 11, Aria "Palesar vorrei col pianto", bars 14–20.

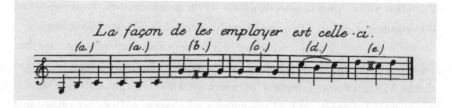

Musical example 32. From Roeser, *Essai d'instruction à l'usage de ceux qui composent pour la clarinette et le cor, ca. 1764, 15.*

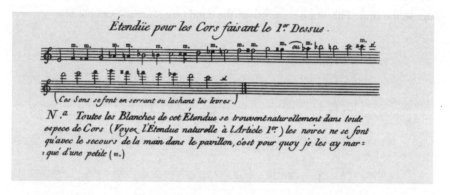

Musical example 33. From Francoeur, *Diapason général de tous les instruments à vent*, 1772, 44.

Hampel certainly played a key role in the development of the hand horn, of which he was undoubtedly a pioneer, but it is conceivable that similar experiments and solutions were developed by other horn players in various parts of Europe. In this respect, it seems worth mentioning Herbert Heyde's opinion (1987b, 47), according to whom Hampel essentially "resumed the experiments done prior to him, deepening, expanding and organizing them and also providing a theoretical method for the implementation [of the technique]."

With regards to the tendency of some scholars to date the introduction of the hand horn well prior to this point, it should be noted that non-harmonic sounds in compositions of the first half of the eighteenth century, which are often undated or dated only on the basis of stylistic considerations, would be played with the *falsetto* (see Chapter 10, p. 84), rather than with the hand technique. In fact, the former technique remained in use long after the discovery of the new option of producing sounds using hand-stopping (for further information, see also Ahrens 2005).

THE CONCERTO BY GEHRA/GEHRING

See online. See Musical example 34 online.

HAND-HORN TECHNIQUE

The first reference to the use of the hand in the bell in a treatise is contained in the *Essai d'instruction* by Valentin Roeser, published in Paris in 1764—three years before the "invention" by Hampel, as mentioned previously,[11] if the cited information by Volek is correct. Roeser (1764, 14), while not explaining the kind of technique actually adopted by horn players, says that the third harmonic can be lowered to written F (in bass clef) and the eleventh to f" by introducing the hand into the bell, "especially with white and black notes" (i.e. long notes). He also considers—albeit very cautiously—that five other sounds outside the natural harmonic series may be obtainable: b, f' sharp, a', b', and c" sharp.[12]

Roeser recommends avoiding the a" (wrongly indicated as g" in the table found in Roeser 1764, 14) because it is too flat, saying "*il n'y a pas moyen de le rendre juste*" (there is no way to make it in tune). It should therefore be avoided as much as possible in chords and in unison with other instruments, which incidentally indicates that it was played without the hand in the bell.[13]

Starting from the subsequent text by Francoeur (1772, 47), this note will also be accepted as a part of hand technique, although the latter practice was still limited to a few sounds of the harmonic series and used either to refine their intonation or to lower them by a semitone with a greater occlusion of the bell. In his instructions for composers (pp. 36–51), Francoeur describes the technical possibilities of the hand horn in a little more detail, also indicating the range obtainable with each single crook on the instrument. He uses the symbol "m" (Fr. *main* = hand, see Musical example 33 above) to indicate the notes requiring hand-stopping, whether obtained through simple tuning adjustment of a harmonic (as with f" and a") or generated

[11] The volume must have been printed by the end of 1763, since on January 9 of the following year it was mentioned in *Annonce Musicale* (Gétreau 2006, 69).

[12] Roeser 1764, 14: "The sounds I have marked [. . .] are too high, but one can obtain them properly by putting the hand in the bell of the horn [. . .]. There are another four or five notes that can be played with the hand, but it is necessary to proceed carefully if one wishes to use them."

[13] An indication that recalls the one contained in Hampel–Punto (*ca.* 1794, 1), where it is stated that "the young composer should take care to never put these two intervals together [f"–a"], as the too low A and the too high F would result in a horrible dissonance."

from a greater modification of the natural pitch (as a, b, a', b', etc.).[14] The complete range of the first horn is reported in the "*Étendüe* [*sic*] *pour les Cors faisant le 1er Dessus*" and that of the second in the "*Étendue pour les Cors faisant le 2d Dessus*" (pp. 44 and 45 respectively), with the clarification that some notes are to be realized "*en serrant ou lâchant les lèvres*" (tightening or releasing the lips, i.e. in falsetto; sounds between c' and e', evidently deemed of unsatisfactory effect, are not included).

He also explains through an example—an "*Ariette*" by Jean-Claude Trial (1732–1771) from the opera *La fête de Flore* (Fontainebleau 1770),[15] transcribed on two staves—which passages are more appropriate for the first and for the second horn, adding that distinguished players such as Rodolphe were able to perform both parts (Francoeur 1772, 51) (see Musical example 35 online).[16] Moreover, in reference to Trial's aria, he states that in the absence of Rodolphe, the solo was performed excellently by Jean-Georges Sieber (1738–1822), a horn player from the Opéra and music publisher. But since it would not be easy to find horn players of similar skill, assigning the *primier cor* parts that are suited to the second and vice versa is not recommended.

Trial's song is particularly instructive because in some fast passages (i.e. bars. 22, 30, 35, etc.), the "m" does not appear, suggesting that in such rapid figurations the eleventh harmonic (f" or f" sharp) and the thirteenth harmonic (a") were obtained using the falsetto, not the hand.[17] The author also remarks (Francoeur 1772, 45) that the series of lowest notes should not be used in the orchestral Tutti because they are too "drowned,"[18] and they must therefore be used exclusively for solos.

---

[14] Actually, in the "*Étendue*" (Francoeur 1772, 44), Francoeur omits the a", but in a subsequent musical example an "m" above that note (indicating the compulsory use of the hand) is found in the slowest passages. Its omission in faster ones suggests a handless practice in the latter cases.

[15] Bachaumont 1777, III, 337, reports that a repeat performance of Rameau's opera *Dardanus* on February 15, 1768 ended with a short aria with horn accompaniment written by Trial, one of the directors of the Opéra. It is quite probable that the piece in question was the *Ariette* later reused by Trial in *La fête de Flore* and that the horn player was the same Rodolphe.

[16] In the printed edition of Trial's *Ariette* (Paris, *Le Marchand*, 1771), there are obviously no detailed performance instructions for the horn, instead there are a few bars present that are not included in the example by Francoeur.

[17] Today, in performances on period instruments, some hornists play f" sharp and a" by withdrawing the hand from the bell and, with a slight pressure of the embouchure, adjusting intonation.

[18] "*Cette Etendue ne pourroit servir pour être dans un Tutti, parce que les Sons en sont trop sourds.*"

The aforementioned *New Instructions for the French-Horn* (London, Longman and Broderip, *ca.* 1780), a booklet that incorporates information from earlier British treatises (Humphries 2000, 51), provides additional insight. It includes valuable information on the mouthpiece (p. 2), the embouchure (p. 4), the most appropriate range for the first horn (p. 6) and the second (p. 7), and the appropriate position of the hand (p. 4). Regarding the use of the latter, it reports that "should you want to make the Cromatic tones, you may hold the horn with your Left or Right hand as near as you can to the Mouth-piece, the Bell to bear against your side, one hand must be within the Edge of the Bell ready to put into the Pavilion or Bell of the Horn as notes may require. [. . .] Mr Ponto [*sic*] and many others, famous on this Instrument, constantly uses this method, by which means the half tones are expressed." The same text recommends different ways of holding the instrument depending on the context: "sometimes in the left arm, with the Bell hanging from the same arm, sometimes with the Bell perpendicular, the method which is generally used in concerts" (p. 3).

The first to explain the technique of the hand in detail was horn player and composer Othon Vandenbroek (1758–1832),[19] author of a *Méthode* (*ca.* 1797) that also encompasses portions of an additional handwritten part (*Suite de la Méthode*, after 1797) as well as instructions provided in his subsequent *Traité général de tous les instrumens à vent, à l'usage des Compositeurs* (after 1803).[20]

According to the title page, this *Méthode* "teaches how to know the range of the horn perfectly, instructs how to attack all semitones correctly, deals with all double tongue strokes, and gives explanations suitable for acquainting all musicians and composers with the instrument, and for how to choose the proper pitch." In addition, the author states—to our surprise—that in the orchestra, the horn gives the pitch to the other instruments (Vandenbroek 1797, 3). He also advises on how to play all semitones and how to produce the different types of "tongue strokes" through the use of syllables (i.e. ta out to ta od to het thi ed, etc.), as is customary in many ancient methods for wind instruments (see Figure 59 online). To clarify how to use the right hand (the one commonly inserted in the bell), Vandenbroek includes two drawings, titled *1er Main* and *2e Main*, which illustrate the two different positions of the hand employed to play stopped notes (see Figures 60 and

[19] His name is spelled in different ways, such as Vandenbroek, Brock, Vandenbrock, Van der Broeck, and others. He was the first horn at the Théâtre de Monsieur and then at the Opéra (1793–1816) in Paris.

[20] The dating of the three texts reflects what is reported in Carter 2005, 97–98.

61). The *1er Main* position is with the hand at the mouth of the bell and "sunk" inside it, with the fingers joined like a spoon, in a way that leaves minimal air passage, thus enabling the player to play d', f', g' sharp, b', c" sharp, and d" sharp, f" sharp with small changes in position. The *2e Main*, which was sunk into the bell as in the previous case, must be shaped with the phalanges retracted to obtain e-flat', f' sharp, a', g" sharp, a", with small variations of position explained from time to time. The notes not obtainable with these positions are carefully discussed in the remainder of the *Méthode* (see Figure 62).

Aside from these explanations, Vandenbroek provides a further one in the addition to his method, the *Suite de la Méthode*, which, according to Morley-Pegge

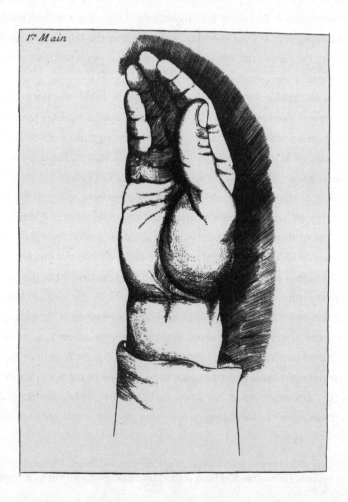

Figures 60 & 61. First and second *"main"* (hand), from Vandenbroek, *Méthode, ca.* 1797, 5, 7.

2.ᵉ Main.

(1973, 95), constitutes a draft of the printed version, but it was apparently written later (see Carter 2005, 97). Here, the author deals with the intonation of some untuned sounds, disregarding the complicated "syllabic" pronunciation described in the printed treatise. Since the latter was a spin-off of the baroque tradition, its omission is a further proof that the *Suite* is a follow-up to, not an anticipation of, his *Méthode*.

Returning to the use of the hand, he observes that professionals adopt different ways to obtain the semitones (*tons bouchés*), although only one system should be employed. While the explanation is not entirely clear, the method he deals with first is defined by him "not the best." It consists of holding the hand at the entrance of the bell with the fingers folded and the thumb held a little apart (similar to the

Figure 62. Vandenbroek, *Traité général*, after 1803, 3 *(Traité)* with the series of stopped *(bouchés)* and "less-stopped" *(pas si bouchés)* notes.

1er Main of his *Méthode*), thus ready to go deeper for stopped notes. The second method *(autre manière)* prescribes the use of the hand only during the stopping action, bringing it outside the bell for ordinary notes. Finally, he explains the last and best system *(autre manière et meilleure)*, with the back of the hand against the inside of the bell and the wrist brought backward for stopped notes. He warns that not all sounds require the same type of occlusion. This, according to Vandenbroek (after 1797, [iv]), is the "more comfortable, more correct, and easier system."

What can be deduced from the *Suite de la Méthode* is the persistence of various methods of use of the hand in the late eighteenth century. This may not only be proof of traditions developed independently but may also reveal that several horn players continued to adopt a completely outdated technique, that is, holding the hand outside the bell and inserting it only when necessary.

This practice is also confirmed in a treatise published in Italy in the same period, *La Scuola della Musica in tre parti divisa* (1800) by Carlo Gervasoni.[21]

---

[21] See the chapter "Lezioni di corno" (Horn lessons) Gervasoni 1800, 319–331. An appendix with a music example can be found at the end of the text, pp. 58–60. Carlo Gervasoni (1762–1819) was a well-respected Italian theorist, music historian, teacher, and organist.

According to him, "the instrument should normally be held with the bell well up, so that the sounds are clean and clear" (Gervasoni 1800, 322). A different position is required when one has to insert the hand to play stopped notes, in which case the right hand must be held "with the fingers held together at the tip to form a concave hand" (p. 329). This technique, where the hand was held near the outside of the bell and put inside only for stopped notes, was apparently still widespread in Italy along with much more advanced systems. Regarding the latter, it is enough to mention the virtuosity required by obbligato parts in Italian operas from the last quarter of the eighteenth century (see below).

Holding the instrument with the bell upwards is also documented in the *Méthode* by Dauprat (1824, II, 158). His method states that before the introduction of the hand technique, horns were played in a manner resembling that of the contemporary hunting horn, that is, by holding them with one hand and with the bell side up (therefore with the "natural" pitch of the eleventh and thirteenth harmonic). Dauprat notes that he saw horn players in theaters near Milan who kept the bell raised during the execution of forte passages. The same effect was required by French composers with the remark "*pavillon en l'air*," such as in a fortissimo passage from *Mélidore et Phrosine* by Méhul (Paris 1794) that has the direction "*Levez les Pavillons*" (ed. Huguet, p. 120). Nevertheless, according to Dauprat, the horn players did not follow this prescription because it raises intonation and increases the weight of the instrument on their lips, impacting the attack of the notes. This practice was instead deemed appropriate, in some musical contexts, by Castil-Blaze (1841, 426). He recalled that the various players (Duvernoy, Domnich, Kenn, etc.) who accompanied works by Méhul and Cherubini raised the bells of their instruments whenever it was necessary to obtain a harsh effect, unlike some contemporary hornists who felt the same practice was inconvenient.

The method exposed by another distinguished Parisian horn player, Frédéric Duvernoy (1765–1838), appears to be similar to the first proposed by Vandenbroek. Duvernoy was one of the most renowned musicians in Napoleonic Paris and among the first teachers of the newly founded Conservatoire of Paris. In his *Méthode pour le Cor* (Paris 1799), he includes a drawing of the hand in the bell that looks like that of Vandenbroek, although there is no description on how to obtain the stopped sounds (see Figure 63 online). Duvernoy also presents a table with all the chromatic notes obtainable on the horn, with or without the hand, from c to c'", and a series of exercises with continuo accompaniment.

The use of stopped notes involves a somewhat different timbre. This was later a favorite argument of the first advocates of the valve horn and often still hampers "historically informed" performances when the modern technique used to play *bouchés* (or "closed") sounds is inappropriately applied. At that time, horn players—and certainly those of the French school—must have been much more accustomed to achieving homogeneity between closed and open sounds, given that in as late as 1835, the *Méthode de Cor suivi du Doigté du Cornet à pistons* by Jean-Baptiste Mengal (1796–1878), contains a paragraph (art. VI) entitled "De l'Égalité du Son." In order to get the most possible equality, Mengal suggests "lightening" open sounds, that is, opening the hand in the bell as little as possible to get the proper intonation of unstopped sounds.

The following description by Castil-Blaze (1825, II, 320–321, s.v. *"Tons Bouchés"*) is particularly instructive as to the uniformity of timbre: "Stopped notes. Sounds which cannot be emitted without more or less closing the opening of the horn with the wrist, d, f, a, b, f, and a, are stopped notes. The great art of the horn player is to strengthen these sounds, weak in their nature, and to diminish the brilliance of the open sounds, so that the sound of the instrument is even on all the degrees of the scale."

Notwithstanding the increased adoption of the hand technique, which remained the purview of great virtuosos, composers of orchestral pieces at this point were still mostly avoiding non-harmonic sounds and even exploited the clarino and falsetto techniques in solo repertoire.[22]

However, in the meantime a peculiar language for the horn was established, with its ever-changing colorful timbre, which has given us all the "classic" literature for the instrument, from Mozart's concertos to the compositions of Beethoven, Weber, Cherubini, and Rossini as well as numerous solo parts in the symphonic and operatic repertoire. This practice also left a strong legacy in the later writing for horn, to the point that the orchestral pieces by Brahms, though written in the main era of the "mechanization" of the instrument, are still intended for hand horn. And he hoped that his famous Trio, op. 40 for Violin, Horn, and

---

[22] This refers not only to the orchestral repertoire, but also to some solo compositions such as the Concerto for Horn and Orchestra by F. J. Haydn from 1762 (Hob. VIId: 3). In some other cases requiring the clarino technique, such as in some of the Twelve Duos for Two Horns by Mozart from 1786 (KV.487, KV.496a), many passages imply the use of the falsetto for adjusting the pitch of the eleventh and thirteenth harmonics.

Piano would be performed with this technique at its premiere (which, however, occurred with valve horn, as we shall see in Chapter 25 online, "Brahms").

This was not an isolated position, however, since upon the retirement of Meifred in 1864,[23] the valve-horn class at the Paris Conservatoire was closed. Even in Italy, in 1881, during the music national conference (*Atti* 1881, 51), the reintroduction of the same technique was advocated.

THE ENGLISH SET OF CROOKS

Beginning in the 1760s, a complete series of crooks based on a new and ingenious system—one or two master crooks with conical bores to which a full set of cylindrical couplers could be added to produce all necessary keys for the instrument—seems to have made its appearance in England.

A text from this time period (Halle 1764, 371), in describing nine different sizes of horns in use at the time, refers to this type of instrument: "The horns in F, or English natural horns, have crooks and pieces to be put into the mouthpipe, and therefore ascend further than the other models." The basis for the idea may have come from Germany or may have been developed in England by German makers who immigrated just before or during the Seven Years War (1756–1763), as the famous "twelve apostles," who moved from Germany to London attracted by the thriving English market, did for the piano.

Baines, citing horns built in London by Rodenbostel and Hofmaster (two are reproduced in his table IX, 2 and 3)—names that clearly establish their owners' national roots—points out that such horns were probably made after the middle of the century by copying German examples equipped with crooks, which had recently been introduced in England (Baines 1976, 157). Today we know that the pair of Hofmaster horns cited by Baines were purchased by Sir Samuel Hellier in 1767 and were initially equipped with an outfit consisting of a few crooks (Frew–Myers 2003, 10–11). Two years later, however, they were entrusted to Mr. Barr "in the Strand," who probably created the full set of crooks (masters and couplers) that have come down to us.[24]

---

[23] The valve-horn class was opened by Meifred in 1833 and continued to run until 1864 (Morley-Pegge 1973, 3–4, reporting 1863). It was then essentially reinstated by François Brémond (1844–1925), French horn player, tenor, and teacher, in 1897, when the hand horn was also taught. From 1903, only the valve horn was taught.

[24] We also mention for the sake of completeness that Eichborn 1897, 9, assigned this pair of horns the hardly credible date of 1735; he probably used the date from Day 1891, 147–148 (No. 308), who noted, however, that the last two digits were missing (cf. Frew–Myers 2003, 10).

Even the introduction of a horn of this type in France seems to date back to 1765. In fact, according to Castil-Blaze 1855 (II, 345), the instrument with "replaceable crooks" (*tuyaux de rechange*) was presented in that year at the then imperial Académie de musique (later the Opéra) by the famous Rodolphe (see below). Since it is untenable that single crooks, already found throughout Europe, were unknown in France, this evidence likely refers to instruments with a complete system of couplers and master crooks (see online, "The year of John Christopher Hofmaster's death").

Returning to London horns by Hofmaster, we note, according to the description found in Baines (1976, 157), that the master crook (about 120cm long) has two loops, placing the instrument in G. The lower keys are obtained using four couplers, and it is possible to obtain the highest keys using an alternative short master crook or a shank for B-flat and a small coupler or a longer shank for A (see Table 9 online and Figure 65 online). Such a system, although particularly popular in Great Britain (Morley-Pegge 1973, 22), was also successful elsewhere owing to its simplicity and economy, at least until the early nineteenth century.

Several variants were developed in various countries, with different arrangements of master crooks and couplers, as well as one with tuning slide and up to eleven individual master crooks, each for a different key.

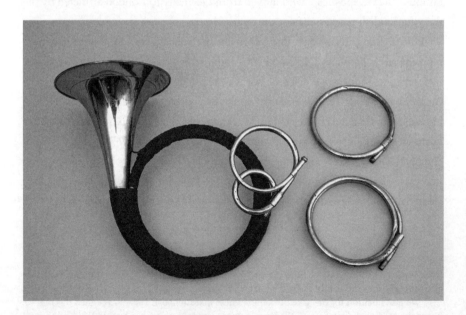

Figure 64. J. C. Hofmaster, *ca.* 1750.

An interesting comparison is allowed by a pair of orchestral horns built in 1807 by Michael Saurle (1772–1845), now in the Museum of the Conservatory of Florence (*La Musica* 2001, 215–217). Crooks and couplers surviving with them differ somewhat from that of the above horns, all the more for the presence of the tuning slide, but Saurle's catalog also shows the economy of the model with terminal crooks when compared to the other models he produced (cf. Hübner 2006, 85) (see Table 10 online). On this informative catalog, see also Part II, Chapter 2, "Three price lists."

To reduce the encumbrance of the latter model, a further variant was devised in 1771 by the Viennese maker Carl Starzer (1733–1789), as announced in the *Wiener Zeitung* of that year (September 18, p. 8):

> Karl Startzer, Imperial and Royal court and chamber horn maker in Vienna, invented a new genre of French Horn with which one may obtain, strongly and properly, 11 keys with no more than 5 crooks and no shanks, that is from high C down to low A. These horns differ from the others in that instead of the usual 11 crooks only 5 are required, and they are also so convenient to be easily carried in the pockets.

Although this system remained in use for a very long time, it presented a major inconvenience for the orchestral performer. As the various crooks were added, the player had to hold up heavier and heavier instruments progressively more distant from their body and less stable owing to the numerous joints of the crooks (see online, "A possible explanation for the success of crooks and couplers").

FOUR HORNS INSTEAD OF TWO

The replacement of the couplers resulted in a quite long and laborious operation in some cases, and opera scores of the second half of the eighteenth century sometimes call for frequent and fast changes of tonality. For this reason, in certain cases, although the score called for only one pair of horns, two were used. Furthermore, it is relatively common to find operas, oratorios, and ballets in which only two horns are required for almost the whole work, but four horns are suddenly called for in one or two pieces, such as in *La Finta Giardiniera* by Mozart (Monaco 1775).

The general adoption of four horns is also confirmed by an anonymous article in the *Revue Musicale* in 1833 (172–173), which also includes the following:

Méhul and Cherubini first introduced this use into the music of the theater, from which it was passed on to the symphony proper. At first there were two horns in the main key and another two in the dominant, for pieces written in major key, or two in the main minor key and two in the respective major one. Then, four horns began to be grouped in different keys, which allowed for much more varied combinations. There are few great compositions nowadays that do not call for their four horns.

The reporter goes on to say that in many cities of the province, owing to the shortage of players, the scores could be performed in an incomplete manner (with two instead of four horns). Even at the Opéra-Comique in Paris, four horns were used only in the *première* performances. In subsequent ones, the horn players, weary from too much effort, took turns resting.

The information is completed by the dates found in Castil-Blaze (1855, II, 347), which states that in 1788, two horns were added to the orchestra. They alternated between themselves and divided the work.[25] Then, in 1794, Méhul called for all four horns together for the first time, but only in the Overture of *Horatius Coclès*.[26]

News about this practice of alternating two pairs of horns, something that is little known in our day and that should possibly be resumed in performances on period instruments, can be found in some texts by Johann Simon Mayr (1763–1845). From *Brevi cenni* it is clear that horn players took turns during key changes and therefore were also able to rest, especially in the ballets. In the *Trattatello* (s.v. "*corno*"), he suggests that large *Cappelle* (orchestras) may have even adopted three pairs of horns: The first one specialized in the keys of B-flat *basso*, C, and D; the second in E-flat, E, and F; and the third in G, A, and B-flat *alto*, since "he who plays in the tonality of B-flat basso and changes [crooks] to play in A alto . . . cannot consider the quality of sound and must be happy to be in tune" (see Rocchetti 2007, 29).

In *Traité général des tous les instruments à vent* (after 1803), Vandenbroek (p. 2) reports that in some orchestras in Germany, there was a pair of horns for alto crooks and one for low ones. In this regard, Van Boer (2000, 116) informs us that

[25] Obviously neither the anonymous writer nor Castil-Blaze could have known that Bononcini had done the same thing in Rome about seventy years earlier (see Chapter 9, p. 67).

[26] Castil-Blaze errs here: in fact, four horns are not required in the Overture—neither in the print version (Paris 1794) nor in the original manuscript (I-Fn A-355.A)—but in the remainder of the opera. In addition, the author called for the "*Pavillon levée*" (bell upward).

in the music collection of the Royal Swedish Opera in Stockholm (now kept at the Statens Musiksamlingar), horn parts copied after 1784—when the second pair of horns was hired permanently at this court—are divided between the two couples. The first one is reserved for pitches from F to high B-flat and the second from F to low C. One example is in *Soliman II* (1789) by Joseph Martin Kraus. The full score calls for only two horns throughout the work, but separate parts show the use of both pairs (Van Boer 2000, 117). The same author also points out some cases (Mozart, *Entführung aus dem Serail*, 1781–1782; Joseph Haydn, *Armide*, 1783) in which horn players do not have sufficient time to change crooks, which is why in these cases the two pairs likely alternated during the performance of the piece. This practice, as already mentioned, would be quite plausible in a period when the most common instruments were furnished with master crooks and couplers, which imply a certain delay in preparing the instrument for the key change.

Of special interest in this regard is a set of four natural horns, all apparently in B-flat size, with oblong-looped crooks for lower keys, made by the Venetian maker Andrea Coin in 1770. These instruments may have been inspired from a specimen in F by Joseph Kerner of Vienna, also preserved at the Venetian Istituto della Pietà, where Vivaldi taught from 1704 to 1740 (Tiella–Primon 1900, 77–80).

16

NEW CROOK SYSTEMS

We now enter a stage of the horn's history that has been more difficult to reconstruct, either because key evidence for the history of the instrument was missing until recently or because erroneous information was given by Gerber in 1792. The latter's faulty reporting has long hampered the understanding of the events we are about to narrate and may have originated from a simple confusion of two models of the instrument, which were both called "*Inventionshorn*."

FORK CROOKS

We must first start from the text by Gerber (1792),[1] well known to English readers thanks to the translation provided in Fitzpatrick (1970, 219–226). Gerber cited a paper dedicated to flute and flute players that appeared in the journal *Magazin der Musik* and was signed "J. J. H. R." (these initials were omitted in Fitzpatrick's translation), easily identifiable as Johann Justus Heinrich Ribock.[2] This essay, published in 1783, does not, however, contain any reference to the horn. Gerber confused it with another article signed with the same initials, published in a subsequent issue of the same magazine, in 1784. Here Ribock, after stressing the importance of Count von Sporck to the history of the horn, adds valuable information on the latest inventions, including crooks that were inserted along the body of the instrument:

---

[1] Art. "von Spörcken," vol. II, 1792, 546–549, here 548–549. A summary of Gerber's historical reconstruction appeared in Bagans 1829, 338, and was translated the following year in *The Harmonicon*, 8 (1830), 23–25 (see Morley-Pegge 1970, 21). On Bagans's name spelling, see Mendel 1870–1879, vol. I, pp. 413–414.

[2] Ribock (1743–1785), a physician and flute expert, was active in Lüchow and in close contact both with J. G. Tromlitz, and with C. F. Cramer, editor of the journal.

It is known that to change tonality, instead of the use of terminal crooks, crooks to be inserted into two short sockets on the inside of the circle were also devised, and, as I understand it, the first horns built according to this system were those of Hanau. With this invention, it has become possible to play the instrument in any key without reverting to terminal crooks, which are too laborious to build. However, with these new crooks, it was still not possible to make small differences in intonation, because the sockets, just one inch in length, soon lost their air-tightness, thus making the performance more difficult.

This description, copied almost verbatim by Gerber, is documented by a surviving instrument built in Hanau by J. G. Haltenhof, whose exact biographical data (born Grossen-Körner, February 23, 1701; died Hanau, April 21, 1783) were recently communicated (*Grove* 2014, s.v.). The specimen, dating back to 1761, is located in Bochum, and has been presented and described in Ahrens–Klinke (1998, 64, no. 50) (see Figure 66). In this instrument, the two ends of the "fork crooks" are connected to two short sockets inside the circle with tenon and mortise terminations (one end of the crook enters into the slot while the other end receives the tenon protruding from the instrument).

It was a significant step forward over terminal crooks, since the unique leadpipe now remained at a constant distance from the player, thus ensuring greater stability of grip, even though it was not yet possible to adjust the pitch, as appropriately pointed out by Ribock. This item, which was also studied by Ahrens for the presence of multiple traces of mute insertion (Ahrens 2007; 2008), can

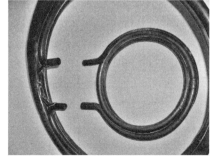

Figure 66. Haltenhof horn, 1761, and detail.

Figure 67. Hampel–Punto, *Seule et Vrai Méthode*, ca. 1794, title page.

therefore be documented as the model described by Ribock and by Gerber, to which we will return shortly.[3]

And although the illustrations of printed music editions are usually unreliable, a probable depiction on the title page of Hampel–Punto's handbook (*ca.* 1794) should nonetheless be mentioned in this context owing to the rarity of the above model (see Figure 67). The instrument here sketched has a design resembling that of older instruments while also presenting a minimal flaring of the bell.

SLIDE CROOKS

We must now consider another Haltenhof instrument, which is instead well known to scholars. It is a horn from 1776 preserved in the Paris Museum (inv. E.1020) that demonstrates that this manufacturer was also on the forefront of the design of sliding crooks. These crooks are conceived for tonalities from E to low B-flat, while higher tonalities (F, G, A, and high B-flat) were obtained with

---

[3] In the hunting castle of Lovecký Ohrada (South Bohemia), two anonymous horns with a fork crook slightly more advanced than that of the Bochum horn are on display. Since the tenons and mortises are longer, it is possible to modify the intonation slightly while the crook remains inside the circle of the instrument. These two items also have the option of inserting a shank or a terminal crook into the leadpipe.

Figure 68. L. B. Coclers (1756–1817), portrait of horn player Pelting (?) with an *Inventionshorn* similar to the 1776 Haltenhof model.

substitute leadpipes that were inserted into the slide crook yard, which went directly to the bell, bypassing the first part of tubing of the instrument. This system, which remained in production with Haltenhof's successors and was imitated by many other manufacturers, definitely allowed the player to adjust the pitch, and even with higher crooks (from F upwards), the distance of the instrument from the player did not change (see Fitzpatrick 1970, 130).

Ribock (1784, 10), probably unaware of the new creation envisaged by Haltenhof, attributes the first appearance of the slide crooks to "new Viennese horns," which were also equipped with a similar device:

In the new Viennese horns, the crook's stems are now from 5 to 6 inches long, thus allowing for a certain sliding of the crooks, which protrude a bit outside the perimeter of the circle and pass close to it. Thanks to these longer stems and through the [sliding] movement, the performer can tune the instrument perfectly, even without stopping playing, when he finds it to be sharp, thus eliminating a defect frequently ascribed to this instrument.

At this point Gerber, after reporting the previous narrative of Ribock, rejects this "new Viennese" authorship, crediting instead the Dresden maker Johann Werner (*ca.* 1710–after 1772) with having invented a horn capable of playing in nine different tonalities (supposedly from low B-flat to high B-flat), fitted with slide crooks, and more, as early as 1755. He also reports that two horns built by the latter and with these types of crooks had been sold to the Gotha orchestra in 1757 by hornist Carl Reinert (1730–1804) for the very considerable sum of 80 thalers.[4]

The attribution of the invention of the slide crooks to Werner, accepted in all subsequent literature and previously also by the present authors, must be questioned, however, on the basis of new and detailed evidence. First, Gerber was not present when the horns made by Werner to which he refers arrived at Gotha (Ahrens 2009, 178). Furthermore, his testimony on the invention of the slide crooks is denied by a good appraiser of the history of the horn, Heinrich Domnich, who instead credits the invention to Haltenhof of Hanau (*Méthode*, 1807, v, fn. 1).[5] The third, and most significant argument, comes from the authoritative pen of Johann Nepomuk Forkel (1782, 205–206), who wrote the following:

The so-called *Inventionshörner*, in which the crooks are not placed right after the mouthpiece but in protruding sockets placed in the middle of the horn, were invented about six years ago. On these instruments and by means of this invention, one can embrace an entire octave [of different tonalities]. Initially this novelty cost from 60 to 80 thalers. Now, one can find *Inventionshörner* from

---

[4] A couple of lesser-known Italian sources refer to this musician: on May 10, 1766, at Palazzo Pitti in Florence, "Carlo Rainard Sassone" played an unspecified concerto for "corno da caccia" (*Gazzetta Patria*, 20 (1766), 78); on July 12, 1767, "Gian-Carlo Reinert, virtuoso of *corno da caccia* in the chamber service of His Serene Highness the Duke of Wirtenberg" played in a duo with Maria Maddalena Reinert, receiving "universal applause," at the Teatro di S. Sebastiano in Livorno (*Gazzetta Patria*, 29 (1766), 120).

[5] "The horn with a slide valve was first made by Haltenhoff, an instrument maker at Hanau, near Frankfurt on the Mein."

16 up to 20 ducats. The Viennese instruments of this type stand alongside those built in Hanau, and it is believed that one can not find better brass instruments than the ones produced in these two places.

Forkel was thus aware that the production centers for the invention horns were Hanau and Vienna, but he did not mention Dresden at all. What is most revealing, however, is that in 1782, he said that they were invented "about 6 years ago," that is, in 1776. Forkel lived in Göttingen, and had the invention of the slide crooks taken place nearly thirty years before in not-too-distant Dresden, this fact would hardly have escaped his attention. In addition, the year 1776 coincides with that of the oldest surviving original instrument equipped with slide crooks, which confirms that the date of invention was right then (or just before), and that this discovery should be definitively attributed to Haltenhof.[6] A further confirmation seems to be the fact, secondary but not less significant, that the firm Haltenhof founded continued production of the model described for more than forty years.[7] (See online, "News on Haltenhof in the *Zeitschrift für Instrumentenbau*".)

Specimens based on the same principle as the Haltenhof horn from 1776 were also built later by other craftsmen. Among them was Jean François Cormery, who before 1788 made an *Inventionshorn* of this type, now located in Paris (Musée d'arts et métiers, inv. 01613) (see Figure 69). This horn, already mentioned in Pierre (1893, 150), still possesses its E-flat, C, and B-flat crooks (the D and E crooks are missing), and the substitute sliding leadpipes for the keys of F, G, A, and high B-flat, which are very similar (if not identical) to those by Haltenhof.[8] The same can be said for a horn of this type by Philipp Ferdinand Korn of Mainz preserved in Basel (inv. 1980.2101, described in Klaus 2000, 6, and fig. 25).[9]

La Borde (1780) called the horn with slide crooks *cor à l'anglaise*,[10] a name already used by Halle in 1764 to designate the type with terminal crooks (it seems

[6] A confirmation to the attribution to Haltenhof from around the same time period can be found in Fétis 1827, 155.
[7] We also mention, for the sake of completeness, the incorrect attribution of the slide valves principle to Michael Wögel (Karlsruhe). He only applied the device invented by Haltenhof to the trumpet, as reported by Schlesinger 1910, 704.
[8] Particular thanks goes to Thierry Maniguet (Paris) for information on this horn.
[9] An item based on a comparable system is the one by Gabler & Krause, Berlin (fl. 1790–1806) preserved in Stockholm, Scenkonst Museet (inv. N42670). See http://www.mimo-international.com/MIMO/doc/IFD/OAI_SMS_MM_POST_5769.
[10] La Borde 1780, I, 254: "There are different kinds of horns. The English type, with slides that serve to lengthen or shorten the tone [tubing] of the horn and in this way to easily tune to

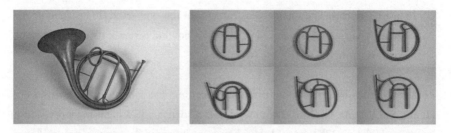

Figure 69. J. F. Cormery, *Inventionshorn* (left) with set of crooks (right).

likely the latter is actually English in origin). Many years later, Dauprat (1824, I, 4, fn. 2) remembered this definition, pointing out that still no one knew the reason for the name. At the end of the nineteenth century, it was again mentioned in a paper by Pierre (1893, 150), who referred to Cormery's model as *"cor à l'anglaise ou à la Punto,"* with a slide used "to lengthen or shorten the pitch of the instrument," that is, with slide crooks.

To summarize, there is no doubt, on the one hand, about the innovative role played by Johannes Werner of Dresden, who, at the suggestion of Anton Hampel, was able to build in 1755 horns playable in nine different tonalities, a design to which the term *Inventionshorn* was applied (although the first design to which the term *Inventionshorn* was applied dates back to 1736: see Ahrens 2015, 451). On the other hand, attributing the invention of the slide crooks to him seems completely arbitrary. In any case, the few surviving instruments made by Werner have a wide hoop, suitable at most for the insertion of terminal crooks but not for the adoption of fork or slide crooks (see online, *"Für unseren sächsischer Kollegen . . ."*).

Even once the conjecture that the slide crooks were invented by Haltenhof is accepted, the role played by the Viennese makers, in particular Anton Kerner Sr. (*ca*. 1726–1806), a leading figure of the Austrian area, still needs clarifying. Kerner, together with Karl Starzer (1733–1789),[11] was the principal maker in Vienna in the second half of the eighteenth century. Horn manufacturing in Vienna was considered to be the most advanced among the various musical instruments, at least until the advent of the golden age of piano making in the 1790s.[12]

---

the pitch of other musical instruments. The horns without slides are cheaper, but also less convenient."

[11] A very informative study on Carl Starzer and the Viennese makers of the second half of the century is to be found in Starzer 1998 (for biographical dates, see in particular pp. 86, 89).

[12] Starting in 1772, Kerner was one of the two court builders in Vienna, together with Starzer (see *Calender* 1772, 472), a city where horns "are built with the utmost perfection" (Hermann 1782, 32, fn. 2).

THE INVENTIVE ANTON KERNER (KÖRNER)

According to information provided in 1824 by Stephan von Keeß, superintendent of the imperial customs, we must credit Anton Kerner Sr. (also Körner in old sources) with some crucial improvements during the years 1782–1783. Von Keeß, praising the work of Kerner's son, his contemporary, describes the latter's father with these words: "The best builder in Vienna is Anton Körner, the court manufacturer, whose father already made several improvements to these instruments 41 years ago" (Keeß 1824, 169). Since information provided by von Keeß is, as a rule, very precise, and since slide crooks are documented six years before these innovations by Kerner Sr., we can categorically exclude the hypothesis that the latter was responsible for their invention. In addition, the aforementioned La Borde (1780, I, 255), while praising Kerner for the production of the "best concert horns," does not refer to him in relation to the slide crooks of what he calls the *cor à l'anglaise* (and more to the point, he does not cite Werner of Dresden either).

The error about the invention of the slide crooks by Werner must therefore be ascribed to Gerber alone, and taking into account his main source of information on horn and horn players, one may be able to understand his motivation. He received much of his data from a manuscript by Carl Thürrschmidt, whom he of course admired first as a horn player but who also sent him "*ganze, geschriebene Bogen, voll merkwürdiger Notizen von deutschen und französischen Meistern*" (entire written sheets, full of remarkable news on German and French masters: Gerber 1814, IV, 403).[13]

In an attempt to find the reason for Gerber's incorrect assertions about the invention of the slide crooks, we submit the thesis that the origin of this error could be a simple misunderstanding of what was written by Thürrschmidt, owing to the different meanings attributed to the German word "*Inventionshorn*" over the course of a few years (see also "Different meanings of '*Inventionshorn*'," p. 151) (see online, "Possible misunderstanding of the term *Inventionshorn*").

Moving on to what is in turn undoubtedly an invention by Kerner, that is, a more practical version of the slide crooks, we should mention at least two literary sources. The first is again Koch's dictionary, of 1802, which reports on a complete set of slide crooks to be inserted in the middle of the instrument, once more calling this model an *Inventionshorn* (Koch 1802, 884):

---

[13] Further documentation of the information provided by Thürrschmidt can be found in Gerber 1812, II, 493.

In the case of the horn, in the last half of the past century an arrangement was made for inserting crooks of the same kind, supplied for all keys, into the middle of the tube of the instrument; thus, with only one instrument all tonalities are obtainable with the corresponding insertion pieces. Such an instrument is usually called an Inventionshorn.

The second piece of evidence is an extensive description made by the aforementioned Stephan von Keeß (1824, 167), who also recalls other horn designs then available on the market:

Once, there were only the so-called *Jagdwaldhörner* (hunting horns) and those a bit smaller for the musicians. Three sizes were used to obtain all keys, something that now, with the *Inventionshörner* invented by Körner (father) in Vienna, one can do with a single horn through the simple substitution of the so-called substitute parts (*Veränderungsstücke*), which consist of nine or ten sections of straight and curved tubing for every horn. With such *Waldhörner*, one can easily play in high C, B-flat, A, G, F, E, D sharp, D, C, and as low as low B-flat. The lower the key, the more coils the extra piece has, while the body of the horn proper has just two loops of tubing. The semitones are obtained by the insertion of the hand into the bell by means of which the air passage can be stopped at will. In addition to these invention horns and the common natural horns, there are also *Concerthörner*, which often differ only in that they have a more refined shape. The additional forked pieces (*Gabelansätze*), which on the common horns were placed inside the hoop, have almost completely disappeared and are still being built only for Russia and Poland. Silver horns, which were once made for the opulence of the hunt, are out of fashion.[14] In fact, the thickness of the silver, which had to be greater than brass, was still insufficient for the wind instruments.

In reference to Kerner's invention, we can also point to an undated specimen, probably from the early 1780s, preserved in Florence (Galleria dell'Accademia, inv. 195) (see Figure 70). Here, the F slide crook (the only one still surviving) also functions as a tuning slide, which was also likely the case for the other slide crooks

---

[14] In the castle museum of Hluboká nad Vltavou (South Bohemia), there is a silver horn that has the inscription "ML Wien 1730," presumably an abbreviation for Michael Leichamschneider on the bell garland, which is finely chiseled with hunting scenes (see Table 4 online).

no longer present today. A short tuning bit is also found at the entrance, while the diameter of the socket (11mm), as well as the ending position of the leadpipe, make the addition of initial tubing indispensable, as in subsequent specimens of this model. Based on this same instrument, Kerner should also be credited with the adoption of a bell (approx. 29cm in diameter) considerably wider than the ones documented prior to that point. Finally, it is not implausible that Kerner may have offered the same instrument with only three slide crooks (high B-flat, middle F, low C) and with two additional crooks of semitone and whole tone to get all other tonalities as an alternative solution, as seen in a later price list by Tuerlinckx (see "Cor solo," p. 153).

We do not know of any Kerner horns with all the crooks present, but one can compare them to similar specimens, such as the anonymous one preserved in the Museum of Lübeck (inv. no. 4422 a–k), equipped with nine slide crooks (high B-flat, A, G, F, E, E-flat, D, C, and low B-flat) and two tuning bits (Althöfer 2000, 151). Another example may be a horn built *ca.* 1830 by Schmidt of Leipzig, on display in London in 1891 with as many as thirteen slide crooks for every key, descending chromatically from high B-flat to low B-flat, including those for A-flat, G-flat, D-flat, and B natural (Day 1891, 148, no. 310).

Probably because of the uneven sound of the longest slide crooks and the high costs of these sets of extra pieces (each single crook needed a different template to be made), an additional model was also developed in Kerner's workshop: a full set of terminal crooks, all independent and conical in shape, ensuring an even timbre

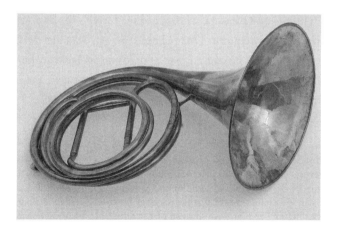

Figure 70. Horn by Anton Kerner.

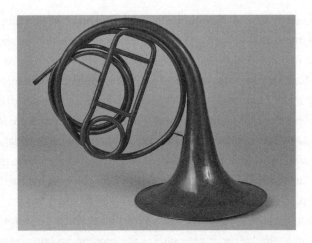

Figure 71. Joseph Kerner, *Inventionshorn*.

and a constant distance from the player, with a single slide crook acting as tuning slide. The construction of this type of instrument was probably made possible by a new metalworking process—probably one that simplified the making and bending of conical tubes, which were until then the result of a hard and laborious forging procedure.[15]

Anton Kerner received Viennese citizenship on January 27, 1751, and then worked in Vienna until the year of his death, 1806. He had six children (Richter 1909–1910), two of them well-known followers of their father's workmanship, Ignaz (*ca.* 1768–1813) and Anton Jr. (*ca.* 1770–1848). A third son, Joseph, probably an elder offspring of Anton's first marriage, may be the builder of the horn illustrated in Figure 71 and the same who signed the receipts for horns and crooks repaired for the Esterhazy court in 1782 (Ebner 1996, 44; Maunder 1998, 176). In his will, Anton Sr. named his sons Ignaz and Anton as heirs to his business, continued under the company name "Anton und Ignaz Kerner"; the other four children received a partial value of the cash assets (Haupt 1960, 149).

---

[15] In this regard, we should also make note of a subsequent invention by a Parisian builder (but the name reveals foreign origins) that took place in France in the year 1800. With it, "the difficult procedure of curving the conical tubes of horns in any number of shapes was made easier. The Parisian instrument-maker Wendel Sandhas hit upon the idea of pouring molten lead into the tubes before bending them, instead of the unreliable mixture of sand, pitch and rosin formerly used" (Brüchle-Janetzky 1988, 32), a process that has remained in use in some places until the present day.

A specimen by Joseph Kerner, dating back to about 1790 (Heyde 1982, 145–146), is based on the design devised in Kerner's workshop. This instrument, held at the Leipzig Grassi Museum (inv. 1686; see Figure 71)—its twin was lost during the war—is, to the best of our knowledge, the oldest example of what would shortly become the typical orchestral type of the invention horn. In this model, whose body is made up of 1½ loops only, the alto C crook is normally constituted by a short tapered straight shank, 15–17cm long (according to Baines 1976, 164, "a cornet A shank, lapped with paper to fit the socket of the horn" was later used for the same purpose), while the other crooks were made from one or more coils. Higher ones were mainly conical, while from F down to low C they were made with a conical initial segment (from 60 to 80cm) firmly soldered to the remaining cylindrical part (low B-flat is obtained using a removable piece of cylindrical tubing added to the low C crook).

With regards to Anton the son, we cannot refrain from reporting a curious fact that has apparently escaped all of Beethoven's biographers: in the same year in which the Ninth Symphony was first performed in the author's presence in Vienna (by which time the composer was completely deaf), instruments by Kerner were "sent to France, England, Russia, etc., and even North America," and he also built "the metal hearing aids that he calls 'mechanical' for those with hearing difficulties which are considered to be the best for the quality of their workmanship" (Keeß 1824, 169) (see also online, "The Bellonci model").

DIFFERENT MEANINGS OF "*INVENTIONSHORN*"

One final note concerns the use in the old sources of the same German name, *Inventionshorn*, for each of the new models subsequently created, each considered, in turn, an effective novelty (see Gerber 1792, 549–550):

a) a model of uncertain features documented in 1736 to which attention was recently drawn by Ahrens 2015, 451;

b) a horn—probably with terminal crooks—invented by Werner in 1755 that could play in nine different keys;

c) the instrument with forked crooks devised by Haltenhof in around 1761 (specimen in Bochum);

d) the horn with slide crooks and independent leadpipes for higher tonalities also created by Haltenhof by 1776 (specimen in Paris);

e) the one invented by Anton Kerner Sr. in circa 1783 with slide and terminal crooks (later specimen in Florence);

f) the one with conical terminal crooks and a master tuning slide, also by Kerner's workshop, of which the earliest known item was made by Joseph Kerner (specimen in Leipzig).

While for all the above models the term "Inventionshorn" was used interchangeably,[16] the last one was also given the name "orchestral invention horn," a fitting definition that it would seem useful to popularize.

AFTERMATH

Long after this chapter of the book had been written, a stimulating exchange of opinions with the expert hornist and researcher Ulrich Hübner added some important considerations to the topics just addressed. In particular, Hübner notes that all the horns of Anton Kerner Sr. so far examined and known to him have no tuning slide at all. The Kerner item in Florence could be more recent than the dates of activity of this maker and, owing to some details, including the singular spelling of the mark, it could even be a counterfeit (perhaps by a craftsman from Neukirchen in Saxony).[17] The horn by Joseph Kerner located in Leipzig also has, according to Hübner, the appearance of an instrument younger than the date proposed by Heyde and accepted by us, and may also be the result of some imitation or counterfeiting.

In appreciation of these and many other suggestions from Ulrich, we simply wish to observe that the preserved instruments represent only a small part of the number of horns that once existed. In any case, it will be a very stimulating task for future researchers to carefully examine and further verify the work of Anton Kerner Sr., of his descendants, and of their possible imitators.

---

[16] It is less commonly known that the model with all slide crooks was also called *Maschinenhorn* (Schubart 1806, 312). See also Heyde 1982, 42.

[17] A piece of evidence supporting Hübner's position is provided by an announcement by Kerner in the *Wiener Zeitung*, August 31, 1771. It is a warning about instruments made in Prague, Leipzig, and elsewhere that falsely bear his name (a detailed, similar admonishment was published in the same journal on December 19, 1789). See Maunder 1998, 176.

COR SOLO

The penultimate model listed above in "Different meanings of *Inventionshorn*" (p. 151) is similar to the one invented in Paris in 1781 by Lucien-Joseph Raoux (1753–1823). It is uncertain if this was completely independent from Kerner's experimentation in Vienna, but it is documented that the new instrument was devised based on suggestions by Carl Thürrschmidt (1753–1797), the horn player idolized by Gerber.[18]

The first occurrence of the name *cor solo* dates back to a Tuerlinckx price list from the 1820s (see below), since Dauprat (1824, I, 4) still did not use this name in describing the model in 1824. The new term was probably a byproduct of the preference accorded to it by soloists with such names as Punto, Duvernoy, Dauprat (his *cor solo* by Raoux is in F-Pmdm), Gallay, Puzzi (his *cor solo* by Raoux is in GB-Lh), Palsa, and, of course, Thürrschmidt. The final two—as described by Gerber (1792, 551)—owned "excellent" Parisian silver horns that cost 100 carolins and were, in all likelihood, built by Raoux. (On the Cor solo see also Scott-Chick-Myers 2019.)

The *cor solo* has a body consisting of two and a half loops, approximately 33cm in diameter, and a long fixed leadpipe (about 135cm). It allowed for remarkable tonal results and an appreciable balance between the different registers while using only a few slide crooks. It was in fact pitched in G (the crook is a short bow of tubing in this case), and other slide crooks can be used for F, E, E-flat and D—the restricted group of tonalities in which the hand technique gives the best results.

The *cor solo* was not intended for orchestras, given the lack of the crooks required there for the other keys, although it could also be employed to this purpose by transposing the parts and using an appropriate crook. The latter was a practice described by Dauprat (1824, I, ii), who states that "the low and high crooks were no longer used, even in the orchestra, where the middle crooks were used to transpose the accompaniments of the pieces written for the other two classes [high and low] of crooks. It is needless to say what monotony of effect, what poverty of sounds, what mistakes of harmony resulted from these continual transpositions." This system therefore limited the resources available to performers and composers. A similarly negative judgment was provided by J. S. Mayr, who

---

[18] Lucien Joseph was the son and successor of Joseph Raoux (1725–1787), one of the leading exponents of the famous family of French makers (see Waterhouse 1993, 318–319). Joseph started work in the mid-century and, like Carlin, another well-known builder (see Vaast 2023), in 1759–1760 he makes "les cors de chasse et enseignent à sonner les fanfares & les autres aires de chasse" (from *Tableau* 1759, 211). On Raoux, see Giannini 2014 and Maniguet 2015.

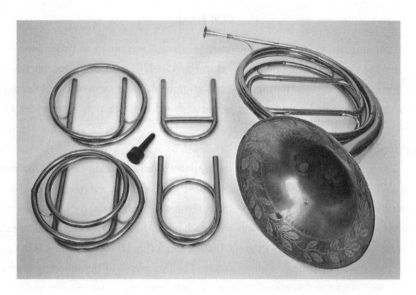

Figure 72. M.-A. Raoux, *Cor solo* with G, F, E, E-flat (on instrument), D crooks, 1826–1827.

INSTRUMENS A VENT EN CUIVRE.

CORS D'INVENTION

la paire avec 9 corps de rechange à poser sur la pompe de *Si b bas* jusqu'à *Si b haut.*	120	—	259	—
dite	dite	à l'embouchure	96	—	207	—
dite	avec 6 corps de rech. de *Ut* jusq. *Si b bas*	66	—	142	—
dite	« 5 « « « « « « *Ut bas .*	55	—	119	—

CORS SIMPLES

dite	avec 4 corps de rechange à l'embouchure	33	—	71	15
dite	en *Fa, Mi b* ou *Ré*	24	—	51	75
dite	grandes trompes (cors de chasse) . .	30	—	65	—

TROMPETTES D'INVENTION

la paire avec 9 à 10 corps de rechange de *Si b haut* jusqu'au *Si b bas*	72	—	155	20
« avec 6 à 7 corps de rech. à l'embouchure de *Sol* jusqu'à *Si b*	40	—	86	25
une Trompette à double coulisse	36	—	78	—
une dite à souspape	30	—	65	—
une « à 6 clefs et corps de rechange en *Fa, Mi b, Ré, Ut*	36	—	78	—

Figure 73. Schott catalog from 1827, horn section.

did not approve of instrumentalists who adopted this system in order to avoid changing crooks, thereby going against the composer's wishes. For example, in works requiring horns in B-flat *alto* (characterized as "witty"), some performers used horns in E-flat with deeper, darker tones (Rocchetti 2007, 29).

Both the "invention" models and the *cor solo* offered soloists greater ease in obtaining the second harmonic, a difficult pitch on several older instruments. Normally, therefore, there were four tonic notes available, something quite unusual among wind instruments.

THREE PRICE LISTS

So far, we have examined the models available at the end of the eighteenth century and the beginning of the nineteenth. Probable contemporary French preferences are summarized in the catalog by the Tuerlinckx company in Mechelen (Belgium), which dates back to the mid-1820s and was published in van Aerde (1914, 335; see also Baines 1976, 164–165). The catalog offers a *cor à coulisse* (with slide crooks) from B-flat alto to B-flat basso ("tous les tons de B hauts à B bas") and a cheaper model of *cor à coulisse* with three slide crooks for high B-flat, F, and C, and another two (terminal) crooks for whole tones and semitones, thus fitted for all keys (a possibility also for Kerner's item in Florence). Furthermore, a *cor solo* with four or five crooks and, finally, two natural horns without crooks, are listed.

A price list by Schott of Mainz from 1825 (Baines 1976, 165), although written in French, presents a summary of the situation in Germany and possibly in Austria. Under "invention horns" (*Cors d'Invention*), an instrument with nine slide crooks from high B-flat to low B-flat ("9 tons à coulisse de Si[bem] haut jusqu'au Si[bem] bas"), another with nine terminal crooks ("à l'embouchure") that must have had a tuning slide since it was listed as an "invention horn," two further models with terminal crooks, an "invention horn" with five crooks (from high C to low C), and a "simple horn" with four crooks are listed. A very similar offer is found in a catalog in the appendix of the 1827 issue of *Cäcilia*, the periodical published by the same company (see Figure 73 above).

Finally, another meaningful list by Michael Saurle of Munich was published by Hübner (2006, 85). Dating back, in our view, to the early 1830s, it mentions the following instruments:

a) an invention horn with ten crooks (from high B-flat to low B-flat, including that of A-flat) that all fit into the slide sockets (90 florins);

b) an invention horn with terminal crooks for all the aforementioned keys (36 florins, about a third of the previous one);

c) a model similar to the latter, but with E and D pitches obtained by adding "a little crook" to those of F and E-flat (30 florins);

d) a valve horn ("ein gromatisches Horn") with all terminal crooks, from high to low B-flat (55 florins);

e) a valve horn ("ein gromatisches Horn") in F with crooks for E, E-flat, D and C that all fit into the slide sockets (50 florins).

We must also note that in the early nineteenth century, the model with all terminal crooks and one slide crook (the second design probably devised by Kerner) had become the most popular in the orchestra, favored by the quick interchangeability of the terminal crooks and the ease of tuning with the slide crook.

For the sake of comparison with surviving items by Saurle, we will refer to one privately owned instrument located in Italy (see Figure 74), originally equipped with all the slide crooks (only that of A-flat is preserved), and one with all the terminal crooks and one main slide crook in Nuremberg (inv. MIR 85) (see Figure 75), both dating back to the late 1820s.[19] The bodies of these two instruments are essentially identical and could therefore be used with both systems, slide and terminal crooks—possibly an original conception by Saurle. Hübner understandably wonders why there was such an enormous difference in price (the first model cost almost three times as much as the second). The pricing may have depended on the aforementioned high costs of manufacturing the slide crooks, since each one required a different template to be made. That such a model would remain in use despite its cost can be only explained by the fact that, while the tuning slide of the cheaper model is effective with higher terminal crooks, with the lower ones, its influence is increasingly reduced, a limit that the horn with all slide crooks obviously does not have (see Table 11 online. On the "chromatic" horns by Saurle, see Chapter 21, p. 248).

[19] A horn very similar to the latter is found in Kremsmünster, Schloß Kremsegg (inv. Piz. 005).

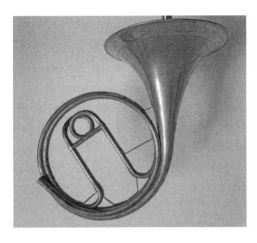 

Figures 74 & 75. Left, horn by M. Saurle; right, horn by M. Saurle.

JEAN-JOSEPH RODOLPHE

Having dealt with the main transformations of the instrument, we will now look at some of the leading figures in the early European dissemination of the hand horn. Among them is the Alsatian Jean-Joseph Rodolphe (or Rudolphe, 1730–1812), a former pupil of the violinist J.-M. Leclaire in the mid-1740s. After having held a position as a violinist in Bordeaux and Montpellier, he went to Parma, according to the biography outlined in Choron-Fayolle (1811, II, 228). Here, under the name Giuseppe Rodolfi, he was admitted to the Reale Concerto on June 7, 1756; he played in the orchestra of the Teatro Ducale from 1757 until October 1, 1760, in both cases as a violinist.[20]

According to Choron-Fayolle, the famous composer Traetta (1727–1779), chapel master of the duke of Parma, wrote the first obbligato horn part in an operatic aria for Rodolphe, who was a virtuoso on the latter instrument too, while giving him lessons in composition and counterpoint.[21] The piece in question is

[20] Gaspare Nello Vetro, personal communication (2012). See also http://www.lacasadellamusica.it/Vetro/Pages/Dizionario.aspx?ini=R&tipologia=1&idoggetto=2822&idcontenuto=2494.

[21] This was not, of course, the first request for an obbligato horn in a vocal composition, but at the time of Choron-Fayolle (1811), the music of composers of the past was practically forgotten. Additionally, note that the content of the "Rodolphe" entry of this dictionary, often reused by later authors, may have been provided personally by the hornist, who was still alive at the time of publication.

"Disperata invan mi affanno" from the opera *Solimano* (Parma 1759), which has been identified and brought to scholars' attention (Rocchetti 2006, 277) (see Musical example 36 online). It is written in clarino style with a virtuoso character and does not require use of the hand, even though the eleventh and thirteenth harmonics do appear.[22] The aria begins with a recitative accompanied by violins I and II, violas, solo horn, and obbligato cello—an extremely rare scoring, by the way—and testifies to a highly developed soloistic treatment of the horn, which Rodolphe may have developed at the duke of Parma's court while serving as a violinist. In any case, his biography reports that at the age of seven, he started studying horn with his father, and ten years later (1747), "he was regarded as the foremost horn player of France."

Rodolphe moved to Stuttgart after October 1, 1760 to continue his compositional studies with Nicolò Jommelli, and remained there until at least the end of 1766. Beginning in 1755, Jommelli had created an excellent orchestra in Stuttgart that employed twenty-four famous musicians (*Grove* 2001, s.v. "Jommelli", § 2), who were then joined by Rodolphe. According to Dauprat (1824, I, 9, fn. 2), Jommelli wrote a demanding aria with solo horn (in F) in the *Olimpiade* ("Lo seguitai felice", Act III, Sc. III, included only in the Stuttgart version of 1761) for Rodolphe (see Musical example 37 online). Because of its large range, Dauprat continues, it caused Rodolphe to develop an incurable hernia owing to the effort required to play in all the instrument's registers. The horn part is full of broken chords and mostly uses the falsetto technique with a limited use of the hand, possibly more sympathetic to the composer than to the soloist (the latter could, however, highlight his skills in virtuoso cadenzas). The range required of the player is in fact very wide, as they must juggle rising to c''' (sixteenth harmonic) and descending to the very low F sharp,[23] obtained by bending the second harmonic.

Another appealing solo by Jommelli is found in the aria "Odo il suon de' queruli accenti" of the opera *Demofoonte* (Act III, Sc. VI), a rewritten version of which was performed in Stuttgart in 1764 (D-Sl = RISM 1001155584; the aria

---

[22] Traetta also wrote another aria with an obbligato horn, "Al giuramento mio," for Rodolphe in the opera *Le feste di Imeneo* (Parma, September 3, 1760) (RISM 858000659).

[23] Notation in such a low register in the treble clef implies the use of numerous ledger lines and must have been somewhat uncomfortable even for the editor of the first edition, which is not free of errors (*Imprimerie de l'Academie Caroline*, 1783). Nevertheless, this was possibly an intentional choice by the composer in order to avoid misunderstandings owing to the octave jump when using the bass clef (see Appendix I online).

alone is also in I-Mc, Noseda 36 O 12) (see Musical example 38 online).[24] The horn is again used mostly in the high register, not unlike in Traetta's writing, with a few notes outside the harmonic series (G, e, f sharp, b, and a') and extensive use of the lowest octave (second and third harmonics). The range covered is from low G to c''' and there is a series of wide leaps, a sign both of the gradual stylistic change that had occurred in solo horn writing as well as of the wide range mastered by the soloist. Particularly noteworthy is the inclusion of an *arbitrio* (or free will) entrusted to the player during their first entry and a cadenza, where Rodolphe could undoubtedly demonstrate all his virtuosity.

The virtuoso then moved to Paris, where he arrived together with the famous violinist Antonio Lolli (*ca*. 1725–1802). Here, on April 19–21 and 23, 1764, he performed a concerto of his own. The performance was reviewed in the *Mercure de France*,[25] and was enthusiastically commended by the French writer Louis Petit de Bachaumont (1777, II, 49): "April 21, 1764. Last week, at the Concert Spirituel, we heard a horn player that amazed all of Paris, Mr. Rodolphe, a musician of the Duke of Württemberg. Never has this instrument been pushed to such a bold extreme, imitating in turn the most tender flute and the brightest trumpet. His tongue strokes are of inexplicable speed, variety, and precision. He seems to perform the most difficult and the fastest music without hesitation."

Domnich in turn states (*Méthode* 1807, iv, fn. 2) that Rodolphe introduced the hand-horn technique to France. In 1765, he would also make known the model with a full set of crooks (Castil-Blaze, 1855, II, 345), probably required owing to the frequent key changes in orchestral playing. In that period, Rodolphe was invited to the Paris Opéra, where on December 4, 1765, the opéra-comique *La Fée Urgèle* by Egidio Duni was performed. In the fifth measure of the aria "Ah! Que l'amour est chose jolie!" (Act I, Sc. V), the solo horn plays b' and a' in succession (as in Gehra's concerto and therefore obtainable with a mute, a stopper, or even the hand) and then a lower d', which could only be played using the hand (see Musical example 39).

Rodolphe must have left Stuttgart permanently in late 1766 or early 1767, for he was a member of the prince of Conti's orchestra in Paris by 1767. He then played both the violin and the horn in the Opéra Orchestra on a permanent basis and

---

[24] The first version, staged in Padua in 1743, does not contain this solo.

[25] The text of the review published in the *Mercure de France*, May 1764, 194, is reported by Morley-Pegge 1973, 173, fn. 3.

Musical example 39. E. R. Duni, *La fée Urgèle*, aria "Ah! Que l'amour."

later joined the Royal Chapel.[26] At the Opéra, on June 10, 1767, Rodolphe performed a now lost aria by Boyer,[27] which contained a part for obbligato hand horn ("Amour, sous ce riant bocage") and was sung by the famous Joseph Legros,[28] who later became the director of the Concert Spirituel (Bachaumont 1777, III, 224).

The virtuosity displayed by Rodolphe is well summarized by two contemporary statements by both La Borde (1780, III, 474) and Francoeur (1772, 51). According to the first, "he has found a way of producing sounds that before him had never been heard on his instrument," while the latter notes that "he commands the range of the first as well as that of second horn at the highest level."

Both features are also found in the obscure *Le Plaisir de la campagne Ariette nouvelle a Corno principalé* [sic], *Violino Primo et Secondo, Basse (Oboe et Cors) ad Libitum* by Pierre Péterlard (Pettelard, Pettelart) le Jeune (1747–1779), a little-known singer and composer from Valenciennes. Most probably written for

[26] Choron-Fayolle 1811, 228, argues that these events had already occurred, starting in 1763, but given other biographical evidence, this seems unlikely.
[27] Perhaps Pascal Boyer (1743–1794), a French writer and composer who lived in Paris writing, composing, and teaching singing and the guitar.
[28] Joseph Legros (1739–1793), French tenor and composer; choirboy at Laon Cathedral. He made his début at the Paris Opéra in 1764 and became the Opéra's leading haute-contre until his retirement in 1783.

Rodolphe, it was performed for the first time at the Concert de Mrs. les amateurs and published in Paris in 1776 (see *Mercure de France*, February 1776, 168). The piece is also notable because the *Corno principale e Obligato in D.laré* (i.e. in D) must play the introduction in A major and then the "arietta" in D. In addition, there is the following meaningful specification: "pour éxecuter ce morceau il faut absolument que le Cor sentende [*sic*] avec la voix" (understanding between the horn player and singer is compulsory to play this piece). The composer has also fully notated two "Capricio ad libitum," useful for understanding the kind of cadence performed by horn players of the time (see Musical example 40 online).

Rodolphe was also active as a composer, a capacity noted appreciatively by Mozart in a letter to his father from Paris on May 14, 1778. He wrote several ballets and, of course, music for horn including two concertos, the first of which was

Figure 76. L.-G. Blanchet, alleged portrait of Rodolphe, signed "Rome 1759."

published in 1779.[29] His theory handbook *Solfège ou nouvelle méthode de musique* (1784) was also very popular and remained in use throughout the nineteenth century.

Finally, a well-known piece of iconographic evidence is a painting by Louis Carrogis (also known as Louis de Carmontelle, 1717–1806) portraying Vachon, Duport, Rodolphe, Provers, and Vernier in about 1770. Here, Rodolphe is pictured with a simple natural horn, as was then customary in solo repertoire. Much less well known is a portrait by the artist Louis-Gabriel Blanchet (1705–1772), painted in Rome in 1759 said to be Rodolphe's (see Figure 76), but with no resemblance to that by Carrogis (Carmontelle), of 1770 *ca.* (see also online, "A forgotten virtuoso").

GIULIO PAER

Surprising as it may be, early diffusion of the hand technique is documented in Italy with Giulio Paer (before 1750–1790), father of the famous composer Ferdinando Paer and son of the trumpet player Michael, from Peterwaradin (today Novi Sad). Michael had moved to Parma in the early eighteenth century and was the one who imparted to the young Giulio the first rudiments of the horn. A long biographical note on the latter is found in Castil-Blaze (1838) and is probably based on information from his son Ferdinando, possibly not without some forgivable exaggeration:[30]

Giulio Paer was able to obtain sounds that the natural horn could not, completing its scale with the trick of introducing the hand into the bell. Its notes were then able to blend with those of the clarinet, oboe, and bassoon in the orchestra, thus forming part of the harmony.

In fact, the horn rarely appeared in music and only for the performance of a few ringing fanfares. Giulio Paër softened the voice of his instrument to the point of charming audiences with his melodious performances, both when facing the musical discourse alone and when playing with the singer. The invention by this horn player was a great sensation in Italy; composers promptly took advantage of the new resources that the transformed horn offered to them and wrote solos for this instrument. Since Paër was still the keeper of the secret and had not taught the art to students, he was called to perform all the cities where they wanted to hear the horn blend with the admirable voice of David the

---

[29] *Almanach Musical pour l'année 1779,* vol. V (Paris, 1779), p. 118: "Concerto pour Cor principal, n° 1 par Rodolphe; *chez M. Sieber.*"

[30] Biographical data on Giulio Paer will be restated more briefly in Castil-Blaze 1843.

father. The *Nitteti* by Gatti presented this double wonder to the enchanted Italians: Paër was required wherever David went to perform the famous and favorite aria "Puoi vantar le tue ritorte," a true concertante piece for tenor and horn. Punto and Rodolphe, are the leaders of our current way of playing, so well represented today by Gallay, Dauprat, Meifred, Mengal, etc.

Aside from the unlikely idea that Paer was the first to make use of the hand, Castil-Blaze's biography is crucial both in that it suggests a relationship between Rodolphe and the skilled horn player from Parma and explains the subsequent flourishing of the most important Italian school of horn playing in this city.

The aria "Puoi vantar le tue ritorte" in the opera *Nitteti* (Mantua, 1779; not 1773) by Luigi Gatti (1740–1817) is in fact found in the original manuscript (I-Bc, FF 99; see Rocchetti 2006, 279), with the heading "for Mr. Giacomo David," the famous tenor (1750–1830). The libretto (I-Bc Lo.9049) confirms (Rocchetti 2006, 8) that the difficult part for obbligato horn, full of virtuosic passages and notes obtainable only using the hand, was indeed performed by Giulio Paer (see Figure 77, and Musical example 41 online).

It is also conceivable that seven years earlier, Giulio Paer may have performed and even inspired the challenging solo for hand horn found in Mozart's *Mitridate*, which premiered in Milan (December 1770), and a meeting between the two may have taken place during one of Leopold and Wolfgang Mozart's two preceding visits to Parma in March and October 1770 (Meucci 2010, 146–147).[32]

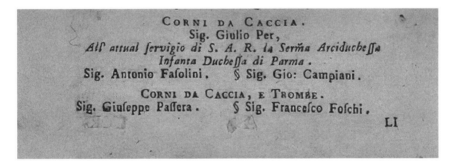

Figure 77. L. Gatti, *Nitteti*, libretto.[129]

[31] The horn obbligato of the *Mitridate* was added at the last minute (cf. Sadie 2006, 296); on the singer D'Ettorre, who first sang that aria, and on the different versions of the same opera, see Wignall 1995.

[32] From the libretto it is apparent that the second pair of horn players also had to play trumpets; Paer, as a soloist, is mentioned above the other four hornists.

Musical example 42. Mysliveček, *Demetrio*, in comparison with Mozart's Horn Concerto.

In that same year, a unique friendship between the young Mozart and the already established Bohemian composer Josef Mysliveček (1737–1781) began after a meeting in Bologna. In Parma, the Mozarts had also heard the singer Lucrezia Agujari (1743–1783), on whose uncommonly wide vocal range Amadeus comments in a letter to his sister on March 24 of that year. Agujari, who long remained in Mozart's memory, then performed the role of Cleonice in *Demetrio* by Mysliveček, which was staged for the inauguration of the theater of Pavia on May 24, 1773. The compositional scheme in this opera is very similar to that of his aforementioned *Bellerofonte* (Naples 1767), with an orchestral introduction to the aria "Alme ingrate" in which a long horn solo, most likely entrusted to Paer, accompanies the virtuosic role of Fenicio (tenor). In comparison to the previous opera, the register in which the instrument plays is lower (some passages are identical but an octave below) and there are many more notes produced using the hand. In measure twenty-four, a new musical theme begins with striking similarities to the main theme from Mozart's Horn Concerto KV.417 (1783), perhaps the composer's tribute to his Bohemian friend (see Musical example 42).

JOSEPH LEUTGEB

Leutgeb (1732–1811), whose surname is written in many different ways (Leitgeb, Leitgel, Liekhgeb, etc.), is known to all lovers of the horn both for the concertos that Mozart dedicated to him and because he was the object of Mozart's jokes, which gave him an unfair reputation as instrumentalist in the long term.[33]

His musical training is not known, but it is certain that in the early 1750s he was in the service of the duke of Hildburghausen and performed in Vienna in 1754 with his orchestra. In the period between November 27, 1761 and January 28, 1763, Leutgeb played as a soloist at least fourteen times at the Burgtheater in Vienna, performing compositions including horn concertos by Leopold Hofmann (June 11, 1762), Michael Haydn (July 2, 1762), and Carl Ditters von Dittersdorf (November 5, 1762),[34] none of which are today identifiable with certainty.[35] This is a remarkable number of solo performances, surpassed in that theater only by those of the violinist and composer von Dittersdorf, a fact that incidentally confirms Leutgeb's uncommon instrumental ability.

Leutgeb's celebrity as horn player and his friendship with Haydn was likely the basis for his enrollment in the orchestra of Prince Esterházy in February 1763, where he was offered a very high salary, resigning however for unknown reasons only a month later. In fact, in the same year, he was hired in Salzburg, where, in August 1763, he had already established a close friendship with the Mozarts.[36]

Until today, little was known about his life between this point and 1770, so it is relevant to present a piece of evidence that was recently discovered from the *Gazzetta Patria* (48 (1766), 195–196) published in Florence. It reports a performance of two horn concertos in the city on November 24 and 26, 1766, that were "so bravely performed by Mr Leütkeph, horn virtuoso in the service of His Highness the Most Reverend Prince Archbishop of Salzburg, who not only received the cheers and the applause of all the people present, but also the signs of great

---

[33] A detailed biography of Joseph Leutgeb (not Ignaz, as he is named in many modern papers) is found in Pisarowitz 1970. The large amount of information discovered by Michael Lorenz (http://michaelorenz.blogspot.com/2013/04/a-little-leitgeb-research.html), who also succeeded in identifying Joseph's baptismal certificate and his birth date, October 6, 1732, should be added to this.

[34] Hans Pizka (http://www.wienerhorn.com/forum/viewtopic.php?f=4&t=157), in addition to providing further biographical information, mentions that these concertos are listed in Philipp Gumpenhuber's "Répertoire," found in the National Library of Vienna.

[35] The surviving Concertino in D major by M. Haydn displays much more modern writing than was used in 1762, including ample use of the hand technique, and therefore cannot be identified as the one mentioned here (see also Chapter 17 online, "Haydn").

[36] In a letter addressed to Lorenz Hagenauer of August 20, 1763, Leopold Mozart reports, "Once since we started upon them, it was in Augsburg, I think, Wolfgang, on waking up in the morning, began to cry. I asked him the reason and he said that he was sorry not to be seeing Herr Hagenauer, Wenzel, Spitzeder, Deibl, Leutgeb, Vogt, Cajetan, Nazerl and other good friends" (see Anderson 1938, I, 39).

admiration from the Sovereigns." We can assume that Leutgeb repeatedly took leaves of absence from his occupation in Salzburg in order to perform as a soloist on tour. Indeed, the music chronicles report that Leutgeb performed in Frankfurt on January 19 and 22, 1770, a city where he had evidently already given other popular concerts.[37] Then, a few months later, he appeared three times at the Concert Spirituel in Paris, again with considerable success.[38]

Subsequently, Leutgeb organized concerto performances with the help of the Mozarts—such as, for example, when they went back to Milan in late 1772 for the preparation of *Lucio Silla*. In a letter to his wife (February 13, 1773), Leopold Mozart praises the soloist, stating, "So far, he has arranged his affairs pretty well and he will make quite a fortune here, for he is extraordinarily popular. If the concert which the courtiers want to arrange for him takes place, I wager that he will get one hundred cigliati on the spot. The Archduke also wants to hear him."

Leutgeb was therefore given the opportunity to perform in Milan, but that was not his last trip to Italy. On May 6 and 18, 1774, he took part in two concerts at the Accademia Virgiliana in Mantua. In the first, he played one of his own horn concertos in E-flat major, now lost; in the second, he played the same concerto again and the obbligato horn part from Mysliveček's aria "Alme ingrate," already interpreted by Paer, this time adapted for the soprano voice of Angela Galliani (Meucci 2010, 147–148).

As mentioned, Mozart literally borrowed the theme of this aria in the first movement of his KV.417 Concerto, which, quite unusually, starts with a theme in the orchestral exposition that does not match that proposed by the horn. This is a peculiarity that seems to have escaped the attention of the many Mozart scholars. The composer also headed the score with an irreverent dedication: "Wolfgang

[37] "Our city can boast, as a matter of fact, that the most celebrated artists and virtuosos have chosen it to demonstrate their gifts and talents to the specialists. We have just had the luck of admiring the violinist Mr. Holtzbogen, concertmaster of Duke Clement of Bavaria, prince and ruler, and the well-known hornist, Mr Leitgeb, of the Principal Orchestra of Salzburg, in a public concert. Both are so great at their art that they are met with approval from all listeners" (from *Post Zeitung*, 15 (Frankfurt 1770), quoted in Israël 1876, 51).

[38] The April 1 concert was reviewed by the *Mercure de France* 2 (April 1770), 141: "Mr. Liekhgeb, musician of the prince bishop of Salzburg, received the applause he deserved owing to the superior talent with which he performed a hunting concerto of his composition . . ." (this piece is lost). The second concert, held in May, celebrated the artistic skills of the hornist even more (*Mercure de France*, May 1770, 164): "Mr. Seikgeb, first horn of H.S.H. the Archbishop of Salzburg, gave two concerts, displaying all possible mastery. He draws sounds from his instrument that surprise even the connoisseurs. He deserves praise for singing the adagio so perfectly, like how the most mellow, the most fascinating and the most correct voice can do."

Amadé Mozart has taken pity on Leitgeb the ox, donkey, and fool, Vienna, the 27th of May 1783."[39] Despite the sarcasm, Wolfgang had a deep bond of friendship with Leutgeb—who, by the way, was also close to the composer during the last days of Mozart's life (Abert 2007, 761)—a friendly relationship that resulted in the creation of some of the most popular compositions for the horn (see Chapter 17 online, "Mozart").

Leutgeb had moved to Vienna by 1777 at the latest when he asked Leopold Mozart for a loan in a letter on December 1 (Schiedermair 1914, III, 279) in order to start a cheese business.[40] Indeed, Leutgeb had married Barbara Plazzeriani (Plazerianin, Placereano, Placeriano) on November 2, 1760. Her father, Biagio, from the Italian region of Friuli, ran a company that produced Italian cheeses and cold cuts, which was, however, sold immediately after his death in 1763. According to research by Michael Lorenz, since there are no traces of subsequent permits or tax payments by Leutgeb as a seller of cheese in Vienna, it is likely that the loan—which Leutgeb probably never repaid—was used, in agreement with Wolfgang, to pay for the new house he had purchased. Leutgeb's cheese shop, on the other hand—which was a blight on his reputation—is just a legend!

Finally, we would like to briefly comment on Mozart's Concerto in D major KV.412 (386B) / 514, long mistakenly believed to be the first in the series but in fact the last, which dates back to 1791 (see Musical example 43 online).[41] Here, Leutgeb was harangued in a way that is truly irreverent—especially for a celebrated instrumentalist at the end of his artistic career. Above the horn part, the following text is penciled in Italian: "To you Mr. Donkey; come on; soon; courage; oh, what a jarring," continuing with a series of provocations and ending with "Thank heaven! Enough, enough!" This is just friendly teasing, but one might suspect that the adoption of the D major key (all other concerts are in E-flat), and especially the limited range of a ninth (from g' to a-flat"), were because of the fairly advanced age of Leutgeb, who was fifty-nine at the time. This remains only

---

[39] A section of the manuscript is lost, but both the first movement up until bar 176 and the entire third movement have been preserved. The missing parts can be recovered from the orchestral parts from the first printed edition (Offenbach, André, 1802).

[40] In this letter, Leutgeb also asks that a horn concerto be composed.

[41] Research conducted by Alan Tyson in 1987–1988 produced a new and surprising dating of the manuscript to 1791, thus within the last year of Mozart's life. We have, more to the point, a complete version of Mozart's first movement—which Tyson believes he may have started to write as early as 1790—and two versions of the Rondo: the one usually performed, attributed to Süßmayr (Mozart's pupil who completed Requiem KV.626), and another incomplete version by Mozart. Neither the second movement nor its sketch has survived.

a possibility, however, because the well-known version was completed by Franz Xaver Süßmayr (1766–1803).

In any case, Leutgeb was one of the leading pioneers of the hand horn, and his undisputed successes in Europe suggest a strong appreciation for the man who was unjustly victimized for a long period of time, as it has been said, by a thoroughly modern interpretation of the ironies introduced by Mozart in his manuscripts.[42]

GIOVANNI PUNTO

The first to publish a biography of Giovanni Punto (1746–1803)—the Italianization of his Bohemian name, Jan Václav Stich—was Dlabacž, who covers him thoroughly in his *Dictionary of the Bohemian Artists* from 1815 (III, s.v.), presenting numerous original pieces of evidence and documenting Stich's unmatched reputation. Stich came from a territory south of Prague belonging to Count Thun, who perceived the considerable musical gifts of the youth and sent him to be trained with the best horn players of the time in Prague and Munich, and then in Dresden, by Hampel. Upon his return in 1764, the young man entered the chapel of Thun but left four years later with other colleagues. Various evidence, including a story that circulated for a long time stating that the count ordered Punto's teeth smashed in (Gerber 1814, 281; Kling 1908, 1068), demonstrate that this was not at all pleasing to the count. Yet there is no proof of such an order to be found in the original sources cited by Volek (1983) and mentioned in Chapter 15. The latter work, as already stated, is to be regarded with caution, as it does not reveal the sites in which the documents are preserved.

Punto then started an exciting career as a traveling virtuoso[43], perhaps the most distinguished one, at least for the hand horn, not to mention his occasional employment as violinist. He also edited the aforementioned Hampel/Punto handbook, a volume of exercises entitled *Etude ou exercise journalier . . . pour le cor* (Paris, Leduc, 1793), and a large amount of music for the instrument (see online, "Punto's role as concertmaster").

---

[42] In addition to the dedication of KV.417, in KV.495 Mozart used inks of different colors. This choice has been interpreted by some scholars as a sign of Mozart's alleged irreverence toward Leutgeb. However, according to other scholars, it is much more likely that Mozart intended to supply some interpretative suggestions for this piece (see Giegling 1987, xiv).

[43] Punto's knowledge of foreign languages surely helped to this goal. According to Dlabacž 1815, III, 213, Punto, in addition to his mother tongue, also spoke German, French, and Italian. On Punto's travels to London in 1772, 1773, and 1788 see Humphries 2021.

However, during the so-called Reign of Terror (1793–1794), Punto retired to Rouen, north-west of Paris, along with other famous musicians, such as the violinist Pierre Rode, the young composer François-Adrien Boïeldieu, and the tenor Pietro Giovanni Garat (*Le Mercure musical*, November 15, 1906, 316). Here, he performed in numerous concerts—during the first period also with Rodolphe Kreutzer—even though, belonging to the Garde Nationale, he was frequently on patrol (Chastenay 1897, I, 182). Punto had already performed in that city in 1787 (*Le Mercure musical*, November 15, 1906, 328), and in 1792, he played the obbligato from *Les Visitandines* by François Devienne and one of his own horn concertos, finishing with a horn quartet and arias with variations (*Le Journal de Rouen*, November 15, 1792, 782) (see Musical example 44 online).

Dlabacž also mentions the *Prager neue Zeitung* from 1801, which included a review of a concert that he himself had attended and that contains a real tribute to the soloist: "according to the opinions of the most experts, a similar demonstration on the horn had never been heard. This exhibition, on an instrument otherwise so arduous, consisted only in singing, as much in the high register as in the low." In this article, another piece of information that may appear of trifling importance is also mentioned during the discussion of Punto's many virtuosic skills—namely, his ability to perform multiple sounds. Nonetheless, it should be reported, because, together with similar performances of the Böck brothers (see Chapter 17, "Duet players and composers" online), it constituted the precedent for the request for these sounds by Weber in his Concertino, op. 45 (see Chapter 18, "Solo concertos in the early nineteenth century" online).

Nearly a hundred years after Dlabacž's text, Henry Kling (1908) devoted an extensive monograph to this great horn player, which we recommend readers peruse, along with all subsequent literature, for more biographical information. However, we wish to particularly mention a recent essay by Thierry Maniguet (2015) dedicated to the makers of the Raoux family, in which a surviving letter by Punto is reported which throws light on his preferences concerning the instrument to be used.

Headed "From the famous Punto to the Citizen Raoux," the letter is addressed from the Hotel de France in Rouen on 27 Brumaire of year 6 (November 17, 1797), and contains an order for a new orchestral horn, probably replacing a *cor solo*. In spite of an incomplete mastery of the written French language, the musician lists precise requirements in terms of the position of the slide, the position of the leadpipe, and even of the overall size of the instrument so as to facilitate the playing with the hand in the bell:

My dear friend,

I beg you to choose for me a good bell, in the same style of the other one. But you must put the slide to your usual and the yard into which the mouthpieces are inserted as high as to be possible to use the hand. If you still want to prepare everything, I do not want to have the slide outside: you will put it to your ordinary.

A thousand honest things to Madame, and to Mr and Mrs Kenn. Embrace your child for me, I am for life, Your sincere friend . . .[44]

---

[44] Johann Wenzel Stich, *Lettre de Jan Stich Punto au citoyen Raoux*, 27 Brumaire an 6 [November 17, 1797], BnF, département de la musique, la-punto jan stich-1 (see Maniguet 2015, 238).

17

THE CLASSICAL REPERTOIRE

Apart from the survival of old-fashioned playing techniques and outdated models of the instrument, and apart from compositions still written in a style bordering on baroque (e.g. Joseph Haydn's Concerto Hob. VIId:3), the early classical repertoire features an increasing abandonment of the clarino style and the constant presence of at least two horns in the orchestra.

Starting in the 1770s, a vast solo repertoire for hand horn was also developed, with the first major concertos by Mozart, Michael Haydn (Concertino), Stamitz, Danzi, and Rosetti (Rösler), serenades for wind instruments, chamber music for solo horn (Mozart KV. 407, Punto's quartets, etc.) and, last but not least, the obbligato passages in the opera, possible clues as to the presence of distinguished players in the orchestra.

Nonetheless, the hand technique initially constituted an expansion of the previous style, not the birth of a new esthetic idiom based on this "manual" resource (Kearns 1986, 104). Examples can be found in some passages of the contemporary solo horn repertoire, such as in Franz Xavier Pokorny's (1729–1794) *Concerto per il Corno Secundo Principale* in E from 1755 (music example in Kearns 1986, 186). The fact that only a few players were accustomed to the new technique is demonstrated, for example, by an anonymous alternative part ("Corno Variante") preserved with a concerto in E-flat by Rosetti (before 1782; catalog no. C41) which avoids the highest notes and some stopped ones (Kearns 1986, 128).

Orchestral parts, in turn, mostly limited the use of the hand to correcting harmonics eleven and thirteen. This could allow for acceptable performances even where, as in small theaters, orchestral forces could be less skilled and less up to date than those in the major venues. In most cases, in fact, the approach to stopped notes was problematic for orchestral players, as the presence of all the other instruments made horn sounds less audible and difficult to tune, thus reducing the possibilities for exploiting the most peculiar features of the technique.

Only when orchestral players became well acquainted with the hand horn could composers unabashedly call for a greater number of stopped sounds and a greater harmonic variety. However, few compositions fully exploited the potential of the new language, namely that of evoking an emotional situation through expressive tunes (see, in this regard, Rogan 1996). The esthetic use of stopped notes in the orchestra dates back to the early nineteenth century, aside from exceptional instances in the last three decades of the previous century.

It is in fact only at the threshold of the new century that orchestral solos involving the hand technique began to be called for on a constant basis, and this coincided with the appearance of the first hand-horn tutors (Duvernoy 1799, Domnich 1807, etc.). Perhaps the earliest example of the genre is encountered in *Médée* by Luigi Cherubini (1797), in which stopped notes help evoke the dangerous atmosphere of the opening scene of the second act.

Even in contemporary chamber music, requests for these new hand-horn sounds began to occur, in small ensembles (trios and quartets), in the serenades with strings, and in the *harmonie* for winds, where stopped notes became more frequent even when the horn stuck to its traditional harmonic function.

HORN CONCERTOS

During the 1770s, further development of the solo repertoire for horn and orchestra took place. Some distinguished players (such as soloists Leutgeb, Paer, and Punto and duo players Palsa and Thürrschmidt and the Böck brothers, among others) began performing in new roles on tour across Europe. They played their own compositions or those by other composers, both of which were a sign of the increasing success of the horn and its repertoire.

The Bohemian composer Francesco Antonio Rosetti (Franz Anton Rösler, *ca.* 1750–1792), who worked in the Hofkapelle of Prince Oettingen-Wallerstein from 1774, was particularly productive. He became Kapellmeister there in 1785 and then moved to Ludwigslust, where he died in 1792. During a stay in Paris (1781–1782), he wrote three of his numerous horn concertos (sixteen concertos for one and six for two horns, among which at least five are lost). These compositions show his musical skill (Kearns 1986, 135) and reveal a more marked independence between solo and tutti than is found in Mozart's concertos. A certain originality is also apparent in the use of harmony, melody, and rhythm, and the pieces also have an effective melodic vein, especially in the slow movements. Kearns (1986, 16) assumes that the concertos for first horn by Rosetti were written for Carl Thürrschmidt, and the two horn players hired after 1780 in Wallerstein, Josef Nagel (*ca.* 1751–1802) and Franz Zwierzina (1751–1825), were the recipients of several concertos for two horns. These certainly included the one in F major (cat. C.61) with the heading "fait pour Messieurs Nagel & Zwierzina" and the date 1787 (Murray 2014, 255) (see Figures 78 & 79 online).

However, it is uncertain whether the two virtuosos were also the beneficiaries of a concerto in E-flat major for two horns with a second movement in E-flat minor (a key that was quite unusual for the period), which was initially attributed to Joseph and then to Michael Haydn, but has been recently assigned to Rosetti (Murray 2014, 260). The concertos for second horn numbered C.53 (see Musical example 45 online) and C.50 were written for Zwierzina and have a different character from the one that was certainly written for Thürrschmidt in 1779 (C.49, one of the most well known today). Rosetti's Concerto C.58 may have instead been written for the Thürrschmidt–Palsa duo. The presence of these horn players at the court of Wallerstein also influenced other composers who wrote for the horn, such as Josef Fiala (1748–1816) and Josef Reicha (1752–1795), Czech composers who worked there from 1770 to 1785.

Solo horn pieces such as those by Michael Haydn (1737–1806), who left a demanding Concertino in D, Carl Philipp Stamitz (1745–1801), and Anton Teyber (1756–1822) were also created by this generation of composers. Teyber's Concerto in E-flat major—which despite being numbered as his first, is not—makes use of a considerable range, up to g''' (*b-flat*" at concert pitch), and a type of mixed writing using clarino and hand technique that recalls the playing skills of Thürrschmidt (similar writing features are found in various horn concertos itemized in Dahlqvist 1991). In addition, we could mention the concertos by Mozart (see below) and those bequeathed by the greatest soloist of the time, Giovanni Punto.

Moreover, there are the compositions by Franz Danzi (1763–1826) who wrote a Concerto in E circa 1790, which was perhaps for Franz Lang (1751–1816) or for Carl Franz (1738–1802), a horn player in Esterháza. Although there are some signs of inexperience in the writing (Kearns 1986, 134), it contains fascinating melodies in the same vein as those by Mozart.

The development of this repertoire for solo horn with orchestra is mostly owing to German composers, while in Italy the prevailing interest for opera led to the creation of many obbligato parts or concertos written by leading orchestral

Musical example 46. E. Nappi's *Concerto a Corno da Caccia*, c. 5r, scoring: solo hn, I vn, II vn, basso.

members, such as the Belloli brothers. A separate case is the *Concerto a Corno da Caccia* (1789) by Emanuele Nappi (1767–1836) from 1789, undoubtedly written for a distinguished anonymous virtuoso, in which a short quote from Mozart's Concerto KV 495 (1786) is cleverly inserted in the final rondo (see Musical example 46). A few years later, in 1797, Nappi composed another concerto (in E), this time for "lira" (a lyre guitar) and horn (RISM 850012831) and presumably for the same soloist, entrusting him with a number of flourishes within the range from c to g" sharp (see online, "Solo repertory for horn mentioned by Choron and Lafage").

CONCERTOS FOR TWO HORNS

The aforementioned duet tradition, to which we will return below, was related to the increasing presence of a pair of horn players in the orchestra and to the practice of the instrument by members of the same family. The emergence of the *sinfonia concertante* for few obbligato instruments,[1] as well as the development of a solo

---

[1] According to Brook 1975, 13, in the period between 1770 and 1830, about 570 concertante symphonies were written by some 210 composers.

repertoire for two horns and orchestra, in turn allowed the most skilled players to perform in private and public concerts, a tradition that had grown rapidly since the middle of the seventeenth century.

It is no wonder that this repertoire was favored by horn players and composers of Bohemian or southern German origins, where the concertante tradition had found particularly fertile ground. At the court of Oettingen-Wallerstein, thanks to the presence of some outstanding horn players hired on a permanent basis or active as traveling soloists (like Punto), a large number of concertos for two horns appeared. They were usually in the tripartite form (Allegro–Adagio–Allegro) and showcased the virtuosity of the players, who experimented with their technical "discoveries." The catalog drawn up in 1858 by Franz Xaver Zwierzina, the eldest son of the horn player Franz Zwierzina, for the sale of music owned by his father,[2] includes nineteen such concertos. However, it is possible to document a repertoire of approximately twenty-six double horn concertos composed by or for members of the Wallerstein Hofkapelle or directly connected in some other manner with that court (Murray 1986, 519).

This relevant repertoire, written between circa 1752 and 1818, includes music by Leopold Mozart, Franz Xaver Pokorny, and other minor composers (a complete list can be found in Murray 1986). In summary, this is a huge quantity of compositions that deserve to be better known and would also allow us to appropriately appreciate the virtuosic skills attained during this stage on the natural horn in a particularly active music chapel (see online, "Horn players at Wallerstein, 1746–ca. 1825 (after Grünsteudel 2013, 15)").

DUET PLAYERS AND COMPOSERS

With the technical and melodic development of the use of hand technique that occurred between the eighteenth and nineteenth centuries, the duet tradition reached its peak.

One famous pair of horn players was formed by Johann Palsa (1752–1792) and Carl Thürrschmidt, whose story is described in detail by Fitzpatrick (1970, 176–178). During their tours, they repeatedly performed in Paris (five times in March 1780 alone). After the death of Palsa, a pupil of Punto, Jean Brun (1759–1809)—

---

[2] "Verzeichniss über jene Horn Musikalien welche in das furstliche Musikzimmer abgeliefert wurden," Rechnungskommissar Franz Zwierzina in Jahr 1858 (Wallerstein Archive, Dienerakten 111, VII, 14b); quoted in Murray 1986, 518.

not Le Brun (cf. Gerber 1812, 532)—took the place of the former in the duo with Thürrschmidt for a few years. Fitzpatrick (1970, 177–178 and 204) also extensively describes the activity of the Böck brothers, who were known for their use of an effective mute and as the authors of a collection of *10 Pièces pour Deux Cors et Basse* in E-flat (Leipzig, 1802), reviewed in the *AMZ* (4 (October 26, 1803), 56) (see online, "The Böck brothers," and Musical example 47 online).

As in the case just mentioned, the duet repertoire was often linked to family traditions, when apprenticeships on the instrument were undertaken by two (or more) brothers, specializing in turn in the roles of first and second horn. A memorable example was that of the Thürrschmidt family, with the founder Johann (born in Leschgau in Bohemia in 1725), his younger brother Anton, the aforementioned and renowned Carl (probably the son of Johann), his younger brother Joseph (active in France), and the latter's son Carl Nicol (born in 1776 in Paris and later also a pupil of J. Brun). Among other numerous examples (see Murray 1986, 512–515), we could cite the Ziwný brothers (Joseph, Wenzel, and Jacob), who worked at the electoral court of Mannheim and later in the chapel of the duke of Württemberg in Stuttgart; the Bohemian brothers Thomas and Georg Hosa, employed by Prince Charles of Lorraine in Brussels; the brothers Johann Peter and Philipp Dornaus, who, along with their father, Christopher Dornaus, constituted the horn section of the electoral orchestra at Koblenz in the mid-1780s; and the Gugel or Gugl brothers (Joseph and Heinrich), whose lives bridged the eighteenth and nineteenth centuries. Less well known are the Petrides brothers, Joseph (1755–after 1825) and Peter (1766–after 1825), whose careers, full of anecdotes, are narrated in detail (see the sections "England" and "The Petrides brothers in Spain and Portugal," pp. 203–209).

Some of the characteristics of the horn duo were that the first horn played mainly in the upper register with the clear but restrained sound derived from a "trumpet-like" embouchure, sometimes climbing up to the twenty-fourth harmonic, while the second horn, by virtue of a proper horn embouchure, the falsetto technique, and the help of the hand, could in turn obtain harmonic results that had previously been unthinkable and a more smooth and powerful sound. Gerber's (1792, 551) statement in this regard is no coincidence: "When a pair of [horn] virtuosos mount the platform, one seems not to hear the sound of brass instruments, but a flute accompanied by a gamba." Gerber also confirms that soloists used simple natural horns without crooks, as shown, for example, in the portrait of Rodolphe painted by Carmontelle and in that of a horn duo in *New*

Instructions for the French-Horn (*ca.* 1780) (see Chapter 12, Figure 55 online). This was certainly a widespread practice at least until the 1780s, after which all these simple models were replaced by invention horns.

If the performers were influential, the composers who created the horn duet repertoire were equally important. A key role among them is obviously reserved for W. A. Mozart and his twelve duets (KV. 487/496a). The story of these pieces is rather complex (cf. Marx 1988), to the point that both authorship and setting for two horns have sometimes been questioned, but nowadays they are unanimously recognized as genuine. In fact, three of them (Nos. 1, 3, 6) are preserved in autograph with the heading "Vienna, 27 July 1786" and the witty clarification "during the billiard game!" In addition, separate parts from an early Viennese edition dating back to 1802–1803, from which the Paris print of 1807 was derived, have recently been discovered (Berke-Flothuis 1999, 26).

The writing is rather varied and mostly ascribable to the possibilities of the Thürrschmidt–Palsa duo described, the first of whom was also a friend of Mozart and hosted him for a couple of weeks during the latter's stay in Potsdam in April 1789 (Abert 2007, 1160). Sometimes anachronistic in terms of writing, the twelve duets may be considered to be at a junction point between the tradition of the baroque technique in pure clarino style (in the Duet no. 1, whose autograph manuscript has survived, the first horn reaches the twenty-fourth harmonic, or *b-flat*" at concert pitch) and the new writing for the classic horn. In fact, the second horn part offers new possibilities for modulation through the use of several notes outside the harmonic series performed using a highly developed falsetto technique while exploiting the use of the hand in the middle register and in chromatic passages (see Musical example 48 online).

Later on, a few other famous composers wrote music for two horns; five duets in a nineteenth-century edition are attributed to Rossini, but their source is, however, unknown.[3] The *Fünf Duette für zwei Singstimmen oder zwei Waldhörner* by Franz Schubert (May 1815), which can be performed by two horns, are quite unusual.

By and large, however, the duet repertoire was created by distinguished teachers of the time, starting with Hampel/Punto, whose method is written almost entirely as a real duet. Vandenbroek in turn left a collection of duets, *Nouvelle Suite d'Airs, Ariettes, d'Opéra et Opéra Comiques, Romances et Vaudevilles arrangés*

[3] In *Grove* 2001, s.v. "Rossini," they are dated around 1806; we add that the first duet was reused in a march contained in the first act of *La donna del lago*, written in 1819.

pour deux Cors, apparently with a didactical goal, to which one can add various collections of duets by Punto, C. Thürrschmidt, F. Duvernoy, J. F. Gallay, L. F. Dauprat (among them *Six Duos pour Cor Alto et Cor basse*), and, last but not least, the *Studio* (twenty-one pieces) for two natural horns titled *il Labirinto* (The Labyrinth) by Luigi Belloli (see online Musical Example 62), as well as the duets written by his brother Agostino, which are mostly unpublished (see also online, "Again from Choron–Lafage (1838)").

THE MUTE

The first known requests for mutes have been mentioned above in the discussion of Hampel (Chapter 15, p. 123), but it was in the last quarter of the eighteenth century that the mute assumed a new role that fitted into the new sounding and expressive ideals for the instrument quite nicely.

One of the earliest pieces of information dates back to 1771, when Adam Kerner of Vienna—perhaps a member of the famous family of horn makers (his first name, not otherwise documented, might be a simple mistake in place of Anton)—supplied some horn mutes to Esterháza (Ebner 1996, 44), where Haydn had been chapel master for ten years. At that date, the mutes may have looked like the two very peculiar leather items preserved in Edinburgh, possibly dating back to just this period (see Figure 80).

The mutes used by the Böck brothers were not very different from these but were made from metal and are described by Cramer (1783, 1,401, fn. 191): "These mutes, less widely used on the horn than they should be, consist of a metal hollow insert covered with thin leather which fits in the bell and thus immediately dampers the sound." The mute invented by Jean Brun, consisting of a cardboard cone open at the tip with a hole at the base, was likely based on the same principle but had a different shape and stuffing. He used it to create beautiful effects in the Adagios (Fétis 1860–1865, V, 242, art. "Lebrun") (see online, "Muted horns in D").

A mute that could simulate the use of the hand is attributed by Gerber (1814, III, 404) to the famous Carl Thürrschmidt in collaboration with the Parisian maker Raoux: "In 1795, he invented a mute for the horn with which one can obtain semitones or stopped notes with the same safety and simplicity with which they are obtained with the hand without the mute. Using it changed the sound of the horn as little as with Hampel's mute." All of this leads us to believe that the mute called for in Beethoven's Rondino WoO 25, written in 1793, was very similar to this type.

Figure 80. Horn mute, eighteenth century.

A detailed description of such a device is found in Fröhlich (1811, 3). It was an empty sphere of papier-mâché with a diameter of 6 inches (15cm) containing "a metal ball covered with leather, firmly connected to a metal wire (Germ. *Draht*) through which one can close off the opening; the thread goes out from the bottom of the sphere [the one facing outwards] and has a graspable eyelet which can be used to play stopped notes."[4]

The same model with an improved mechanism was described in even more detail by the same author many years later (Fröhlich 1834, 7, fn. 14):

The mute was originally made of wood, with a narrower top that went inside the horn tube and a back that was fairly wider, like a skull. It was closed but had a small opening in the center to permit the outlet of the air. Since the wood

---

[4] A possible reconstruction of Fröhlich's mute is proposed in Smith 1980, 4, but it shows the thread on the side of the mute entering into the bell. It is evident that the thread must be on the opposite, external side. Dr. Smith's website, see http://www.hornsmith.net/horn_mute.html, also contains a revised version of his pioneering dissertation (Smith 1980).

gives a harsh, unpleasant sound, the Böck brothers made use of a hollow brass mute covered with fine leather. Today, the mute is usually an empty sphere of cardboard with a diameter of about 6 inches and an open neck or pipe that is inserted into the bell of the horn. In order to obtain stopped sounds, there is a metallic rod inside connected to a leather ball with which the cavity of the neck can be more or less occluded when needed. The rod, which comes out below the sphere, is equipped with an eyelet with which one can control the passage of the air, neither more nor less than is the case with stopped notes.

Given the importance of the issue and the lack of modern acquaintance with this device, it may be worth quoting that Frölich's description of this "mechanical mute" is reported almost word for word by Schilling (1834, III, 633) and summarized by Bernsdorf (1856, 646–647) (see Figure 81):

It consists of a hollow sphere of cardboard, usually covered with cloth and approximately 6 inches in diameter, attached to a tube that enters into the bell. A rod connected to a disc passes through the ball, which allows the hole of the tube to be occluded so as to allow the horn player to obtain stopped notes with the damper as well. At the end, the rod has an eyelet bulging out from the bottom of the sphere.

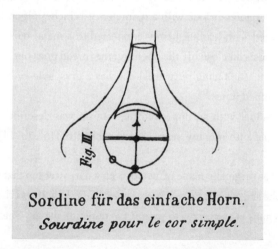

Sordine für das einfache Horn.
Sourdine pour le cor simple.

Figure 81. Mute for natural horn.[5]

---

[5] This testimony, which only recently came to our attention, can be inspiring to all players involved in historically informed performance.

Although it may seem surprising, Dauprat 1824 (II, 151–152) considered the use of the mute to have ended, but its many subsequent uses, especially in the twentieth century, prove him wrong:

> Since good artists are becoming able to modify the tones of the horn almost at will through the hand, lips, and breath, they no longer use the sourdine and it is no longer in favor. Without a doubt, with it, one obtains a pianissimo effect which can surprise listeners, but this foreign body changes the quality and timbre of the tones and lowers their pitch noticeably when placed in the bell, which it fills up almost completely.

A less biased opinion is expressed, in turn, by J. S. Mayr in his *Brevi cenni* (*ca.* 1824; see Rocchetti 2007, 28):

> At times a cardboard tube called *sordino* or *sordina* is inserted into the bell to give the instrument a darker sound and create a so-called *echo*, because by repeating the same musical phrase first loudly, then with the mute, the second one seems to come from far away like a natural echo. Some players are even able to produce this echo effect without the aid of a mute.

Finally, there is the invention by Benjamin Millgrove of Bath (evidently a cultured man, since he was among the subscribers to Burney's *General History of Music* in

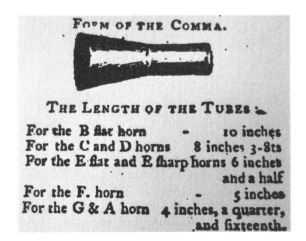

Figure 82. "Comma" device by Millgrove.

1776): the "Comma" device, described in detail in *The Monthly Magazine* (November 1797) with a corresponding illustration (see Figure 82) was designed to produce notes outside the harmonic series accurately without them sounding stopped. It was formed by a cylindrical tube of tin welded to a conical one. The cylindrical part, 5cm (2") in diameter, entered into the bell and, depending on the size of the horn, varied in length from 10cm up to 25cm (B-flat basso size). The conical part increased from a minimum diameter of 5cm to a maximum of nearly 10 and was more than 16cm long. By holding the mute "Comma" inside the bell with a cupped hand over the opening of the conical part, it was possible to lower the pitch of sharp notes.

HAYDN

See online.

MOZART

See online.

BEETHOVEN

See online.

18

THE HEYDAY OF THE HAND HORN

From the very beginning of the nineteenth century, the widespread adoption of the hand technique helped lead to the birth of a new and unique idiom of the horn, characterized by a greater palette of timbres and new expressive possibilities and focused on the middle register, in which an increasing number of instrumentalists were now able to play a complete chromatic scale. In the imagination of a skilled composer, this new possibility became an effective means of expression, allowing for a melodic style that definitively freed the instrument from its ancient hunting roots. The progressive dismissal of the clarino register gave way in turn to a wider use of the instrument, as demonstrated by the progressive increase in the number of solo concertos for horn (or two horns) and by the many obbligato passages in operatic arias as well as in the symphonic repertoire. Meanwhile, new criteria in bell design and the bell's substantial expansion allowed for more precision and a greater variety of sounds in the middle and low register with the systematic inclusion of the second harmonic. These improvements, which constituted a remarkable achievement from a technical and expressive point of view, actually slowed down the diffusion of valves for at least the first half of the nineteenth century.

Therefore, we must revisit Fitzpatrick's (1970, 126) assumption that the discovery of the hand technique gave way to its immediate and widespread adoption starting in the mid-eighteenth century and to an equally rapid change in the shape of the horn. All the considerations listed testify to the fact that the process was in fact far slower.

COR ALTO, COR BASSE, COR MIXTE

Throughout the classical period, there was a marked distinction between the role of first and second horn. Usually, the first horn was trained in the use of the high register (commonly from the fifth to sixteenth harmonics, and at times up to the twenty-fourth) according to the clarino tradition, with which we have repeatedly dealt. On the other hand, the second horn specialized in the low register, where the greater distance between the available harmonics implied a more developed falsetto technique and hand technique. This specialization began to spread at the orchestral level and in the solo repertoire, with duets and concertos specifically written for one of the two roles. With the birth of a stable training tradition, specialization began to be learned during the apprenticeship, as documented by many handbooks, in particular by those adopted at the Paris Conservatoire. In these publications, differences of mouthpiece (Duvernoy 1799, 2) and embouchure between the two genres, among other things, were codified: the first horn—later called *cor alto* by Dauprat (1824, I, 7)—was to use a narrow and short mouthpiece, with an embouchure similar to that of the trumpet (⅓ on the upper lip and ⅔ on the lower one), and for the second horn—which Dauprat called *cor basse*—the mouthpiece had to be a bit broader and deeper and ⅔ of the upper lip and ⅓ of the lower were used.[1]

In addition, Dauprat (1824, I, 2) states that a large bell is more convenient for the *cor basse* and a narrow bell is better for the *cor alto*, since it is useful for the high register.

As already observed by Morley-Pegge (1973, 95), the fact that a clear distinction between the roles of first and second horn was established starting with the earliest appearances of the great orchestral tradition of the instrument is down to the difficulty that most players faced in playing across the whole range of the horn. A specialization in one register was "mandatory," and was influenced by the trumpet-like embouchure of the first horns, which was the opposite of that of the second horns.

When the hand horn became more widely used, the need for this marked distinction between registers was mitigated, and so a new role began to take form among professionals and amateurs: the *cor du milieu*, as defined by Vandenbroek (after 1803, 2), which was subsequently referred to as *cor mixte*. This was essentially a performance technique involving the reduction of the range to less than two

---

[1] Similar considerations were made in Italy, independently, by Gervasoni 1800. In the chapter "Lezioni di corno," he underlines the two distinct roles of the horn on the basis of different embouchures ("imboccature"), in this case referring to the position of the mouthpiece on the player's lips. Thus "the first [horn] normally holds the mouthpiece down and the second up; in this way the first proceeding upwards brings the mouthpiece down as needed and the second, proceeding downwards, brings the mouthpiece up as needed" (p. 324). Gervasoni indicates that the instrument should normally be held with the bell facing up (p. 322) so that the sounds are clean and clear; but the position would also likely be more comfortable if it is necessary to insert the hand to obtain stopped notes (p. 329).

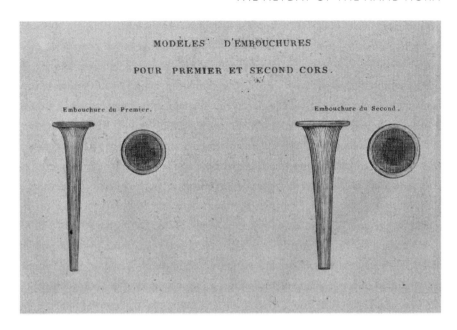

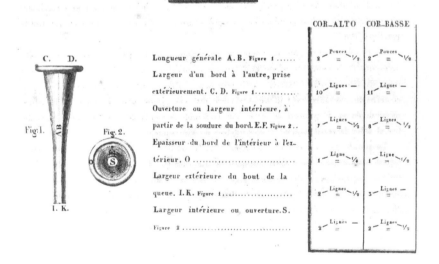

Figures 83 & 84. Above, Duvernoy, *Méthode* (1799, 2), mouthpiece models for first and second horns; below, Dauprat, *Méthode* (1824, I, 12), proportions of the mouthpieces for *cor alto* and *cor basse*.

octaves, between e' and c'''—as confirmed by Vandenbroek (*ca.* 1797, 2) ("*Gamme du cor du milieu*")—instead of the three and a half octaves used previously (see Figure 85 online). A consequence of the development of the hand technique and the cantabile style associated with it, this limitation, which is not addressed in instruction books, is occasionally overcome in some *cor mixte* solos, while others are restricted to an even more limited range.[2]

The tonal balance between open and closed sounds is greater in this register than in the rest of the range, and the changes in taste then in progress eased this choice, which also ensured a greater precision in performance. In addition, Vandenbroek (after 1803, 2) argues that because of the popularity of the *cor du milieu* the *premiers cors* could no longer easily go up into the high register.

Criticized by various instrumentalists and composers beginning with Domnich (1807, vi–viii), the *cor mixte* was actually a temporary stage in the esthetic development of the instrument, and in fact most subsequent handbooks return to the previous division of roles, that of *cor alto* and *cor basse*. Dauprat (1824, I, ii) states that the introduction of the *genre mixte* seemed to move the horn toward its decline because many musicians who were able to perform solos were ineffective at playing orchestral parts. With the new technique, in fact, all parts written for high-pitched horns were transposed into F or into a central key, leading to the need for a new method of training for instrumentalists. To this regard, Snedeker (2021, 49–50), points out that "A range or style of playing called '*cor mixte*' was frowned upon by some, but there is a lack of information and conflicting evidence/reports of who was responsible and whether this was a criticism of a range, set of techniques, or style of playing that some found objectionable."

FRÉDÉRIC DUVERNOY

The celebrated Frédéric Duvernoy (1765–1838) played a prominent role in the *genre mixte*, and his devotion to this sort of style earned him both fame and criticism. The criticisms by Domnich (1807, vii–viii), and those from an anonymous review of his *Méthode* in the *Gazette Nationale ou Le Moniteur Universel* (139, May 16, 1808) do not mention him directly but clearly refer to him. Another article that expressed dislike for the *genre mixte*, published in *AMZ* (1824, 658 ; a review of Dauprat's

---

[2] Nowadays, no one would dare criticize the range of many solos that are part of the most important repertoire of the horn, such as that in the Andante cantabile in Tchaikovsky's Symphony no. 5, which is written entirely within the ninth between e' and f" sharp.

method), on the other hand, does use his name. Here, the reduction of the horn's range, acceptable—according to the writer of the article—only for those who play solos, not for the usual orchestral accompaniment of the horns, is personally attributed to Duvernoy (see also online, "A forgotten method and his author").

If, on the one hand, Dauprat (1824, I, ii) criticizes the *genre mixte*, on the other (Dauprat 1824, III, 48–49) he praises Duvernoy by comparing him to Punto and Brun ("Lebrun," as he spells it). He also notes that most horn solos in the *ballets* and *divertissements* performed at the Opéra were either written by Duvernoy himself, the *cor solo* in that theater since 1801, or dedicated to him (Fétis 1860–1865, III, 100) (see Table 13 online). Even Castil-Blaze (1825, I, 151) compares Duvernoy to Punto and Dauprat, asserting that the artistry of these virtuosos had given the horn a new vitality, enriching it with a multitude of sounds that its nature seemed to reject. He then presents (p. 154) a singular definition of the *genre mixte*, as he recalls that some masters devoted to this genre, such as the famous Duvernoy, were able to play in a mixed style, embracing part of the *cor alto* and part of the *cor basse* register.[3]

Duvernoy's celebrity certainly also grew owing to the esteem of Napoleon (Fétis 1860–1865, III, 100), who wanted him to be the first horn in his Chapelle-Musique (Castil-Blaze 1832, 175) together with Domnich, Colin, and Vandenbroek.[4] An extensive description of this special relationship between Napoleon and Duvernoy is contained in Luca Delpriori's (2007/8) dissertation, which includes a great deal of information on the role of the horn in the Parisian salons, as well as details of the harpists Dalvimare and later Nadermann. Duvernoy was also the performer of the solo written by Paisiello in the Mass for the Emperor's Coronation (December 2, 1804) (see Musical example 49 online),[5] and his fame grew further in the following years, to the point that his name was displayed on the posters for the performances in which he took part.

[3] "Some famous masters, such as M. Duvernoy, have a mixed type that encompasses both registers." In Duvernoy's *Méthode*, although the range generally used is from C to a", both the *Gamme chromatique* and some duets or trios arrive at c'" (sixteenth harmonic), as was the case, albeit more rarely than in the past, in some parts written for Parisian orchestras.

[4] Many years later, in 1830, Duvernoy is listed as "solo" with Mengal and Dauprat in the other chairs, while in the "Musique de la chambre du Roi Charles X," Duvernoy was the sole horn player (Castil-Blaze 1832, 231–234).

[5] "Paisiello had introduced a duet in 'gallant' style, for harp and horn, performed by d'Alvimare and 'Frédéric' in his mass, probably upon the request of Madame Bonaparte" (Reichardt 1896, 385). As one can see, Duvernoy was simply known as Frédéric at the imperial court.

Among these, the best known is the premiere of *La Vestale* by Spontini (Paris, 15 December 1807), where the name of the composer is lacking and that of the singers is in the background, while "*M. Frederic Duvernoy exécutera les solos de cor*" is clearly visible. Less well known is an announcement for a performance of Mozart's *Don Juan* at the Académie impériale in 1805 (see Figure 86 online). It amazed a later reviewer for *Le Figaro* (144, January 8, 1922), who noticed that on the poster for the performance, the following sentence was found above the list of singers: "*M. Frédéric Duvernoy exécutera un nouveau solo de cor de sa composition dans le troisième acte*" (M. Duvernoy will play a horn solo of his own composition in Act III).

Returning to *La Vestale*, in addition to the solo reproduced in Morley-Pegge (1973, 208–209), another long solo accompanied by harp and orchestra is found in the second *Divertissement* of the Finale, recently published as a detached piece for horn and harp. This piece was most likely inspired by the one written for Duvernoy (or by Duvernoy himself?) in the *Divertissement* in Act III of *Le Triomphe de Trajan* (Paris, October 23, 1807) by Jean-François Lesueur (1760–1837), which definitely demonstrates the extreme virtuosity of the player (see online, "*Une anecdote musicale*," and Musical example 50 online).

In the meantime, a kind of entertaining and easy listening music in which horns and harps often had prominent roles was circulating in Paris. It was well suited to the bourgeois class, which was in a phase of rapid and progressive expansion after the French Revolution and whose foremost and most authoritative representative was the emperor himself.

One unusual and instructive description by an illustrious diarist of the time, Mme Chastenay, attests to the fame reached by Duvernoy in the parlors of the French capital, mentioning him using his first name alone (Chastenay 1897, II, 130–131):

The *musique d'etiquette* that I have found everywhere since that moment until I left Paris, consisted of Frédéric with his horn, Naderman with his harp, or sometimes, during the first period, d'Alvimare. The pieces for those pretty evenings were composed, so to say, with an eye on the timing: nothing long, and consequently nothing truly developed; nothing disagreeable, and consequently nothing profound; but pleasant things, all in all, and, in the lack of passionate expressions, a type of graceful smile of the arts. It was by means of these events that the arts were brought back a bit into common habits and the people became accustomed to them.

These "habits" are reflected in the compositional style of many pieces for horn and harp that use the wind instrument in a restricted range so as to avoid intrusiveness and also to preserve the delicacy of sound.

Typical of Duvernoy's performance was the use of a single crook, that of F (an anticipation of the valve-horn setting) even when playing sections in other tonalities, such as E-flat or C. The option was preferred by a number of Parisian composers, since the F crook, replacing that in the key of the piece, could avoid stopped notes in favor of open or semi-closed ones, with a greater timbric homogeneity. In addition to the fascinating beginning of Cherubini's *Chant sur la Mort de Joseph Haydn* (1805), inspired by the alleged death of the great Viennese man, the solo in the opera *Milton* by Spontini, performed five days before Paisiello's Mass, is an interesting case. Here, the use of the horn in F (*Hymne*) in the key of E-flat (the two orchestral horns are in fact pitched in the latter key) allows some stopped sounds to be avoided. Among them is an a" (*c*" at concert pitch), which is fully closed on the E-flat horn and therefore dull and sharp-pitched but open and in tune on the F horn (see Musical example 51). Dauprat himself (1824, III, 95)

Musical example 51. G. Spontini, *Milton*, horn in F and in E-flat compared.

found the F crook useful in some cases, since in the key of C major, it is possible to use fewer stopped notes than with the C crook. He also notes that apart from F crook, the E and E-flat crooks were the most commonly used in the accompaniment of vocal soloists.

In addition to long obbligato parts, the compositions from early nineteenth-century Paris also contain solo passages and phrases assigned to the orchestral horns. Something similar may be said for Milan (which was governed by the French throughout the Napoleonic era) thanks to the presence of Luigi Belloli and the creativity of Simone Mayr. This implies an increasing use of stopped notes in the secondary parts (as well as in many works by Méhul; see Coar 1952, 21) and a particular attention to the combination of horns pitched in various tonalities (as in Isouard's operas). In any case, starting in 1797, the major soloists were hired in the orchestra especially for solo playing (Castil-Blaze 1855, II, 352):

> These musicians did not struggle to sustain long notes or double the part of violin or cello as their colleagues did. The soloists rested during the tutti sections of the symphony and were only heard during the performance of their instrumental song. Several of these players belonged to the orchestra of the Opera.

Regarding these solos, Dauprat (1824, III, 50) emphasizes that in the orchestra the performer should "refrain as much as possible from accompanying before the moment when he is forced to stand out in a difficult obbligato piece." He concludes the volume by affirming that "in the dance pieces, and since Mr. Duvernoy was at the Opera as a solo horn, the domain of the instrument has been extended because of the skill of this performer. Solos with various characters, duets for horn and harp, and concertante pieces for various stringed and wind instruments were as advantageously placed as they were skillfully performed."

Finally, we should not forget the increasing repertoire for solo wind instruments. One noteworthy example is the nearly one hundred pieces for wind quintets (fl, ob, cl, bn, hn) created in Paris for Dauprat by Antonin Reicha (1770–1836) following a model successfully tested by Giuseppe Cambini (1746–1825) (see online, "Dauprat on Reicha").

DAUPRAT'S METHOD (1824)

This additional quotation prompts us to describe the frequently cited treatise by Louis François Dauprat (1781–1868), published in 1824 in three volumes. It constitutes the most complete method ever dedicated to the hand horn, and, in all likelihood, to the horn in general. Here, every single aspect of practicing and training (vol. 1), of soloistic technique (vol. 2), and of all the issues that composers may face in dealing with the instrument (vol. 3) are discussed (see Figure 87 online).

A singular depiction of the unsurpassed quality of Dauprat's treatise is provided by authors from the time period, beginning with the aforementioned anonymous extended review published in *AMZ* (1824, 657–666), which concludes with the following:

> All in all, it is neither a work for those who play the horn for pastime or to perform some fanfares, nor for professionals who use it as a second instrument, but for all those who want to study the horn thoroughly and appear in performance; for those who already possess a certain degree of virtuosity, particularly for those who teach it (they will find materials that will save them burdensome work in these volumes); and finally, mostly the third book, for all composers and conductors who do not play the instrument.

In this regard, we can also quote the long description by a non-instrumentalist composer, Joseph Fröhlich (1780–1862), who duly commends the method, although he experimented with the esthetic results of Punto and Domnich's teaching more successfully (Fröhlich 1834, 8, fn. 16):

> The present author, as the director of a musical institute, has had the occasion to see many students instructed by a master taught based on the principles of Dauprat's method, while others are trained according to Punto and Domnich's technique. The former easily performed the most difficult passages that one can imagine using the stopped sound technique. The latter had a more beautiful sound and their result was far more magniloquent, if commensurate with the character and possibilities of the instrument.

In conclusion, in the post-revolutionary period the horn acquired a completely new and prominent status in the French capital thanks to the contribution of many skilled performers, almost all of whom were pupils of the Conservatoire. The teachers there included scholars such as Vandenbroek, Duvernoy, Domnich, Dauprat, and last but not least Jacques-François Gallay (1795–1864), a renowned composer and author of a *Méthode* published in 1845 whose studies are still appreciated today (see online, "Gallay's 'enharmonic scala' ").

THE GERMAN COUNTRIES

With regards to the German countries, we should once again mention Beethoven, who was responsible for a substantial step forward in the esthetics and writing for orchestral horns,[6] using the instrument in a manner approaching the "romantic" role characteristically played by the horn in successive orchestral compositions: not merely a voice used to fill in the harmonic texture (as in the First, Second, and Fourth Symphonies), but also a melodic resource (Trio from the Third Symphony and from the Eighth Symphony), a powerful reinforcement (final theme of the seventh symphony), an effective calling instrument (Trio from the Eight Symphony), and an evocative voice (solo from the Sixth Symphony, inspired by the Swiss *ranz de vaches*).[7] The horn was also able to suggest a mysterious summoning, as in the well-known fourth horn solo in the Ninth Symphony. Undoubtedly written for a hand horn, it once again demonstrates Beethoven's ability to exploit all the resources of the instrument, this time with a difficult scale in A-flat (*C-flat* at concert pitch) assigned to the instrumentalist who was expected to be the least tired by the long work (at least for the period) (see online, "On the fourth horn solo," and Musical example 52 online). The same may be said for the *Missa Solemnis* (St. Petersburg, 1824), in which the first horn takes some rests (e.g.

---

[6] The fundamental studies of Theodore Albrecht provide more information about several compositions by Beethoven and the names of the horn players who participated in some early performances. With regard to Symphony no. 3, two interesting notes written in the composer's handwriting appear on the title page of the score prepared by the copyist of the Theater an der Wien (where it was first performed on April 7, 1805): "The third horn is written in such a manner that it can be played by a first [*cor alto*] as well as a second [*cor basse*]" and "The three horns will be positioned in the orchestra in such a way that the first horn is placed in the middle between the two others" (quoted in Albrecht 2003, 43). According to Albrecht 2003, 45, Benedict Fuchs (1765–1828), Franz Eisen (1771–1822), and Michael Herbst (1778–1833) performed in the premiere of Symphony no. 3. Perhaps this was the same horn section that played the aria with solo horns in *Fidelio* (Albrecht 2006, 58).

[7] The first performers of the Fifth and Sixth Symphonies were Herbst and Fuchs on December 22, 1808 (Albrecht 2006, 59).

in the Sanctus) while his second and the second pair take over more demanding parts.

We have already discussed the alternation of two pairs of horns when the score requires only one. Beethoven not only calls for this substitution in *Fidelio*, but also introduces new options in the modified 1814 version (Albrecht 2006, 61–62): in the famous aria (Act I, No. 9) "Komm, Hoffnung," originally conceived for a section of four horns, he subsequently preferred a trio of concertante horns with the reinforcement of the bassoon, more suitable for the low register (the latter instrument allows for a security and full sound that could not be obtained using the horn, at least before the introduction of valves). The horns, in the key of E, are launched in chromatic evolution with arpeggios up to the sixteenth harmonic and with diatonic scales ranging over two octaves (see Musical example 53).[8]

The treatment of the four concertante horns (I and II in F, III and IV in C) in the aria "Will unser Genius" from *Die Ruinen von Athen*, op. 113 (1812) is slightly different. The first horn still plays the main role, but their colleagues are frequently called to compete, often supported by the bassoons (see Musical example 54 online).

C. M. von Weber's writing is more pictorial. His works are pervaded by a strong sense of nature that finds one of its greatest expressions in the evocative voice of the horn. It is enough to recall *Der Freischütz* (Berlin, 1821) with its hunting fanfares or with the overture itself, whose main theme is divided between the two pairs of horns (the first in F, the second in C) (see Musical example 55 online).

Another example is the moving call of the horn (in D) of the knight Huon with which *Oberon* (London, 1826) begins. This is a feature also found in works conceived for the hand horn by other German authors, such as *Hans Heiling* (Berlin, 1833) by Heinrich Marschner (1795–1861) with the solo at the beginning of the overture (see Musical example 56 online), and Konrad's aria "Gönne mir ein Wort der Liebe."

The parts in Schubert's symphonies do not contain innovations in terms of writing for the instrument, but we can point out the unusual use of the A-flat (alto)

---

[8] The passage is reproduced by Gevaert 1885, 209, who states that "this latter scale, which rises diatonically up to the 16th sound, cannot be performed except by artists of great skill." Beethoven could have been inspired by exercise No. 108 in Domnich (1807, p. 54), which distributes the scale between three horns in order to facilitate its performance.

Musical example 53. Beethoven, *Fidelio*, Leonora's aria, with marked stopped sounds.

crook in the second movement of the Fourth Symphony (1816) and the uniqueness of the beginning of Symphony no. 9 (1825–1828), where the two horns in C (in unison) present the theme, which contains several stopped notes, without any orchestral support (see Musical example 57 online). This solo was undoubtedly conceived for the natural horn, since there are no elements suggesting the use of the valves, as in other compositions by the same author (see Chapter 23, "Schubert's songs: a case study" online). Moreover, in post-restoration Vienna, the natural horn continued to be the instrument of reference at least until the death of Michael Herbst (1778–1833). He was the last great Austrian virtuoso and teacher of this model, the first performer of the aria "Komm, Hoffnung" from *Fidelio* (Fitzpatrick 1970, 215), and the author of a lost manuscript method for horn (Fétis 1860–1865, IV, 301).

The horn solo in *A Midsummer Night's Dream* (1843) by Felix Mendelssohn, with two accompanying bassoons, is particularly appealing. It was written for natural horn, of course, as is much of Mendelssohn's music, although he also called for the valve horn (as we will see in Chapter 23, "Two valve and two natural horns," p. 279).

The instrument also played a pivotal role in mixed string and wind chamber music compositions, such as in Beethoven's Septet, op. 20 (cl, hn, bn, vn, va, vc, db), Conradin Kreutzer's op. 62 for the same ensemble, Franz Lachner's piece for this ensemble with flute instead of bassoon, Schubert's Octect (cl, hn, bn, 2 vn, va, vc, db), Ferdinand Ries's op. 128 (pf, without vl II), the Nonetto, op. 31 by Louis Spohr (fl, ob, cl, bn, hn, vn, va, vc, db), the Concertino by Franz Krommer, op. 13 (fl, ob, 2 hn, vn, va, vc, db), and others. We will not add any other examples here as the repertoire is truly immense, but we refer the reader to bibliographic literature (in particular to Brüchle 1970, 1975, 1983 and Dempf–Seraphinoff 2016) as well as to the many internet resources available nowadays.

THE ITALIAN OPERA

The history of the hand horn in Italy is less well known than in other European countries, even though it is apparent that there were many excellent instrumentalists. This is demonstrated by the many obbligato solos in the operatic repertoire, which is by far the most widespread and appreciated in that country (see Table 14 online).

Some of the first occurrences are thanks to the temporary presence of a visiting virtuoso, as in the case of Mozart's *Mitridate* (1770), Luigi Gatti's *Nitteti* (1773), or Mysliveček's *Demetrio* (1773), rather than the birth of a solid tradition, but from the 1780s, the existence of reputed horn schools, at least in the cities of Milan, Venice, Rome, and Naples, should be recognized.

Naples is presumably the place in which a true hand horn tradition first settled, as a number of obbligato parts come from there starting with *Bellerofonte* by Mysliveček (1767) and continuing up to the works written by Rossini for the San Carlo Theater, with a gradual transition from a pure clarino style to an increasingly demanding use of the hand technique. In Rome, however, a stable school must also have been formed soon after, as the hornists soon had to tackle virtuosic passages, as are found in *Li due baroni di rocca azzurra* by Cimarosa (1783), which contains a demanding solo reaching the twentieth harmonic (see Musical example 58). Subsequent works written in Rome includes the arduous solo by Rossini in his *Matilde di Shabran* (1821) and the expressive cantabile writing in *Torquato Tasso* by Donizetti (1833), which already leans toward a fully romantic idea of the instrument.

A prominent figure on the operatic scene between the two centuries was undoubtedly J. S. Mayr, who wrote sixty-eight operas that were mostly performed in Venice and Milan. His huge output is accompanied by an interesting manuscript treatise dedicated to the horn (*Brevi cenni intorno al . . . corno da caccia*) from circa 1824, which remained unnoticed until some years ago (Rocchetti 2006). In his operas, Mayr entrusted several solos to the instrument, at least when a celebrated soloist was available and especially when writing for Luigi Belloli (see "Luigi Belloli," p. 197). Many virtuosic passages for the horn (or horns) are also found in his sacred music, in which, again depending on the availability of outstanding soloists (in several cases the Belloli brothers—see below), he experimented with the tonal and expressive possibilities of the instrument.

Another Italian opera composer who reserved important roles for our instrument and who must be mentioned is Ferdinando Paer (1771–1839), the son

Musical example 58. Cimarosa, *Li due baroni di rocca azzurra*, first horn solo in E-flat.

of the horn player Giulio (see above), whose music is full of solos for wind instruments, just like that by Mayr. The solo in *Circe* (Venice, 1792) is undoubtedly a significant example, with arpeggios and scales in various tonalities, while in *Agnese* (Parma, 1809; Act II, Uberto's aria "Ah come è buono") the second horn, after having performed various *bravura* passages, is also used in a particularly expressive way (see Musical example 59)—for instance, to emphasize the text "Son stordito, son oppresso" (I'm stunned, I'm oppressed) through a stopped appoggiatura, a practice that is well documented in that time period but was lost completely with the advent of the valve horn (and therefore should possibly be resumed).

Even Gioachino Rossini's father, Giuseppe, was a horn player whose instrument, built in Paris after 1812 by Courtois frère, was presented to the Conservatory of Naples by the hornist Edoardo De Angelis where it is preserved (*Dal segno al suono* 2010, 278). According to Fétis (1864, VII, 320), Gioachino started playing the horn at the age of ten, performing the second part in the orchestras in which his father was a member, before devoting himself to composition. His interest in the instrument is documented by the fact that almost all his works contain challenging solos for the natural horn. Apart from the most well-known passages, such as the solos in *Italiana in Algeri* (Venice 1813), the horn quartet of *Semiramide* (Venice 1823), or the calls on the stage in *Gugliemo Tell* (Paris 1829), one must also take into account the long challenging solos in *Otello* (Naples 1816), *Armida* (Naples 1817), the aforementioned *Matilde di Shabran* (Rome 1821), and those written for the Teatro alla Scala and therefore for Luigi

Musical example 59. F. Paer, *Agnese*, Uberto's aria, second horn in E-flat.

Belloli: *La pietra di paragone* (1812), *Aureliano in Palmira* (Milan 1813), and *Il Turco in Italia* (Milan 1814) (see online, "The first solo performance of *Matilde di Shabran*," and Musical example 60 online).

The most important Italian horn school in the second half of the eighteenth century, is that of Parma and the nearby Fontanellato, where some of the prominent soloists were trained: Giulio Paer, the Belloli brothers, the Paglia brothers, Giovanni Puzzi, and Luigi Pini, the latter profusely referenced in Chapter 20.

LUIGI BELLOLI

"The singular mastery of Mr. Belloli, whose manner of singing with the horn could surely be [a] model to those who wish to distinguish themselves among the crowd of singers . . ." (*Il Poligrafo*, September 15, 1811, p. 384). This comment, published immediately after the performance of the aria "Deh quel rigor" in the opera *I pretendenti delusi* by Giuseppe Mosca (1811), testifies to the artistic level of one of the most renowned Italian hornists and the first horn teacher at the Conservatory of Milan, who began teaching there as soon as the institute was established (1808).

Little is known about the musical training of Luigi Belloli (1770–1817),[9] which, at least in the beginning, he possibly shared with his brothers Giuseppe

---

[9] Humphries's statement (2000, 19) that Luigi Belloli was a pupil of Punto is untenable as the latter never stayed in Parma. Nor can we agree with Fitzpatrick 1970, 191, who believes that Luigi was the first Italian exponent of the Bohemian horn school without any concrete evidence in support of this thesis (cf. Chapter 16, "Giulio Paer," p. 162).

(1775–*ca.* 1845) and Agostino (1778–1839), both famous horn players.[10] However, in 1786, Luigi was hired by the wind band of Parma at the modest salary of 202 lire per month (Goli 1834, 11, fn. 1). There, he probably improved his instrumental skills, which allowed him to subsequently join the Ducal orchestra of the same city in 1790. In Parma, he surely came into contact with instrumentalists such as Giulio Paer, who may have taught him the hand technique. Finally, in 1803 he was hired as first horn at the Teatro alla Scala under the recommendation of concert master Alessandro Rolla, a role that he maintained until his death.

The skillfulness of Luigi Belloli is documented by the numerous solos written for him during his tenure at La Scala (e.g. those by Mayr—see Musical example 61 online—and Rossini) and by his own compositions for horn, among which the difficult concertos for one or more horns and orchestra stand out. His concertos also entered the repertoire of other instrumentalists, as in the case of his likely student Giovanni Puzzi, who performed one of them at the Favart Theater in Paris in 1814 (Strauchen 2000, 120, fn. 11). Another outstanding example is the *Gran concerto per corno da caccia*, dated June 17, 1816 (Ms. in I-Mc; copy and four other concertos in I-Ria), whose range of four whole octaves demonstrates— together with other music for horn that Belloli wrote as well as the obbligatos written for him—that Belloli was not a performer of *cor mixte*,[11] as stated in Morley-Pegge (1973, 103) (see online, "*Cor mixte?*").[12]

Aside from his concertos, we must add other compositions by Luigi Belloli, including the aforementioned *Labirinto* for two horns (see Musical example 62 online) and several ballets inspired by the collaboration with the Imperial Royal Academy of Dance in Milan, with which his brother Agostino Belloli also

---

[10] The February 1, 1794 *Gazzetta Toscana* (p. 18) describes Giuseppe Belloli as an "excellent professor of *corno da caccia*" who "cleverly [performed] a concerto, which gained the admiration and received the repeated applause of the large audience owing to its supreme difficulty and sweetness." We have found little other documentation on the life of Giuseppe, who left some handwritten compositions, including horn trios and quartets, others for chamber groups, and finally a *Notturno* for natural horn and piano or harp. Agostino in his turn took over Luigi's position both as first horn at La Scala (from 1819 to 1829) and as horn teacher at the Conservatory of Milan (starting November 28, 1817). He wrote many ballets that were performed at the Teatro alla Scala and numerous exercises and compositions for horns, some of which were published at the time by Ricordi.

[11] See, for example, *Giornale del Taro*, April 20, 1813, 146: "the range of three octaves, which encompasses the scale of this instrument, has no limits for him."

[12] Antonio Tosoroni, a student of Luigi's brother Giuseppe, testifies that Luigi Belloli "was the first to show that it is possible to play the whole range of this instrument with only one mouthpiece" (Tosoroni 1850, 33).

collaborated (Tozzi 1978, 53–55). Luigi also had two sons, Giovanni (1794–after 1846) and Giacomo (1795–1855), who were both hornists and his students at the Conservatory (see online, "An early female horn player").[13]

Unfortunately, we have been unable to locate Belloli's method for the instrument. We have at least two authoritative testimonies about its manuscript: one by the anonymous reviewer of the Dauprat method (*AMZ* 1824, 657) and one from Lichtenthal (1826, IV, 460), who, in referring to this method, states that "[its] existence is confirmed by the brother of the author."

Finally, the instrumental and artistic skillfulness of Luigi Belloli can be briefly summarized by quoting an excerpt from his biography, written by Gervasoni (1812, 88) when Belloli was still alive:

> He is especially excellent at producing the half-step tones using the hand, emitting them with utmost purity and with an amazing speed. He adds to his rare ability in performance excellent taste in the composition of instrumental music, of which he produced a huge quantity. His concertos for natural horn are very much appreciated by all who are intelligent about music.

LOW-PITCHED CROOKS IN ITALY

The use of various sizes of horns in the same composition was also adopted early in the Italian operatic repertoire. The keys of G, F, E-flat, D, and C are documented together as early as the mid-seventeenth century, such as in the *Ifigenia in Aulide* by Jommelli (Rome 1751); he also called for B-flat basso shortly thereafter in *Enea nel Lazio* (Stuttgart 1755).[14] In the last quarter of the eighteenth century, it eventually became common practice in this context to use almost all the crooks from high B-flat or A to low B-flat.

Many scores also testify to the Italian composers' interest in experimenting with new expressive moods and new sounds, particularly through the use of low pitches. Their dark and mellow sound can be particularly impressive and more

---

[13] A duet performed by the young Bellolis (said to be eleven and twelve, but actually slightly older) is reported in the *Corriere milanese* of April 11, 1809 (p. 348). Personal data on the members of the Belloli family living in Milan can be found in the *Ruolo generale della popolazione di Milano 1811* (Milan, Archivio storico civico).

[14] The score (I-Nc Rare 7.7.25) has at fol. 74v (Choir: "Invan l'abissi") the indication "corni in Bfa" (horns in B-flat). This can only mean B-flat basso, otherwise at some points the horn would play an octave above the violins.

effective than the ringing and penetrating high sizes, perhaps even because they allowed the instruments to be less "invasive" at a time when the orchestral pit in the modern sense did not yet exist. In particular, it is apparent that the use of the keys from E-flat to low B-flat was becoming more frequent, and later even A and A-flat were used. The constant presence of two pairs of horns also favored the use of two different pitches (E-flat/B-flat, D/A, C/B-flat, etc.). The second pair, usually the lower ones, improved the entire section's timbre owing to the resonance of the natural harmonics of the instrument—an effect later obtained with valves as well, and still used today in the horn section of the Vienna Philarmoniker Orchester. The compass of the horn in this repertoire is generally limited from the fourth to the twelfth harmonics, a range that may effectively be exploited with the hand technique.

Like the key of D-flat, normally obtained through the addition of a coupler to the D crook (Mahillon 1907, 33), the key of low A must have required the use of a similar gimmick, since specific crooks for this pitch have never been found. An exhaustive explanation in this respect is reported in the essay on instrumentation by Marx (1847, 84), which states, "Through a special yard designed to lengthen the tubing (although better and with surer intonation would be the case with the adoption of an appropriate terminal or slide crook), the intonation of every size can be lowered by another semitone" (according to Marx, the keys obtainable in this way are those of A basso, B basso, D-flat, G-flat, and A-flat alto).

In Italian operatic scores, the use of low crooks is not only found in the ensemble pieces, but also in several solos, including the obbligato in Rossini's *Aureliano in Palmira* (Milan 1813). Here, the aria "Cara patria," written for Belloli, calls for the demanding crook of low C and includes a rich assortment of arpeggios and stopped notes in the *cor alto* range, from the fourth to the sixteenth harmonic (see Musical example 63).

The solo for low C horn in the Overture of Donizetti's *Don Pasquale* was written much later. Staged in 1843 at the Théâtre Italien in Paris, we only mention it here to remark that it was most likely conceived for the natural instrument.[15] In France, in fact, the tradition of the hand horn lasted a very long time indeed, as documented by the *Rapports* (II, 1856, 669) of the 1855 Universal Exhibition,

---

[15] The discomfort of a solo for low C horn can be witnessed by a set of orchestral parts of *Don Pasquale*, repeatedly used by the Dresden court orchestra since 1844 (RISM 270002081). Here the horn solo is replaced once by the first clarinet in A and on another occasion by the first flute.

Musical example 63. Rossini, *Aureliano in Palmira*, horn solo in C, written for Belloli.

which state that "in the French orchestras, the valve horn is used only for exceptional occasions."

In any case, the two lowest pitches constitute the most unique aspect of the matter. As for the key of A, it was documented in St. Petersburg (where many Italian composers were active) as early as 1770, when Mareš devised a combination of tonalities distributed between two horns, one covering the keys from low A to high G sharp and the other from low C to high B (see Chapter 19 "Transitional systems"). This may seem to be an early date for the crook of A basso, but it is in fact coeval with an article from the *Wiener Zeitung* (September 18, 1771, p. 8; see Chapter 15, p. 137) in which reference is made to crooks from C alto to A basso.

The crook of A basso is also implied by the setting of Giuseppe Sarti's opera *Alessandro e Timoteo* (Parma, 1782), in which small ("piccoli") horns in *Are* (in A) and very small ("piccolini") horns in *Bfa* (B-flat) are called for, together with big ("grandi") horns in *Bb* (B-flat basso). One can thus presume that "big" horns in A basso also existed. A similar case is found in Act III of Sarti's opera *Fra i due litiganti il terzo gode*, staged at the La Scala Theater in Milan in 1782, where "small horns in A" are found (see online, "*Corni piccoli* in E-flat").

Likewise, the horns in Mayr's *Un pazzo ne fa cento* (Venice, 1796), are likely not in A alto, as they would sound in unison with the two clarinets where the winds (2 cl, 2 hn, bn) play alone for a while (Act I, Duet no. 2). Performing the part an octave lower, in A basso, they would instead comply with the usual writing for these instruments (including chamber and military music). In any case, the pitch of A basso is definitely encountered in an opera at least in Act II of *Armida* by Rossini (1817).

In case of ambiguity, it was crucial to precisely indicate whether the high or low crook was to be used in order to avoid any potential misunderstandings. In *Dom Sébastien* by Donizetti (1843), the published instrumental parts dating from the same year (Paris, Bureau Central de Musique) have the explicit indication "*en la bas,*" which was obviously written to avoid having them played an octave higher, since the horns "*en La*" are also called for elsewhere in the score. In other circumstances, when the choice was unquestionable, Donizetti simply called for horns in A (and also B-flat) without explicitly indicating the low register, as in the two Parisian operas *La fille du régiment* and *La favorite*, both of 1840.[16]

It seems, therefore, that the simple request for B-flat and A horns was normally understood in reference to low sizes and that only when the high pitches were meant the composers explicitly stated their intentions (see Appendix II online). A conclusive confirmation in this regard is found in Gassner (1838, 29): "If there is no specific indication of 'high' or 'low,' but only Horn or Horns in C, A or B, it always refers to low pitches."

Both the A basso tonality, and even the lower A-flat basso, are in turn mentioned in Antolini (1813, table IV, ex. no. 22). The oldest occurrence of the latter in a score is once again in music by Rossini, the *Stabat Mater* (first performance 1842; score by Schott fils, Mainz). No. 2 calls for "Cors en Lab bas" (the first pair being "en Mib"), and the part is entirely playable using the hand-horn technique. This prescription fully matches the one found in Verdi's *Nabucco*, which was written at almost the same time (1841) and calls for a pair of horns in the same key of low A-flat (with the other two in E-flat and sometimes in F).[17] Further evidence comes from a statement by George Hogarth in *The Musical World* (4(46), January 27, 1837, 83): "the *low* A-flat horn (the lowest in use) sounds them [the notes] a tenth lower than they are written."

However, it is likely that by 1842, some players had adopted valves in order to obtain the lowest keys or to quickly change the pitch, especially when the composer

---

[16] Dauprat 1857, 110, probably refers to this kind of request when recalling the recent introduction of the A and B natural crooks in France.

[17] The lack of known instances of A-flat basso crook prior to these late examples call into question the mention of this crook by Antolini 1813 (possibly a misprint?).

left little time to change crooks, as in Donizetti's *La fille du régiment* (Paris 1840). Instances like this probably constitute the "exceptional occasions" for which valve instruments were used, as mentioned in the aforementioned *Rapports* from the 1855 Parisian Exhibition.

With regards to the lowest A-flat key, we should add that in some cases this pitch was not originally called for by the composer and instead resulted from a transposition made to render the part more comfortable for some singers. An example is found in *Lucia di Lammermoor* (Naples, 1835), where the key of A-flat basso is the consequence of a lowering of the aria "Spargi d'amaro pianto" in Act II. Since it was transposed by a full tone with respect to the original, the key of the second pair of horns is changed from B-flat to A-flat basso (and the first pair from F to E-flat). In this case, the alteration does not actually involve a significant change in sound and esthetics, which instead occurs in the duet "Il pallor funesto orrendo" (Act I). Here, the three solo bars in the third horn end up a seventh above what the composer imagined since the low A horn is transposed to high G. On other occasions, the horn parts were even transposed, possibly by a more punctilious copyist, to low G, and in all likelihood the example quoted by Humphries (2000, 37) from Bellini's *Norma* (Milan, 1831) is an instance of the latter case and therefore in an unexpected, and certainly mostly uncomfortable, tonality.

Finally, it is possible that from time to time Italian composers made use of these unusual keys to simplify their work, which was often carried out in very short time by notating the horn parts in the same key as the score. Such a practice would allow the parts to be written within the staff, thus speeding up the process and reducing the use of ledger lines, and accidentals also, as much as possible. The hornists could then perform using crooks other than the ones called for in the score. Although this implies a change or loss of the tone, this is—incidentally—the general situation commonly experienced in present-day performances.

ENGLAND

The center of musical activity in England has always been London, where, between the end of the eighteenth century and the early nineteenth century, players who had emigrated from the German territories were numerous. They occupied important places in the major London orchestras, as the Royal Philharmonic Society, where Peter and Joseph Petrides, Thomas Leander with his sons Lewis Henry and Vincent Thomas, and George Kellner worked, among others (Strauchen-Scherer 2006, 248–249). However, others were, of course, of English descent, such as Henry Platt, James Rae, and many others.

Some of the surviving instruments dating back to this period are German models, even though they were sometimes made by local builders who were often themselves of German origin. They resemble the constructive style of the aforementioned Hofmaster, with which they share the system of terminal crooks and couplers, but with a wider throat for the bell and a master crook. One example is an instrument by William Sandbach (fl. 1809–1835) located in Edinburgh's Music Museum (inv. 0203). It was ordinarily used by Cornelius Bryant, or O'Brien, in the Covent Garden Opera Orchestra (*ca.* 1815), and therefore is possibly the instrument heard at the first performance of Weber's *Oberon* (London, 1826) (see Figure 88). Another similar horn was made by Thomas Key (fl. 1807–1855; mark: "T. Key / Superior / London") and is part of the Bate Collection of Oxford (inv. 62). A third horn is marked "Smith & Sons Fecit" and attributed to John Smith of Wolverhampton and distributed by the same T. Key (illustrated in Morley-Pegge 1973, table III/2).

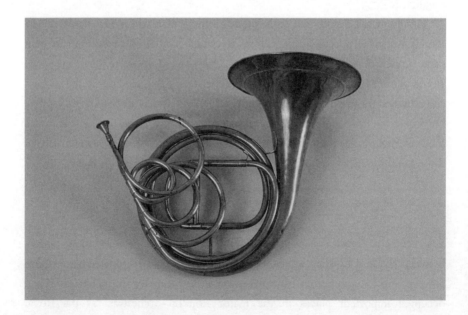

Figure 88. W. Sandbach, invention horn with terminal crooks, Edinburgh, 1810–1830.

The most prominent players in London in the first two decades of the century were the aforementioned Petrides brothers, who, after having spent fifteen years on an uninterrupted European tour, settled in the British capital in 1802 and remained there until 1825, when they eventually returned to their native Bohemia. However, when Italian hornist Giovanni Puzzi moved to London in 1816 (Strauchen-Scherer 2006, 249), this heralded a real flood of novelty and change.

GIOVANNI PUZZI

Born in Parma on May 24, 1791,[18] Puzzi entered the House of Education of nearby Fontanellato, founded in 1802 by the philanthropist Count Stefano Sanvitale (1764– 1838), in 1808 as an "Étudiant du Dessin et du Corne de cache [*sic*]."[19] Enrolled in the instrumental music school attached to the institute, he studied under the guidance of Francesco Paglia (*ca.* 1772–1821), the first horn in the Real Concerto of Parma, who certainly played a key role in his primary instrumental training.[20] Subsequently, Puzzi came into contact with Luigi Belloli, of whom he claimed to be a student— thus confirming what Dauprat (1824, II, 158) asserted—as can also be inferred from the heading of the Ms. *Arie con Variazioni Pour Corno In Elami avec un Adagio pour Introduction e Polacca* (. . .) *composto da Luigi Belloli mio Maestro* [composed by my teacher Luigi Belloli] (. . .) *1813 Parigi* (RISM 400066400).

The first traces of a brilliant career as traveling soloist date back to 1811, with a performance of a concerto for *corno da caccia* in the Cremona Theater, for which he earned the remarkable sum of 332.14 lire (Santoro 1995, 92). Another occasion was a concert on January 7, 1812 at the Imperial Theater of Parma, where he performed with great success. From that moment on, he began his career in the major European cities. Count Sanvitale took him to Paris in 1812 (Adorni 1840, 53), where he was introduced to the court by Paer (Whitaker 1907, 217) and where he also achieved remarkable success, including his hiring as first horn at the renewed Théâtre Italien on September 7, 1815 (*Gazzetta di Parma*, October 21,

---

[18] Parma, Archivio vescovile, *Liber baptizatorum 1791–1792* (birth date to be corrected in many general repertoires). Puzzi died in London on March 1, 1876.

[19] Parma, Archivio di Stato, Sanvitale, busta 905/A, list of pupils, n.d. but 1810.

[20] Francesco Paglia was a member of a family of horn players from Colorno, near Parma (see Gervasoni 1812, 215). He was the son of Federico, who was the brother of another Francesco. Their biographies are yet to be fully verified despite the forerunning studies of Gaspare Nello Vetro (https://www.lacasadellamusica.it/Vetro/Pages/Ricerca.aspx?tipologi a=1&idoggetto=1921&idcontenuto=2166).

1815). A review of his skillfulness was published in the *Journal de Paris* on September 19, 1815 (see also *Gazzetta di Parma*, October 17, 1815):

> Could it be possible, without being unfair, to forget the great talent of Mr. Puzzi, who draws such a bright result from the most ungrateful among the instruments? What pure and sweet sounds does he obtain from the horn, which he enlivens with his breath? What clarity! What mastery!
>
> He makes fun of the difficulties. He faces them and assaults them with such courage and luck that one cannot perceive them, so to speak, unless when they are overcome. His modesty then emphasizes his admirable skill, of which he seems not be aware.

The following year, the newspaper *Le Constitutionnel* (145 (May 24, 1816)) published a review of *La clemenza di Tito* KV. 621 by Mozart performed at the Théâtre Royal Italien (Salle Favart). The performance also included an aria composed by Paer ("Se all'impero, amici dèi"),[21] in which "the accompaniment of

Musical example 64. Paer, aria and choir with obbligato horn for Mozart's *Clemenza di Tito*, "Se all'Impero amici Dei", Act II, Sc. VIII.

[21] See the manuscript copy in I-Mc Part. Tr. Ms. 261, vol. 2, fol. 76, with the heading "Aria e coro con corno obligato del M.tro Fer.do Paer nella *Clemenza di Tito* se all'Impero amici Dei'."

the horn, performed with perfect mastery by Mr. Puzzi, instills a unique charm" (see Musical example 64).[22]

Perhaps Parisian music life was somewhat unsuited to Puzzi, whose acclaimed appearances seem to be closely linked with the Italian circles in Paris. Whatever the case, after the fall of the Napoleonic Empire, he was invited to come to London by the duke of Wellington (Whitaker 1907, 218). Here, within a few years, Puzzi became the first horn at the King's Theater, in the orchestra of the Philharmonic Society (1821–1824), where the Petrides brothers had worked shortly before, and at the Concert of Antient (*sic*) Music (1823–1826). A decade later, he founded the Classical Concerts for Wind Instruments (1837).[23] From 1826 on, Puzzi began to be involved in opera management as well, leading the company of the Lyceum Theater between 1836 and 1838. He traveled throughout Europe both to engage singers and to pursue his own solo career, performing a wide repertoire that included arrangements for solo horn from the best-known Italian operas. His repertoire, partly written by him or dedicated to him (such as the Sonata di Bravura Concertante, op. 13 for horn and piano by Cipriani Potter, circa 1824, or Ignaz Moscheles's Introduction et Rondeau Écossais, 1825) reaches the limits of virtuosity on the natural horn and on the *cor basse* in particular,[24] in the genre of which Puzzi was the most distinguished virtuoso among the generation following Punto's.

Puzzi also had a dramatic influence on the London horn milieu, to the point that the local players abandoned the German horn models in favor of the Raoux instruments.[25] The extreme conical shape of the opening of their bells allowed for better balance between stopped and natural sounds and therefore a clearer and sweeter tone.

[22] An obbligato horn part is also found in Agnese (Parma, 1809) and matches Puzzi's abilities; it is also probable that Paer wrote for Puzzi both the short cantata L'odalisque (Ms. in I-Baf) and the serenade "O notte soave" for SATB, hp (or pf), hn, vc, and db that Puzzi performed in the concert hall of Manchester on October 25, 1837 (*The Musical World*, 7(86), November 3, 1837, 123).

[23] Further information on Puzzi's music career after his move to London can be found in Strauchen 2000.

[24] The performance of the Sonata, op. 17 by Beethoven in London in 1837 provides further evidence of this capacity that Puzzi shared with Punto, Dauprat, and other distinguished soloists (Kroll 2014, 218).

[25] Not only did the Petrides brothers switch to this model, but Friedrich Adolf Borsdorf and Franz Paersch also both had to switch to Raoux horns when they settled in England in 1879 and 1882 respectively (Fitzpatrick 1970, 191, fn. 1). From 1861 the instruments were brought to London by a student of Dauprat's, Antoine Victor Paquis, Raoux's successors' agent for the English market (Strauchen 2000, 184–185).

Three instruments by Raoux that belonged to Puzzi are still preserved: a *cor solo* by Lucien-Joseph Raoux dated 1814 (Carse Collection at the Horniman Museum, London); an orchestral model built in 1821 by L.-J. Raoux, subsequently purchased by Friedrich Adolf Borsdorf (1854–1923) (Royal Academy of Music, London);[26] and a *cor solo* with the bell directed to the left by Marcel-Auguste Raoux made in 1826 or 1827 and presented to Puzzi as a gift from the king of France (Horniman Museum, London; see Figure 72, p. 154).[27] The choice of French models characterized the British horn school and lasted until the 1950s, when Dennis Brain decided to put aside his Raoux–Labbaye in favor of a single horn in B-flat/A by the famous Gebrüder Alexander of Mainz (now located at the Royal Academy of Music).

Figure 89. P. Toschi, *Portrait of Puzzi*.

[26] A set of valves were added to this horn and it became Borsdorf's (1854–1923) usual instrument. Borsdorf was a professor at the Royal College of Music and at the Royal Academy of Music, first horn in some of London's leading orchestras, and one of the founders of the London Symphony Orchestra in 1904 (see http://archive.is/43BjG).

[27] This instrument is the mirror image of other horns, which are normally gripped by the left hand (Martz 2003).

The first teacher when the Academy was founded in 1823 (Strauchen-Scherer 2006, 255), Puzzi can be considered a leading figure in the modern English horn school. He was famous, it seems likely, for the melodious taste and technical skillfulness that was the basis for the success of many instrumentalists trained in Parma, such as Rodolphe, Paer, Belloli, and Paglia. This is a technique that was most likely divulged in his *Nuovo metodo di imparare a suonare il corno*, which is mentioned in Regli (1860, 427) but has unfortunately been lost.

THE PETRIDES BROTHERS IN SPAIN AND PORTUGAL

We will now go back slightly in time to deal with the Petrides brothers and their adventurous career in Spain and Portugal. They first came to Barcelona in 1794 and moved permanently to Madrid in 1799. Their series of concerts also included performances at the court of King Charles IV, who directed the orchestra (first violin) accompanying the Petrides (the remuneration received by the two hornists for these "royal" performances was commensurate with the wealth of their hosts). Then they moved to Lisbon, where they remained for some time. There, they were hired by the Italian Opera and gave a number of concerts with great success. They even performed in front of Prince Augustus of England, who paved the way for their move to London in 1802, where they settled permanently. As always, they gained great success there as well. Their life is narrated—almost certainly using information they themselves provided—in the *Dictionary of Musicians* by John Sainsbury (1824, II, 283–285), which concludes, "Thus, after a wandering and eventful life of fifteen years over the greatest part of Germany, all Italy, Sicily, Malta, France, Spain, and Portugal, the Petrides have, for the last twenty-two years, been settled in London; and we have heard them declare that they soon, very soon, found England to be the best, the most generous, and most hospitable country under heaven."

AMERICA

One of the major music centers in North America can be identified as Charleston, South Carolina, where one of the earliest public concert organizations, the St. Cecilia Society, was founded in 1762 (Sonneck 1907, 16). Here, on October 16, 1765, Thomas Pike performed two concertos for horn and two for bassoon, probably written by the performer, and concluded with a horn concerto by Hasse.

A few years later (1773), there are accounts of another horn performance by Mr. Stotherd, who came from Dublin and had already given recitals in New York City on January 9 and February 9, 1770 (Sonneck 1907, 170 and 181). As in the case of Jonas Green (see Chapter 11, p. 209) and of Mr. Pike, Stotherd was an amateur music enthusiast who also appeared in public as a guitar player and singer (Sonneck 1907, 22).

The activity of Lewis Vidal was instead of a professional nature. In 1774, he described himself as the "first player on the French horn in the Court of Portugal" (Bridwell 2004, 28, quoting the *South Carolina and American General Gazette of Charleston*, SC, September–October 1774). Victor Pelissier was in turn an accomplished professional (Marseille 1756–?New Jersey *ca.* 1820). He moved to Santo Domingo in 1789 (Camier 2009, 5380) and later emigrated to North America in 1792 at the latest (Saloman 1978, 94). Defined by Gilbert Chase (1955, 121) as "the most prominent of the French musical emigrants," he was known primarily as a composer but also performed on the horn several times in Philadelphia and then in New York. Chase was also a member of the Old American Company, the first fully professional ensemble active in North America.

At the beginning of the nineteenth century, American music life, apart from that in the theaters, continued to be animated by both civilian and military bands and by many music clubs as well, with the presence of hornists who had emigrated either along with English and French regiments from the Old Continent or simply in search of luck on their own. This was the case for Sigismond Proechel, a horn player with the New Orleans French Opera, who tied for the second prize in Dauprat's class at the Conservatoire National in Paris in 1826, or Jean-Emmanuel Michault, who won awards in Domnich's class in 1811 and in 1812 before emigrating to America. However, only from 1825 are there records of immigration from German territories (Bridwell 2004, 30–31).

Of the patrons of the music clubs, we may refer to Samuel Holyoke (1762–1820), author of *The Instrumental Assistant* (1807) (see online, "The First Handbook From Overseas?), to which we can add another very similar text, *The Instrumental Director* (1819) by Ezekiel Goodale (1780–1828?). According to Snedeker (1995, 162), one of the most interesting points in this publication is the indication of how to handle the instrument. The text states that the first horn is to hold it from the left and the second from the right so that "the two bells will be together; which enable them to hear each other equally, and, if blown with equal strength (which ought to be particularly attended to) will blend the tones so as to give effect of one instrument." Once again, this is the same description as was reported in the *New Instructions for the French Horn* (*ca.* 1780), here updated for the benefit of the hand-horn technique.

SOLO CONCERTOS IN THE EARLY NINETEENTH CENTURY

See online.

SONATAS FOR HORN AND PIANO

See online.

19

TRANSITIONAL SYSTEMS

We have seen that in the second half of the eighteenth century, the hand technique gradually allowed for new possibilities, making the horn a nearly chromatic instrument by the end of the century. Its peculiar language was characterized both by natural sounds and by stopped ones with a different tone, also used for special timbral effects. However, not all instrumentalists were capable of bringing the best out of the horn using hand-horn technique. Especially in orchestral performances, a complete chromatic scale between the second and the fourth harmonics was not always available in an effective way. Sometimes this range was only partially obtained, and sometimes it was obtained only on low-pitched sizes of the instruments.

The desire for fully chromatic instruments that could be used to play in the middle and lower registers was surely shared by some composers and instrumentalists, thus stimulating the conception of new mechanical systems. Since other brass instruments had disadvantages like those of the horn—the trombone being the unique exception, but it was confined to the evocation of the afterlife and supernatural scenes (Wills 1997, 158)—a series of attempts to fulfill this desire according to the features of the different instrumental categories occurred (for the trumpet, see Altenburg 1795, 111–112).

The earliest example of a horn equipped with a mechanism for playing chromatic notes is found in the *Amorschall* of the Bohemian Ferdinand Kölbel (*ca.* 1700/1705–*ca.* 1778). For a long time, it was thought to have been fitted with keys like those of woodwind instruments, but the discovery by Alexander Stepanov (Tarr 2004, 16–17) of three sketches of the instrument made by Jacob von Stählin in 1766 shed new light on this invention and suggest that it could be considered a precursor of the valve mechanism. However, the description of the instrument by Stählin (1770, 176), who had also had the opportunity to listen to Kölbel play and to witness the long process of the development of the invention, does not leave much room for doubt: "He succeeded in furnishing the horn with finger- and keyholes [*mit Griff- or Klapp-Löchern*], like the oboe, the bassoon, etc. Their closing and opening allowed all tones and semitones in a range of two or three octaves, as with any other wind instrument with fingerholes."

It may have been a mechanism made up of a few (apparently six) keys used to obtain non-harmonic sounds and with some "crooks" that were presumably intended for changing the pitch. A long "rectangular" transversal crook that ran across the body of the instrument may also have been used to move between them (no written music, which could clarify how the mechanism worked, is known to exist).[1] The documentation available so far suggests therefore that the *Amorschall* may not have been equipped with proper valves. It is far more likely, as suggested by Tarr (2004, 17), that it was a kind of primordial omnitonic horn with the type of switcher made by Labbaye many years later (see below).

Stählin also provided a biography of Kölbel, which was later expanded by Gerber (1790, I, 742–743; 1792, II, 550) and by other authors (Schilling 1841; Bernsdorf 1856, s.v. "Amorschall"). The inventor had worked on the development of his idea for a decade and, together with his son-in-law Franz Haensel (1726–1805), finally had the opportunity to perform at the court of Catherine II, obtaining great success and praise from the then master of the royal chapel, Baldassare Galuppi. Stählin (1770, 186–187) also explains why, in his view, the invention was not pursued further: First, neither Kölbel nor his relative Haensel ever revealed how their device functioned to anyone; the mechanical system was so complex that it could not be replicated by another builder, except with considerable expense; and finally, the instrument was so different from the ordinary horn that it required thorough study even by the most talented and fearless horn players.

Some years later, in 1771, a couple of Bohemian musicians (Kölbel and his son-in-law Haensel?) made a tour in Germany and Vienna playing a *taille d'amour*, of which the *Avant Coureur. Feuille hebdomadaire* (1771, 385–386) provides the following description: "It is a kind of horn, but with keys along the tubing, bent in a rectangular shape [*tuyau, qui se replie en quarré*].[2] Using these keys, one can

---

[1] A Trio for Clarinet. Cornu De Schass et Basso Dell M Kölbel. a Wien (RISM 450002769), probably written by Ferdinand Kölbel, is found in the Musikabteilung of D-DS. In this case, however, the horn part, written in the most demanding part of the clarino register (horn in D), is fully playable on an ordinary model of natural horn.

[2] This word was mistakenly read and transcribed as quarté, but the correct reading is *quarré*, the old form of the present French *carré*, i.e. "square" or "rectangle" shape.

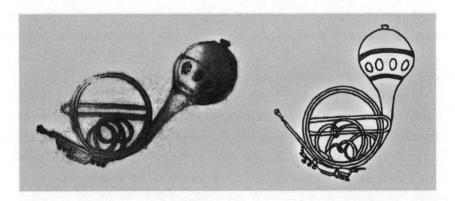

Figure 90. Sketches from Porfiryeva–Stepanov.

obtain differently modulated sounds, as with the clarinet. This instrument is very promising, and it shares—in a very nice combination—features of the ordinary horn, of the English horn and of the oboe." By comparing the above descriptions with the sketches of the *Amorschall*, one is tempted to interpret the "*tuyau, qui se replie en quarré*" as a reference to the transverse crook. It is much more probable, however, that the above description refers to the earliest angled basset horns, such as those with brass bell produced by the inventors Anton and Michael Mayrhofer (see Shackleton 1987).

Whatever the case, the long transverse crook of the *Amorschall*, similar to a tuning slide, was probably used to select the length needed for each different tonality. In order to press and handle the six keys or buttons, both hands may have been needed, with each hand operating three keys (the mechanism, however, is cleverly concealed in the drawing). The bell was probably held in a totally unusual position, resting against the body of the player rather than put on their leg so as to mitigate the timbre change due to the holes in the tubing. This also justifies the adoption of the perforated bell "cover," which was probably soldered to the remainder so as to avoid annoying noisy vibrations (see the discussion of Bergonzi's keyed horn below).

We also have, once more, an account from Gerber (1792, II, 550) about a second chromatic horn experiment, again referring to Stählin (1770). This experiment was performed by the aforementioned Johann Anton Mareš (1719–1794), a horn player and pupil of Hampel, cellist, and music director active in St. Petersburg. He invented the "Russian horns," which were capable of producing one note each, but could also produce melodies and even chords within three or four octaves using sixteen or more sizes played in turn (see online, "Louis Spohr on the Russian horns," and Figure 91 online).[3] Mareš exploited the same principle to obtain another ambitious result—that of combining one or more pairs of horns pitched a third minor apart. By distributing the sounds of the scale alternately to the first or the second of the pair, it was possible in fact to fill in many gaps in the harmonic series (Stählin 1770, 188–192) (see Musical example 65 online).

An instrument based on the same principle was patented by the Englishman Charles Clagget (1733–1796), who officially registered it on September 15, 1788 under the heading "Chromatic Trumpet and French horn." The new idea here was connecting two instruments of different size (trumpets or horns), a semitone apart from each other, with a valve that directed the air into one of the two. In the pamphlet *Musical Phenomena* (1793), the author explains his patent, adding a drawing of a trumpet of this type; however, this is insufficient for clarifying how the switcher operated. The London and Bath audiences had the opportunity to listen to several performances carried out with this instrument, but without the success hoped for by Clagget (see online, "An unfortunate inventor").[4]

KEYED HORNS

Several accounts of holes applied to the trumpet are known. One of the oldest is reported by Altenburg, who describes an instrument with one hole allowing the performer to play the eleventh and thirteenth harmonics in tune (Altenburg 1795, 112). Baines (1976, 190–191) dates this information back to about 1760, the period when Kölbel conducted his experiments on the horn in St. Petersburg, a sign that wide-ranging research was underway in order to expand the capabilities of brass instruments.

A more extensive application of keys to the trumpet might have taken place in Dresden around 1770, according to information contained in Schubart (1806, 310: see also *Grove* 2001, art. "Keyed Trumpet"), while a trumpet equipped with transposing holes (one for each tonality down to low B-flat, closed by a revolving

---

[3] A detailed discussion on Mareš and the Russian horns can be found in Hinrichs 1796; see also Findeizen 1928–1929, chap. 16.

[4] An ample discussion of the subject, with some considerations on how Clagget's invention worked, can be found in Morley-Pegge 1973, 26–30; see also Brownlow 1996, 22ff.; and also the papers by Durkin, Humphries, and Nex presented at the Galpin Society Annual Conference 2022 (http://www.euchmi.ed.ac.uk/gxtta.html).

collar, with the exception of this last key, which was covered by a key) was built in London by William Shaw in 1787 (Baines 1976, 190). In 1791–1792, Nessmann in Hamburg produced in turn a keyed trumpet that was appreciated by Gerber (1813, III, 571). The effectiveness of these experiments is confirmed by Haydn's E-flat Concerto (1796), composed for an instrument of this type and entrusted to the expert hands of Anton Weidinger.

Weidinger himself would also try out the use of keys on the horn (*Klappenwaldhorn*). His twelve-year-old son performed on this instrument for a Viennese audience, as reported by *AMZ* on December 29, 1813 (p. 844). Another *AMZ* article from September 20, 1815 (cols. 638–639), by Gottfried Weber (a German theorist who will be cited later in relation to the idea of a horn with a master slide) states that the inventor and mechanic Schugt of Cologne successfully played on a keyed horn of his invention by the end of 1813, and reports that the instrument was capable of producing a chromatic scale.

As for the preserved items, we should mention a couple of *Inventions-klappenhörner* that are probably of Bohemian origin (Freemanová 2006, 222) and date back to circa 1800. They have three keys and a tuning slide and are now located in the Musikinstrumentenmuseum in Basel (inv. nos. 1980.2056 and 1980.2057); one of them is reproduced in Brüchle-Janetzky (1976, fig. 179) (see Figure 92).

Returning to England, in 1810 the pharmacist and inventor William Close (1775–1813) received a gold medal and, on November 2, 1811, a patent (No. 3505) for "Improvements on Trumpets of different denominations, namely the common trumpet, the French horn or tenor trumpet, and the Bugle horn."[5] He then sold the idea to the maker Thomas Percival who seemingly renewed the patent in 1812 for what was called the "Polyphonian horn." *The Monthly Magazine or the British Register* (33, Part I (1812), 468) speaks of the latter as an instrument with finger holes and what could be the first water key ever: "The former of these improvements the inventor accomplishes by tubular appendages provided with finger-holes: the latter by so affixing very small pipes to those flexures of the instruments in which the water collects, that the fluid may flow out spontaneously." The most detailed and appealing description of the mechanism is, to our knowledge, contained in the

[5] In 1812, *An Introduction to the Art of Playing the Polyphonian Trumpet, Improved French Horn, and Bugle. With a Collection of Airs* was on sale in London (cf. *Antiquarisches Bücherlager von Kirchhoff & Wigand in Leipzig*, vol. 61, 1862, 9).

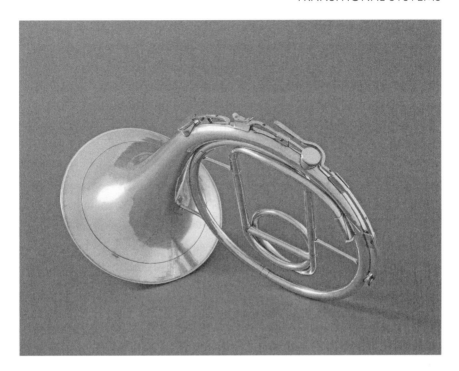

Figure 92. Anonymous keyed invention horn, first quarter of the nineteenth century.

magazine *The Repository of Arts, Literature, Commerce, Manufactures, Fashions, and Politics* (10 (July 1813), 98), and it deserves an extensive quote:

> The first of these improvements, which has long been desirable to musicians, is accomplished by tubular appendages, connected with the main channels of horns and trumpets, and provided with finger-holes, which are *open* when the instruments produce the notes of their original scales, and variously closed for those that are supplementary. The second particular of the invention is obtained, by affixing very small pipes, or tubular appendages, to those parts, or flexures of the instruments where water collects; in such manner, that the fluid may either flow out spontaneously, or be expelled through the same by the performer occasionally blowing into his trumpet without sounding, and holding it in a proper position for the ducts to convey the water.—The finger-holes are added to each instrument upon a new principle. They are not contained in the side of the *main channel*, as already intimated, but in a pipe communicating with it. By several peculiarities of construction, the larger additions have been reduced to such compact sizes, as to be no encumbrance;

and the holes brought, into a convenient compass for fingering, which is so easy a process, that, for the most useful supplementary notes in the principal key of each instrument, it may be acquired in half an hour by an intelligent performer. Indeed, by a systematic simplification of the fingering, whole strains may often be played on the trumpet with the movement of a single finger. The instruments constructed with these improvements are appropriately denominated *polyphonian*.

In *AMZ* (38 (1815), 636), the correspondent from London also reports an original explanation for the absence of the keys: "The reason why the inventor has avoided all the keys is, as he says, to avoid the damage which the keyed instruments would be subjected to when used as military instruments on horseback, as they would be thrown out a great deal. However, I suspect that it was mainly because a patent already exists for the keyed bugle horn, yet this does not apply to the trumpet and the natural horn."

So these instruments had finger holes and no keys,[6] and the former was practiced on "tubular appendages" connected to the main tubing of the instrument. However, no item of the kind is known to survive, and the system, it seems, was not followed up on; however, owing to its originality, it might deserve more attention on the part of modern scholars. The same may be said for the keyed horn devised by the aforementioned Mr. Schugt of Cologne, as reported in the *AMZ* of 1815.

A few years later, in Italy, Benedetto Bergonzi (1790–1839), a descendant of the well-known family of Cremonese luthiers and a pupil of Luigi Belloli, exhibited a horn with four keys operated by the left hand (Rocchetti 1990). In order to make the sounds emitted through the keyhole uniform—the main problem with keyed brass instruments—he soldered a tiny reversed cone called a *trombino* (small trumpet, or small bell) around it.

Bergonzi was not inspired by the experimental models discussed, which he could hardly have had direct knowledge of, but by the keyed trumpet, which was widely disseminated in Italy and for which he had written some compositions. He performed repeatedly with his keyed instrument, obtaining contradictory

---

[6] Pearn – Gardner-Thorpe 2005 seem to assume that keys had been adopted, in particular pp. 41–42, but this is because of an arbitrary use of the term "keyed brass instruments" to refer to items that only had finger holes.

reviews,[7] and it is probable that his *40 Capricci* (ed. Ricordi 1830) was written for this invention (see Figure 93 online).[8]

OMNITONIC NATURAL HORNS

A considerable challenge that the players of the hand-horn era had to deal with was changing crooks, a procedure that took some time to be accomplished. There were understandable disadvantages with sets of crooks and couplers (the cheaper system), which often had to be dismantled and reassembled in different combinations and were therefore relatively time-consuming, even without the frequent need to refine tuning at each change of crook. Terminal crooks for all tonalities, ready to handle from their case, were more advantageous. This was also true for a complete set of sliding crooks, whose high price, however, was not justified by the results obtainable. In addition, the crook to be applied could have a different temperature than the instrument that had been played up to that point. Especially in colder periods, this could mean that the pitch could change. Therefore, as we have previously seen, when the score did not leave one pair of players enough time to replace their crooks, another pair of players could be added to the orchestra to fill the gap.

All these impediments probably propelled the search for a device allowing for the use of all, or at least most, of the crooks simultaneously, and the possibility of changing between them instantaneously. This happened at the beginning of the nineteenth century, when several mechanical systems appeared, making that rapid change truly possible. These instruments, called *cors omnitoniques*, or horns in all keys, were mainly produced in France and Belgium, and also made their appearance in England.

However, they did not gain real success since they were heavy, expensive, and difficult to manage, and also because they had to compete with the set of terminal crooks, which was available at the same time, and later on with valves. Nevertheless, perhaps because of their ingenious mechanical solutions, several models of omnitonic horns were devised over the time, and many items are still preserved.

---

[7] A negative review appeared in the AMZ from July 1822, while, conversely, J. S. Mayr viewed a concert given by Bergonzi on this instrument very favorably (Rocchetti 1990, 162–163).

[8] A modern reconstruction of this instrument can be seen on Richard (Dick) J. Martz's website: http://rjmartz.com/horns/bergonzi/ (as of April 3, 2022).

The first known model was built in Paris by J.-B. Dupont in 1815. The crooks of B-flat alto, A, G, F, E, E-flat, D, and C are fixed to the instrument, each with its own leadpipe and independent crook. A sort of rack collects the row of all the leadpipes so that the instrumentalist has only to put the mouthpiece into the chosen one, which is then activated by a lever that directs the air in the appropriate tubing. The instrument was relatively heavy, especially when compared with the models normally used by the horn players of the period, and it also lacked the capability to reach the frequently requested key of B-flat basso (see Figure 94).

Three years later, Dupont also patented another omnitonic model (French Patent No. 892) based on a completely different principle. Here, the crooks—the ones mentioned previously plus the low B-flat—share the mouthpiece and the body of the instrument so that the mouthpiece must never be moved from its placement. The crook change occurs using a long indented lever that runs all over

Figure 94. J.-B. Dupont, omnitonic horn, *ca.* 1818.

the body of the instrument in an elliptical (non-circular) shape. Dupont subsequently decided to offer his patent to Jacques-Charles Labbaye (active in Paris between 1815 and 1848), who included that model in his price lists (1819), and a specimen by this builder is still preserved at the Paris Museum (see Figure 95).

The Belgian Charles Sax (1791–1864) also experimented with the construction of an omnitonic horn, and in 1824, he put on the market an equally odd model equipped with the same nine tones as the instrument previously described. In this case, the instrument is similar to the ordinary natural horn, with a single fixed leadpipe, while a telescopic tenon, to which eight crooks are connected, allows the performer change the tonality while moving it to determined positions along its axis. The horn was patented in 1826 by an agent named Stuckens, and reproductions of the patent designs of both this model and the previous one are offered in Morley Pegge (1973, 58–59; a whole chapter is devoted to an in-depth discussion of omnitonic horns) (see Figure 96 online). The *cor omnitonique* by Sax, which also has a key to facilitate moisture expulsion, had some success, and a positive review appeared in the *Revue Musicale* (1833, 172–174).

Among the models without valves, perhaps the last one conceived was the "Radius French horn" devised by the Englishman John Callcott and probably

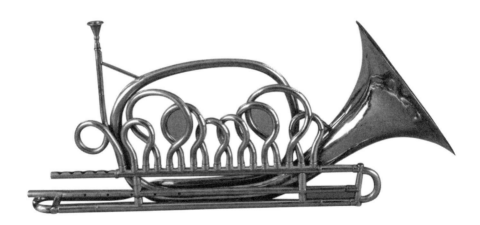

Figure 95. J.-C. Labbaye, omnitonic horn, *ca*. 1820.

made by Thomas Key of London (the instrument was presented at the London Great Exhibition of 1851).[9] Thanks to a radial telescopic tube, which could be connected to the series of small receivers placed throughout the four spiral coils at the distance of a half tone from each other, it was possible to play in all the keys from B-flat alto to B-flat basso, while the tuning crook provided the correct pitch (see Figure 97 online).

However, the experiments did not end there, and in fact, despite the lack of success of these models, omnitonic horns continued to be experimented with until the end of the nineteenth century, well into the era of the valves (see Chapter 24, p. 286).

TROMBONE-LIKE CROOKS

A completely different and almost isolated experiment was performed by Christian Dickhut (fl. 1811–1830), a hornist, guitarist, and composer active in Mannheim. His invention, a horn equipped with a main slide, was presented in the *AMZ* of November 18, 1812 (759–764) by Gottfried Weber (1779–1839), a German composer and theorist who was perhaps most attentive to the changes then underway for wind instruments. The slide could be pulled out by about "half a span" with the left thumb and was drawn back by a watch clock spring. Though the system could not render the horn completely chromatic, it allowed the performer to avoid the less-stopped pitches—or "easier stopped sounds," as Mayr called the tones obtained by partial occlusion of the bell—and improved the intonation of out-of-tune notes, such as the eleventh and thirteenth harmonics. Weber's article draws attention to the solos in the finale of Sarti's opera *Fra due litiganti* and in Beethoven's Third Symphony, where the use of this device allows the performer to play with good results the *ff* final theme. The author concludes by remarking that the mechanism is easy to use and that he cannot explain why it is so little known.

A similar invention is described by E. Goring in *The Repertory of Patent Inventions and Other Discoveries and Improvements* (vol. 36, London, 1820, 350–353). The author reports on an experiment by Thomas Percival, who had applied a main slide to the bugle horn and suggested that a horn could be constructed

[9] The horn-shaped omnitonic trumpet built by Jacques Christophe Labbaye fils (mid-19th century) located in the Sterns collection was probably inspired by this horn model and offers the keys of F, E-flat, D, C, and B-flat.

based on the same principle. A conjectural drawing is also included (it is not known whether this instrument was ever created) (see Figure 98 online).

Various factors hampered the diffusion of these experimental instruments, none of which were of further consequence, nor, apparently, with any direct link to the contemporaneous invention of the valves. In fact, the cost and labor required for such mechanisms inhibited the achievement of their goal, especially since, in the meantime, the hand technique, with which similar and even more satisfying results were possible, was becoming increasingly appreciated.

PART III

PART III

20
VALVE HORNS

After the attempts by Kölbel and Clagget, we must wait until the beginning of the nineteenth century for new experiments with valves capable of effectively diverting the air stream into an additional portion of the tube in order to prolong its length. The most important piece of information in this regard dates back to December 6, 1814, and is contained in a letter addressed to King Frederick William III of Prussia by Heinrich Stölzel (1777–1844), a horn player in the band of Prince Louis Augustus of Pless (today the Polish Pszczyna, in Upper Silesia). Here, he calls for the recognition of his invention, which he arrived at after many attempts in the July of the same year.[1] However, the idea, although with a different technical solution, seems to have started with Friedrich Blühmel (1777–ca. 1845), a miner and bandsman from Waldenburg (today the Polish Wałbrzych, in Lower Silesia), even though the former had greater determination and certainly more economic resources to dedicate to the ingenious concept (see also Grove 2001, art. "Blühmel").

A new musical era was approaching with the advent of a device that was destined to dramatically change the practice of music, albeit not with the economic advantages hoped for by the people who conceived it. As this mechanism was perfected and its use spread, it came to define the modern family of brass instruments, which, in the second half of the nineteenth century, would join the orchestra. New instruments began appear, such as the tuba and a whole set of flugelhorns with very different shapes and sizes of tubing, although the latter would not find a stable place in the symphony orchestra.

In brass bands, especially military ones, valve instruments soon became widespread because they allowed for faster learning and easier handling, in some cases even allowing the player to hold the reins with one hand while on

---

[1] The letter in question, as well as the archival documentation referred to below, is cited here on the basis of the transcripts reported in Heyde 1987a (an English translation of this and other important documents on the invention of the valves can be found in Ericson 1997).

horseback. But their adoption by professionals and virtuosos, who were highly specialized in the hand-horn technique and certainly unwilling to welcome the newcomer, turned out to be much less smooth.

THE INVENTION OF VALVES

After the letter from Heinrich Stölzel to the king of Prussia, the news of the application of the valves to the horn appeared in the *Allgemeine Musikalische Zeitung* on May 3, 1815 (cols. 309–310) in an article signed by Gottlob Benedict Bierey (1772–1840), the music director of the Wrocław Theater (today in Poland) (see Figure 99 online). He had examined Stölzel's horn and described it as having "two levers operated by two fingers of the right hand." In addition, the timbre was "very similar to that of the natural sounds, and preserves the character of the natural horn." Finally, Stölzel had requested a patent for this new invention. The news was reported again shortly afterwards by the *National-Zeitung der Deutschen* (Gotha, May 24, 1815, cols. 421–422), an information magazine in which a section of the *AMZ* article was quoted, a sign that the discovery was considered to be relevant to fields beyond the musical field. Subsequently, on November 26, 1817, the *AMZ* published another article (cols. 814–816) signed by Friedrich Schneider (1786–1853),[2] in which Stölzel's invention was also praised. These sources were apparently influenced by Stölzel's remarkable talent at promoting himself and his business, as evidenced also by an autographed letter of his, dated March 6, 1819 (Ahrens 2015, 456), with which he sent two of his horns to the Grand Duke of Weimar (which were, however, sent back two weeks later). Blühmel, who most likely had made the discovery first, remained instead in obscurity.

CONTEMPORARY DOCUMENTATION

Fortunately, numerous documents on the invention have been preserved and can be found in the Berlin State Archives (Geheimes Staatsarchiv Preußischer Kulturbesitz), where they have been carefully examined by Herbert Heyde (1987a, 12–21). Heyde also confirmed the loss of the sources related to Blühmel's valves

---

[2] An English translation of this article can be found in Brüchle-Janetzky 1988, 74–75 (see also Ericson 1997, 71).

previously held at the Oberbergamt zu Berlin (quoted by Rode 1860, 242; they were already considered missing by Mahillon 1893, I, 283).

A year after his first request to the king, Stölzel filed a petition to the Ministry of Finance on December 29, 1815, requesting a fifteen-year privilege for all Prussian states. The answer, dated February 1, 1816, was that the three written statements he had attached to support the request, one of which was drafted by the aforementioned superintendent Bierey, were insufficient to grant the request. To that aim, it was necessary to produce technical drawings or a sample of the instrument, which evidently had not been exhibited until then.

Two years later, on February 19, 1818, Stölzel, who had in the meantime moved from Pless to Berlin, made the request again. Owing to illness and, above all, the fact that his horn was not owned by him but by the prince of Pless, it had not been possible for him to produce a specimen. Now, equipped with a new instrument, he was able to submit it for the ministry's examination and perform some musical examples with it.

However, just a day earlier, on February 18, 1818, Friedrich Blühmel, who, according to authoritative testimony, had been experimenting with valves since 1811–1812, made an analogous petition. In the end, the ministry decided to issue a Prussian privilege registered to both, dated April 12, 1818. The two inventions, which had similar objectives, differed in their mechanical solutions since one was based on the tubular valves, which took thenceforth the name of Stölzel, and the other used box valves (Heyde 1987a, 16, 18). We will see that, contrary to common belief, the tubular valves were in all probability invented by Blühmel and the box valves by Stölzel, although the later terminology suggests the opposite. This could be explained by the fact that when Stölzel made an agreement with his rival—paying a sum of 400 thalers, together with the bandmaster Wilhelm Wieprecht, for exclusive use of the Prussian privilege—he could adopt the mechanism as such, independently from the valve model, which is also why other subsequent patents were rejected (*Grove* 2001, s.v. "Valve").

Among the documents examined by Heyde is a long clarifying statement by Blühmel that we will summarize here (the full text is found in Appendix III online) as it seems to be a crucial piece of evidence that he was the original inventor of the valves.

Blühmel had begun by playing the violin but was unable to progress with this instrument owing to the nature of his work as a miner, which affected his hands; he therefore dedicated himself to the horn and the trumpet, and his attention was soon focused on the shortcomings of these instruments' harmonic series. His solution to the problem was inspired by nothing less than the air conduits of the foundries and blast furnaces he had seen during a stay in Upper Silesia (hence in the region of Pless). He discussed the idea with competent people who supported the possibility of applying the same principle to the instrument's tubes, lengthening or shortening the path traveled by the air through the instrument in order to obtain the sounds not found in the harmonics series.

Once he decided that two valves would be sufficient for the new mechanism, Blühmel, who in the meantime had returned to Waldenburg, first tried to work the metal himself. He later had to resort to specialists, but he still did not obtain the desired result. The first successful experiments, the outcome of a collaboration with a master smith named Richter, consisted of simplifying and reducing the size of the device. This was successfully implemented on a trumpet in 1816, and he was finally able to produce all natural and chromatic sounds on a specimen with two valves.

However, after the installation of new air ducts with pressure valves in Waldenburg's mines in 1817–1818, he decided to try another solution. The new mining devices gave him a hint for how to perfect the closing and opening devices with which he had equipped a trumpet and a horn, drawings of which he attached to the petition. Owing to a lack of time, it was not possible, however, to apply the same mechanism to other types of instruments, although the process was ongoing. Finally, Blühmel requested a ten-year patent for horns, trumpets, and trombones with valves, enclosing nine authoritative attestations that confirmed that he was the inventor of the device. Moreover, in February 1818, he had a two-valve horn and a three-valve trombone under construction in the Berlin workshop of J. C. Gabler. A detailed description of these valves has been preserved, but the drawings that Blühmel attached to his explanatory notes have been lost, so Heyde has proposed a graphic reconstruction of the respective mechanism (Heyde 1987a, 18; see Figure 100 online).

Both the details of the story reported and the careful reference to the mining machinery that inspired the valve mechanism support the idea that Blühmel was the originator of the idea. A not irrelevant detail is the fact that he spent a period of time in Upper Silesia, where Pless is found (a stay also confirmed by a piece of evidence reported below). He could there have met Stölzel, who was perhaps one of the "competent people" to which he refers in his statement, and the latter could have then independently developed the invention. Finally, the aforementioned documentation includes an attestation by the master of the mining district of Waldenburg, a certain Gerhard, about the fact that (a) the first experiments by Blühmel dated back to 1811–1812 (further confirmation that the idea, at least in its original form, began with him), and that (b) they initially concerned a valve mechanism that was completely different from that for which the patent was now being requested (Heyde 1987a, 19).

We must not forget, however, that Stölzel was already using a valve horn in 1814, as documented by three different sources, including that by Bierey in the aforementioned article in the *AMZ* (1815). This horn, as it seems, was not owned by him but rather by the prince of Pless for whom he worked, and only later would he have one of his own.

Faced with this situation, the Ministry of Craft and Trade (Ministerium für Gewerbe und Handel) wisely decided to have the two men sign a mutual recognition agreement when granting the right. The agreement is dated April 6, 1818, and is reported in full here:

> To the illustrious royal ministry for labor and commerce with utmost submission, we represent that, following our previous petitions of the 19 and 18 February this year, we have both agreed to cancel the pending request for the rights concerning the priority of our invention for the horn, the trumpet and the trombone, and to renounce our right to raise any objection of any kind and joint request a shared patent with the name "invention of the firm Stölzel and Blühmel." Because of this agreement, the undersigned Stölzel promises to the aforementioned Blühmel, for the exclusive right to use this patent, a unique and unrepeatable compensatory allowance of 400 thalers, of which 200 thalers will be provided in cash when the right is obtained and 200 after the end of one year, with which the co-signatory Blühmel agrees not to make further use of his discovery or any claim.
>
> Owing to this agreement, the petitions regarding the rights to the discovery in question have become superfluous.
>
> Therefore, we pray that the most excellent royal ministry ensure that the license individually requested by each of us is instead assigned, as soon as possible, and handed over to both, valid for ten years throughout the Prussian monarchy, with us as sole inventors and with the company name "Stölzel & Blühmelsche Erfindung." In fact, it turns out that others have unexpectedly come across our invention and are making the discovery public in their

exclusive interest, with which our economic advantage turns out once again to be questioned, as unfortunately happened with the disclosure made by Hein, State Trumpeter.

With the most profound respect, we remain the most respectful servants of the Royal Supreme Ministry.

Stölzel	Blühmel
musician of the Royal chapel	bandsman

The patent was thus granted to both within a few days, on April 12, 1818, and it does not seem irrelevant to point out that it concerned two different devices, as documented in the brief anonymous news item that appeared in the *AMZ* (29 (1818), col. 531). The article specifies that Stölzel and Blühmel had performed "two different improvements." After being compensated with money, Blühmel remained in the shadows for the next ten years, only reappearing in 1828 with a request for a new patent for a completely different device, a rotary valve.

We will not discuss the functioning of the valves in detail, given that the main modern texts on the subject provide an irreproachable description and also contain clarifying diagrams and drawings (see also Chapter 21, p. 237). We simply note that the principle of a temporary deviation of the air due to the activation of the valve, which makes the air travel along an additional path, usually increasing the total length of the tube and thus lowering the pitch of the instrument, remains (see Figure 101 online).

It should be added that contrary to popular belief, the invention of box valves is likely attributable to Stölzel and that of tubular valves to Blühmel. In this regard, it is interesting to note what Blühmel himself states in a document dated 1828 (see Appendix III online): "I found it necessary to give the exclusive rights to Stölzel in exchange for a payment of 400 thalers, my co-partnership in the patent, and so my original invention of tubular valves (*Röhren Ventile*)—which were invented before Stölzel's box valves (*Kasten Ventile*)—has remained in use unchanged until today."

In the same year, Fétis confirmed this based on information provided by Louis François Dauprat (1781–1868) and Joseph Emile Meifred (1791–1867), and he also provided a clear illustration of the copy of Stölzel's box valve made by Schuster of Karlsruhe (Fétis 1827, 157; see also Chapter 22, p. 258, Figures 124 and 125).

Something similar would be recorded in 1845 by the bandmaster Wilhelm Wieprecht, whose personal involvement in the events narrated will be examined in detail (see Chapter 22, p. 260). In addition, F. G. A. Dauverné, in his *Méthode pour la trompette* of 1857, says (p. xxii) that he was among the first to receive a trumpet with tubular valves in 1826, adding the following enlightening caption to the figure of the instrument (Dauverné 1857, xxv, fig. 10, caption): "Trumpet with 3 pistons, system by Stölzel, whose primitive invention is attributed to the Silesian Blühmel, model sent to France by Spontini in 1826" (see Figure 102 online).

It should be noted, however, that Blühmel himself, by presenting his patent application in 1818, described his instruments to the ministry as using *"Ventil-Kästgen,"* which Heyde (1987a, 18) understandably interpreted as box valves, also presenting a possible reconstruction of both mechanisms (see Figure 100 online). Whatever the circumstances, it is clear that once the economic agreement between the two had been reached and the aforementioned 400 thalers had been settled, Stölzel was entitled to freely exploit the model that he judged the more functional, possibly the one that still bears his name.

A price list (*Preis-Courant*) of the valve instruments produced by Stölzel is found in the two instrumentation treatises by August Sundelin (1828) with a warning stating that, in order to prevent abuse, his instruments were marked with a special trademark (see Figure 103 online). However, this is not documented by any preserved specimen.[3]

The chromatic horn or "*Chromatisches Waldhorn*," the first and most widespread name of the new model, is not discussed by Sundelin in the volume devoted to the orchestra and is instead treated in the volume on band instrumentation (Sundelin 1828b, 38): "In these musical corps there are often also two so-called chromatic horns, namely a first and a second. They are always in F and therefore quite similar to the ordinary F horns, so a fifth below the clarinet in C. With the appropriate valves, they can emit all the semitones and tones of their register, which in actual pitches covers the range from *A* to *c"*. [. . .] As already stated, the chromatic horns in F never change their size, since there would be no reason to do so."

Sundelin, who lived and worked in Berlin like Stölzel, thus confirms that in 1828 the valves had been adopted only in wind bands. Stölzel, who in the meanwhile had been hired in the court chapel, in turn highlights the difficulties he had found

---

[3] A modern, little-known, and particularly original text (Schreiber 1938, 179) claims not only that Blühmel was the original inventor of the valves, but also that Stölzel published his *Preis-Courant* (1828) only after the invention of conical valves by the Berlin mechanic Hützner (perhaps a misreading of the name "Blühmel"?).

in Berlin and in Prussia in introducing the valves to professionals in his petition for an extension of the patent in 1827, since (a) the hornists, accustomed to the hand horn, did not want to change their performing technique; (b) the music composed up until then had not been written for the valve model; and (c) composers were not yet familiar with the new instrument. For these reasons, his initial patent was not very successful, and only recently had the use of the valve horn began to spread a little more widely (Heyde 1987a, 70; see also Ericson 1997 for some translations of full passages).

A little later, the valve horn was listed in a dictionary by Andersch (1829, s.v. "Stölzel"), who again assigns all merit to Stölzel alone, adding, however, an interesting detail: Carl Maria von Weber was the first to recognize the qualities of the new valve instrument and to advocate for a demonstration by Stölzel before the king of Saxony in 1817.[4]

However, a letter from the composer Adolphe Charles Adam (1803–1856), reported in the preface of Meifred's *Méthode* (1840, iii–iv) and dated June 3, 1840, testifies that at the date the *cor chromatique* was not yet used at the Berlin Opera House, where his opera *Die Hamadryaden*, featuring a horn quartet in the overture, had been recently staged (see Musical example 66 online).[5] He therefore had to have the fourth horn part (evidently written for the valve horn) played on a tuba, an instrument he considered suitable, which had the same sweetness of the horn and all the energy of the trombone (see also online, "News from the *Neue Berliner Musikzeitung*").

A LETTER BY SPONTINI

The most authoritative information on the invention of the valves and on the relationship between Stölzel and Blühmel comes from a long letter by Gaspare Spontini dated April 3, 1840, and addressed to the Académie des Beaux-Arts in Paris. The institution had been asked to acknowledge some new valve instruments by a few Parisian craftsmen and wanted to determine whether they were original according to the opinion of the celebrated resident partner in Berlin.

---

[4] A brief account also appears in the Hoffmann dictionary (1830, 429–430), which also gives Stölzel all the credit for the design of the new instrument.

[5] The quartet had already been included in Adam's *La fille du Danube* (third "tableau"), whose premiere took place in Paris in 1836.

The letter contains an objective report, based on three interviews with the protagonists of the invention, following a thorough examination of their instruments, which was performed by "disassembling and reassembling them." Spontini asserts that even though Stölzel and Wieprecht (see below) had paid Blühmel to obtain permission to use the invention and adapt it to other types of brass instruments, the majority of the credit for the invention of the valves was due to Blühmel himself. The letter in question, still located at the Académie des Beaux-Arts in Paris, is quoted in full by Kastner in his *Manuel général* (1848, 190, fn.) and briefly reported with further considerations in his review of Urbin's horn method (Kastner 1854). Here are the salient passages (see further in Meucci 2021, and Snedecker 2021, 66):

The inventor Stölzel, who you have mentioned, made all the oral and written statements necessary to me, as did the inventor Wieprecht. They are both Royal Chapel musicians and received the first indications on the *pistons* [valves] about 25 or 26 years ago, from the inventor Blühmel from Silesia. Later on Blühmel, following a payment of about three thousand francs, granted the right to continue use of the invention of pistons in Prussia and to obtain patents or rights to apply these pistons to all brass instruments without exception first to Stölzel and then to Wieprecht.

The result of my many questions, the close examination of all his inventions, disassembled and reassembled, and the instruments played during our three sessions, give me the following conviction: all the pistons or valves, applied to the horn, the trumpet and the cornet (which is nothing but a small horn in high Bb), were without exception invented and applied as a set of two or three to the above three instruments as well as to various low brass instruments and even to trombones in Prussia and throughout Germany. These valves, in various forms, have received a good number of progressive modifications and improvements here in particular, which means that it is not realistic—and on this point also Mr. Adam agrees—to think that someone could have invented them or further perfected them in Paris in 1839, especially after the examination of a two-piston cornet we have before our eyes which was made at the Courtois brothers' factory, rue du Caire in Paris, 1835.

[. . .]

I sent numerous horns, valve trumpets, and cornets with two and three pistons or valves (which were thus introduced for the first time in Paris) from

Berlin to Paris, from 1823 to 1831, including to Mr. Barillon, to the horn teacher Mr. Dauprat, to the bandmaster of the guards Mr. David Buhl, and it is on the basis of these specimens that some Parisian manufacturers thought they had invented or perfected, while they only imitated and copied.

(See online, "News on Stölzel and Blühmel in the *Zeitschrift für Instrumentenbau*.")

21

FURTHER VALVE SYSTEMS

Following the discoveries of Blühmel and Stölzel, various other types of valves were designed and tested. One of the very first, and so far the least well known, was the rotary valve invented by Luigi Pini of Fontanellato in 1821, a solution devised much earlier than Blühmel's own rotary valve, which dates back to 1828, and will be discussed later (Chapter 21, p. 248).

With regard to pistons, the famous Viennese valve, designed by Riedl and Kail in 1823 and perfected by Uhlmann in 1830, deserves a separate treatment. Equally well known is the robust Berlin piston valve by Wieprecht, patented in 1833. Finally, in 1838, F. Périnet's piston appeared; this was very successful on all brass instruments and is still mostly used today.

Despite the many other valve systems developed over the course of the nineteenth century, we will concentrate only on the ones mentioned, which are particularly relevant for the subsequent history of the horn, and on a few other models that are currently less known. For the rest, we rely on the many studies dedicated to valves, from the pioneering work of Mahillon (1893, 282–292) to that of Carse (1939, 62–80) ("The mechanics of brass instruments"), from the authoritative synthesis in Baines (1976, 206–219) to the monumental treatment of Heyde (1987a), and from the "valve" article of *The New Grove Dictionary of Music and Musicians* (2001) written by E. Tarr to the text of Ahrens (2008b), which discusses, among other things, the social and economic implications deriving from these inventions.

Tarr also takes the opportunity to address imitations and copies, adding, among other things, that the Stölzel valve "was very soon copied by J.F. Anderst (St Petersburg, 1825)"—actually 1822, as we will see later (Chapter 21, p. 241)—and that the same can be said of "Labbaye and Halary (Paris, 1827), Pace and Köhler (London, after 1830), and even James Keat for Samuel Graves (Winchester, NH, c1837)."

THE UNIQUE VALVES BY PINI

The earliest rotary valve was conceived at the latest in 1822 by Luigi Pini (1790–1848)—sometimes erroneously called "Bini" in German sources (Gathy 1835, 219; Schilling 1836, III, 635). Like Puzzi, Pini was a pupil of Francesco Paglia (*ca.* 1772–1821) in the horn school of his hometown, Fontanellato near Parma (see Chapter 18, p. 205). A specimen of his model of valve horn, built in 1822 by Lorenzo Dall'Asta, active in nearby San Secondo, is preserved in the Museo della Musica of Bologna (inv. no. 1847) and bears the inscription "submitted to Her Majesty the Archduchess of Parma" (see Figure 104). This instrument aroused great surprise at the time of its restoration from Ursula Menzel (1988–1989) and during the preparation of the museum catalog by John Henry van der Meer (1993, 78–79), as it presented a system of valves that was unknown to scholars, but the discovery did not receive international attention. The instrument is characterized by a unique mechanism—two rotary devices for each of the two valves—moved by toothed wheels driven by long rods; furthermore, it is also equipped with valve slides, which successive builders and inventors later claimed to have invented.

With reference to such an early and unique instrument, dating back to only a few years after the first official mention of a valve horn, we would like to highlight an article published by the *Gazzetta di Parma* on February 9, 1822:

Mr. Luigi Pini, an amateur *corno da caccia* player, a student of the former Sanvitale school in Fontanellato, his fatherland, pupil of Maestro Francesco Paglia of Parma, assisted by the distinguished Professors Simonis and Gesuit, had the honor of presenting to Her Majesty, our high-honorable sovereign, a *corno da caccia* of his own invention built under his direction by the talented maker Lorenzo Dall'Asta of San Secondo.

This horn has eight touch keys, and with a single crook in B-flat basso, the player can play in thirteen keys with a chromatic scale, that is from the B-flat alto to the B-flat basso, without putting in or pulling out a crook whatsoever. The player can switch from one to another quickly, even without removing the lips from the mouthpiece, and there is also a slide for the different tunings.

On December 16, 1821, the inventor of this Horn showed it to his teacher, then to the *Professori* in the service of his Majesty [. . .] and on the 21st of the same month, as stated previously, he had the honor of presenting it to the Her Majesty, from whom he received a sign of her munificence, and the venerated

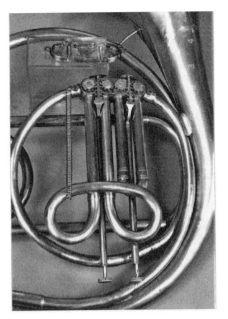

Figure 104. L. Dall'Asta, horn with two rotary valves, 1822.

sovereign order to produce an instrument of the like. He is already working on this specimen, and it will be completed by the month of May of the current year, 1822.

The reported description of the *Gazzetta di Parma* was repeatedly borrowed, starting with Lichtenthal (1826, I, 211). However, the statement that "This horn has eight touch keys, and with a single crook in B-flat basso, the player can play in thirteen keys with a chromatic scale" does not fit the 1822 specimen preserved in Bologna (today at the Museo della Musica, formerly in the Museo Civico Medievale of the same city). The discordance is discussed in the catalog of the collection (Meer 1993, 79): "The horn described above does not have B-flat (*Bfa basso*) as fundamental and does not have eight keys. Therefore, either Lichtenthal has reported incorrect information about the instrument or Pini also invented a B-flat basso horn with eight keys which was also dedicated to the Duchess Marie Louise."

The preserved item is thus possibly the outcome of the "venerated sovereign order," bearing the date 1822, and not 1821 (that demonstrated to Her Majesty on December 1821 should have been finished by the date), and in fact it may match a modified or refined second design.

According to Dacci (1888, 8), the duchess of Parma, Marie Louise of Austria, who was shown the instrument on December 1821, "had left [to Pini] a modest donation and sent the instrument to the Imperial Music Academy in Vienna for the requisite approval," evidently referring to the first item built, which is today lost. Dacci and some other Italian late nineteenth-century sources also maintain that this invention was resubmitted with some changes and passed as Austrian. This opinion, however, is incorrect, and probably came about because the Austrian rulers in Italy promptly validated Riedl's 1823 patent (see below), which also had double valves but was based on a rather different system, that is, the Viennese one.

An instrument by Lorenzo Dall'Asta was also evaluated, approved, and praised at the Milan Conservatory on June 26, 1823. On this occasion, Pini also performed with this instrument, on June 30th at the Teatro Re (Chiappori 1825, 132) and on July 3rd at the Theater of Canobbiana (Chiappori 1825, 84). In addition, on June 28, 1828, he participated in a concert in Bologna at the Teatro Comunale (*Teatri Arti e Letteratura*, 6/218 (July 10, 1828), 169), where he performed together with three students of the "Sanvitale school of Parma." The musicians played some quartets for horns, a concerto with variations for the "two horns of new invention," played by Pini and Colombi, and a horn concerto composed by Giovanni Alinovi, once again for the Pini valve instrument, performed by Massimiliano Colombi (the music has been lost).

In 1824, two other Italian makers, Carlo Bernardi and Giacomo De Luigi, submitted a valve horn with features similar to those of Pini's to the Istituto Lombardo di Scienze, Lettere e Arti, requesting a patent for their invention (Rocchetti–Rossi-Rognoni 1998, 12). The instrument, which was also equipped with two double rotary valves,[1] again prior to Blühmel's, was given "honorable mention," the commission having found it particularly functional when "pitching it in the various keys without changing the crook."[2]

---

[1] The description preserved in the archives of the institute states, "Simple construction with only four keys," but the specification "only one or two keys must be pressed, depending on the key in which you want to play" makes it clear that the instrument did not have four separate valves. The valves were apparently double valves, like those by Pini.

[2] For the sake of completeness, we should also mention another Italian horn with two rotary valves. The instrument may have come from the same workshop, and it too is preserved in Bologna (anon., inv. 1840; see Meer 1993, 79–80).

ANDERST OF ST. PETERSBURG

One of the oldest and less known set of valves is documented by a group of nine instruments, including two horns, located at the Cultural History Museum in Kuopio, Finland. Our knowledge of these instruments is thanks to the studies of Paul Niemistö and to an exhibition held in 2009.[3] These instruments are the work of Johann Friedrich Anderst (1804–1871?), a German-born builder active in St. Petersburg, who adopted a type of valve that imitates the ones "used in water and air ducts" (Niemistö 2009, 18). We conjecture that these valves were directly inspired by Blühmel's early experiments based on the air ducts adopted in the mines in Waldenburg, a "totally different" mechanism with which Blühmel experimented and later abandoned in favor of pressure valves (see also Appendix III online). It is worth mentioning that Anderst was a German living in St. Petersburg (where the German-Bohemian Anton Dörfeldt had been working as a band master since 1802),[4] and finally, that Anderst himself, like Blühmel and Stölzel, soon moved on to pressure valves.

The "butterfly" valves on these instruments have a central pin with two lateral wings that rotate around the pin. They are controlled externally by a lever with a unique type of movement, similar to that of steam engines, which makes the valve rotate 90 degrees with respect to the rest position. The air normally flows through the main path, but when the valve is pressed, the butterfly turns and diverts it through the additional tubing of the valve. The horn from this group of instruments (inv. 8929:2) is pitched in F and is described along with all the other specimens in Niemistö 2009. Another instrument (inv. 614), curiously called a "bassocorno" (Niemistö 2009, 17 and 53), is said to be pitched in low C (16'). The length stated, however, is not compatible with the photo of the instrument reported therein. Another reason why these items are interesting is the general adoption of three valves, a timely solution created right after Sattler's in 1819 (p. 243).

A second group of brass instruments with Anderst's mark is located in the Museum of Theater and Music at the Sheremetev Palace in St. Petersburg. It includes a horn with three piston valves for the right hand, dated 1822 (inv. 1536). It is probable that, after a temporary adoption of the butterfly valves, Anderst—

---

[3] See https://pages.stolaf.edu/niemisto/j-f-anderst-brass-instruments/.

[4] For information on the musical relationships between Berlin and St. Petersburg, in particular those regarding musical bands, see Tarr 2004, 33–34.

Figure 105. J. F. Anderst, horn, *ca.* 1820, and butterfly valve (Kuopio, Cultural History Museum, inv. 8929:2).

who was only eighteen years old at the time—switched to the much more reliable mechanism of the Stölzel valves (as we call them even though, as shown, they were in all probability invented by Blühmel).

EARLY VIENNESE VALVES BY RIEDL AND KAIL

An initial prototype of the Viennese system seems to have been created by Christian Friedrich Sattler from Leipzig (1778–1842). As documented by *AMZ* (1819, 416), Sattler had already successfully applied three Stölzel valves to his *chromatische Waldhörner* (perhaps based on the 1818 three-valve trombone by Blühmel-Gabler, see above), thus obtaining a greater number of sounds in the low register. Furthermore, the mechanism was operated by the left hand, and so the horn could be held in the usual manner, allowing for use of the hand technique.

A later illustration of one of his trumpets with two valves of a different design can be found in the *AMZ* (1821, 411), but the drawing shows only the long and narrow tubes that the transmission rods pass through, with the respective return springs (see Figure 106 online). The mechanisms of the two valves are concealed by two semi-cylindrical guards and could therefore also be of a type other than the Viennese one.

In any case, in 1823, an effective idea likely similar to this one was tested in Vienna. The valves were now operated by paddles and controlled by more effective return springs. On November 1, 1823 (*Grove* 2001, s.v. "Valve"), the builder Joseph Felix Riedl (*ca.* 1788–1837) and the horn player Joseph Kail (1795–1871) obtained a ten-year privilege for the first version of what would become the Viennese system of valves, thus paving the way for a long and glorious tradition. This patent, when announced in Italy (it was evidently valid for the entire imperial territory), led to an unjust accusation against an unknown Viennese maker of having plagiarized Pini's system (Dacci 1888, 8).

The mechanism is probably the one reproduced in the *Hornschule für das einfache, das Maschinen- und das Signalhorn* by Andreas Nemetz, or Ondřej Němec (1799–1846), published by Diabelli in Vienna in 1829, in which the instrument clearly shows Riedl's mark (see Figure 107 online). The Viennese double valve (*Doppelschubventil*) was soon introduced with some variations in Bohemia (see Figure 108 online), in Mainz, in Southern Germany, and in Saxony, and also led to subsequent repercussions (see online, "Riedl and Kail's Italian patent").

THE CONTRIBUTION BY UHLMANN

The Viennese maker Leopold Uhlmann (1806–1878) created a fairly functional variant of Riedl and Kail's system and applied it to a model with a structure very similar to the natural horn built by his firm (see online, "The controversy never stops," and Figure 109 online). The most important novelty was that the three double-piston valves (later called *Wiener-Ventile*, *Wiener-Maschine*, or even *Pumpenventile*) were laid adjacent to a straight yard of tubing that ran along the side opposite the levers. These valves were similar to the previous ones but had the particularity of being pushed externally by long transmission rods, which were returned by effective ribbon springs (like those used in antique clocks). In the rest position, the air passed through the tube in a completely straight line without any constraints. When the button is pressed, it follows a transversal path with two right-angle deviations for each valve (Uhlmann obtained a privilege of five years for this model, starting from July 12, 1830) (see Figure 110 online).

Of the single horns in the standard keys, the Viennese model is the only one to have been retained after the advent of the double horn and is still used today by the Vienna Philharmonic Orchestra. Numerous hornists are also adopting this model for performances with historical instruments, although it was not actually widespread even in the nineteenth century. Like some types of German-made horns (see Chapter 24, p. 281), it has a larger bell and flare than is average for other horns, but instead has a rather small internal diameter: 10.5mm for models from the second half of the nineteenth century, then increasing to 10.8mm at the beginning of the twentieth century. The mouthpiece is a not very deep funnel with a thin rim and a larger throat (Ø *ca.* 5mm) than the average modern mouthpiece.[5]

A distinctive feature of the model is that it still uses terminal crooks, abandoned by all other modern models. Today, the F section is used almost exclusively—this is the usual key for the hornists of the Viennese Philharmonic—which gives the horn section of this orchestra its characteristic timbre. The F crook is entirely conical but shorter than that of the usual F crook used in the French model horn, pitched a tone higher than the Vienna instrument (see Figure 111). The crook of high B-flat (9 feet), rarely adopted for special circumstances, is a simple and short shank that, once inserted, makes it necessary to replace the valve slides with shorter

[5] See http://www.pizka.de/mpiece.htm.

ones made ad hoc.⁶ The way that this short high B-flat "crook" is constructed (some makers provided two crooks of different sizes in order to get slightly different tuning), with its marked tapering associated with the instrument's peculiar tubing and its wide bell, distorts the horn's timbre, making it similar to that of a flugelhorn or a trombone, which is why many orchestral conductors disapproved of its use.

For a long period, an E crook was also used, at least according to Berlioz-Strauss (1905, 299; 1948, 280), who mentions that hornists specialized in the roles of second and fourth horn used this crook when the first and the third used A crooks.⁷ Some makers also provided one or two A alto crooks and corresponding slides—useful for compositions such as Beethoven's *Fidelio*, Symphonies no. 2 and no. 7—but the present-day set-up with only the F crook was already recommended by the Lewy brothers in their letter on the Uhlmann/Riedl dispute (see online, "The controversy never stops").

The model with double pistons was not the only product of post-restoration Vienna, as some makers, including Riedl himself, whose instruments were very popular and widespread in Italy, had a series of other models in their catalogs designed primarily for the export market.

According to Mendel's *Conversationslexikon* (11, 1879, 4), it was Johann Strauss Sr. who introduced Viennese model horns and trumpets to Berlin when he visited the city with his orchestra in 1835. However, the hornists of the Berlin Opera House had not yet passed to the valve horn in 1840, as documented by Adam's letter to Meifred (1840, iii) cited above.

VARIATIONS ON "WIENER-VENTIL"

Other makers applied the Viennese valves to the horn prior to and after Uhlmann, introducing a series of different solutions and obtaining more or less effective results. Among them is Carl August Müller (1804–1870), who was born in Adorf,

---

⁶ In fact, the Viennese valve model could not be used in C alto, thus confirming that in Vienna, Haydn's parts could no longer be performed in high C after the mid-nineteenth century at the latest.

⁷ The re-edition of Berlioz' treatise edited by Richard Strauss (1904; English translation by Theodore Front, New York, Kalmus, 1948; reprint 1991) states, "Horn players now use almost exclusively the horns in E, F, high A and high Bb (incidentally, it requires practice to change the bright and sharp tone of the horn in Bb into the soft and noble timbre of the horn in F)."

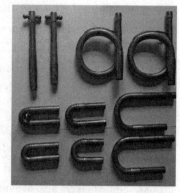

Figure 111. Erste Wiener Produktive Genossenschaft, Viennese horn with duplicated shanks (B-flat), crooks (A), two sets of valve slides (B-flat or A size), and F crook with original mouthpiece, first quarter of the twentieth century.

Saxony, and settled in Mainz in 1824. Here, in 1827, he began a close collaboration with the Schott & Söhne Company, building valve instruments.[8] He adopted Riedl and Kail's valves, operated by keys with flat springs underneath, such as those used on woodwind instruments at the time (a system known in Saxony as *Klinkendruckwerk*). The mechanism was covered externally by a tin guard in order to prevent dust from entering the valve. However, the weakness of the flat spring suggested that, as Uhlmann had already determined, a more robust watch spring should be adopted, in order to draw back the rod connected to the pin that drives the pistons. This new type, early devised in around 1830, was called the *Neumainzer Maschine* (new mechanism of Mainz). This gave rise to a terminology directly dependent on Müller, namely that of the "old" Mainz mechanism (with the spring below the key) and the "new" one (Heyde 1987a, 46–47). Only one valve horn by Müller equipped with this new mechanism, and dating back to about 1835, seems to have survived (see Figures 112 and 113). Müller and Uhlmann were also the first to apply valves to all types of brass instruments, including low brass, thus contributing to the eventual takeover of keyed models well before the middle of the century (Rühlmann 1851, 250).

[8] This date is confirmed by the inclusion of a "cor à pistons, nouvelle invention" (valve horn, new invention) in the Schott instruments catalog found in the re-edition of Domnich's *Methode* of 1828 (for the latter date, cf. *Troisième supplement des Nouvautés en musique . . . Schott . . .* November 1828, attached to the journal *Cäcilia*, 1828).

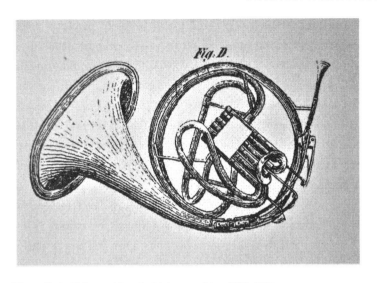

Figure 112. Müller's (?) horn with early *Mainzer* machine, 1828–1830.

Figure 113. *Neumainzer* machine horn by Müller.

Michael Saurle of Munich (1799–1872) also certainly played a role in this experimentation, as documented by a two-valved trumpet dated 1829 at the Metropolitan Museum of New York (inv. 89.4.1098); a horn illustrated in Pizka (1986, 402), with an unusual upside-down arrangement of the halftone valve slide; and a horn dated 1836 auctioned on eBay (2012), featuring a *Neumainzer Maschine* with the two double pistons pushed by a unique type of traction.[9] It is also worth mentioning that Saurle constantly adopted watch springs, apparently highly functional, in all known instruments of his manufacture (see also online, "A Viennese horn in New York City," and Figure 114 online).

The Viennese system was also used by some Belgian makers, with the innovative adoption of pistons with spiral springs (see online, "On 'spiral' springs"), to the point that the system became known in Paris as the "système belge" or "pistons belges." These valves were used on trumpets and especially trombones, despite the well-known "disadvantage of containing angles that harm the quality of the sound," as stated by Pierre (1890, 260–261) (see Figure 115 online). The same system seems to have also been applied to the horn by Ferdinand van Cauwelaert in 1847 (Cools 2005). In any case, there is no basis for the hypothesis that this variant can be traced back to Sax (Mitroulia–Myers 2008, 134).

ROTARY VALVES BY BLÜHMEL (1828) AND RIEDL (1835)

Despite the fact that Luigi Pini introduced rotary valves as early as 1821–1822 (see Chapter 21, p. 238), the system that passed down through history and was later to become the most reliable and widespread on horn instruments was again invented by Blühmel. This is supported by the hypothesis that the anonymous horn preserved in Markneukirchen (Musikinstrumentenmuseum, inv. 1175) is really of his manufacture, as Herbert Heyde maintains in his outstanding book (1987a, 29 and photo 1) (see Figure 116 online).

Blühmel and Stölzel may have already had the idea for a rotary mechanism in 1818, but they did not include it in their initial patent application, probably intending to reserve it for further privileges. Indeed, when the rights expired in 1828, both presented their own device of this kind. Nevertheless, only Blühmel submitted proper documentation and probably a sample item (now lost) to the Prussian Ministry of Commerce. A lot of information can be obtained from the

---

[9] See http://www.horn-u-copia.net/instruments/a2/Michael-Saurle-1836-FH.jpg.

long accompanying text (reported in Heyde 1987a, 28–29), along with an extensive critique of the valves then in use and of the improvements made by the new model Blühmel presented. Among other things, Blühmel states, "My efforts were crowned by a felicitous result, and I am now in possession of a device that meets all expectations; with it I have always regained well-deserved recognition for the chromatic instrument on my tours, which has often been questioned up until this point" (see Appendix III online).

The rotary valves were later modified by J. F. Riedl in Vienna in 1835 with a design very similar to the one then definitively in use (see Heyde 1987a, 31–32). The most reliable description is found in the text approving the patent, reported in the *Jahrbücher des kaiserlichen königlichen Polytechnischen* (Vienna, Gerold, 1837), 479 (see Figure 117 online):

2264. Joseph Felix Riedl, wind instrument maker in Vienna (Stadt, No. 731); for the improvement of all metal wind instruments in which the six flow diverters installed up to now on these instruments are replaced by a single valve for every two diverters. The construction of the valve, with the way that it loops around, prevents the air from reflecting back and forth as it eliminates the sharp corners at right angle along the air path. The tubes of the instrument only curve gently and the valve is designed so that the air turns around and goes back into the curved tube and does not ever make a right angle along the path. Even when passing through all three valves and all the tubes, the air always continues on a curved path avoiding all sharp edges, remaining the same, not interrupted, and not disturbed in its vibrations. The emission of sound, which itself becomes more beautiful, fuller, and purer, owing to the considerably less effort required on the part of the player, is greatly facilitated. For five years, from September 25th.

We should note one more subsequent fundamental improvement, which has become more and more common: the cords driving the mechanism. "A further development was the 'American string action' (Ger. *Schnurmechanik*), patented in 1848 by Thomas D. Paine of Woonsocket, Rhode Island, and also taken up in 1855, on Kail's suggestion, by Wenzel Schamal in Prague" (*Grove* 2001, s.v. "Valve").

THE VALVES BY MORITZ AND WIEPRECHT (1833)

The description of the various valve systems contained in the *Berliner Musikalische Zeitung* (29 (July 19, 1845)), written by the band director Wilhelm Wieprecht (1802–1872), has led to Wieprecht always getting the credit for an additional model of valves, the Berlin pistons. However, Heyde (1987a, 23) believes that this valve was invented by Stölzel in 1827, although the latter failed to obtain a patent. Wieprecht instead succeeded in obtaining one in 1833 with his *Steckerbüchsenventile* (pin capsule valves), later known as *Berliner Pumpen*. They were made by Johann Gottfried Moritz (1777–1840), a craftsman with whom Wieprecht produced an entire family of brass instruments. Some of these are marked "Wieprecht & Moritz" and became common in Prussian bands. Given their robustness, Wieprecht's valves proved to be fairly functional for low brass instruments, especially bass flugelhorns and tubas, but they were also applied to all the other instruments and were used until the early twentieth century. In Sweden—a land particularly connected to the traditions of Berlin—tubas with Berlin pistons remained in vogue until the 1950s (Baines 1976, 212).

These valves are similar in operation to box valves but are built with a durable and large cylindrical housing, in such a way that allows the air stream to be on one and the same plane and with no constrictions (see Figure 118 online) (see online, "Wieprecht vs. Sax").

THE PÉRINET DEVICE

In 1838, Etienne François Périnet, a former journeyman in the Raoux workshop active between 1829 and 1860,[10] developed a new piston valve in which the air column does not pass along the cylindrical tube (as in Stölzel's or in the Viennese pistons). Instead, oblique paths are used that ensure greater fluidity of the air stream, reducing the number of corners in the air column experienced with the aforementioned valves. The dimensions are larger than that of the Stölzel valve and smaller than in the Berlin model, but the inner diameter is in any case larger than the main tubing of the instrument (see Figure 119 online).

The patent application was presented on October 27, 1838 (Brevet d'invention No. 9606-6587) and approved on May 6, 1839 (Mitroulia–Demoulin–Eldredge

[10] Despite the fame and importance of this French inventor, his personal information and biographical details are as yet unknown.

2008, 217), even though the success of these valves came only from the early 1850s (Eldredge 2002, 352). During the five years of validity of the patent (1838–1843), Périnet stipulated a five-year contract with some Parisian builders, including Courtois, Halary, and Labbaye, for use of his invention. The builders could buy the valve sets from a certain Sassaigne, the probable inventor of the Périnet piston (Dumoulin 2007, 236) (see online, "Sassaigne who?").

Subsequently, this type of valve was again perfected in France by some members of the Courtois Company and by Gustave Auguste Besson (1820–1874), who, on July 31, 1854, obtained patent No. 20350 for a "Périnet cornet." In England, according to Morley-Pegge (1973, 48), Joseph Pimlott Oates (fl. 1850–1872) patented some variants of this valve in 1858. Starting in 1848, another main feature of the most common valve horns in France became, as we shall see, the third ascending valve, while models built in or exported to England normally continued to use a descending third valve.

These were ultimately the two countries in which the Périnet valve had the most effective success, at least until the adoption of the double horn, on which it could not be effectively applied. For many other instruments, especially trumpets and cornets, the Périnet piston has become the valve *par excellence* owing to its manageability and functionality.

VALVE SLIDES

The application of valves implies the presence of the additional portions of tubing necessary to lengthen the instrument's air column by a semitone or more. On early models, these additional yards were soldered to the main tubing and could not be removed. In fact, these instruments were pitched in a specific key and intended to be used chromatically without exploitation of the hand technique. Subsequently, the simultaneous use of the crooks and the hand made the presence of valve slides mandatory; especially when the instrumentalist used the valves to replace crooks as if it were an omnitonic horn.

Although the concept of the valve slides has long been attributed to the Parisian manufacturer Labbaye, who supposedly implemented an idea by Meifred (Fétis 1827, 158–159), to our knowledge the first instrument equipped with these devices is the model designed by Pini and made by Lorenzo Dall'Asta, whose 1822 horn was discussed previously.

Finally, we should mention the first appearance of the valve slides also in America. They were introduced by Nathan Adams (1783–1864) in 1824 with his "Permutation trumpet," discussed further below.

TWO AND THREE VALVES

Despite the usefulness of three valves, makers initially had to settle for two, the one nearest to the performer lowering the pitch by either a semitone or a tone. The increase in weight and above all the lack of reliability of early valves, with corners that hindered air passage, meant that makers had to use as few as possible (Meifred 1840, 80).

However, two valves alone—a semitone and a tone, a tone and a half when used together—are not enough to offer the full range of sounds of the horn. A few would require the help of the hand,[11] or the use of the falsetto, both techniques that horn players at the time, well trained on the hand horn, were certainly versed in (even though Kastner 1844, for example, makes no mention of them) (see Figure 120 online).

In the *Gamme du Cor à Pistons* contained in the expanded edition of Mengal's *Méthode* (Paris, *ca.* 1840, 50), the author suggests performing C#, D, and D# using *falsetto* and playing the a-flat as an open note, "barely raising the sound with the lips," as stated much earlier by Duvernoy (1799, 24). Fétis (1837, 72) notes this problem with the two-valve horn and suggests introducing a third two-tone valve (see below, p. 254). Without this third valve, the player had to combine the use of the valves and the hand (closing the bell "*à trois quarts*") or put on a different crook.

In the first half of the nineteenth century, French and Belgian instrumentalists mostly preferred horns with two valves, to which the first methods for valved models were also dedicated. Numerous models with two valves by French or Belgian makers such as Halary, Goudot, Gautrot, Charles-Joseph and Alphonse Sax, Michel Rivet, Charles Mahillon, and others have survived (see Figures 121 and 122). Rare examples by English builders such as Thomas Percival and Charles Pace (London, 1830–1834) (see *The Harmonicon*, 8, 1830, 320), are documented as well.[12] There are also a few

[11] The a-flat must be performed open as for natural horn by lowering the a by one semitone (first and second valves pressed and bell partially closed). The D-flat is "always defective despite the joint action of the pistons and the hand in the bell. Only an experienced artist can play it in a satisfactory way" (Kastner 1844, 14, "Tablature du cor à 2 pistons").

[12] For an item by the latter maker see http://museumcollections.rcm.ac.uk/collection/Details/collect/1258.

Figure 121. Goudot jeune, two-valve horn, 1842.

Figure 122. Two-valve horn, from a rare English version of Gounod's *Méthode*.

surviving German (Johann Gottfried Kersten, Michael Saurle) and Italian instruments (anonymous horn in the Museo della Musica in Bologna and the one by Apparuti mentioned below). As for North America, in *Dodworth's Brass Band School* (New York, 1853), the horn in E-flat reproduced on p. 22 still has two valves, but in the 1880 Busch & Dodworth band list of instruments, a three-valve "Improved French Horn in F with double movable slide for E, E-flat and D, or Pistons or Rotary valve" is also included.

It is also significant that the author of the "Horn" entry in the first edition of the *Dictionary of Music and Musicians* edited by George Grove (I, 1879, 747), after having dealt extensively with the natural horn, only briefly addresses the valved model, including a picture of a French instrument with only two Périnet pistons; on the other hand, in circa 1881, Charles Roth of Strasbourg constructed horns with F and E-flat crooks with only two rotating valves (see Figure 123 online).

We have already seen that the introduction of the third valve on the horn was thanks to Christian Friedrich Sattler of Leipzig, and this is authoritatively confirmed by Chladni (1821, 398). This text also mentions the compass of Sattler's instrument, confirming that it had a one-and-a-half-tone third valve (see also Schreiber 1938, 179).

TWO UNCONVENTIONAL THIRD VALVES

Fétis (1837, 72) in emphasizing the shortcomings of the two-valve horn, states that he hopes that a third valve ("adopted in Germany, but not in France") will be introduced, which he suggests should lower the pitch by two tones. This experiment is actually known to have existed (Heyde 1987a, 81), even though we do not know of fingering tables contemplating it, nor surviving specimens with this feature (however, a two-tone slide could have later been replaced by the usual tone-and-a-half one). It could be observed that this two-tone valve would be particularly effective on the G horn, commonly used in France, on which it became possible to obtain the following keys with three valves (two tones, one semitone, one tone): G, F (t), E (t + st), E-flat (2t), D (2t + st), that is, all the keys usually used by the French *cor solo*, and occasionally also G-flat (st), C# (2t + t), and C (2t + st + t).

A far more unusual solution was initially adopted for some time in Germany in the mid-1830s with the application of two different semitone valves, the usual one for lowering C to B and another one that was a little longer to shift from B-flat (the common one-tone valve) to A. Actually, the second semitone should be, in terms of the air column, a little bit "longer" than the C–B semitone, so that the series of harmonics obtained is in tune and not slightly sharp, as would occur using the other semitone valve.[13] The advantage obtained is actually rather limited if one considers the notes that are lost in the lower register without a valve for the minor third, and indeed it was soon given up in favor of the usual system, as accurately reported by Weber (1835, 92–93). Once again, the aforementioned system is not documented by any surviving specimens. However, unusual slide length, as Fétis's two-tone slide, is difficult to trace back on preserved items, since a later replacement with a usual one is always possible.[14]

Some clues suggest that the model was conceived by C. A. Müller of Mainz, given his acquaintance with Gottfried Weber (1779–1839), the author of the article mentioned above, and given their mutual collaboration with the firm Schott of Mainz; for the latter company, Müller built instruments and Weber edited the magazine *Cäcilia*, which contained the reported text. If this hypothesis is correct, then the alleged attribution of the invention of the third valve to Müller (see Weber 1835, 104) could be traced back to a simple misunderstanding. As erroneous as it may seem in general terms with reference to the third-valve invention, it would be fitting enough if referred to this particular valve system.

TWO VIENNESE PRICE LISTS

To give an idea of the variety of horns on the market, and of their diffusion, we examined three price lists from Tuerlinckx, Schott, and Saurle in Chapter 16 (p. 155). The last one, which is a little more recent than the others (from the early 1830s, as it seems), already offers two valve instruments and lists their respective prices (for information on the currency, see online, "The value of money"):

d) a valve horn ("ein gromatisches Horn") with all terminal crooks, from high to low B-flat (55 fl.);

e) a valve horn ("ein gromatisches Horn") in F with crooks for E, E-flat, D and C that all fit into the slide sockets (50 fl.).

---

[13] As is common knowledge, the issue still exists today when two valves are pressed down together, especially the second and third valves, which gives a sharp result.

[14] Let us mention here two further unusual specimens: a horn made by J. G. Moritz in the Berlin museum (No. 4366) and an anonymous one in Dick Martz's collection (http://rjmartz.com/horns/anon/anon.htm). Both are supplied with five crooks and valve slides of one tone, one semitone, one tone (the latter a bit longer than the other one-tone crook). Possibly (with F crook): F, E (st), E-flat (t), D (t + st), Db (t + longer t), C (t + st + longer t).

We now add two other sources of this type, related to the most famous makers in Vienna, Joseph Felix Riedl and Leopold Uhlmann. The first of the two lists, Riedl's (copy in I-BGc), dates back to somewhat before 1835, the year in which he introduced the rotary valves that are neither listed nor illustrated here (the ones pictured are all Viennese valves):

> 1 pair of natural horns with all their respective crooks, mouthpiece and shanks, soldered in silver 110 CM (*Conventions-Münze*)

Among the horns "with no valves or keys," namely *Inventionshorns*, there are still six different models, at 70, 60, and 40 CM each pair (attested by specimens in museums and private collections with tuning slides and crooks marked "I" and "II").

The Uhlmann catalog dates back to 1848 at the latest (see Heyde 1987a, Abb. 34–35) and lists the following items among the "chromatic piston instruments":

Horn in C with nickel silver pistons and sleeves (60 fCM)
Horn with nickel silver pistons and sleeves [10 crooks][15] (70 fCM)
Horn with silver pistons and sleeves (120 fCM)

The other "chromatic instruments" included "a bass horn in C, with 4 crooks, in B-flat, A, A-flat, G, and to be used in place of the horn" (36 fCM), likely for use in bands. Obviously, Uhlmann also offered natural horns: one "in C alto with 10 crooks" from high B-flat to low B-flat (30 fCM) and one in "high Bb with master crook and 9 crooks" from A to low Sib (40 fCM).

---

[15] Here, there is certainly a typo in the original text: "10 crooks" is found on the line above, but it obviously concerns the more expensive of the two horns, the 70 fCM one. This is supported by the image of the 60 fCM instrument, which mentions only five crooks, from E to low B-flat (which implies that the remaining five higher crooks cost 10 fCM).

22

REPORTS BY CONTEMPORARIES

After reviewing the main inventions related to the valves, we now move on to three reports on the early history of these mechanisms. They are based on information provided by professionals (the article by Fétis) or are written by them (Wieprecht and Meifred). Therefore, they are perhaps less objective than Spontini's aforementioned testimony; nevertheless, they are firsthand and very early evidence, certainly useful for historical reconstruction. In addition, a long essay by Julius Rühlmann, a trombonist from Dresden, is also summarized here, as he offers an elaborate critique of the different valve systems in use at the mid-century, declaring himself already totally in favor of the rotary valves.

AN EARLY DESCRIPTION BY FÉTIS (1827)

Fétis claims that Stölzel, after having invented the *cor à pistons* in 1815–1816, submitted his idea to Schlott in Berlin to have it developed, and that the object of his invention was box valves (Fétis 1827, 156):

> His invention consisted of two small boxes placed on the master crook, each containing a perforated brass element [piston] resting on a spiral spring. As long as the spring was at rest, the brass piece remained pushed upward, so that the holes did not coincide with those of the additional tubes designed to lower the pitch of one, two or three semitones; but when the fingers pushed the piston, the holes coincided allowing the air to circulate, and the effect was guaranteed.

He adds that the great horn player Christoph Schunke (1791–1856) from Karlsruhe, who was in Berlin when Stölzel presented his invention, invited a maker in his city, Friederich Wilhelm Schuster (1798–1873), to reproduce it. The latter, following

Stölzel's example, applied the mechanism to the tuning slide of a *cor solo*, with a series of disadvantages reported in detail by Fétis. The main one was that, with this model, only the keys produced with the valves (F, E, E-flat, and D) could be obtained, since the tuning slide was designed to accommodate the two pistons and therefore not interchangeable. Therefore, the hornist could not use the higher pitches (Bb–A–G) and lower pitches (low C and B-flat) and was forced to transpose parts written for these crooks. The constant use of the valves also changed the natural sound of the horn and since the tuning slide had to be moved to tune the instrument, the hand operating the valves had to change position too, making everything less comfortable. Fétis also offers the clearest representation known of this device, which matches that of a mechanism by this maker preserved in Brussels (inv. 1310, reproduced in Baines 1976, plate XIII/3). But, as can sometimes happily happen, by the time this chapter was long completed, we learned of Ulrich Hübner's discovery and acquisition of a genuine Schuster horn fitted with these valves.

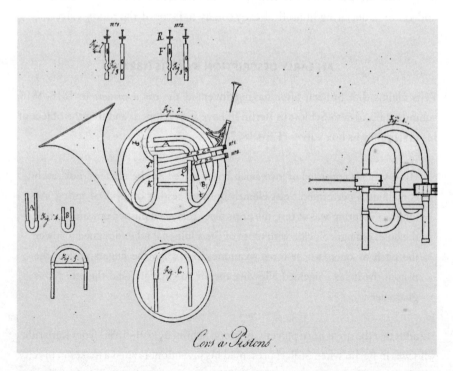

Figure 124. The horn by Labbaye (left), and the Stölzel box valves imitated by Schuster (right).

Figure 125. F. W. Schuster, horn with square valves, Karlsruhe, *ca.* 1850.

The next to enter the scene is Joseph-Émile Meifred (1791–1867), a horn player at the Opéra and in the musical chapel of the French king, who also undertook a practical training in manufacturing at the school of arts and craftsmanship of Châlons-en-Champagne.[1] He wanted the valves applied on the main tube of the instrument, bringing the tuning slide back to its original function, so that the crooks were once again available for changing keys. Fétis also reports that the manufacturer who brought Meifred's ideas to life was the Parisian builder Labbaye, who exhibited his horn at the Exhibition of Industrial Products in 1827. On this model, the highest key was G, which was obtained by pushing the slides to the end (Fétis 1827, 159); he also assesses that this horn "retains the properties of the old instrument and adds all the missing ones." In other words, the player could use the valves to make the horn fully chromatic or to quickly change keys and use the hand technique for the remainder (see online, "Dauprat and the *cor à pistons*," and Figure 126 online).

[1] For more information about Meifred, we draw readers' attention on his biography by Frédréric Champlon, which can be found at https://patrimoine.gadz.org/gadz/meifred.htm.

THE PERSONAL RECOLLECTIONS OF WIEPRECHT

A well-known version of the following story originated with Wilhelm Wieprecht. It was published in the aforementioned 1845 issue of the *Berliner Musikalische Zeitung*, translated into French by Kastner (1848, 190, fn.), and finally reprinted in Kalkbrenner (1882, 89–91).

Wieprecht began by challenging the originality of the piston valves used by Adolphe Sax and provides his personal recollection of the early history of the valves. He at first credits the invention to both Blühmel and Stölzel, adding that although he knew both personally, he was unable to determine to whom the original idea should be assigned. However, the rest of Wieprecht's detailed narration seems much less objective, probably because of his personal involvement in the affair and his close relationship with Stölzel and with the Berlin makers in general. This raises some doubts about the reliability of some points of his report: namely (a) the attribution of both the oldest models of valves to Stölzel, even though one must have been the work of Blühmel, otherwise there would have been no reason for the former to pay the latter; (b) the fact that Blühmel is mentioned only as the inventor of the rotary valves presented in 1828; (c) the fact that he gave part of the sum to pay off Blühmel, as documented by the aforementioned letter by Spontini; and finally, (d) his personal interest in his own pin capsule valves (*Steckerbüchsen-ventile*, or *Berliner Pumpenventile*). Notwithstanding all of this, the remainder of his narration proves extremely useful for better evaluating the events we are dealing with (Wieprecht 1845a, [3]):

> In the year 1816 or 1817, Stölzel appeared in Berlin with a three-valve chromatic horn.[2] He declared himself the inventor of this instrument and obtained a ten-year privilege for the territory of the Prussian monarchy. The art connoisseur Count Bruhl, who was superintendent of the royal theaters at the time, hired him as a horn player in the royal chapel. In order to use his ten-year privilege, he established a relationship with the instrument makers Griessling & Schlott. Valve instruments of all kinds were built by these makers, but unfortunately they were very weak in sonority and therefore initially had little success.

---

[2] This is evidently an error, since Stölzel's horn, unequivocally described by Bierey (see Chapter 20, p. 228), was equipped with two valves. Nor does it seem possible, if it did have three, that this could have been ignored in the paperwork for his request for a patent.

Stölzel had made several attempts to perfect the valves, such as with the box piston valves (*Schiebe-kastenventile*)[3] in which the air moves along a circular path. These proved impractical, however, and he eventually returned to tubular valves (*Röhren-Schiebe-ventile*).

All the musicians in Berlin were decidedly opposed to the discovery. Abroad, however, above all in Russia, France, and here and there also in the Austrian states, it was well received. I went to the workshop of Griessling and Schlott daily and personally supervised some improvements of the external construction of the instruments.

The period of the patent was about to expire and the competitors could therefore go about their work undisturbed when the bandsman Blühmel arrived from Silesia in 1828 and presented the first conical rotary valves (*konische Drehbüchsenventile*).

He requested a privilege but was rejected because one had previously been given to Stölzel for a similar mechanism. Blühmel produced documents that proved Stölzel had bought the invention from him ten years before; however, it was not possible to conclusively ascertain how true this was, and Stölzel remains therefore as the first creator of chromatic brass instruments in the eyes of the world.

Blühmel's conical devices differed only externally from Stölzel's first box piston valves (*Schiebe-Kasten-Ventile*), while their internal construction was the same, and therefore both represent the essence of the discovery.

When comparing these inventions to one other, Blühmel's valves are preferable owing to the strength and evenness of sound that they provide since the air-stream runs within a loop of tubing without obstacles and the sound waves remain intact in the instrument. This does not happen in Stölzel's tubular valves, which break the path at a right angle, even though the latter offers many advantages in terms of practicality. To combine both properties, the beautiful sound and the ease of execution, I transformed the rotary valves into pin capsule-valves (*Steckerbüchsenventile*), and with this new tool, chromatic instruments soon became common in our military bands, especially cavalry bands.[4] Another

---

[3] This assessment, and even more the one that follows a few lines later ("Stölzel's first box piston valves"), confirm the opinion that the invention of the box valves is likely attributable to Stölzel and that of the tubular valves to Blühmel.

[4] According to Baines 1976, 224, in 1837, the "B-Hornists" of the Prussian Jäger Guards were already supplied with horns in high B-flat.

valid improvement was made by a man from Prague, whose name is however unknown to me. He made Blühmel's rotary valve smaller and equipped it with a spiral spring (*Spiralfeder-Druckmaschine*),[5] thus giving this rotating mechanism an appropriate ease of execution. In any case, these valves found little success in military use because they proved too fragile. Because of this, my perfected pin valves are preferable owing to their simple and durable casing.

Apart from his aforementioned partiality, Wieprecht is particularly instructive with regard to the main valve models that had been experimented on at the time when he was writing: the box and tubular valves, both deceptively attributed to Stölzel; Blühmel's conical rotary valves; the pin valves of his design; and finally the rotary valves invented by "a man from Prague," obviously the well-known Joseph Kail (see Heyde 1987a, 30), who constantly collaborated with the company of J. Riedl, the first maker of the modern rotary valve.

A THOROUGH SURVEY BY MEIFRED

The frequently cited Meifred provides us with another relevant narration, which dates back to 1851. Meifred's text contains an update of the facts, partially those involving him personally, reported in Fétis (1827). He also presents a detailed survey of the various types of valves built up until the mid-nineteenth century, evaluated from the standpoint of a French instrumentalist and teacher, a staunch supporter of their validity, and the principal valve experimenter in Paris (see Figure 127).

Meifred talks about the first *trompette aux pistons* Spontini sent to Paris in circa 1826 ("pistons" is used here as an overall synonym for valves) in order to introduce the instrument to the Opéra musicians. He adds that these pistons did not allow the air to follow along a direct path owing to various "corners" (fig. 1 of Meifred's table, Figure 127). These "corners" deprived the instrument of its peculiar color and sound, so it could no longer be considered a trumpet but rather a new instrument with new sonic capabilities. In 1827, Dauprat and Halary asked that a box-valve horn (*boites rectangulaires*) (fig. 2 of Figure 127) be sent from Germany, and Spontini sent them a horn by Schuster of Karlsruhe, which had an air path that was less tortuous. The instrument, pitched in F, could also play in the additional

---

[5] This was a true spiral spring, like the ones used in old clocks. Later, it would become the standard type for these instruments (see online, "On spiral springs").

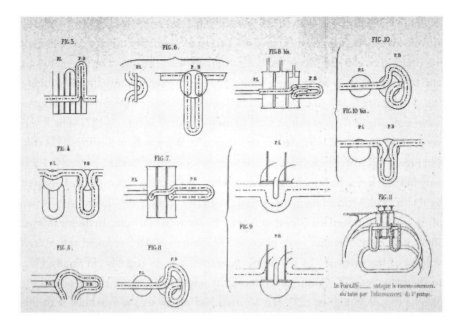

Figure 127. J. E. Meifred, *Notice sur la fabrication . . .*, 1851, table.

keys (*tons fictifs*) of E, E-flat, and D, which were obtainable using the two valves. However, the instrument was heavy and lacked the sound quality offered by crooks, so Dauprat decided not to play it (see also Morley-Pegge 1973, 34).

Meifred boasted having suggested that Halary apply the valve slides (*coulisses*) in 1827—already experimented by Pini, as seen—and design the instrument in a more "elegant" shape, a model that was then copied by other makers. However, this horn did not have all the qualities he desired and required some improvements to allow the air to circulate more freely within the instrument.

In 1832, the double-piston system was imported to Paris (fig. 3 in Figure 127), but its tubing involved a series of broken and narrow curves, to the detriment of the acoustic properties. In that same year, Riedl's rotary valves entered the scene (fig. 4 in Figure 127). These valves did not have angles and offered a more linear path to the tubes connected with the valve mechanism, but they were very expensive to make, so they did not enter in general use, at least in France. In 1833, Arsène Deshays invented the *valvules ou clapets*, which "change the path of the air without the need for any additional tubing" (Meifred 1851, 8), a delicate mechanism based on two shutting doors that is not clearly illustrated in Meifred (fig. 5 in Figure 127) but is clarified by a technical drawing provided in Dumoulin (2006, 80) (see Figure 128 online).

In 1835, Halary introduced the *plaques mobiles* system, based on the rotary movement of a perforated disk to which two short U-shaped tubes were soldered; the rotation of the disk made the holes coincide with the ones that divert the air into the valve tubing, while in rest position, the air passed through the main tubing (fig. 6 in Figure 127). On October 27, 1838, Périnet obtained the patent for his *gros piston sans angles* ("great piston without angles," fig. 7 in Figure 127), which was very similar in operation to the one introduced by Wieprecht in Berlin in 1834 (fig. 8 in Figure 127). Meifred claims to have seen Wieprecht's "Berlin" pistons in Paris only in 1840, but to be unable to ascertain whether Périnet's invention was inspired by that model. Meifred maintained that the Périnet piston was the more effective of the two, and indeed the course of history has proven him right. In the meantime, some new developments took place in 1842, when Halary reduced the overall volume of the invention by designing new straight paths (fig. 8bis in Figure 127). In the same year, M. Coëffet introduced the *soupapes ou clapets* that replaced the pistons (fig. 9 in Figure 127), but Meifred had never seen horns built with this system and did not express judgments in this regard. Another piston valve, similar to the Berlin one, was experimented with by Sax in 1843 on a three-valve horn (figs. 10 and 10bis in Figure 127), but this instrument was much heavier and duller in sound. Finally, Halary equipped the instrument with the third ascending valve (fig. 11 in Figure 127), which would prove to be particularly successful in the near future (see Chapter 24, p. 283). Lastly, Meifred stressed that the valve horn should not eliminate the stopped notes, and that it was an anomaly to use both natural and valve horn in one and the same orchestra.

RÜHLMANN'S OPINION

Julius Rühlmann (1816–1877), a trombonist in the Dresden court orchestra, in turn offered an authoritative evaluation of the main systems in use in German countries in an 1851 text, which does not reveal any partiality of the kind we lamented in Wieprecht's account. He praised the new possibilities offered by the adoption of the valves, stated that he hoped that key systems from the low brass instruments would be abandoned completely, and declared the hand-horn technique obsolete and to be used only for compositions expressly written for it.

Rühlmann's contribution included his pioneering position in favor of rotary valves and a careful description of the three valve systems that he considered worth mentioning: (1) the *Büchsenventile*, that is, the Stölzel valves; (2) the *Röhren-*,

Schub-, or *Hebelventile*, that is, the Viennese valves; and (3) the *Cylinder-* or *Drehventile*, that is, the rotary valves, the most reliable in his opinion.

Rühlmann later returned to the same subject in another paper in 1870 (and in a little-known sequel in the 1872–1873 issue of the same magazine, *NZfM*), reaffirming his position from twenty years earlier and adding that in recent times, a fourth type of valve had been introduced, the ascending valve, although it had not received much notice, at least in the German countries.

In the last part of this essay (Rühlmann 1870, 318–320, 325), he offers a very detailed description of the Stölzel valve, reminds readers that Sattler was the one to add the third valve, and concludes by remarking on the main disadvantage of the Stölzel system, namely the fact that the spiral spring tended to deteriorate. C. A. Müller from Mainz worked on a solution for the problem. In 1830, he came up with the idea of using clock springs (actually, Uhlmann of Vienna may have thought of the idea first) and, instead of pistons, two short perforated tubes: "These airtight tubes that move up and down inside the main tubing constitute the second category of valves," the "*Röhren- oder Schubventile*," that is, the Viennese valves. Here, the author evidently refers to the refinement of the *Neumainzer Maschine* (Chapter 21, p. 245), as the Viennese valve had already existed since 1823. Finally, Rühlmann reports that some German makers, and at the same time apparently also Sax Jr. in Paris, came around to the idea of the rotary valve, of which he also gives a detailed description, in 1840.

The French, English, and Belgian players preferred pistons (in particular the *Büchsenventile*) to rotary valves, since for trumpets, trombones, and tubas these valves are in fact preferable, but the same cannot be said for the horn. If the French, as Rühlmann stated, looked down on the so-called *genre allemand* (as they define rotary valves), this was because of the misconception that they were more difficult to move and came to a complete stop more slowly. They were indeed more expensive than pistons, which incidentally have a fuller sound, but rotary valves guarantee easier and more secure movement.

Rühlmann then paid fleeting attention to Viennese valves, repeating that there is a right-angled path in the tubing, and moved on to praise all the advantages of rotary valves. He then wondered if they are placed at the appropriate point in the tubing and remarks that Červený of Königsgrätz (the Czech Hradec Králové) might have found an additional solution with the *Tonwechselmaschine*, a sort of multiple diverter designed in 1846, which had not yet met with much acclaim (see Figure 129 online).

23

EARLY MUSIC LITERATURE

The first music conceived for the valve horn was probably written by Stölzel himself, but it has not survived. The same may be said for the *Variationen und ein Concert für das von Stölzel erfundene chromatische Horn*, composed in 1817 by Friedrich Wilhelm Berner (1780–1827),[1] the first piece documented for the new instrument. It was performed in Berlin on July 1, 1818 (*AMZ* 1818, 597).

The *AMZ* (November 1818, 790–791) informs us that on October 16, 1818, a concerto for four horns by Georg Abraham Schneider (1770–1839) was first performed in Berlin.[2] This concerto had a first horn part to be played on a chromatic instrument (by F. Bode of Schwerin), while the other three (Andreas Schunke,[3] Heinrich Lenss, and a certain Pfaffe) were performed on natural horns. The concert was repeated on November 7 and December 14—for the third performance, the valve horn part was performed by Bliesener, from Berlin—while the last documented performance took place in 1825 with Andreas Schunke (valve horn), his sons Julius and Carl, and Heinrich Lenss. According to the publisher Robert Ostermayer, this concerto is the one preserved in the library of Darmstadt, which he recently published.[4]

---

[1] This information is reported in the biography of the composer (Berner) published in the journal *Eutonia, eine hauptsächlich pädagogische Musik-Zeitschrift*, Breslau, Grüson, 1829, I, 304. The same information is also reported in Hoffmann 1830, 32 "Für das von Stölzel erfundene chromatische Horn, Variationen und ein Konzert. 1817."

[2] See http://www.french-horn.net/index.php/biographien/93-georg-abraham-schneider.html.

[3] The Schunke family, whose founder was Johann Gottfried, counted a great number of hornists over the course of four generations (see also Fitzpatrick 1970, 214–215). Among them, the first to be particularly interested in the valve horn was Christoph (active in Karlsruhe), the same hornist who actively devoted himself to the improvement of the valves (Fétis 1827, 157).

[4] See http://www.corno.de/shop/concertos/Horns-orchestra/rom039.html?XTCsid=1d 5d57aeedb3861f211f37e4ee599f18; according to Ericson (http://www.public.asu.edu/~jqerics/vh_first_works.htm): "The work itself would appear to have be written for natural horns; the first part, while playable on the natural horn, is nevertheless a soloistic, obbligato line compared to the other horn parts, and thus may have been intended to demonstrate the unique ability of the valved horn to perform these lines without stopped notes."

Another example—the music has again been lost—is the Concerto for Three Horns by "a hornist named Lenss" (Heinrich?), which premiered on November 26, 1819; one of the Schunke brothers (Andreas) performed the chromatic horn part, as reported in *AMZ* (December 1819, col. 874).

In Italy, a very early appearance of the valve horn took place in the presence of the duchess of Parma, Marie Louise of Habsburg, on December 21, 1821, when Luigi Pini played his new instrument. The enterprise was repeated on June 26, 1823 at the Milan Conservatory (see Chapter 21, p. 238) with a fair amount of success, but no composition by this horn player is known to have survived either.

Back in Berlin, on January 11, 1823, a Septett by Nithard (?), with four horns, one of which was chromatic, valve tenor horn, clarinet, and trumpet, was performed by Belke ("chromatic tenor horn"), Ludging ("clarionet obligato"), Bogans (probably Bagans, "single trumpet obligato"), and then Glaseman ("chromatic French horn"), Blusenn, Plaffer, and Koppfasack ("french horns").[5]

On March 9, 1828, the Parisian public had the opportunity to listen to the valve horn for the first time in the inaugural concert of the Société des Concerts, with a solo composed and performed by Meifred (Snedeker 1994, 7), whom we have repeatedly mentioned and to whom we will return.

As far as England is concerned, we have no information regarding solo performances on the valve horn until 1835, the year when Lewy performed in London with his chromatic horn, as reported by *The Court Magazine*.[6] Later on, there was a performance by Lewy on the chromatic horn and by Puzzi on the natural horn: an anonymous reporter was impressed by Lewy, although the performance of Puzzi was also pleasant and admirable.[7]

---

[5] See the *London Quarterly Musical Magazine and Review*, 5 (1823), 408. The same announcement also reports that the son of a certain Griebel (?), a boy of twelve years, played the horn masterfully.

[6] *The Court Magazine* (7 (1835), 44): "On the 25th ult. [May 1835] Mr. Eliason's concert took place at the residence of Dr. Elliotson, in Conduit-street."

[7] *The Court Magazine* (7 (1835), 88): "Mr. Lewy – We call the attention of our readers to the extraordinary performances of this gentleman upon the chromatic horn. For power, effect, firmness of embouchure, and the expression of pathos and feeling on this most difficult of instruments, Mr. Lewy has never been surpassed. Sig. Puzzi, with his pure quality of tone and beautiful cantabile, wins our delight and admiration; but Mr. Lewy, by the passionate character be imparts to his notes, and by his power of modulation, kindles emotions which, till now, we did not think his instrument capable of producing, except in orchestral combinations. In our next, we purpose giving a description of the chromatic horn."

SCHUBERT'S SONGS: A CASE STUDY

See online.

See Table 15 online, "Provisional list of the earliest solo performances with chromatic horn (not including repetitions)," and online, "An exception for Vivier."

INTRODUCTION INTO THE ORCHESTRA

The first unquestionable appearance of the valve horn in the orchestra is found in the opera *La Juive* (1835) by J.-F. Halévy (Rogan 1996, 61) (see Musical example 67 online). Four hornists are called for in some parts of the composition, while, according to the original score, the use of the valves is required from the second pair only. Castil-Blaze (1855, II, 347), identifies the original players as Duvernoy and Meifred. However, as Duvernoy would have been sixty-nine years old at that date, it is fair to assume that this was his homonymous nephew (cf. *Annuaire* 1833, 219). In any case, the composer's intention was to have two instrumentalists play the *cors simples* (natural hand horns) and two the *cors à pistons*.

Halevy also considers the possibility of replacing one of the *cor à pistons* with an ordinary horn and changing its key (see full score, ed. Schlesinger, Paris, n.d. [1835], "Introduction," 38): "The Es in the second horn are written for a valve horn; if there is none in the orchestra, the second horn will have to change to C." In any case, the valve horns are used in a similar way to the aforementioned examples, as chromatic instruments in the middle-low register where the hand horn is not very effective. The crooks are not abandoned (even on the *cor à pistons*), and the stopped sounds are more relevant from the esthetic point of view, since hand stopping is non-compulsory, but adopted when requested by the composer.

On the other hand, we have seen that in 1823 Spontini began to send valve instruments from Berlin to Paris, and in particular horns for Dauprat. As early as 1827, valve trumpets were used in *Macbeth* by Hippolyte Chelard (1789–1861), and in 1830, Berlioz used a pair of *cornet à pistons* in his *Symphonie Fantastique*.

In terms of the way that valves were used, we have seen they were not expected to be exploited as they are today. The tradition of the hand horn and the predilection for its multifaceted timbre, resulting from the alternation of open and closed sounds, prevented composers and horn players from unconditionally accepting the solely "open" sound of the valve instrument.

Therefore, two hybrid techniques for use of the valve horn seem to have been adopted: one in which the valves are used in place of crooks, and the remainder is played as if the instrument was a hand horn; and another that calls for an episodic use of the stopped notes. This second technique required that new symbols be adopted in order to designate which notes should be stopped. A graphic solution (the sign "+"), which is probably attributable to Wagner and his Dresden horn player, Joseph Rudolph Lewy, was devised. All this further justifies the adoption of the F valve horn, which is the most comfortable and effective, as well as the most sonorous, for the dual exploitation of the hand and valve horn (see Chaussier 1889, 14).

A few scores written in the era of the hand horn were later revised by the authors themselves, this time explicitly indicating the use of the hand technique. An example can be found in the 1845 Bärenreiter printed edition of the *Symphonie Fantastique* (1830) by Berlioz, who notes that the B-flat basso horns in the fourth movement should "faites les sons bouchés avec la main sans employer les cylindres" (play these notes stopped with the hand, without using the valves). Thus, when the piece was originally written in 1830 there was no need to indicate the stopped sounds, but this had become compulsory in 1845.

EARLY HANDBOOKS FOR "CHROMATIC HORN"

The adoption of the valve instrument was favored, as already seen, by the possibility of performing a complete chromatic scale in the low register, an operation that was indeed quite difficult on the hand horn. Therefore, even orchestral players progressively switched over to the new instrument, as made apparent by the publication of handbooks for natural horn that also include a short section on the valve instrument. Of these, the oldest were those by Dauprat (1828), Nemetz (1829), and Meifred (1829b; dedicated in particular to composers).

Full instruction books written only for the valve horn have their feasible forerunner in Meifred's *Première étude* of 1829 (see Figure 130 online);[8] then there is a handbook written by none other than Charles Gounod (*ca.* 1839), followed by methods by Meifred (1840), Kastner (1844), Haumuller (J. A. Hanmüller) (1844), and numerous others listed in Table 16 online (many French treatises are now available on IMSLP

---

[8] The front page of the latter, with the illustration of a two Stölzel valve horn, together with praise of the maker Antoine Halary, has been included in a recent work (Mürner 2016, 224–225, figs. 1, 2), but without further details.

owing to a monumental contribution by user "Puzzi22"). A detailed scrutiny of all these methods and of those later published in Paris can be found in Snedeker (2021).

In addition to these manuals, we should mention two more: the expanded edition of Mengal's handbook of 1835 with a one-page section on the valve horn (*ca.* 1840), and a brief valve-horn method by Asioli (1840). It seems that only a single copy of each of the latter two volumes has survived.

In 1835, Jean-Baptiste Mengal published *Méthode de cor*, focused on the natural instrument, including a picture of a *cor solo* very similar to the one in Duvernoy's *Méthode*. But in the later reprint of the same text (*ca.* 1840) (see Figure 131 online), a page containing a "*Gamme du cor à pistons*" together with the illustration of a two-valve horn and the respective fingering table was added. This very model, equipped with two Stölzel pistons, is also reproduced in Kastner 1844, and in Haumuller 1844, and all of these reproductions may be based on the model (Raoux?) shown in Gounod's handbook of 1839 (for the latter see Figure 122, p. 253).

The *Transunto dei principj elementari di musica e breve metodo per corno a macchina* by Bonifacio Asioli deserves its own treatment (see Figure 132 online). In this short handbook (one of a series dedicated almost to every principal instrument), the same image of the Riedl and Kail valve horn reproduced in Nemetz's handbook is included (see Figure 107 online). This provides further confirmation of the aforementioned close relationship between Vienna and Milan, even though in this case the name of the maker (Riedl) was erased.

It is to Charles Gounod that we owe, as mentioned, the first extensive method entirely dedicated to the valve horn. Wondering about the reasons for the great French composer's publication about an instrument not explicitly called for in his music, Daniel Allenbach (2015, 205) brilliantly guessed that it may have been because Gounod had recently been awarded the Prix de Rome (1839). The illustrious recognition may in fact have inspired maker and musician Marcel-Auguste Raoux (1795–1871) to commission the young composer of the aforementioned publication to aid in the production of his company's horns.[9] The entire operation may have been accelerated by the imminent publication of a handbook by Meifred, who supported the competing manufacturer Antoine Halary. The race for primacy would thus also explain the hasty publication and considerable

[9] In the same year, 1839, Gounod also published *Six Mélodies pour le cor à pistons avec piano* dedicated to Marcel-Auguste Raoux.

number of errors. Furthermore, Allenbach identifies the instrument depicted (and therefore also that pictured in the other three methods mentioned) as a horn by Raoux (cf. Figure 122, p. 253).

The contemporary *Méthode pour le cor chromatique ou à pistons* by Meifred 1840 (see Snedecker 2006), also entirely dedicated to the chromatic horn, in turn contains a depiction of the horn with two rotating valves that had been conceived not long prior by Antoine Halary. The identification of a surviving specimen of this was recently reported.[10]

Finally, the studies for horn solo published in 1833 by Georg Kopprasch (fl. 1800–*ca.* 1850) deserve mention. Some of the sixty studies of the op. 6 for "Cor-Basse / second Cor," still part of the study repertoire of many horn players today, suggest a performance with the chromatic instrument, probable fruit of the

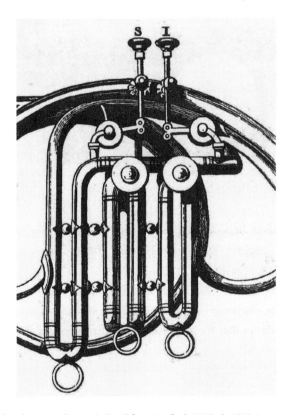

Figure 133. Halary horn, mechanism's detail from Meifred, *Méthode*, 1840, i.

[10] The two slides of these valves look identical, but part of the tubing on the second one is bent backwards, so that what we see from the front is a double U with a ring at its base that is soldered to the tube to facilitate extraction.

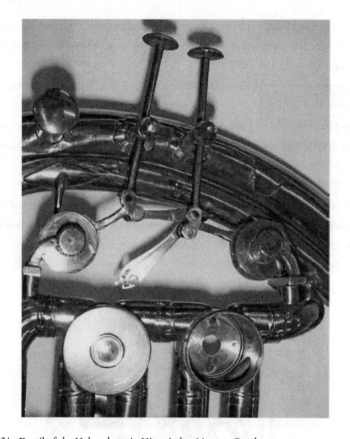

Figure 134. Detail of the Halary horn in Historisches Museum Basel.

direct acquaintance between Kopprasch and Stölzel in Berlin (see Ericson's website, "The original Kopprasch Etudes," https://www.public.asu.edu/~jqerics/original_kopprasch.htm).

Starting in the early 1850s, despite the discordant opinions on the use of the valves that will be discussed later, the publication of manuals mainly intended for the valve horn shows that the way was eventually paved for the new chromatic instrument.

A REVERSED "CHIRALITY"

With the success of the valves, new advocates of the recent model, which, eliminating the unique technique of the hand horn, could be learned and played by anyone who had practiced any other brass instrument, were acquired. Therefore, horns with right-hand mechanisms, as usual in almost all other valve instruments, began to be made available. Consequently, their bells faced left, the opposite direction with respect to the usual—although not exclusive—one for the hand horn.[11] An interesting paper by Richard J. Martz about this subject appeared in *HBSJ* (2003). He examined a substantial number of specimens, both natural and valve horns, which were made to be held with the right hand, thus documenting that it was possible to play in a position that mirrored the one most rooted in horn-playing tradition. In fact, not even the most authoritative natural horn teachers were so rigid as to force all the students to grip with their left hands (think of Duvernoy, Domnich, Dauprat, etc.). In fact, no exclusive approach was ever advocated in teaching in orchestral practice, despite the fact that this could possibly result in the bells of two horns facing each other.

Martz also reproduced two portraits of Italian hornists, Luigi Brizzi and Luigi Belloli—the latter of whom, identified via conjecture, is on the cover page of this book—which both show the instrumentalists with their horns on their left, albeit not during a performance, which makes these pieces of evidence somewhat less reliable.[12]

HAND HORN VS. VALVE HORN

We have already observed that the most immediate repercussions of the invention of the valves mainly occurred in the wind band where, thanks to the recent device, new instruments that could expand the repertoire were introduced. These instruments also allowed for a shorter apprenticeship in comparison with that of other natural instruments.

[11] Currently, no horns with right-handed sets of valves intended for orchestral use are on the market. However, in various countries, including Italy, they are common in bands and usually given to younger apprentices. They are generally pitched in E-flat with an F master slide, which is advantageous because the fingering is the same as on other band instruments.

[12] It is noteworthy that Luigi Brizzi (1737–1815) performed on a "baroque" horn at the end of the eighteenth century– that is, an instrument with no crooks and no master slide, narrow tubing and a bell slightly wider than the models from the first half of the century. On the other hand, the horn embraced by Belloli (?) is folded in two loops with tuning slide tubes that do not cross and left-handed owing to the position of the crook with respect to the body of the instrument. This type of instrument was built, for example, by Michael Saurle (see Chapter 16, Figures 74 and 75).

Acceptance in art music occurred much more slowly, however. In fact, professionals had to adapt to a new performing system, and the music already written for natural horn required performance techniques suited to that instrument.

Unlike the aforementioned authors of valve-horn handbooks, many others, especially some distinguished teachers, took against the new invention, as also occurred with some models of woodwind instruments (for example, think of the resistance toward the Müller clarinet or the Böhm flute). Many composers and concert reviewers were also opposed. On several occasions they rejected the invention, arguing that the hand horn, full of possibilities for different colors and sounds, was already effective and was perfectly sufficient as a solo instrument. Some examples, mainly limited to the German-language countries, are reported by Ahrens (1986); in his survey of the chromatic brass instruments, he summarizes the main arguments that were then made in favor of the hand horn as follows (Ahrens Engl. ed. 2008, 10):

First, there was the different sound of the valved instruments, to which for a long time the public could not or would not become accustomed. Second, there were the new techniques that soon expanded the scope of the instruments and did not correspond to the idiom of the classical horn and trumpet. And third, there was the new tone color that resulted when one gave to the trumpet or the horn a melody in the middle or low register and combined it with other instruments.

Opponents of the valves included teachers such as Joseph Fröhlich, who in 1834, in the contemporary most important historical account of the horn, aside from Gerber's written forty years earlier, totally ignored the invention, which was by then already widespread. A year later, the same attitude can be found in an explosive outburst in an article that appeared in the *NZfM* (1835) with the signature "C. Rdt, Ludwigslust." Here, the new valve instrument is deprecated and the "*Karlsruher Ventiler*" (the "valve man" of Karlsruhe), in all probability Andreas Schunke, is reproached for having abdicated his talents as an excellent natural horn player and devoted himself, instead, to the "monotony" of the new device. At most, the anonymous author of the article, most likely a skilled composer, states, use of the valve horn must be confined "to the role of the fourth player in the horn quartet" (see online, "Who is hiding behind the pseudonym C. Rdt?").

Another position of radical resistance to the misuse of the valves for older repertoire is found in an instrumentation book by Ferdinand Gleich (1816–1898), from which the following extensive quote is taken (Gleich 1853, 37):

As on the trumpet and the cornet, the invention of the valves has found a home on the horn. Although perhaps the valves have caused very little loss features in the sound for these instruments, quite the opposite is true for the horn, which has almost completely lost its noble character and, in place of its beautiful tone colour, has assumed a by no means enviable kinship with the bassoon. However, the horn is used by almost all modern composers: Meyerbeer in his last operas, Wagner in all his dramatic works and in others, R. Schumann in his symphonies, etc. It is regrettable, however, that the beautiful, noble, vaporous sound of the natural horn has almost disappeared from our orchestras with the introduction of the valves, since only some players consider it necessary to adopt it for the oldest compositions and especially in those written specifically for it. Most performers play everything with the valve horn and, moreover, transpose everything, each horn part, onto the F valve instrument, probably to spare the effort of replacing the crooks! For compositions that are intended and written for the valve horn, and that would be impossible to perform with the natural horn, this is certainly appropriate, but using it in Beethoven's and Weber's compositions is vandalism.

A further document that is overtly in favor of the natural horn but partially accepts use of the valves is found in the hitherto unknown *Metodo per corno da caccia sì semplice che a pistoni* (Manual for both natural and valve horn) by Luigi Frontori, published in Naples just before 1849 (p. 4) (see Figure 135 online):

Piston valves must therefore be used only to obtain the notes that are missing on the natural horn or in cases in which can they be played only with the greatest difficulty. Therefore, the player should try to avoid using the benefits of the three valves too frequently, especially in the high register, if there is no need for it, since in this way he will deprive the instrument of its unique value, which is that of the delicate sweetness of the stopped notes unobtainable with the use of the valves, or he will transform the soothing sound of the corno da caccia into the strident blast of trumpets and trombones.

The situation in France was in turn quite different. Here, the class of *cor cromatique* at the Paris Conservatoire was opened in 1833 and closed with Meifred's withdrawal in 1864. It was then essentially reopened by François Brémond (1844–1925) in 1897 and definitely reactivated only in 1902, while the hand horn continued to be studied, admired, and used extensively until the beginning of the last century (Morley-Pegge 1973, 3–5; see now Snedeker 2021, 176–189) (see also online, "The features of the sound of the natural horn").

A meaningful change in this regard comes from Chaussier (1889, 13), who still maintains at first that "the natural horn can not be eliminated from use without causing the most serious loss to a good performance of the pieces of the ancient masters." He adds, however, that even though the *cor à pistons* may have previously had some flaws, instrument makers had recently made great progress and so "a *cor à pistons* definitely possesses the same quality, the same beauty as a *cor simple*" (p. 11).

In France, therefore, instruments equipped with both valves and crooks remained in use longer than elsewhere, in particular the model called *cor sauterelle*, on which it was possible to transform a natural horn into a valve horn by adding a "valve mechanism" to the tuning slide. The instrument was available with two or three piston valves, and in the latter case the third valve could be either ascending or descending (see Figure 136). This solution, however, was not brought about by a preference for the tonal properties of each individual crook, since "French" horns with the ascending third valves were missing some keys (low C and B-flat, high A and B-flat) when the device was used as a simple substitute for the crooks.[13]

In any case, the prolonged preference for the hand horn in France is still documented in the twentieth century through compositions such as the famous *Villanelle* by Dukas (1906) or the *Pavane* (1910) by Ravel, to which we will return later (see Chapter 24, p. 286) (see online, Kalliwoda, op. 51, and Musical example 68 online).

BOTH HAND AND VALVE HORNS IN THE ORCHESTRA

In the period encompassing the forty central years of the century, concluding with the transformations that took place with Wagner's *Ring* (completed in 1874), new instruments and new instrumental techniques became part of an ever-increasing

---

[13] When the valve horn was used as a natural horn, the slides of each valve needed to be "fine-tuned" to the correct tuning pitch.

Figure 136. *Cor sauterelle* by M. A. Raoux, descending third valve, *ca.* 1850.

orchestra. In the case of the horn, the simultaneous presence of valve and natural instruments soon required alternative denominations, such as *natural horns, cors ordinaires, cors simples, Naturhörner,* and *corni semplici* on the one hand and *chromatic or valve horns, cors à pistons* (French generic term for valves), *Ventilhörner, corni a macchina,* and *corni a cilindri* on the other.

Initially, a single valve horn was often used in the quartet, a solution considered acceptable even by the very conservative C. Rdt (alias Reissiger? See online, "Who is hiding behind the pseudonym C. Rdt?"). Later on, however, a pair of valve horns was normally used in combination with two natural horns, an arrangement that, if restored today, could offer stimulating results in terms of the sound produced.

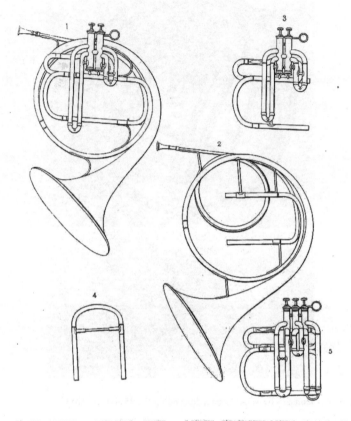

CORS D'HARMONIE DE RAOUX   5
MILLEREAU , Breveté , Seul Fabricant

N° 1   COR à 2 PISTONS. ____ 2 COR SIMPLE ou NATUREL. ____ 3 COULISSE ou MÉCANIQUE MOBILE à 2 PISTONS s'adaptant sur le Cor simple,
4 COULISSE D'ACCORD du COR SIMPLE. ____ 5 COULISSE ou MÉCANIQUE MOBILE à 3 PISTONS, s'adaptant sur le Cor simple

Figure 137. *Cor sauterelle* by Raoux Millereau, from the *Grande Méthode* by Garigue, *ca.* 1888 (three-valve ascending, and two-valve descending models are shown).

An example of the first of the two possibilities is found in the aforementioned pioneering use of the configuration by Franz Schubert (*Nachtgesang in Wald*, 1827). In the orchestra, it was Halévy (*La Juive*, 1835) who made at least partial use of the possibilities of the chromatic horn in the low register and later of a mixture of natural and valve horns. Additionally, we have already mentioned Robert Schumann's interest in the chromatic horn in his *Jagdlieder*, op. 137, written in 1849, in which he explicitly calls for three *Waldhörner* (I–III) and a *Ventilhorn* (IV). However, he too soon came to prefer the use of two pairs, valve and natural (see online, "The pivotal role of Schumann," and above "Hand horn vs. valve horn," p. 273).

Owing to the presence of both natural and valve instruments, the composer's palette was greatly expanded: the classic tone color of the natural horn and the peculiarity of the stopped notes, which could be sweet or more metallic (those completely closed) could be preserved; the low register of the valve horns, useful for obtaining notes that are uncomfortable to obtain on the natural horn with security and good intonation, could be exploited; modulations to distant keys, which require a greater number of alterations and therefore of stopped notes on the natural instrument, could be afforded while continuing the use of the crooks and their tone color and sound differences. Audiences and critics therefore became gradually accustomed to the "new instrument," as evidenced by several writings from the period, including those by Gevaert, Romero, and others (see the definitive endorsement of the valve instrument by Billert [C. B. 1875]).

TWO VALVE AND TWO NATURAL HORNS

Felix Mendelssohn-Bartholdy's writing for horn offers a possible initial example of this dual use of the instrument. He generally preserved the traditional features of the natural horn—think of the beautiful and long solo in *A Midsummer Night's Dream* (1843)—but in the "Scottish" Symphony, which was completed in 1842, two pairs of horns were allegedly adopted, one ordinary pair (in C and A) and a second pair with valves (E, F, D), at least according to the example reported in Gevaert (1890, 178; actually, the autograph score does not contain an explicit request for chromatic horns) (see Musical example 69 online).[14] In any case, the parts themselves suggest this solution since the writing would be rather daring for natural horns alone. The solo third horn is doubled by the cellos in the Adagio (bars 74ff.), evidently to cover any "imperfections" of the valve instrument and to ensure a more homogeneous tone color, which is much more difficult to create with the natural horn although the parts are playable on it. The theme of the Allegro maestoso assai (Finale, bars 396ff.) is particularly effective. If entrusted to a pair of valve horns, it can be performed with open sounds in the middle register

---

[14] Elsewhere, Gevaert (1890, 141) mentions the solo by a pair of chromatic horns in E at the beginning of the last section of the symphony (Allegro maestoso assai), but in the first printed score, they are in D (Breitkopf & Härtel, [1842], plate no. 6823). In the autograph manuscript, the solo in the second pair (horn in D) is clearly a later addition.

and at a piano dynamic. The theme is repeated at a forte dynamic in the upper octave by the pair of natural horns in A alto. Finally, when the four horns (doubled by violas and cellos) play in unison, an attractive mélange of open and stopped notes results (bars 444ff.). The resulting sound merits replicating in modern performances (see Musical example 70 online).

The aforementioned distinction between the two pairs was quite usual for some time, as Gevaert (1863, 92) already remarks in an earlier publication: "For some years, the artists in charge of the third and fourth horn parts have generally been equipped with a piston valve instrument," adding that "the custom is to write for two ordinary and two piston valve horns" (p. 93, see also Romero 1871, 56 and below, p. 291, fn 9). A complementary judgment is proposed also in Gevaert (1890, 246). In discussing the disposition of "Le Grand Orchestre Dramatique" in Wagner's operas, he witnesses that at the time in Germany, at least two of the four hornists in the orchestra played valve instruments.[15] Gevaert (ibid.) also adds, "The adoption of valve horns in place of natural ones, which was at first partial and subsequently became widespread, provided the advantage of rendering the annoying couplings of the crooks, a procedure of very limited efficiency, useless."

On the other hand, the continued use of natural horns in the middle of the era of the valves, the progressive development of orchestral writing, and the increasingly complex harmonic textures forced the adoption of unusual combinations of crooks on certain occasions, especially in opera. This had also some spin-off on the temperament. In his *Relazione*, Florentine composer Baldassarre Gamucci (1877, 89) reports that "some have also observed that the mixture of valve horns with natural horns is not sensible because the former, especially with stable tuning, necessarily use equal temperament and the latter the natural harmonics, so their intonation cannot conform perfectly."

THE PIVOTAL ROLE OF SCHUMANN

See online.

---

[15] According to the same Gevaert (1890, 247–249) the first printed edition of *Lohengrin* calls for pairs of natural and valve horns in various sections of the score. This, however, is not the case (cf. Breitkopf & Härtel edition, *ca.* 1850). Probably Gevaert makes reference here (and also elsewhere in his *Cours méthodique*) to a French edition we weren't able to identify.

24

VALVE DISSEMINATION: A REGIONAL OVERVIEW

Not only the type of horn model, but also the type of valves—the set of three probably more than the set of two—followed local customs, which had become increasingly more differentiated from the middle of the century. Although generalization is always somewhat hazardous, let us try to sketch out here some regional or national trends in the hope they may be useful for focusing on at least some local habits and orientations.

GERMANY (PRUSSIA, SAXONY, BAVARIA)

Despite the great number of experiments and new inventions, a preference for a particular type of valve had already been established in German-speaking countries at the middle of the century. In Julius Rühlmann's 1851 aforementioned essay, he takes only three systems into consideration: the Stölzel valves, which were already falling out of favor in his opinion; the Viennese double pistons, whose limits he emphasizes; and finally, rotary valves, for which he states his unequivocal preference (p. 249):

> This is therefore the best way, since here not even the slightest part of the air stream is dispersed. The rotary valve only turns around and does not push forward as in other valves, and it also allows for the most extraordinary virtuosity with a tone that is closer to that of the natural instrument. The items made in recent years by L. Uhlmann in Vienna leave almost nothing to be desired, both in terms of the rotors and also of the movement of the rods.

Subsequently, rotary valves became the most widespread type of valve in Germany, and the authoritative Oscar Franz (1843–1886), who lived in Dresden, states in his *Grosse theoretisch-practische Waldhorn-Schule* from 1881, also published in English in 1906 as the *Complete Method for the French Horn*, that (here p. 9) the models with Viennese valves had fallen out of use.

Kastner (1837, 47) reports in turn that the German-made valve horns were pitched in F, and an additional comment of his seems worth mentioning: "Experience has proved that it is difficult to tackle the high pitches and the low ones with this single crook," so the high B-flat, A, and G crooks and the low D, C, and B-flat crooks should remain in use. Several years later, Kling (1865, 77) observed, "I advise the employment of G, the A, and the high B-flat crooks whenever these are indicated by the composer. By their aid, the passages will be rendered with great ease, more clearly and with a truer tone than when they are transposed on the [valve] F horn."

The most common single horn model in F was normally equipped with slide crooks for the keys of F and E-flat and sometimes also G, which also served as tuning slides. The mouthpiece was strictly conical, with an edged throat; the inner diameter of the bore was about 11.7mm, which is wider than on all other models of the period, while the bell reached remarkable dimensions.

Instruments with terminal crooks were also common, starting from high B-flat (in this case a short straight shank). A few makers equipped some models with valve slides with very long tenons that were therefore suitable both for high pitches and the lower keys of F and E-flat. A nickel silver reinforcement garland on the bell, similar to the one applied to Viennese horns, embellished the instrument and improved its acoustic qualities. The sound, which is much more impressive and darker than the French model, could be as harmonious as the Viennese one.

One feature specific to Southern Germany is a unique arrangement of the valves called the "catholic" or Bavarian arrangement. In this system, the valves lower the pitch by one, two, and three semitones respectively, instead of the usual succession of two, one, and three. This system was the subject of an informative article produced by Joe R. Utley and Sabine Klaus (2003).

Finally, as far as teaching is concerned, we can note that in Germany, as well as almost everywhere else, the natural horn was never completely forgotten during the nineteenth century. Oscar Franz, for example, began the aforementioned *Waldhorn-Schule* with studies for the hand horn and then continued with those for the valve instrument (see also online, "From Vogtland to the whole world").

AUSTRIA

Throughout the Austro-Hungarian Empire, models with Viennese valves prevailed. This also explains their diffusion in Italy until at least 1860, while the country was still under Austrian rule (rotary valves subsequently prevailed, as we have seen for Germany). Regarding the use of valves, it seems appropriate to note a statement made by the admired Austrian bandmaster Joseph Fahrbach, who in 1869, in his *Vollständige Horn-Schule für das einfache und Maschin-Horn*, declared himself definitively against the uneven effect of the "old custom of stifling the harmonics with the hand."

The Viennese "machine" has been described extensively in this book. After the Kail–Riedl patent and the fundamental improvement by Uhlmann, it did not undergo substantial modifications. It is a system that initially involved some notable defects, including the fact that it leaked water, leading to the name *Spritzerventil* (spray valve), but it was later brought to mechanically unsurpassed results. Rühlmann (1851, 249), however, speaks of Vienna valves in negative terms, recalling that they "have the disadvantage of temporarily diverting the flow of air and not being sufficiently airtight, as well as not being adaptable to all brass instruments."

As we know, the model equipped with these valves has remained in continuous use up until the present day in the major Viennese orchestras. Over the course of its history, skilled artisans have built these instruments, including, in addition to those previously mentioned, Anton Dehmal (d. 1907) and the Produktive Genossenschaft der Musikinstrumentenmacher, a cooperative that flourished until 1940 (see Figure 111, p. 246). All these builders, including Uhlmann himself, also produced models equipped with rotary valves with the same concept and the same features as the double-piston horn (see Figure 138 online).

Today, several makers manufacture the instrument, and it is enjoying a growing revival owing to historical performance practice, although it is sometimes adopted under not entirely appropriate circumstances. We might also add that a fun-loving first horn of the Vienna Philharmonic, when asked about the advantages of this model with respect to other systems, used to answer, "A few less years of life . . ."

THE FRENCH PERSPECTIVE

In France, the prophet of the valve horn was the previously mentioned Joseph Meifred, who deserves full acknowledgment for his first public performance on the new instrument in 1828, the first publication of an anthology of studies (1829a), and a handbook for novice composers (Meifred 1829b).[1] While mostly dealing with the natural horn, the latter also includes a brief section on the valve horn (pp. 30–31), the implement with which "all the inconveniences of the stopped sounds disappear, as well as the gaps in the diatonic and chromatic scale," allowing the horn player "to choose freely whether to use stopped or open notes when faced with the different music passages."

His more extensive discussion of the valves is found, however, in an ignored article from the *Encyclopedie Pittoresque de la Musique* by Adolphe Ledhuy and Henri Bertini (Meifred 1835). Here the author, ten years after the introduction of the valves in France, asserts that the abolition of the *corps de rechange* (crooks) had been a major impediment to the success of the new instrument. The same charge could be made about the change in notation, at least until he devised a new mechanism awarded with a medal in the Paris Exhibition of 1827 (the model built by Labbaye and illustrated in Fétis 1827; see Figure 124, p. 258). Meifred also compares the natural horn to a piano on which only a few keys give good sounds, while the others are dull or out of tune. The *cor à pistons*, on the other hand, produces only notes that are in tune, including f" and a", for example, and renders the muffled ones fully voiced. It allows the player to fill in the gaps in the harmonic series with sharp and flat notes; it also allows them to choose between open and stopped sounds, while facilitating performance in the low register. In order to demonstrate these unique features, Meifred added a separate insert with musical examples for the *cor basse*, including some echos (*sons bouché*) that cannot be performed on the natural horn.

A few years later Berlioz affirmed in his *Grand Traité d'instrumentation et d'orchestration modernes* (1843–1844, 186), where he dedicates only one page to the chromatic horn, that the three-valve instrument was already in general use in Germany. In *Méthode*, his contemporary Georges Kastner (1844, 14) added that, while the valve horn was usually pitched only in F in Germany, crooks remained in use in France after the valved instrument entered into widespread use, as the latter "contains all of the qualities and properties of the older one while correcting its shortcomings."

In the reprint of his *Méthode* (1849), Meifred declares himself in favor of a new three-valve system with an "ascending" third piston, an invention by Jules Halary Jr.

---

[1] On Meifred's detailed output to 1840, see J. G. Kastner, "*Correspondenz*," *Jahrbücher des Deutschen Nationalvereins für Musik und ihre Wissenschaft*, 2 (1840), 358–359.

(cf. Meifred 1851, 9–12) that later achieved long-term success in France and Great Britain. In the resting position, the third piston allows the air to pass through its corresponding slide, thus producing the F harmonic series. When pressed, it shortens the instrument by a whole tone, putting it in G and therefore allowing the player to use the keys of G, F#, and F, as well as E/E-flat/D (the latter three implying the use of the first and second valve). This arrangement improved some sounds in the high register, which were now easier to obtain and had a more uniform tone, and also allowed for all of the keys of the *cor solo*.

We can consider this to be the true "French" model. The instrument sometimes had the set of valves attached on the tuning slide, which could therefore be removed and replaced with a simple slide in order to obtain a true natural horn (the *sauterelle* model mentioned in "Hand horn vs. valve horn," p. 273) (see Figures 139 and 140 online). Some makers also provided a "descending" third valve with its corresponding one and a half tone slide (Baines 1976, fig. 41). In this case, the player needed to replace the terminal crook at the mouthpiece with one that was a tone longer in order to correctly pitch the instrument in F.

Raoux maintained a prominent position among Parisian makers and was the only firm that kept the same constructive features, including bore and bell diameters, for the horn during the entire period the company was in business. It was still well respected even when sold to Labbaye in 1857, after a dispute with Sax. The average internal bore of these instruments varies from 10.8 to 11mm and the sound is clear and balanced, albeit rather rough in the low register, around the third harmonic. The mouthpiece, which was entirely conical, has a slight double taper on some models and was no longer constructed from a metal plate, as was the case for many earlier French instruments, but rather turned out from a single piece of brass. The Raoux company was taken over by Millereau in 1878 (these instruments, despite Morley-Pegge's criticism, had first-class build quality and sound). The firm then passed under the ownership of Hermann Schoenaers in about 1898, who continued to use the Raoux-Millereau brand until 1931, when it was bought by the Selmer Company (1858–1941) (see also Figure 141 online).

Another leading and historically relevant company in France was Gautrot,[2] which obtained various patents, starting in 1846, including a forward-looking compensation system called *systéme équitonique* in 1864 (Morley-Pegge 1973, 48). However, in the same year the company produced "cors

[2] A comprehensive overview of the French brass instrument production and industry of the second half of the century can be found in Grenot 2016.

d'harmonie ordinaire a 10 tons" alongside instruments equipped with two or three valves.[3] In all likelihood, the valve instruments were mostly used with the hand-horn technique (i.e. with the pistons only exploited for switching keys), since in France this technique remained in use for much longer than elsewhere in Europe.

The famous solo in Ravel's *Pavane pour une enfante defunte* (1910), in which a *cor simple en sol* is explicitly called for (i.e. a natural horn or a valve horn used with the hand technique only), was conceived for a "French" horn. Dukas's *Villanelle pour Cor avec accomp.t d'Orchestre ou de Piano* (1906),[4] dedicated to Monsieur François Brémond, on the other hand, requires mixed use (see Musical example 71 online).[5]

OMNITONIC VALVE HORNS

Omnitonic horns provide indirect evidence of the continued use of the hand horn in France and in Belgium. We have already discussed omnitonic natural horns, but we will now dedicate space to instruments equipped with valve mechanisms, even though it is not always easy to assign all models to the first or to the second category.

Gautrot, mentioned previously, ventured into the production of *cors omnitoniques* with valve systems starting from 1846, obtaining various patents until at least 1855. The company also created a *cor transpositeur* with a central switcher valve, which was reasonably considered by some to be a conventional imitation of previous models (Pontécoulant 1861, II, 512) but nevertheless remained in production, with or without valves, until at least 1878 (see Figure 142 online).

As with "natural" omnitonic horns, the market for these valve models was predominantly the Franco-Belgian one, although there were makers and inventors

---

[3] Gautrot ainé, *Catalogue des instruments de musique*, Durand & Cie, Paris, Oberthur et Fils, 1878. See https://brasstacks.de/gautrot-aine.html.

[4] The first part of this composition should be performed "sans les pistons," that is with the hand technique, while the second part requires the use of the valves to produce open, stopped, and also muted sounds. It uses all of the technical, virtuosic, and timbral capacities of the instrument and therefore of the performer, covering the entire range of the horn and reaching the sixteenth harmonic in the brilliant finale.

[5] A price list from Schoenaers-Millereau (Paris, 1910) shows the various models recommended by François Brémond (1844–1925) in his re-edition of the *Méthode* by Dauprat. The horn has three valves, and the third could be ascending, descending, or both (the "patented" third system is not described, but the third valve probably had two different mechanisms). A right-handed instrument was also available (see Chapter 23, "A reversed 'chirality'," p. 272), as was a complete series of crooks: high b-flat, a, a-flat, g (in one loop or two), f#, e, e-flat, d, c, low b-flat (one piece), half-tone shank, and whole-tone shank (the price list is reproduced in Martz 2003, 204).

in other geographical areas. One example comes from Italy, where Giuseppe Pelitti Sr. presented, together with other new brass instruments, an omnitonic horn in 1845. He made further modifications to the instrument in 1855. It featured a small rotating valve with a handlebar used to deflect the air stream and obtain one of the keys indicated on the cover, an idea that closely resembles that of the *Tonwechselmaschine* patented by Červený in 1846.

But the history of the omnitonic horns was not yet finished and, even after these experiments, other inventors tried to design new models. This continued into the era of double horn, which offered the possibility of obtaining all pitches from high B-flat to low natural B.

A unique model that still deserves mention as a precursor to the modern double horn was conceived by Henri Chaussier (1854–1914), a renowned horn player and soloist. He had been in Berlin in the 1880s and witnessed the practice, which he deemed unacceptable, of playing the F horn only and of transposing all parts, even the oldest ones, written in other tonalities. In order to preserve the timbres of the crooks, he conceived a new double-pitched model that allowed the player to play from C to F# and, by moving a fourth rotary valve, to switch to F, thus transforming the instrument into a chromatic horn with three pistons. Not yet satisfied, Chaussier also imagined an additional model with a mixed system of four ascending and descending valves, which allowed the player to play in all keys from high to low B-flat with some adjustments of the slides. It was a kind of *cor omnitonique* called the *système Chaussier* (Brussels, MIM, inv. 1312) that, when presented to a committee of prestigious musicians on April 11, 1891, was met with acclaim (see Figure 143 online). However, this did not result in any further success (Morley-Pegge 1973, 63–66; Hübner 2016).

Since they never obtained any real relevance outside the Franco-Belgian market, these valved omnitonic horns are only briefly discussed here. For more details, we direct readers to Morley-Pegge (1973), which dedicates an entire chapter to the subject, to Dick Martz's well-documented website (http://www.rjmartz.com/horns/), to Maury's 2016 paper, and also to other sources available online.

BELGIUM

Belgium's proximity to France and especially the invasion of French troops in 1792 were the basis for many cultural choices that were made at the beginning of the nineteenth century and continued after Belgium gained independence in 1830.

Thenceforth, new musical schools and new conservatories were created that allowed some famous musicians, who had settled in France in order to complete their musical training, to return home. The teaching system was based on that of France, and the instruments preferred in that country were adopted (Billiet 2016, 328–330).

The main difference in Belgian teaching when compared with French teaching was that students were given general training that was mostly aimed at solid basic standards instead of virtuosity. After 1830, the leading Belgian manufacturers—Charles Sax, Van Engelen, Tuerlinckx, Mahillon, and van Cauwelaert—also began to produce chromatic instruments on a large scale (see Figures 144 & 145 online). After having almost entirely neglected the natural instruments, the conservatoires forced horn apprentices to return to practicing them, as this training was reintroduced in around 1850 (Billiet 2016, 333–334). In fact, the firm Van Engelen Frères, founded in 1813, still had in its catalog of 1907 a "cor simple à 10 tons" besides horns with two or three descending pistons, with or without crooks ("4 tons").[6]

The chromatic horn also had its advocates in Belgium. Fétis (1854, 318), after registering French horn players' criticism of the valve horn, states:

> Although the quality of construction of a horn provides the raw material for a beautiful sound, this is only achieved when the artist who uses it has feelings, and when the constitution of his lips meets all the necessary conditions. M. Artôt [Jean-Désiré, 1803–1887], professor at the Conservatory of Brussels, who possessed the most beautiful sound that could be heard on the natural horn, lost none of this precious quality when he adopted the valve horn, and he transmitted this talent to his students. Other artists, I confess, have a heavy, dry or fluffy sound on the piston horn, but where they had a better one on the natural horn is to be ascertained.

Years later, reporting on the Paris Universal Exposition of 1867, Fétis (1868, 289) explained that the valve horn was played badly in French orchestras and that:

[6] See https://www.horn-u-copia.net/library.shtml, s.v. van Engelen

Most composers cannot write for this instrument. In Belgium, where brass instruments are played particularly well, the piston horns are excellent. There is no more beautiful sound, precision and equality then that of the four piston horns of the Brussels Conservatory anywhere to be found.

Belgian horns were made with the stylistic features typical of the French ones, both in the use of two or three Stölzel, Périnet, or Sax pistons and in terms of their diameters and bell flares. In some cases, the third ascending piston was also used.

Omnitonic models also achieved a certain success in the country. One example is the "independent pistons" horn invented by Adolphe Sax (a Belgian, but French by adoption), who presented it at the 1867 Universal Exhibition with Fétis's (1868, 529–530) expected approval. It was Louis-Henri Merck (1831–1900), however, who popularized this independent valve model, which in the meantime had conquered its definitive form, in Belgium. He is also the author of a *Méthode pour le cor à 6 pistons indépendants* written for the same model, which "many hornists despised because of its weight and a supposed complication of fingering" (*Avant-propos*), but the criticism was apparently sound, and the model was completely unsuccessful (Billiet 2016, 337–338) (see Figure 146 online).

GREAT BRITAIN

The tradition of the hand horn also prevailed for a long time in Great Britain, despite what is reported in a paper entitled "On the French Horn" by a certain "I. P." published in *The Harmonicon* (8, 1830, 320). After mostly dealing with the natural horn, he recounts that two English makers, Pace of Westminster and Percival of St. James Street, had already experimented with a two-valve system for completing the scale offered by the instrument. And indeed we know of an 1830–1834 horn by Charles Pace (1803–1867) with two Stölzel pistons (London, Royal College of Music, inv. no. RCM0164) (see Figure 147 online).[7] Thomas Percival (1790–1848) is said to have experimented with valves on low brass instruments as well, according to the aforementioned article and another signed by the same author (*The Harmonicon*, 8, 1830, 281).

---

[7] See http://museumcollections.rcm.ac.uk/collection/Details/collect/1258.

The sparsity of valve horns in Great Britain in the mid-1830s, however, is confirmed by the surprise of the chroniclers who attended Lewy's performances in London in 1835. A couple of years later, the critic and musicologist George Hogarth (1783–1870) dedicated an article in *The Musical World* to the hand-horn alone (4/46 (January 27, 1837), 81–85), commenting on its acoustic features, praising the peculiarities of the instrument, and maintaining that it was "necessary, where possible, to avoid the use of stopped notes" (p. 83). On the other hand, an anonymous correspondent in the same magazine (*The Musical World*, 5/53 (March 17, 1837), 8) reported that he had recently listened to a performance by a certain Mr. Perry, of whom nothing more is known, which included a fantasy for valve horn, in which "he executed the chromatic scale through the whole compass of the instrument, with a perfect equality of tone in every note."

Evidently, the presence and activity of the great Italian soloist Giovanni Puzzi, praised by Hogarth himself, played a decisive role in supporting the continued use of the hand horn in London. Hogarth mentions in addition (*The Musical World*, 4/46, January 27, 1837, 85) "Messrs. Platt and Rae, who are generally associated as first and second horn in our orchestras, [and] are worthy members of the body of wind-instruments which is not rivalled in Europe."

In 1846, however, an announcement for a "three valve Sax French Horn" patented by Thomas Key of London and purposely modeled on the example of Sax valve instruments appeared (Mitroulia–Myers 2008, 101). In addition, the invention of a "Compensation valve-rod" was announced in 1849. The device was to be applied to cornets, trumpets, and horns (see *The London Journal of Arts and Sciences*, 34, 1849, 297) and was probably inspired by Sax's *compensateur*, that is, the valve slide designed to correct intonation. The instruments built in this way were publicized by Key (see e.g. *The Indian News*, May 25 1849, p. 237) because they were "made upon a new principle; the wind, until the valves are brought into play, having a free and direct passage to the bell, which no other valve instrument yet possesses, and gives a greater freedom to the tone."

In the period after 1850, while the natural horn remained in use, valve horns became more and more common and widespread, at least for soloistic use. This is also confirmed by the 1868 *Chambers's Encyclopaedia* (V, 417, s.v. "horn"), which also includes an illustration of a three-piston horn, perhaps built by Pace: "The valve-horn is now generally used as a solo instrument with a greater effect than the common horn."

British players still preferred the two-valve model over the three-valve model at least until the end of the century, so much so that in the first edition of the *Grove* (1879, I), the aforementioned entry dedicated to the horn contained an illustration of a horn with only two Périnet pistons.[8]

Around the same time, the English composer and critic Ebenezer Prout (1835–1909) states in his *Instrumentation* (Prout 1877, 45) that two models are currently in use "in our orchestras: the natural horn, sometimes, [. . .] and the chromatic-, valve-, or ventil-horn," "the use of which is now very general" (p. 50). He also emphasizes (p. 51), "Many modern composers use the ventil-horn exclusively; while some go so far as to write for it only in the key of F. Many of our orchestral players also always use the F horn, and transpose by means of the pistons the music written for a horn in any other key. This plan is by no means to be recommended."[9]

About twenty years later, Prout (1898, I, 195) would state that the natural horn had been completely supplanted by the valve instrument, though "it must be admitted that the quality of tone of the valve horn is slightly inferior to that of the natural instrument." He also added an illustration (p. 193) of a horn that is clearly French made with three Périnet piston valves.[10]

The market was generally favorable to horns imported from France, especially those by Raoux and Thibouville-Lamy, which were very popular at the beginning of the twentieth century (see Figure 148 online). Hornists who emigrated to England therefore had to adapt to local esthetic preferences. The German-born soloist Adolf Borsdorf (1854–1923), a pupil of Oscar Franz, switched to the French Raoux model once he moved to London in 1879 (Strauchen-Scherer 2006, 263–264). The same can be said for Franz Friedrich Paersch (1857–1921), who emigrated to England in 1882. The reason for this transition from the German model to the French one is summarized well in a statement by a colleague of Aubrey Brain, Thomas R. Busby: "Cow's horns, we call 'em" (Morley-Pegge

[8] A two Stölzel-piston horn is also depicted in the English translation of Gounod's *Méthode*, which was still on sale in Britain as late as 1890 (Humphries 2000, 39, fig. 37). Morley-Pegge 1973, plate VI, contains depictions of five instruments with two valves, two of which are of English construction.

[9] This opinion was fully shared by Vittorio Ricci, the editor of the Italian translation of Prout's text (Milan, Hopli, 1892, 72, fn 2), who complains about the indiscriminate use of the F horn and the abandonment of crooks. Ricci instead advocated the use of two natural and two valve horns in the orchestra.

[10] On p. 195, there is also a scientific explanation of the reason why the intonation of first and second valve used together is incorrect.

1973, 4). Alfred Edwin Brain (1885–1966), who emigrated to the United States in 1923, and his aforementioned brother Aubrey Brain (1893–1955) also played on descending French model horns with three pistons.

In fact, the idea of the color of the natural horn never fully left Great Britain. In his Pastoral Symphony no. 3 (1922) (see Musical example 72 online), Ralph Vaughan Williams (1872–1958) wrote in the finale of the second movement an evocative horn solo to be performed with "natural notes only." Here, the seventh harmonic (with flat intonation) creates a particularly sad atmosphere, imitating the long solo of the "Natural trumpet in E-flat." Twenty years later (1943), Britten would also start his *Serenade*, op. 31 for tenor, horn, and strings, a piece written for Dennis Brain (see below), with the solo horn purposefully playing natural harmonics.

ITALY

To understand the uniqueness of some Italian choices, we should remember that the local instrumental schools aimed at creating a sound fully capable of blending in the most acclaimed repertoire in the country, namely vocal and operatic performance. This attitude was not only applicable to the horn, but also to many other orchestral instruments. In Italy, in fact, students were trained to "sing" with their instruments, and the principal skills required were the ability to improvise, to perform some extemporary ornamentation, and even to perform duets with singers. The manner in which this goal was achieved and the preferred model of the instrument used to achieve it was not so relevant as abroad. This was probably the reason why there was less resistance to the use of the valves than we have encountered elsewhere.

The instruments conceived in Italy, in addition to the aforementioned early experiments by Pini and some others of which we have little evidence, include an isolated example: the two-valve design conceived at the latest in 1832 by Antonio Apparuti (1799–1844), one of the most refined Italian makers of the time. The same Apparuti performed a *Concerto per corno* on his chromatic instrument on December 10, 1832 at the Opera House of Modena (*Il censore universale dei Teatri*, N. 7, 23-1-1833, p. 27). The music, now lost, was written by the young composer and conductor Alessandro Gandini (1807–1871). A single horn by Apparuti is preserved in the Civic Museum of Art in Modena, his hometown. It is equipped with two Stölzel valves and terminal crooks and is clearly based on French models, although the development of the bell and its tapering are slightly more pronounced than on instruments by Raoux (see Figure 149 online).[11]

Some ten years later, the Ricordi Company published Fermo Bellini's (1804–1865) *Teoriche musicali su gli istromenti e sull'istrumentazione* (1844). He briefly addresses the valve horn (*corno a chiavi*): "This instrument, however, will provide great service to the field of instrumentation in the future, since it tends to provide well-resonating and powerful low notes, and once manufacturers have eliminated the imperfection and uncertainty of many of its sounds and has been made perfect in every aspect, it will be treated as an unparalleled new instrument."

Significant improvements were also made in Italy by the Pelittis, Giuseppe father and son—the major Italian brass makers and businessmen of the nineteenth century—whose instruments had huge impact on the market. Their manufacturing standards followed the Austrian path until the 1850s, when they abruptly abandoned the double-piston system (a thorough history of the company is found in Meucci 1994). Thereafter, as illustrated by the examples reported below, horn players in Italy largely preferred instruments equipped with rotary valves (cf. Pierre 1890, online ed. 2011, 184).

The Pelittis and other Italian makers are also due the credit for having produced a unique model of valve horn at length. The latter was initially built by Riedl of Vienna upon the request of the Florentine hornist Antonio Tosoroni, and made the use of the hand inside the bell impossible.

ANTONIO TOSORONI

Antonio Tosoroni (Florence 1787–1855), a pupil of Giuseppe Belloli (1775–1845), brother of the famous Luigi (see Tosoroni 1850, 33), began his career on the natural horn. In 1822, he shocked the Danish composer and diplomat Rudolph Bay both with his mastery of the instrument and the agility he displayed in playing it as if it were a flute. The composer had the opportunity to attend one of Tosoroni's performances in Livorno, and he then invited him to give a series of concerts in Copenhagen, later accompanying him to Kassel, where Tosoroni joined Spohr's orchestra for a period of time.[12] Once he had returned to Florence, Tosoroni

---

[11] See https://it.wikipedia.org/wiki/File:Antonio_Apparuti,_Corno_in_Sib_alto,_Museo_Civico_di_Modena,_1831-1845.jpg.

[12] "Never have I heard such virtuosity as his. His masterly treatment of this instrument was like a flute" (Humphries 2000, 25, quoting Rudolph Bay, *Af Rud. Bay's Efterladte Papirer*, vol. 3: *Musicalsk Rejse, 1842–1843*, ed. by Julius Clausen, Copenhagen, Gyldendalske, 1921, 41).

suddenly switched to the valve horn, adopting a two-valve instrument built by Halary in Paris and purchased for him by the Grand Ducal Court on November 11, 1829 (Onerati 1994–1995, 37). The instrument was equipped with seven crooks, two silver mouthpieces, and a case. The *Extrait d'un traité inédit du cor a pistons* of Dauprat and some studies by Meifred, perhaps the *Première étude raisonnée dans tous les tons majeurs pour le cor à pistons* (see Chapter 23, "Early handbooks for 'chromatic horn'," and fn. 8, p. 269), were purchased along with it. Tosoroni performed with this new instrument for the first time in a public concert on April 16, 1831 (*Gazzetta di Firenze*, 50, April 26, 1831, 4) and on various other successive occasions. However, Halary's horn apparently did not fully meet Tosoroni's expectations, as he designed a new model with a fixed leadpipe, three rotary valves, and slide crooks for the keys of G, F, E, and E-flat, which was made by the Viennese maker Josef Felix Riedl and illustrated in his *Metodo per Corno a 3 pistoni* of 1846 ("pistons" should be understood as valves, as we already observed in France) (see Figure 150). This model is unique because it was impossible for the player to place their hand in the bell since the valve block, operated by the right hand, is located close to the bell. This also makes it impossible to play stopped notes, which implies a clearer and less muffled tone.

Along with the adoption of the chromatic horn, Tosoroni also suggests giving up the traditional dualism between *corno alto* and *corno basso* roles and adopting the same mouthpiece for both registers. He also aimed, in fact, to obtain a homogeneous tone among orchestral horns, which could produce a certain inequality of sound color owing to the notes obtained with the hand.

Tosoroni's choice of totally abandoning the natural horn, even on a training level (see his 1846 *Metodo*), represented a radical change that could not escape criticism, such as that of the aforementioned Rudolph Bay (see also Brummitt 2013). A fan of the natural horn only, twenty years later he once again had the opportunity to attend a performance by the soloist of a violin concerto transcribed for horn. Despite his obvious admiration, after the passage reported above (p. 293 and fn. 12), he states that he strongly disagreed with his "friend" Tosoroni's decision to change over to the valve horn.

The reputation that Tosoroni acquired in the role of first horn at the Teatro della Pergola in Florence (where he performed from at least 1825 until February 1846); the publication of his *Metodo per corno a 3 pistoni*, published simultaneously in Florence by Berni and in Milan by F. Lucca, in 1846; and the 1851 release of a fundamental practical treatise on orchestration in which his sound ideals are fully

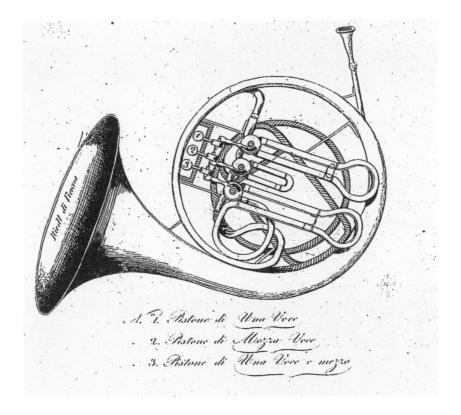

Figure 150. Riedl horn, from Tosoroni's *Metodo*, 1846.

expressed are all evidence of the appreciation that he received. In fact, he established a solid horn-playing tradition in Florence that was continued by his student Francesco Paoli (1820–1870)—the occupant of his teacher's orchestral post from February 15, 1846, and the author of a method entitled *Idea del Corno a macchina* (1849) (see Figure 151)—and later on by Felice Bartolini (*ca.* 1845–1903), in turn a pupil of Paoli.

This practice was widely adopted elsewhere in Italy.[13] The *Metodo teorico-pratico per corno a macchina* published in 1873 by Vedasto Vecchietti (1844–after 1904)—first horn at the Apollo Theater in Rome and a professor at the Santa Cecilia Conservatory from 1875—illustrates a similar model, with the rotary valves in a peculiar triangle arrangement, made by Leopold Uhlmann of Vienna.

---

[13] See Martz 2003, 200–201, or http://www.rjmartz.com/horns/roth/roth.htm.

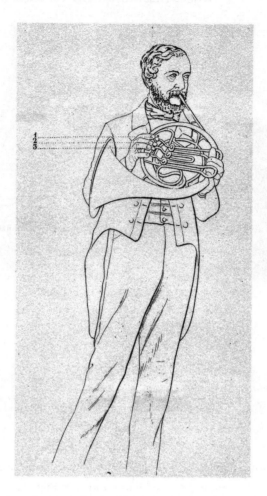

Figure 151. Horn player, from F. Paoli, *Idea del Corno a macchina*, 1849.

In addition, the existence of a right-handed instrument supplied with Berlin valves is also reported (Brüchle-Janetzky 1976, 262).

Not all Italian horn players, however, adopted this arrangement, as evidenced by the *Metodo progressivo per Corno da Caccia a tre cilindri* of Antonio Canti (1878), for example. Canti recommends using valve horns made by Giuseppe Pelitti of Milan, which could be right or left handed (see Figure 152 online).

Many other Italian players, even when adopting the usual left-hand fingering, also neglected to use the right hand to modify the tone, instead using it to hold the instrument. Only when explicitly requested by the score did they introduce the hand into the bell to obtain stopped sounds. All in all, the basis of this choice was found in a conception of the timbre that relied on melody and expressiveness rather than on the sound colors that could be obtained with the hand.

Although this preference for avoiding the use of the hand may have been widespread in the country of Belcanto, it did not satisfy reviewers associated with other traditions. An enlightening example is found in the opinion of a strenuous supporter of hand stopping, the composer and musicologist Hermann Eichborn (1847–1918). In a booklet dedicated to this topic, he boldly declares himself to be opposed to the Italian habit of playing with the bell open (Eichborn 1897, 18–19), apparently ignoring the esthetic reasons behind this choice.

Meanwhile, the practice of the natural horn was almost completely lost in Italy. This is highlighted by Vittorio Ricci who, in the Italian translation of Prout's instrumentation book, reports that "unfortunately this instrument, has been completely abandoned in Italy and replaced by the valve horn" (*Strumentazione*, Milan, 1892, 61, fn. 1).

However, at the 1881 congress of Italian musicians in Milan, the natural horn was praised and deemed useful as a training resource, to the point that the assembly stated that it hoped it would be reintroduced in academic study programs (Atti 1881, 51). Later, this was actually put into effect through the (re)addition of compulsory "hand-horn" exams in Italian conservatories, even though this turned out to be more of an idealistic acknowledgment than an effective restoration of the old performance practice.

The "Italian sound" subsequently maintained its distinct connotation for a long time owing to fine instruments by Pelitti, Ferdinando Roth, and, later on, by the craftsman Giovan Battista Cazzani (1846–1920). The latter built, among other models, a three-valve single F horn with a tuning slide equipped with a semitone valve useful for playing stopped notes with more comfortable fingerings (for example those in E and B major keys) and for avoiding transportation while playing in E (see Figure 153 online).

SPAIN

The Spanish point of view on the valve horn is reflected by the opinions expressed by Antonio Romero y Andía, a clarinetist of the Real Capilla and a professor at the Royal Conservatory of Madrid. He was the inventor of the Romero clarinet mechanism and the author of seven methods for various instruments. In his *Memoria sobre los instrumentos de Música*, written on the occasion of the 1862 International Exposition in London, he states the following (Romero 1864, 19):

Spain did not present any wooden or metal wind instruments at the London International Exposition, which is not surprising considering that the particular conditions of our country do not allow for the organization and support of large factories that produce such objects that can compete with foreign ones. First because our army, even though respectable in proportion to our population, requires few instruments; second, because our geographical situation, our roads, and our commercial relations with foreign countries do not favor export; third, because in our country the immense moral and economic usefulness of encouraging the masses of laborers, workers and young people in general to form musical societies was not yet understood. This would provide them with a useful and pleasant means of education, providing a distraction from idleness with its fatal consequences for which, although experienced by everyone, no remedy is sought. In this way, they could get used to treating each other with intimacy, to getting to know each other, to admiring each other, and to interacting without violence.

In 1871, Romero published in Madrid what he truthfully claims to be the first handbook for horn in Spanish (*Método de trompa de pistones o cilindros con nociones de la mano*, see Figure 154 online). Previously, these methods were preferably imported from neighboring France, where some publishers included a Spanish translation alongside the French text—see the *Méthode élémentaire de Cor à pistons* (*ca.* 1844) by Haumuller, for example.

For the compilation of his *Método*, Romero made use of the assistance of distinguished local instrumentalists: Manuel Hernandez, retired first horn of the Teatro Principal of Cádiz; Miguel Sacristá, former professor in the Conservatory of Music in Madrid and emeritus of Real Capilla; and Miguel Rejoy, horn player in the Sociedad de Conciertos and in the orchestra of the Teatro Nacional of the Court Opera.

After emphasizing the limits of the natural horn, Romero assigns the invention of the valves to Stölzel, stating that they allowed for an improvement on the instrument by discarding several crooks in favor of A-flat (alto), G, F, E, E-flat, and rarely, A (alto) crooks. He also notes (Romero 1871, 56) that in the major orchestras there are two *trompas de mano* and two *de pistones*. This allows the sound of the first ones and the great advantages of the latter to be exploited. In military music, however, only valve horns were commonly in use.

On the other hand, the hornist of Valencia, Luis Font y Mirapeix (1845–1911), the first horn in the Teatro Real as well as a professor at the Royal Conservatory of

Madrid, wrote an unpublished manuscript entitled *Breve raseña historica sobre el origin y progresos de la Trompa* (Madrid 1882, E-Mc 1-15185).[14] Here the application of valves to the horn in 1814 is assigned to Blühmel (fol. 7v) and the development and application of this device to other brass instruments to the firm Griessling & Schlott of Berlin, probably relying on Spontini's long letter reported in Kastner (1848, 190). He then mentions the new valve made by Blühmel in 1828 and the invention of the "system of rotary valves" by Uhlmann and Riedl (1830–1832), which raised the horn and all the brasses to the highest degree of perfection. Font also makes note of Meifred's invention, which was made together with Labbaye between 1827 and 1833 (but we know that the partnership was much shorter), and the *transpositeur* mechanism invented by Gautrot in 1855. He concludes the section dedicated to valves with a brief mention of Sax's improvements. In addition, Font maintains that it is crucial for students, besides learning to play with valves, to be well practiced on the hand horn, with all its peculiarities of natural and stopped notes. Further, he advises his pupils (Font 1882, 28–29) to start with the three-valve horn with the E-flat crook and only to alternate it with the hand horn from the third year. Font also suggests adopting the three-piston model built by Millereau of Paris, which favors a nice, soft, and in-tune sound. The final part of the manuscript is dedicated to the practical study of the instrument, divided into six years of apprenticeship.

FROM THE NEW WORLD

Until the 1850s, the model of horn commonly used in America in the performance of art music continued to be the natural one. Woodbury (1844, 116–118), for example, includes a table with the range and a brief description of the natural horn with crooks in his *The Elements of Musical Composition*.

Within forty years, however, the situation completely reversed. Coon (1883, 130) states that the natural horn was rarely used, instrumentalists preferred the valve F horn, and dance-music composers wrote using only the latter size of the instrument. On the other hand, "those who aspire to the classical style, still adhere to the 'old way'". Rollinson (1886, 265) cursorily informs us that "the ventil-horn, or valve-horn, is in common use."

---

[14] We wish to express our heartfelt thanks to Javier Bonet (Madrid) for informing us about this important unpublished manuscript.

What had happened in the meantime could be introduced by a chapter of the *Brass Band School* by Allen Dodworth (1822–1896), the inventor of a cornet with five valves, which first addressed an evolving situation through a description of the valve types then adopted on band instruments in North America (Dodworth 1853, 13):

> There are many kinds of valves at present in use, but as no valve has yet been invented possessing all the desirable qualities, many more will no doubt be introduced. The valve most in use at present time, is such as all Sax Horn have, called "Cylinder" [here in the sense of piston valve]; these for common valves are preferable to any other, being durable and easily repaired. "The Valve Ordinaire" [Stölzel valve] is such to attached to most French Cornets; the "Perinet" valve, is sometimes attached to the same instrument, and somewhat resembles in appearance to "Ordinaire." The German double valve, is found on most German made Trumpets, Post Horns, &c. The Rotary valve is daily coming into use, with many different arrangements of machinery to turn them, all possessing more quickness and activity than any other valve, but at the same time are much more delicate, and difficult to repair.

As for the horn, Dodworth includes a fingering table of the instrument (from g to c''') equipped with two valves of the Berlin type (on p. 22). Moreover, he also includes the fingering for low g#, a note that was missing in the two-valve instrument (or obtained with the help of the hand). In fact, notwithstanding the picture, the chart refers to a three-valve instrument, with the fingering for valves 2+3 (see Figure 155).

The availability of valve instruments in America remained mainly connected to the import trade, to the point that in around 1860, a good 50 percent of the production of the Vogtland (Saxony) was sent to the USA (Myers 1997, 116). One of the principal dealers was Klemm & Bro. Company, originating from Markneukirchen and musical instruments retailers in Philadelphia. The situation is summarized in a communication by Bob Eliason reported by Snedeker (1997, 167, fn. 36):

> As to availability of the valved horn in USA in 1830, I can only say that in sources I have searched, no specific reference was found. Although Nathan Adams may have been experimenting about that time, no American-made

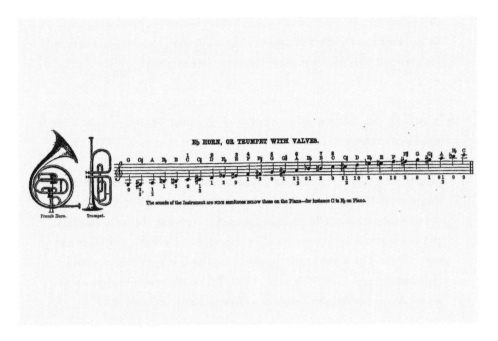

Figure 155. A. Dodworth, *Brass Band School*, 1853, 22.

valve instruments of any kinds were commercially available to my knowledge before 1837. Imported valved horns might have been available, but I have not seen any advertisements for them that early. Even for the next 30 or 40 years American makers were stuck on the valved Saxhorn that they hardly made any trombones, much less French horns.

The overwhelming quantity of imports is criticized by Dodworth (1853, 12), who, in the paragraph "Selection of a good instrument," states that he opposes the arrival of band instruments from the Old Continent:

The French makers have deservedly high reputation, but they *do not all make good ones*. The German had a decidedly bad reputation, but do not make bad ones, as some of the finest instruments are manufactured by German makers; however, it is not now necessary to import brass instruments as formerly, as it is conceded by nearly all, that the finest quality of instruments are now made here, by our American manufacturers. We have also French and German makers residing among us, who make instruments equal in every respect to those imported, with this advantage, in having them made here, the resident makers are naturally more anxious to make and retain a good reputation, than those abroad, who usually make by the dozen for this market.

Not surprisingly, some makers included testimonies by renowned musicians in their catalogs that attested to the quality of domestic instruments in order to promote local production:

"Gentlemen,—The French Horn, made for me by yourselves, is without exception the finest instrument I have ever played upon. Having performed upon the best of French Horns, manufactured in the world, I can unhesitatingly pronounce yours the most superior. Possessing remarkably fine tones, free and very correct. The workmanship is perfect, and the action of the rotary valves light and sure. HENRY SCHMITZ, New York." (*Illustrated Catalogue of the Boston Musical Instrument Manufactory*, Boston, Hollis & Gunn, 1869)

As for valve experimentation in America, one of the country's first researchers was Nathan Adams (1783–1864), who invented a sort of flap or vane valve that worked as part of a pair in Lowell, Massachusetts, in 1824–1825 (Eliason 1970, 86). This mechanism was applied to what was called a "Permutation Trumpet," a specimen of which, dating back to 1825, is preserved on the USS *Constitution* museum ship. The idea is entirely independent from those developed in Europe (Baines 1976, 213) and is earlier than the similar French experiment by Deshays that took place in 1833. The mechanism was applied to a three-valve F trumpet that was also supplied with valve slides, an idea that predates Meifred's analogous device by several years but not the pioneering valve slides by Pini and Dall'Asta. A quite different type of rotary valve was also devised in 1825, perhaps by Adams, and adopted on a trumpet in the Don Essig collection (University of Central Missouri, Warrensburg). Again according to Eliason (1970, 91)—who could not find any examples, however, of the use of these valves on the horn—there was no particular interest in America in local development of the valve mechanism until the 1840s, since instruments continued to be imported or made locally with rotary valves and two pistons in the Viennese style.

In 1848, however, Thomas Paine, a tuba player from Smithfield, Rhode Island, patented an elaboration on rotary valves for the cornet.[15] Thereafter, other

---

[15] See http://www.google.com/patents/US5919.

experiments became more and more frequent. Eliason (1970, 93) notes of other inventions, including that of J. Lathrop Allen (flat-windway rotary valves) in about 1850. This type of valve had a narrower (but longer) body than Riedl's Viennese model and continued to compete with the Viennese design in America until the 1870s, when the Périnet piston eventually prevailed.

It may also be useful to draw attention to a pamphlet published by the instrument maker Isaac Fiske in 1868 (see Figure 156 online). The pamphlet claims that a new rotary valve of the author's invention is more effective than previous systems. We do not know if such an ingenious model was adopted on horns, but it was certainly used on cornets and other instruments.

After the 1880s, brass production companies developed rapidly, mostly to provide instruments for fanfares and civilian or military bands. One example was Conn in Elkhart, which was founded by Charles Gerald Conn in 1877 and had become a major enterprise by 1883–1884. Pepper in Philadelphia, founded by James Welsh Pepper in 1876, started as a publishing house and then evolved into a brass factory through a partnership with the English industrialist Henry Distin (1819–1903), who emigrated to the US in 1877 and moved to Philadelphia in 1882 (Waterhouse 1993, s.v.). He was the second of the four sons of John Distin, and he first found fame as a member of the hugely famous and important Distin Family Quintet. They were among the first to popularize the saxhorn family in England.

To conclude this short section dedicated to the New World, we want to remind readers of some considerations by Otto Langey (1851–1922), a composer, conductor, and cellist of German origin, who emigrated to America in 1889 (see Figure 157 online). In his new country, he republished some of his handbooks for instruments, including the *Newly Revised Tutor for French Horn* in which he explains (Langey 1890, 6) that:

There are French Horns with two and with three valves, the latter being generally adopted now, because capable more perfectly to render in time the entire chromatic scale, especially the lower notes, some of which can not be produced on the two valved instrument. Some old players are still opposed to the entire use of valves, because they argue, that the character of the original sound suffers in consequence. By comparing however, a chromatic scale played on either instrument, it will be found that the preference must be given to the valved Horn as it renders every note with equal clearness.

The method follows the principal guidelines for the ones in use on the Old Continent: training on the natural horn, then the use of the hand, and finally the valve horn. The text is accompanied by studies by distinguished horn players, including Agostino Belloli, Gallay, Gugel, and others, along with duets and major orchestral excerpts.

HIGH B-FLAT HORN

The ever-increasing requirements of the music of composers such as Wagner, Tchaikovsky, Bruckner, Mahler, and Strauss contributed to players' need not only for a valve instrument, but also for one more comfortable to play. This would make it easier to play in the high register, which had become more and more necessary after the pause in writing for the *cor mixte* and the experimentation with the middle-low register that followed the adoption of the valves.

Late in the second half of the century, some performers therefore began to use horns in B-flat alto (nine feet) and A alto, thus transposing their parts, which were generally notated in F and E at the time. The high-pitched instruments were less tiring to play because of the shortness of the tubing and the use of lower harmonics and provided more "security" in the upper register, although they did involve a radical change in the tone of the instrument. This was more dramatic for models built in German countries owing to their larger tubings. In France, England, and Belgium, a narrower bore and bell diameter assured a more homogeneous timbre, even when high pitched instruments were used.[16] The aforementioned change in sound when using the B-flat and A sizes was not favorably received by many conductors (Morley-Pegge 1973, 115), including Carl Reinecke (1824–1910, for a long time active at the Gewandhaus in Leipzig) and Hans von Bülow (1830–1894, Hofkapellmeister in Hannover and later the head of the Berliner Philharmonic from 1887 to 1893). Notwithstanding the opposition to this practice, it offered greater security in performance for both the first and the third horn in the orchestra.

A sort of dispute that arose at the end of the century between Josef Lindner, professor in Würzburg and principal horn in Meiningen, and Richard Tornauer,

---

[16] French, English, and also Italian players were not pushed to use B-flat valve horn because domestic composers did not challenge them with extreme difficulties and because the symphonic repertoire was less frequently performed than the operatic repertoire (in the latter, horn parts require less physical endurance and use the high register less). Many horn players still used horns with crooks in the operatic repertoire for scores written by earlier composers or to avoid transposition.

hornist in Cologne, is informative in this regard. In an article published on August 20, 1898 in the *Deutsche Musiker-Zeitung* ("Hie F-Horn, hie B-Horn, was ist recht?" [Here F-horn, there B-flat-horn, what's right?]) Lindner openly takes a position in favor of the B-flat horn. He clarifies that it should be equipped with a long leadpipe, around 96–98cm in length, and not with a short shank, 10–12cm long, inserted to change the F horn into B-flat.[17] In this way, an appropriate tone can be obtained, however bright it may be. He also suggests replacing the third valve with one long enough to produce the harmonics of F so as to increase the number of keys available with the valves and to produce the corresponding series of harmonics with proper intonation. Finally, while complaining about the difficulties of contemporary music, Lindner notes that Franz Strauss himself, "*der Joachim auf dem Horn*," played with the B-flat horn under the guidance of Wagner at the Munich Opera, and the same could be said of some of his most renowned pupils, such as the Reiter brothers and Bruno Hoyer. This was also the case for Dr. Kaim's orchestra in Munich, where Messrs. Rebky and Albert, first and third horn, performed with the B-flat model.

Tornauer's reply primarily observes that the majority of horn music from the past was written in several keys and that in German operas the low keys of the horn are used more frequently. It is also apparent that most composers prefer the timbre of the F horn, however flawed it may be. The B-flat horn is therefore the choice of players who want to obtain greater security with the result of a less interesting performance. With its bright and metallic tone, the B-flat horn is most suitable for passages like "Siegfried's horn call." Tornauer then relays Gumpert's assertion about the attack of the c''' in the second movement of Beethoven's Fourth Symphony that,[18] although risky with the E-flat or F crook, can be made safer with the A-flat crook.[19] He finally states that while hornists in Southern

---

[17] On the Viennese horn, the adoption of a short B-flat crook also makes the sound like that of a flugelhorn or trombone when compared to that of a full B-flat horn with a long leadpipe.

[18] Friedrich Gumpert (1841–1906), often referred to as Gumbert in printed text, was first horn at the Gewandhaus in Leipzig from 1864 to 1899, where he was hired by the conductor Reinecke (Pizka 1986, 154). He was also a professor at the local conservatory and author of various handbooks, including a *Hornschule* translated into various languages.

[19] Anton Horner (1877–1971), a pupil of Friedrich Gumpert (see Ericson 1998, 31, who reports part of a letter by Horner from 1956), tells how Gumpert did not routinely use the B-flat horn but rather used other crooks more frequently. Even though Gumpert used a B-flat crook for the horn call in *Siegfried*, he used the A crook for Beethoven's Symphony no. 2 and the E crook for *A Midsummer Night's Dream*. On the other hand, some orchestras did not accept the use of the B-flat horn in auditions at the time, even though specialists, when talented, were held in high esteem.

Germany prefer to use the B-flat horn, others prefer the F horn. Richard Strauss's revision of the instrumentation treatise by Berlioz (1905), in which Strauss pays particular attention to the B-flat horn, provides confirmation of this particular "southern" preference.

The period in question featured the progressive acceptance of a new sound ideal, one which we would call "late symphonic style." During this period increasing adoption of the B-flat and A horn has been recorded, as well as—it should be added—the disappearance of the nostalgia for the "old custom of stifling the harmonics with the hand" (Fahrbach). However, some theorists still did invoke the latter technique in order to correct the pitch, facilitate trills, and darken the timbre of the instrument (Eichborn 1897, 20–21).

The dismissal of the hand horn coincided with the introduction of the "timbral" use of stopped notes. In fact, some composers chose to intentionally write notes that were to be performed with this technique using indications such as the German *gestopft*, the French *bouché*, or the Italian *chiuso*. The "+" sign to be found in some works by Wagner, who codified its use in the preface to *Tristan and Isolde* (published in 1859), was also used. In this regard, Rimsky-Korsakov's (1922, I, 22, note ii) statement (posthumously published) appear conclusive:

> From the middle of the 19th century onward the natural brass disappeared from the orchestra, giving place to valve instruments. In my second opera, *The May Night* [1878] I used natural horns and trumpets, changing the keys, and writing the best notes "stopped"; this was purposely done for practice.

25

A FEW LEADING COMPOSERS

We now want to examine how some distinguished composers wrote for the instrument, beginning with the pioneering use of chromatic horns in Wagner's *Ring Cycle* and in the music of Verdi, the two opera composers of the nineteenth century whose works are still the most commonly performed around the world.[1]

Later on, we turn to the main venue where the valve horn began to take over, the symphonic concert hall. After the initial push by a few distinguished German composers, Mendelssohn and Schumann among them, the mechanized instrument was constantly requested by the great composers of the second half of the century, including Tchaikovsky, Bruckner, Mahler, and Strauss. Brahms, however, was the exception. He remained attached to the natural horn, although his prescriptions in this regard were soon circumvented both in the orchestra and by soloists.

See online for in-depth case studies of each of the said composers, set aside Mendelssohn, whose early attemps are discussed in the main text.

[1] Source: www.operabase.com.

26
DOUBLE HORN

Notable developments in the production of valves resulted in increasingly reliable instruments, which were preferred by the new generations of hornists and were continually put to the test by the increasing difficulties of the scores of the time. So, after having opted for instruments with two and then three valves, pitched in F, G, and then in B-flat, a successful new experiment led to the birth of a model destined to become the favorite of the hornists of the twentieth century: the double horn, created in 1897 by Kruspe of Erfurt. This German firm developed a new and promising model that brought together two independent instruments with two different airstream paths and two sets of valves of the proper length for their respective keys but only one mouthpiece with no crooks, a single body, and a single bell (and obviously with a valve for switching from one side of the tubing to the other).

FULL DOUBLE HORN

The double horn with two sets of slides, one for each of the two main sizes of F and B-flat, was in fact invented by the maker Johann Eduard Kruspe (1831–1919) of Erfurt,[1] who built it in 1897 together with his son Fritz (*ca.* 1862–1909) and with the artistic collaboration of Edmund Gumpert, third horn in the Hofkapelle in Meiningen and nephew of the famous Friedrich Gumpert of Leipzig.[2] The innovation was long confused with that of a "compensating" double horn, in which the size of F is obtained by lengthening the main B-flat section through the

[1] Heyde 1987a, 181. From 1899 to 1909, several makers attempted to create double horn models: Friedrich Butti (Riga), C. F. Schmidt (Berlin, then Weimar), Albert Pappé (Leipzig, patent No. 193161 of 1906 for F/F high horn, see Waterhouse 1993, s.v.), Otto Tiedt (Hagen), and Gebr. Alexander (Mainz).

[2] This is also discussed in an article signed "r." in the *Deutsche Musiker-Zeitung*, 1898 (cited by Pizka 1986, 288–291).

use of an additional stretch of tubing. The error, reported by Dick Martz, is described on his website in the following words:[3]

> Both Anthony Baines . . . and Herbert Heyde . . . incorrectly state that the first double horn by Kruspe was a compensating horn, but neither gives a citation for this statement. [. . .] Unfortunately this error has since been spread throughout subsequent publications, including the official catalog of the exhibition of Kruspe instruments at Erfurt in 2012, and, of course, throughout the Internet.

Martz's claims are fully confirmed by the article "Ein neues Doppelhorn" by Hermann Eichborn. The article appeared in 1899 and describes and illustrates the first double horn by Kruspe, which had a switching system (F/B-flat) based on two twin valves that operated simultaneously (see Figure 158). One was located upstream with respect to the rest of the valves and one downstream (*ZfI* (1899–1900), 98).[4] This instrument was granted a patent for the German states (Deutsches Reichs Gebrauchsmuster, No. 84240 dated November 13, 1897). Drawings and a description of the horn are available on Martz's website.[5]

Just a few years later, the success of this initial experiment was already evident, and in the 1907 edition of *The Metronome* Gustav Saenger (1865–1935) emphasized that in the meantime, "innumerable experiments have been made in order to combine the qualities and technical advantages of a B-flat and F horn into one instrument" and that the double horn "[was] the talk of modern European Horn players and bids fair to revolutionize the playing of the instrument to a great extent."

On the early models, the tone of the B-flat side was rather strident and differed from that of the F side, but later makers realized that by slightly increasing the diameter of the tubing, they could improve the response on both sides and reduce the imbalance between the two sides to a minimum.

[3] See http://www.rjmartz.com/horns/drgm232038/.
[4] A similar system was adopted by Alexander for some models of *descant horn* still on the market (see below). Similar projects by Paxman were later abandoned.
[5] See http://rjmartz.com/horns/DRGM84240/#back1 and http://rjmartz.com/horns/kruspe_097/.

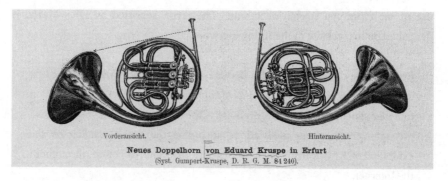

Figure 158. Double horn by E. Kruspe.

COMPENSATING DOUBLE HORN

Although the compensating double horn was mistakenly thought to have been invented prior to the double horn (possibly because the same principle had already been applied to other brass instruments), it was instead its subsequent and advantageous variant. As it turns out, the initial idea for a compensating double horn came from the Alexander brothers of Mainz, as confirmed by Dick Martz on his website:[6]

> No evidence has been found that there was ever a compensating double horn in the modern sense prior to 1906 when the instruments by Gebr. Alexander (Model 102) and Ed. Kruspe (Gumpert-Kruspe, D.R.G.M. 295 125) were introduced.

On this model, the B-flat side has its own full set of tubing (in some cases with its own master slide) and the F side is obtained through an additional portion of tube that forces the airstream to travel through both sections of each valve slide. The additional part of the tubing, associated with that of the main one, "compensates" for the base length of the instrument in order to lower the pitch by the required amount (in other words, the F harmonic series "depends" on that of B-flat). A thorough description of several models of both full double and compensating double horns with simplified diagrams of their operating system can be found in Heyde (1987a, 181–187).

[6] See http://rjmartz.com/horns/DRGM84240/#note3.

In London, David James Blaikley (1846–1936), a skilled inventor and the manager of the Boosey Company (Smith 2003), patented a double compensated horn (Morley-Pegge 1973, 51). It was based on the "Raoux" model and equipped with four piston valves in 1912 (GB # 28599, reproduction in Pizka 1986, 351), but only ten specimens were manufactured (Myers 2002, 407).[7] The Boosey Company subsequently produced instruments equipped with this mechanism. They formed part of the "Sotone" production line, based on the French rules of construction widely appreciated in London.[8]

In Paris, the double horn was in turn built by the Thibouville-Lamy factory in around 1930 (Morley-Pegge 1973, 51). The traditional ascendant system was adopted on a model designed by Louis Vuillermoz (1898–1953), the son of one of the Conservatoire's famous teachers, Édouard (1869–1939), who switched to the new model at the end of his career. According to Lucien Thévet (see *Larigot*, May 2022, 38), Thibouville-Lamy, at the request of Vuillermoz Jr., created two items in F/Bb with an ascending system around 1924 but the company considered this model unprofitable and decided to discontinue its production. French and Belgian instrument builders sometimes applied this double mechanism to the body of older natural horns that had evidently fallen into disuse and were restored by equipping them with pistons and double slides. The model—even when built from scratch—kept the clear and sweet tone of the "French" horns by the renowned Raoux. An interesting example is shown in Figure 159.

The same model also allowed for an easier high register, with the pitch of (high) C obtainable using the third ascending piston.[9] The Couesnon Company, according to their 1934 catalog, in turn put a double ascending horn called the "Nouveaté" on the market.[10] It was equipped with three pistons and a rotary valve for switching the key. Soon after, Selmer of Paris (1935–1936) also began to market a double horn model. Despite having wider tubing than the traditional French standard, this model, which as usual had pistons, did not hold up to the competition of German models, already adopted by some leading Parisian horn players by 1940 (Baines 1976, 225).

[7] Blaikley had already patented a compensating valve system (GB #4618) on November 14, 1878. He used it on several brass instruments but, as it seems, not the horn.

[8] See http://www.rjmartz.com/horns/sotone/sotone.htm.

[9] The model allowed for all the keys from C alto to D, but C# could only be obtained by partially closing the bell with the hand. G, F#, C, and B' had better intonation than on descending double horns.

[10] See http://www.rjmartz.com/horns/Couesnon_045//.

 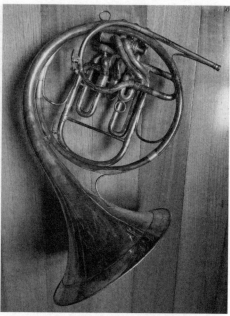

Figure 159. A compensating Raoux horn with a mechanism added in *ca*. 1925 on what was previously a natural horn by Raoux.

The double compensating horn, which is still used by students, has the advantage of making the instrument lighter and cheaper thanks to the use of a smaller length of tubing.

THE MAIN MODELS

Over the course of a century of experimentation, a plethora of double-horn models was presented to the market, allowing the instrumentalist to choose the model that they felt was best suited to their artistic needs (or, in some cases, the most fashionable). Although many models were put on the market, we feel that it is enough to draw attention to the main four—three full double horns and one compensating horn—which could all be easily identified based on the type of switching valve, usually operated by the left thumb of the performer.

KRUSPE MODEL

In 1899, Anton Horner, a pupil of Friedrich Gumpert of Leipzig and the first horn of the Pittsburgh Orchestra, bought his first Kruspe double horn (Morley-Pegge

Figure 160. É. Vuillermoz portrayed with a Selmer compensating double horn.

1973, 54, fn. 28), thus marking the beginning of the adoption of this model in America. However, it did not completely satisfy the excellent American horn player, who considered it "rather temperamental in operation." Kruspe therefore replaced the two twin valves with a single switching valve between the two main sections of the tubing. He called the model "Horner,"[11] and placed it on the market

[11] According to a letter by Anton Horner published in http://www.rjmartz.com/horns/ Kruspe_080/, the latter ordered the horn that eventually took its name from Kruspe during the Sousa band's stay in Europe for the Exposition of 1900 (for more information on the Horner/ Kruspe model, see the *Deutscher Musiker Zeitung* from August 20, 1898, quoted by Pizka 1986, 279–291).

in 1902 (see Figure 161 online).[12] The rotary switching valve is here positioned upstream with respect to the valve mechanism—toward the player, that is—and numerous variations of this model, which was, by and large, the prototype for most subsequent ones, were marketed, including some adapted to local traditions and preferences. In fact, the 1930 Kruspe Company price list contains as many as fifteen horn models, nine of which are double horns! (See online, "Kruspe's double horns,' and Figures 162 and 163 online.)

Many manufacturers promptly adopted the principle of the Kruspe system while adding some original modifications. The company Alexander of Mainz, for example, secured German patent No. 220741 for a double horn on May 30, 1909. This instrument also had a switching valve upstream from the main valve block, but all of its tubes were positioned on the same plane (a six-way valve) and not on two different levels. This is the horn that is still known worldwide today as the "Alexander Mod. 103."

SCHMIDT MODEL

In the year 1900, Carl Friedrich Schmidt of Berlin (1852–1924) created the double horn model bearing his name, which was equipped with a Périnet piston placed crosswise under the keys of the three main valves.[13] It was especially successful in America,[14] where it was imported by Carl Fischer and chosen by Pellegrino Lecce,[15] who had been first horn of the Chicago Symphony Orchestra since 1929 and was later the solo horn at the Metropolitan Opera in New York (the horn section was then composed almost entirely of Italians). Carl Schmidt's instruments are still very popular among professionals, especially in America, and have been sold for considerable prices. Some current manufacturers still produce this model.

---

[12] See https://www.hornsociety.org/ihs-people/honoraries?view=article&id=53:anton-horner-1877-1971&catid=26..

[13] See https://de.wikipedia.org/wiki/Schmidt_%28Blechblasinstrumentenbauer%29.

[14] See http://www.rjmartz.com/Horns/Schmidt/cfschmidt.html#ref5.

[15] Pellegrino Lecce (1896–1989) was a refined horn player—Farkas himself says he was a master of the horn and of life (see Schweikert 1990, 83–84, for much biographical information). He studied the horn at the Conservatory of Naples, first with C. De Stefano (1906–1908) and for another four years with "Cavalier" (an Italian honorary recognition) Eduardo De Angelis, the author of an important four-volume handbook. In 1912, Lecce moved to the United States, where he continued his studies under the guidance of another famous Italian-American hornist, Franck Corrado.

Although the position of the piston produced a certain discomfort, this model was somewhat successful in Europe and especially in Italy, where it was initially imitated by G.B. Cazzani's company. The new company Rampone & Cazzani, founded in 1920, later produced it on a large scale. The soloist Domenico Ceccarossi (1910–1997) performed on a horn built by Rampone & Cazzani that was faithfully based on the Schmidt design for most of his career, eventually donating it to the National Museum of Musical Instruments in Rome (inv. 2871) (see Figure 164 online).

Even some French models were based on this principle with pistons instead of rotary valves. A less well-known horn of which only a few specimens were made by Alexander features the addition of a tuning slide for the B-flat section, which is missing on similar models by other firms.[16]

GEYER MODEL

A design with a rotary valve placed downstream from the others was instead successfully produced later on by Carl Geyer (1880–1973), who made about 1,400 items in Chicago from 1920 onward, when he set up as an independent maker. Many other companies included horns based on a similar principle in their catalogs. In fact, this model's design is linked to Richard Wunderlich (1860–1934), another maker of German origin with whom Geyer had previously worked after having been trained in Markneukirchen. Wunderlich advertised, "We can transform your Single F horn into a perfect Double French horn at a little cost" (Langwill 1993, 437, s.v. "Wunderlich").

This model, which owed its initial notoriety to the Chicago Symphony Orchestra—Chicago being the city where Geyer operated—still enjoys some success. Its lack of tight curves, alongside its straighter tubing, is considered to be a crucial factor for facilitating response. In addition, it is more esthetically pleasing than the models belonging to the first two groups described (see Figure 165 online).

"WALZEN" MODEL

Some models that were successful among professionals were made with a compensation system featuring a switch valve placed almost at the center of the

[16] See http://www.rjmartz.com/Horns/denaro/.

instrument transverse to the slides of the main set of valves. It intersected with the main valve slides, allowing for the opening and closing of the air passage in an additional section of tubing. This model was called the "walzen" (German for roller, barrel, or drum, as defined by Dick Martz).

One of the first patents based on this device was obtained on April 29, 1909 by Otto Tiedt of Hagen in Westphalia (Deutsches Reich Patent No. 222527: Double brass instrument, created by combining two instruments of different pitch in one instrument) (see Figure 166 online). The long transverse cylindrical switch valve is supplied with eight air pathways. When at rest, they only allow the airstream to pass through the valve slides of the B-flat side. When the thumb lever is pressed, the air is allowed to travel through the extra ones, thus adding the path length necessary to obtain the F pitch.[17]

In 1925, Carl Lehmann and Erdmann Chemnitzer patented a horn (Deutsches Reich Patent No. 440308: *Switching valve for brass instruments*) that also has a transverse cylindrical valve but uses a different compensation system. When the valve is activated, the airstream enters an extra section of tubing below the cylinder, thus lengthening each section of tubing just enough to obtain the F size.[18] This model, whose operation is described in detail in Gregory (1961, 93: "horn with horizontal valve"), did not have much success; but a similar one created by Josef Lidl (1864–1946) in Brno and subsequently distributed by the company Amati of Kraslice, which took over the brand in 1948, did.

Several manufacturers tried to make their own variants of this particular system. Kurt August Knopf's dates back to 1929 (see Figure 167 online). Knopf (1900–1945) separated the action of the longitudinal valve (here used to switch between the two sections together with a fourth rotary valve) from that of the three slides of the main valve set. This compensating model, featuring some similarities with a full double horn, remained in vogue until the end of World War II.[19]

Another variant, rooted in the French tradition, was based on the use of pistons for the three main valves and a rotary switching valve. Called the "Radio Wonder Hoorn," it was manufactured by the Dutch firm De Prins (Antwerp) and was sold in the period between the two World Wars (see Figure 168 online).[20]

---

[17] See http://www.rjmartz.com/horns/walzen/1909-4-29-Tiedt.pdf.
[18] See http://www.rjmartz.com/horns/walzen/1925-11-24.pdf.
[19] See http://www.rjmartz.com/horns/walzen/Knopf-1.jpg.
[20] See http://www.rjmartz.com/horns/DePrins_092/.

Figure 169. G. B. Cazzani, compensating double horn, *ca*. 1920, with marks "ditte riunite" (united companies), "sistema brevettato" (patented), and "Sole Agents for Great Britain/The Louis Musical Instrument Co. Ltd./= London =." Right, detail of the lever that operates the F section and the tunable second valve.

The Mahillon Company also proposed its own model with three Périnet pistons and a long horizontal piston. One specimen made before 1937 is located at the Brussels Museum (inv. 2002.031).[21]

August Dummuscheit was granted a patent for an instrument following the same principle that used only rotary valves (three for the B-flat section, one for the switcher, three for the F section) on May 11, 1930 (see Heyde 1987a, 186).[22] The same idea was revived by Giovan Battista Cazzani (1846–1920) with only six simple valves and an ingenious system that allowed for opening the F section and for tuning the second valve, otherwise without a slide. This model was also imported in London by the Louis Musical Instrument Co. Ltd. (illustration in Morley-Pegge 1973, 4, plate VIII) (see Figure 169).

A REGIONAL OVERVIEW

As had already happened with the single horn, the double model (full or compensating) made it possible to obtain better performances than previously. Better voice in the mid-low register with the instrument pitched in F and in the higher one on the B-flat side meant that passages requiring high degrees of agility and virtuosity became feasible in the register in which the horn is often associated

[21] See https://carmentis.be:443/eMP/eMuseumPlus?service=ExternalInterface&module =collection&objectId=113389&viewType=detailView.
[22] See http://www.rjmartz.com/horns/walzen/1930-5-11-Dummusheit.pdf.

with cellos. In fact, some notes that were previously only playable in falsetto became easily obtainable (F, E, E-flat, etc. in the classical notation), as did those with less stable intonation . The approach to the high register was also facilitated, albeit in this case with some timbral compromise. Anton Horner—the aforementioned double horn pioneer in America—claimed to have adopted the B-flat section only in the high register "because the tone is not so mellow and of as good a quality in the middle register and lower register, being harsh and hollow" (Gregory 1961, 45). This practice is still used by many horn players, especially in America.

For composers in the early twentieth century, however, the potential of the horn remained substantially unchanged since the new models did not introduce unprecedented performance features (as happened, e.g., with the advent of the valves in comparison to the hand horn), nor radical changes in range (as occurred during the transition from the baroque horn to the classic one). They therefore continued to write habitually for "F horn" (some also used other keys for ease of writing), well aware that the instrumentalists would decide whether to use the single horn in F or in B-flat or even one of the two sides of the new double model.

The adoption of the double horn, full or compensating, took place in compliance with the esthetic choices that suited each country and the local manufacturing tradition. The German hornists researched and experimented with a dark and full-sounding tone by increasing the bell flare and the tubing, to the point that the diameter of the cylindrical tubing of the Alexander 103 model was increased to over 12mm. In Germany, as already mentioned, many professionals who occupied the place of the first or third horn in the orchestra preferred to use single B-flat horns with a valve for stopped notes (cf. p. 327) due to their lightness, both in weight and response. In Austria, the traditional F horn model with Viennese valves was one of the favorites.

For a long time, the French hornists played with a clear tone, influenced by their type of embouchure and production, to which a constant vibrato was added in the post-World War I period.[23] British players also kept their tone clearer than the German one but did not use constant vibrato. In Italy, where horns were built according to German principles, the tone had to nevertheless remain soft in order to comply with the esthetics of the predominant operatic tradition. However, power was also required for the symphonic repertoire, such as in Ottorino

---

[23] The first to use the constant vibrato in performance systematically was Jean Devémy (1898–1969), according to George Barboteau (cf. *THC*, 6/2, May 1976, 23–30).

Respighi's scores (e.g. *Fountains of Rome*, 1916). In America, the predilection toward a darker and gloomier sound was also reflected by an increase in the size of the tubing. To further darken the sound, horn players put the instrument on the thigh, thus exploiting the absorption of their clothes while using the hand in a bell of increased proportions.

The German B-flat single horns with a stopping valve were eventually equipped with an additional fifth valve for the F harmonics, invented in the United States in 1914 by the Italian-American horn player Lorenzo Sansone, who established his own workshop in New York in 1925: "The World's Largest French Horn House" (see Figure 170 online).[24]

In France, there was no interest in the manufacture of double horns and probably no interest in their use until the late 1920s, since the study of the valve horn had been only recently reintroduced in the country. F horns were traditionally preferred, with an ascending third valve that allowed the player to obtain the key of G. On these models, it was possible to use the higher B-flat and A crooks, but the instrument evidently was then used as a natural horn, since there is no evidence of wide diffusion of slides short enough to match these high keys, as were available for some German models. As we have seen, only in the 1930s were compensating double horns equipped with piston valves, an ascending third valve, and a wider bore introduced in France. In any case, the German double model finally began to spread here as well, starting in the middle of the century (Baines 1976, 225).

In Britain, the single three-valve horn (of French design, or even production) continued to be used in the first half of the twentieth century. This model was the favorite of Aubrey Brain, principal horn of the BBC Orchestra (1928–1945). As mentioned, he used a "Raoux model" built by Labbaye (Baines 1976, 222). Even Dennis Brain (1921–1957) used only the single horn, at first in F (model Raoux–Labbaye), and later switched to a B-flat single instrument with a valve for stopped notes made by Alexander (see below). Further evidence of this predilection comes from the *Grove Dictionary* (I and II, "Horn") and from Schlesinger (1910). Her article "Horn" (for a long time the finest paper in English on the instrument)

---

[24] Lorenzo Sansone (1881–1975) emigrated to the United States in 1903. There, he played in some of the most important American orchestras, teaching horn at the Juilliard School from 1920 to 1947 (Sansone 1975; Caluori 2005). In 1914, he invented this particular model (which was also included in the 1930 Kruspe price list). It was made by the German-born manufacturer Wunderlich (Chicago), who became a faithful collaborator to many first horn players. Further information and a reproduction of a catalog of Sansone's firm can be found at http://www.rjmartz.com/horns/Sansone_028/.

portrays a "modern horn" (a single three-piston horn) built by Boosey & Co. In the orchestration handbook by the British composer Cecil Forsyth (1914), only the three-valve horn is referenced, and Forsyth recommends a model produced by Boosey & Co. (see Forsyth 1914, 85, plate III) equipped with a terminal F crook and three "Automatic Compensating Valves" or "pistons which mechanically correct the error in piston combinations," an invention of D. J. Blaikley (see online, "The horn models described by Forsyth").

Visits to London by German orchestras, such as the Berlin Philharmonic in 1927, certainly provided new incentive to make changes. This continued to the point that Sir Thomas Beecham, upon the foundation of the London Philharmonic Orchestra in 1932, forced the horn players to adopt the "wide-bore double horn" that had been common in Germany for years. It is also said that under pressure from Sir Hamilton Harty, the Hallé Orchestra was equipped with similar instruments. In 1930, Alan Hyde, afterwards a member of the LPO, promoted the Alexander 103 (Baines 1976, 225), the standard model reproduced by Boosey & Hawkes for the English market, which was also adopted in the 1950s by the BBC Symphony Orchestra (Gregory 1961, 44).

In Italy, the double horn based on a pattern similar to the Schmidt had been built by the firm Giovanni Battista Cazzani since the 1910s. It was quickly adopted among professionals, as demonstrated by *La Scuola moderna del doppio Corno in Fa-Sib* (1922) by Carlo Fontana (1864–1933).[25] Referring specifically to the operatic repertoire, he suggests keeping the hand inside the bell in order to obtain a "more mellow" sound and to be prepared for stopped notes, in marked contrast to the tradition of the Tosoroni school (see above). He also encourages the student to practice on both sides of the horn, which he called "*senza pistone*" (without piston) or "*con pistone*" (with piston) (see online, "The first tutor for double horn?").[26]

In contrast to the players mentioned here, other horn players, especially in Central and Southern Italy, continued to follow Tosoroni's example well after the

[25] The first horn at the Teatro Regio in Turin and a professor at the city's conservatory from the late 1800s to the early 1900s, Fontana is author of, among other things, *Metodo completo teorico pratico per corno a macchina ed a mano, diviso in tre parti* (Turin, Calco-litografia salesiana, 1898) and *Raccolta dei principali Passi e a-Soli per Corno di opere teatrali e sinfoniche di Maestri italiani e stranieri, estratte dalle partiture originali d'orchestra, preceduta dalla storia del Corno e da cenni biografici dei più valenti professori* (Milan, Ricordi, 1914).

[26] *Pistone* was the term used to refer to the fourth piston valve, which acted as a diverter valve for the B-flat and F sides of the Schmidt horn. The same term is still sometimes used in Italian to refer more generally to this very valve, regardless of its type.

Figure 171. Hand position in the bell, from G. Mariani, *Metodo popolare per corno da caccia, ca.* 1890.

middle of the twentieth century, either by avoiding inserting the hand into the bell or by using it inside the bell as a simple sustaining function, as seen in the illustration of a horn handbook by Giuseppe Mariani (1840–1904) (see Figure 171). The same attitude was finally witnessed by Anthony Baines, presumptively during the 1960s.

In describing how the principal horn of the Rome opera house played with his hand resting on the outer edge of the bell, he also commented, "Yet Italian playing can be as fine as any" (Baines 1976, 225).

Definitively overcoming the Italian operatic imprint was the scholarship and the mastery of the greatest Italian *maestro* of the past century, Domenico Ceccarossi (1910–1997), who judged the former way of playing to be incorrect and anachronistic (Ceccarossi 1957, 9). His long and illustrious soloistic career, which involved various European countries, including England, is also documented by a huge discography (see Cagnoli 1987).

SOLO AND CHAMBER REPERTOIRE

In the early decades of the twentieth century, the solo repertoire for horn was secondary and written by authors of little international resonance. Starting in the 1930s, however, a major revival occurred. One of the composers who contributed was Paul Hindemith, with a Sonata for Horn and Piano in 1939 and, later, when he was a professor at Yale University, three other solo compositions: the Sonata for Althorn or Waldhorn or Alto Saxophone (1943), which contains some lines that player and pianist have to speak before the fourth movement starts; the Concerto for Horn and Small Orchestra (1949), where the horn part plays a melody that is a musical representation of a poem; and the amazing Sonata for Four Horns (1952), with a final movement that contains variations on *Ich schell mein Horn* (I play my horn). The previously mentioned Concerto for Horn and Orchestra no. 2 by Richard Strauss (performed August 11, 1943 at the Mozarteum by Gottfried von Freiberg) also dates back to this period. It was followed by Concerto, op. 65 by Othmar Schoeck (1951) and another demanding solo piece, the concerto by Reinhold Glière (1951). This latter piece was dedicated to Valeriy Polekh, who performed its *première* and who also created a long and appealing cadenza that is generally played by other soloists owing to its beauty and performing palette.[27]

Chamber compositions that permanently entered the horn repertoire are rarer, while new and variable instrumental combinations began to overtake the standard groups that had previously enjoyed the preference of the composers. Ever-

[27] An article published in THC, 29/3 (May 1999), 39–40 ("The Birth of the Glière Concerto") also contains some information on the soloist. Polekh performed the concert for the first time in Leningrad on May 10, 1951 under the direction of the composer, and in 1952, he recorded it with the orchestra of the Bolshoi Theater, again conducted by Glière.

changing jazz combos should also be added to this list. Although they offered the horn only a marginal role, they had considerable influence on the writing of many avant-garde composers, a matter we will discuss (see Chapter 28, p. 331).

One stable chamber music ensemble commonly called for in modern times, however, was the wind quintet (flute, oboe, clarinet, horn, and bassoon) (see Table 17 online). Many compositions gave this quintet new life after a previous short period of importance during the full Romantic period. In this repertoire, the horn is treated in the most disparate ways, both solistically and in dialogue with the other instruments, with a great variety of technique, range, and dynamics used. Composers frequently had a particular horn player in mind when writing the solo part, generally the one who was the first to perform the score. One example is the aforementioned *Serenade* by Britten (1943), explicitly written for Dennis Brain, who played it on a single F horn, since the beginning calls only for the F series of natural harmonics (see online, "Dennis Brain's horn," and Musical example 73 online).

Other composers were also inspired by Dennis Brain, but aside from Britten, only Paul Hindemith's aforementioned *Concerto* (1949), Gordon Jacob's *Concerto for Horn and String Orchestra* (1951), and Francis Poulenc's *Elégie in Memory of Dennis Brain* (1957) permanently entered the repertoire.

27

THE HORN IN THE SECOND HALF OF THE TWENTIETH CENTURY

Except for descant horns, which we discuss below (p. 326), there were no significant changes in the construction of the double horn during the second part of the twentieth century. Since it was eventually usually adopted at both student and professional levels, the model underwent only minor improvements and refinements of individual components.[1]

Instead, the scale of production was progressively expanded, with huge investments allowing for experiments and more effective manufacturing techniques. Builders attempted to improve response, tone, and intonation by increasing the taper of the mouthpiece and the flare of the bell. The expensive system for making the bells by seaming overlapped tabs and gussets was dismissed in favor of a cheaper bell pressed on the lathe and soldered to the body of instrument;[2] cylindrical tubes were made only through die plates—therefore without longitudinal soldering (seamless pipes)—and tube bending was experimented with through innovative systems (including a mixture of ice and salt tested by the Kalison Company in Milan). Modern machines allowed builders to

---

[1] Experiments with multitonal horns based on the same principle as omnitonic valve horns viewed from a modern perspective were attempted by the Alexander factory and by Mark Veneklasen (an American horn player and inventor) among others, but they had little consequence.

[2] The modern bell built on the lathe has, from the structural point of view, features that are the opposite of the bells made from sheet metal thinned by hammering and soldered on a seam. Spun bells are thicker at the ends of the bell (about 0.4mm) and thinner where they are soldered or screwed to the body (about 0.3mm). Hammered bells are instead thinner at the ends (even 0.3mm) and thicker at the junction point. For the latter reason, it was common for many years for metal garlands to be added to the edges of hammered bells; bells were also sometimes embellished with engravings. The timbre of the instrument is influenced to a certain extent by this difference in construction.

obtain a precisely calibrated leadpipe flare in mere seconds,[3] leading to the abandonment of the old drawing systems. With compressed air and the adoption of moldings and steel balls inserted under pressure, the bending of tubes was much improved, speeding up the procedure considerably. Several parts of the instrument were increasingly manufactured outside the main factory, thus reducing the cost of producing various models and also influencing the structure of the instrument, which was partially adapted to prepackaged components. New research was conducted on improving the quality of alloys, and for some time, especially in America, instruments made entirely in nickel silver had a degree of success.[4] Recently, the German maker Engelbert Schmid has produced horns in four different alloys,[5] as well as a nickel-free model designed for those with an allergy to this metal. The most modern laboratory equipment has also been used by some manufacturers, for example, to identify constructive flaws with an electronic sound simulator in order to obtain essentially flawless specimens.

In short, the work is now conducted in a manner that is quite different from the traditional procedure, where small defects could also become the merits of an instrument. On the other hand, performers are forced to achieve absolute precision and perfect intonation by pressing timetables in the recording studios, or even by simple comparison to "perfect" recordings. A certain "flexibility" of the instrument, long considered a peculiarity, is now seen by some as a defect, while

[3] Different tapering of the initial part of the horn influences the tuning of some harmonics. This is always one of the biggest problems when using crooks on natural horns. Slower flaring offers greater dynamic possibilities while decreasing the effectiveness of the high register (see Jeffrey Agrell, "Horn Design 101," *THC*, 32/2, February 2002, 65–67, who cites the advice of the American maker Walter Lawson).

[4] Nickel silver, which can be made with different proportions of the various metal components (60% copper, 20% zinc, 20% nickel; 67–18–15%; or 63–27–10%), is a much harder alloy than brass. It has been used since the late nineteenth century for parts subject to particular wear (tenons and mortises on valve slides, crook receivers, and some parts of the valve mechanism) or simply as decoration.

[5] Usually, the most common alloys are yellow brass or common brass, which is approximately 70% copper and 30% zinc (about 80% of the horns are produced with this material), gold brass—or red or rose brass—an alloy with a greater presence of copper (85–90%) said to give a darker sound richer in harmonics, and nickel silver (see fn. 4, above), which has a lighter and brighter tone at loud dynamics. Sterling silver may be added (92.5% silver and 7.5% copper), but E. Schmid was the only one to do so. Schmid claims that the metal is corrosion resistant and states, "[It] sounds noble and doesn't get too aggressive or edgy in fortissimo. It speaks very easily in piano with a rounded sound, (ideal for lyrical passages). In fortissimo the sound stays round but is more tiring to play than the other alloys." Other manufacturers make instruments or parts of them with ambronze (84% copper, 14% zinc, and 2% tin, a softer alloy than gold brass) and nickel bronze (89% copper, 9% zinc, and 2% tin).

the choice of a given model is in some cases less the result of esthetic choices than of the fashion of the moment. In this regard, the test proposed by Barry Tuckwell in 1971 at the Horn Week of Pomona College in Claremont, where the celebrated soloist was blindfolded together with Jim Decker and Ralph Pyle in order to try different horn models in front of the attendants, is eloquent. Twelve models of double horns were tested,[6] and the final result can be appraised directly from Tuckwell's words: "The overriding result was that a player sounds the same no matter what horn he is playing" (Kloss–Anderson 1997, 41).

THE DESCANT DOUBLE HORN

The execution of very high parts in which the horn is pushed toward the upper limits of its range (such as in the *Christmas Oratorio* by J. S. Bach or in some symphonies by Haydn and Mozart) led some hornists to adopt instruments pitched higher than the already extreme B-flat: single F alto (six feet) and G alto horns. Well after Gumpert's aforementioned use of a single B-flat alto horn for Siegfried's horn call, and later even F alto single horn, Alexander created a G alto horn in 1906 (with an extension for the key of F) for Händel's *Judas Maccabeus* and Bach's B Minor Mass, both performed at Mainz Festival that year (Baines 1976, 226). Instruments of this type were occasionally used in military bands, since they allowed for an easier approach to the horn during the limited time of conscription.

For a long time, F alto horns—which were favored owing to the fact that fingering was generally simpler than on those in G—were the only possibility for confronting the extreme high register. Taking inspiration from double F/B-flat horns, Schediwy's workshop (Ludwigsburg, see *Brass Bulletin*, 83, 1993, 37) created what could be the first high B/F double horn before 1944 (see Figure 172).

This model had no immediate follow-up, but after World War II, however, in 1955, the Milanese firm Kalison created a model in B-flat equipped with a fourth valve that switched the instrument into F alto (Heyde 1987a, 112) (see Figure 173 online). This horn, on the one hand, used fingering similar to that of the F/B-flat horn and, on the other, allowed the player to maintain the usual tone of the B-flat horn, using the F alto side only for few notes or isolated passages. A major problem was, as was the case for the double F/B-flat model, the notable discrepancy in sound

---

[6] Schmidt, Geyer, Knopf, Kruspe, Kalison, Holton 180, Holton 179, Alexander and Alexander silver, Reynolds, and Conn (new 8D and prewar 8D).

Figure 172. F. Schediwy, B-flat/ F high double horn, before 1944.

between the B-flat side and that of F alto, which was of course brighter, clearer, and poorer in harmonics, with a tone similar to that of the cornet. Later, however, improvements in manufacturing made it more balanced, with much less difference in tone between the two sides, especially through the refinement of the leadpipe taper.

Many makers spent time and money to create a new B-flat/high F model and some horn players began to use this instrument in the orchestra, at first only for the baroque and classical repertoire and later also for more recent music. The instrument, however, has some additional drawbacks in the lower register: the sounds between F and B' (concert pitch) on the F alto side (the first harmonic of each position) have a very different and unpleasant tone. Moreover, stopped notes on the B-flat side, sometimes unavoidable, are out of tune and call for convoluted alternative fingerings. To mitigate these flaws, a fifth valve was added so that stopped notes could be played in tune. This valve, already seen for many years on B-flat single horns, added about three quarters of a step of extra tubing (stopped notes are usually avoided on the F alto side because they raise the pitch by a full step). In some cases, the switching valve may come with a much longer alternative slide that pitches the instrument in low F (or a sixth valve is added). In this way, the instrument becomes a kind of triple horn (see below), although playing in low F calls for the help of the hand and for alternative fingerings.

The double horn in B-flat/F alto is quite common today, although in recent years it seems to have been almost entirely supplanted by the triple horn (see below), a sort of panacea for all the struggles of a modern horn player! Many also advocate the use of descant horns, but other authoritative voices (such as Tuckwell 1983, 56) have stepped back from the indiscriminate use of these instruments, especially by the second and fourth horns in the orchestra. Although to common listeners, and even to many conductors, the tone of high-pitched horns is not remarkably different from the usual horn sound, each horn player is able to recognize when the F alto side is used during performance, despite improvements made by many makers in the production of these models. From a purely acoustic perspective, the upper harmonics are more present and the lower ones are attenuated, making the overall sound of the horn section in the orchestra smaller (quite the opposite of the majestic timbre of the Vienna Philharmonic horn section with its F horns).

The double B-flat/F alto horn is based on the same principle as the double F/B-flat but exists only as the complete version, not compensated. The leadpipe is very short and promptly widens to reach the average diameter of the tubing. On some models, it is like a small extractable tube—equipped with a screw clamp to prevent sliding—which provides the F alto side with its own sort of master slide. Usually, these are instruments with rotary valves (it appears that no specimen of the kind was built with pistons). However, the Finke Company devised a model with a unique piston located along the initial section of the leadpipe for switching between the B-flat and F sides. In addition, some manufacturers offer a smaller bell for baroque and classical repertoire or chamber music and a wider one for Romantic and modern music.

In 1988, hornist and inventor Peter Steidle presented in the magazine *Brass Bulletin* (62, 1988) a polytonic instrument on which, thanks to a complex variety of slides and valves, it is possible to obtain several keys including B-flat and E-flat alto. He considers the latter solution to be more functional than those just described owing to the distance of fourth, instead of fifth, between the two sections, which are therefore closer to one another and more even in sound. Another advantage is that on this horn it is possible to use a longer leadpipe with less pronounced tapering than on the double B-flat/F alto model. This improves the tonal result in forte passages—which in F alto can sound quite harsh—and also the intonation.

Fingering is convenient too, since some alternative fingerings on the E-flat alto horn are equivalent to the usual ones on the F alto horn. A model of the kind was also produced by E. Schmid (*Brass Bulletin*, 94, 1996, 47), who also published a series of musical examples from the orchestral repertoire in which it is profitable to adopt the E-flat alto horn (see Figures 174 & 175 online).

THE VENTED HORN

Alongside the developments of the double horn, we must point out the invention of a new model: the vented horn. As seen, the descant double horn was developed to deal with the demanding and high-pitched baroque repertoire. The revival of ancient music, in addition to fueling the construction of copies of ancient instruments, has prompted some instrumentalists to adopt the same expedient experimented in the 1960s by trumpeters for the "baroque" trumpet, that is, some holes along the bore of the natural instrument. The holes—without keys—have the purpose of adjusting the intonation of some harmonics and allow the performer to play other notes out of the natural series. In London in the 1970s Timothy Brown was the first to apply them to the horn and John Webb also created a model of "baroque horn" equipped with four holes—usually closed in the rest position by a screw cap with a rubber ring seal (O ring, for DIY lovers)—in order to pitch the instrument in G, F, E-flat, and D, the most common tonalities of the baroque repertoire. By choosing the appropriate crook, the instrumentalist opens the single hole corresponding to the required size and then operates with their fingers to obtain the desired sounds. The opening of a hole creates a virtual shortening of the air column, giving rise to a series of higher harmonics. In this way it is possible to avoid the use of the hand technique while performance accuracy, sought after especially for recordings, is increased, even though this trick has no historical foundation. Further information can be found in Humphries (2000, 47), who also deals with the practice of the natural instruments, and on Richard Seraphinoff's website, which reports on an essay of his that appeared in *THC* (27, November 1, 1996).

TRIPLE HORN

Last born among the most widespread models of the modern horn, triple horns are proving to be remarkably successful and can be considered to be an evolution of the double B-flat/F alto horn with the addition of a fifth valve and appropriate tubing for the harmonics of low F. The instrument was developed in 1958 by the English horn player Richard Merewether (1925–1985) with the support of the Paxman Company in London. For many years, the same company has been producing double and triple horns with different diameter cylindrical tube sections with the aim of improving sound quality and ease of execution (see Figure 176 online).[7]

A double lever operated by the left thumb allows the player to select among the three different tubing sections. The three main valves are each equipped with three different sets of slides. It is easy to imagine how complex the work of making and bending the tubes may be for such a model and how the considerable amount of tubing affects the weight. Triple horns can come in both the complete version and in a lighter, compensating version. Moreover, in 1982, the manufacturer Alexander patented a new design for a three-way valve devised specifically for the triple horn,[8] which allows for a lighter instrument, and which is still marketed with a new design (model 310) (see Figures 177 and 178 online). Engelbert Schmid has in turn marketed a triple horn in F/B-flat/E-flat alto that, for the same reasons explained with regards to the B-flat/E-flat alto horn, some find more functional and lighter than the other triple horns, and that is gaining remarkable popularity among professionals.

An advantage of triple horns is the fact that they allow the hornist to play in three different registers, even though some weight is added to the instrument. Many instrumentalists are in fact not particularly concerned about this issue in view of the ease of playing the high register, a constant concern of brass players today. Moreover, the technical improvements made on these models have certainly rendered the triples more competitive than double ones, and some professionals consider them to be the instrument of the third millennium. For many other professionals, however, double horns remain the standard owing to their more balanced timbre. On the other hand, almost all agree that the triple should be strongly discouraged during training. Finally, in recent times, methods and handbooks for descant horns have been published, and some compositions have been explicitly conceived for this model or take into account the possibility of its adoption.[9]

---

[7] This model seems to be no more sought after by professionals.

[8] A patent for a similar valve model dating back to 1975 was awarded to Nakamura Satoshi (illustration in Pizka 1986, 353).

[9] The *Hommage à Brahms* Trio (1982) by G. Ligeti for violin, horn, and piano, written for the hornist H. Baumann, deserves special mention in this regard. It calls for a double horn (F/B) or even a triple (ad libitum) and for a performance technique not unlike that of the natural horn. In fact, natural harmonics are required, and their intonation should not be "corrected." The hand-horn technique, of which Baumann was a pioneer in modern times, is also used.

28

THE REPERTOIRE OF THE SECOND HALF OF THE TWENTIETH CENTURY

The improvements achieved with the invention of the double horn have brought the horn to a new level of technical perfection and performance. Musical performances changed rapidly after 1950 owing to stylistic and formal innovations in composition, openness toward new music styles (pop, jazz, rock, etc.), and the experiments of avant-garde composers, who not only changed the musical language, but also the way of writing for each individual instrument. New performance practices have been experimented with and adopted on the horn (vibrato, flutter tongue, wavering in pitch, blowing into the instrument, glissatos, etc.), although some were derived from older techniques—such as the glissandos of harmonics and use of the hand for timbral effects—or have been borrowed from jazz.

Remarkable success has also been obtained by some brass bands and above all from brass quintets (two trumpets, horn, trombone, and tuba), which have created their own repertoire, first relying on transcriptions of famous compositions and then on original pieces written specifically for them.[1] Examples include the Philip Jones Brass Ensemble, Canadian Brass, Empire Brass, London Brass, German Brass, Austrian Brass, and London Symphony Orchestra Brass.

SOLO AND SOLOISTIC REPERTOIRE

In the second half of the twentieth century, the solo concerto for horn and orchestra does not appear to have had much success, even though several authors have composed for the most distinguished soloists (see Table 18 online).

---

[1] Some examples: Malcolm Arnold's *Quintet for Brass*, commissioned by the New York Brass Quintet; Elliot Carter's *Brass Quintet* (1974), for the American Brass Quintet; Peter Maxwell Davies's *Brass Quintet* (1981), commissioned by Empire Brass; and James MacMillan's *Adam's Rib* (1995). Quintets accompanied by other instruments include Michael Torpe's *Copper* (1988, with orchestra) and Iannis Xenakis's *Eonta* (1964, with piano) and *Khalperr* (1983, with percussion).

The horn was particularly popular as a solo instrument, however, with a repertoire connected—probably with no awareness by modern composers—to nineteenth-century "concerto" studies, usually written by the instrumentalists themselves. Examples include those by Belloli, the several collections by Gallay, and the *Konzert-Etüden* for valve horn by Oscar Franz. Thus, after a lack of interest in the early part of the twentieth century, several composers in the second half of the century turned their attention to the solo instrument. In 1956, Giacinto Scelsi (1905–1988) wrote his *Quattro pezzi per corno in fa*, which required great dynamic and rhythmic ability and took advantage of the instrument's many expressive possibilities: open/closed/echo sounds, bending (upper and lower quarter tones), vibrato, and so on. This type of writing was unparalleled—at least from the compositional perspective—until the "Appel Interstellaire" by Olivier Messiaen (see Musical example 74 online), a revision of an earlier piece included in *Des Canyons aux Etoiles* (first performance in New York City on November 20, 1974) and the less well-known *Monologue* by István Láng (1974). In the experimental field, the horn has repeatedly been paired with electronic equipment, both by hornists/composers and by composers in search of new expressive possibilities. Examples are: Randall Faust's *Horn Call for Horn and Electronic Media* (1978), Douglas Hill's *Thoughtful Wanderings* (1990), Paul Basler's *Dance, Fool, Dance!* (1998), on the one hand, and Tera de Marez Oyens's *Konzert für Horn and Tonband* (1980), Emely Zobel's *Flodigarr* (1984), Barbara Heller's *Domino* (1984), Violeta Dinescu's *Es nimmt mich Wunder . . .* (1984), and Viera Janárčeková's *Yan* (1995), on the other.

Other pieces show more common styles, such as the *Sonatine für Horn* (1964) by Hans Erich Apostel; *Music for Solo Horn* (1965) by Bruno Reinhardt; and *Fantasy for Horn*, op. 88 (1966) by Malcom Arnold. More recent examples include *Dieci capricci* (1977) by Domenico Ceccarossi, *Vingt etudes concertantes* by Georges Barboteau, and *Sea Eagle* (1982, for Richard Watkins) by Peter Maxwell Davies, *Cynddarred Brenddwyd* (Fury–Dream) for solo horn by Heinz Holliger (2004) and the "Capriccio for Radovan 'il sogno di un cacciatore' " by Krzysztof Penderecki, written in 2012. Many other less well-known and unpublished compositions could certainly be added to this list.

New and unique ideas have also arisen with the revival of the natural horn, such as in Hermann Baumann's *Elegia* (1984) (see Musical example 75 online), Bernhard Krol's *Moment Musical*, op. 103 (1987), Francis Alun's *The Dying Deer: An Elegy* (1990), Vitali Bujanovski's *Ballade* (1991), Lowell Greer's *Het Valkhof*

(1991), Jeffrey Snedeker's *Goodbye to a Friend* (1997), Jeffrey Agrell's *September Elegy* (2001), and others.[2]

THE HORN AND JAZZ

Through US military bands, jazz arrived in the Old Continent and met with immediate success after World War I; however, it was after World War II that new styles and also new media made jazz even more popular. Several composers also experimented with the use of new instruments in addition to those that were already well established in the jazz idiom, such as the orchestra of Claude Thornhill, which included the horn with a certain regularity immediately after the 1940s (Dean 1997, 221).

In addition to these first appearances, arrangements for big bands by renowned musicians such as Gil Evans and Stan Kenton also included the horn, although it was rarely used as a solo instrument. According to Schuller (1992, viii), the first horn player to perform in a jazz recording was Jack Cave in Artie Shaw's *Frenesi* (1939). Some American instrumentalists saw abandoning the orchestral position and embarking on a jazz career as a possibility. One of them was John Graas (1924–1962), who, having been dismissed from the Indianapolis Symphony Orchestra in the late 1940s, moved to California and began recording his own jazz albums.

It was a long time before the horn obtained its own jazz identity, but according to Patrick Gregory Smith (2005, 2), things changed when a modest African American man from Detroit decided to devote himself entirely to a solo career with his horn. He was Julius Watkins (1921–1977), an extraordinary virtuoso in the genre, as Dennis Brain was for classical music. He was also nicknamed the "Joachim of the Jazz Horn," an imitation of the nickname given to Franz Strauss in the classical field. It is said that Watkins was an advocate for the transition from a sporadic presence of the horn in jazz music to a regular one and of making the horn a standard member of chamber ensembles. His style, different from that of Graas, encompassed a great melodic vein, with moments of strong intimacy and total exploitation of the many technical and virtuosic possibilities of the horn. In 1949, he performed with this instrument—he had initially played the trumpet—in

---

[2] For detailed information on horn solo literature, readers are directed to Dempf–Seraphinoff 2016.

an album with Kenny Clarke and later had the opportunity to work with some of the greatest jazz icons of the time: John Coltrane, Miles Davis, Gil Evans, Dizzy Gillespie, Charlie Mingus, Thelonius Monk, and Oscar Peterson. Miles Davis's "Birth of the Cool," which calls for the presence of the horn, then played by Gunther Schuller (1925–2015), also dates back to the late 1940s.[3]

In the early twentieth century, jazz exerted considerable influence on the works of Stravinsky, Milhaud, Debussy, and Weill, just to name a few, and in the second half of the century, ventures into this genre by several classical musicians became increasingly more common. Some hornist-composers have created their own compositions inspired by jazz, including, in addition to the aforementioned Gunther Schuller, Bernhard Krol (1920–2013), David Amram (b. 1930), Lowell Shaw (b. 1930), Douglas Hill (b. 1946), and many others.[4]

Finally, other hornists who have developed their own personal languages and styles in the jazz field, experimenting with electronic techniques as well as with the most innovative practices, include Tom Bacon, Vincent Chancey, Rick Todd, Tom Varner, Arkady Shilkloper, Mark Taylor, and Ken Wiley.

America remains the fulcrum of the jazz horn, which is also taught at the university level. John Clark (b. 1944), professor of horn at the State University of New York at Purchase (2001–2008), published *Jazz Exercises for French Horn* in 1993 with the clear intention of pushing students to expand their abilities and address this particular repertoire. Douglas Hill (b. 1946), horn professor at the University of Wisconsin in Madison from 1974 to 2011, is the author of several compositions and studies for horn, many of them inspired by jazz. Jeffrey Agrell (b. 1948) is another horn player who has combined his career in orchestra with his jazz interests, not only through his participation as an instrumentalist, but also with a series of interesting popular articles on the subject. Dale Clevenger (1940–2022) combined his prestigious orchestral career with work in the field of jazz, performing every Wednesday evening in a club in Chicago for seventeen years. Finally, Jeffrey Snedeker (b. 1958) recently contributed to the success of the horn in the jazz field

---

[3] At the age of seventeen, Schuller became the first horn of the Cincinnati Symphony Orchestra, moving to the Metropolitan Opera Orchestra two years later. He interrupted his well-established career in 1959 to devote himself entirely to composition and conducting, with soloists such as Dizzy Gillespie, Miles Davis, and John Lewis. Schuller also wrote a renowned manual on horn technique and was awarded several prizes, including two Grammys and the Pulitzer (1994).

[4] For a paper on compositional trends in this field in America and a list of works composed between 1970 and 2005, see Rooney 2008.

with an album (*Minor Returns: Tribute to the Horn in Jazz*, 2010) dedicated to many of those mentioned above and to those who contributed the most to the role of the horn in this musical genre.[5]

THE HORN AND THE MOVIES

While addressing the repertoire of the modern horn, we would also like to include a brief mention of the instrument's role in film music, especially with reference to America, where it enjoys a considerable reputation in the studios. In some cases, this provides excellent job opportunities, as is also the case with the musical. For a long time, the horn has been used in film music predominantly owing to its evocative role and its connection with the hunt, just as occurred when it was first introduced into the orchestra, but in more recent times its presence has effectively underlined battle scenes and victorious and heroic roles, such as in the movie *Gladiator* (2000, directed by Ridley Scott).[6]

The production of soundtracks is closely linked to the film studios, for which the most important place is of course Hollywood (Faulkner 1971, 22), leading to horn players who gravitate to the Los Angeles area.[7] Among the many names that could be cited are certainly those of James Stagliano and Vincent DeRosa. However, more than the protagonists, it seems relevant to stress the esthetic change that occurred in movie music with the transition from the single F horn, initially adopted, for example, by Alfred Brain,[8] to the single B-flat horn, which he and Wendell Hoss adopted (the five-valve model devised by Lorenzo Sansone) before eventually switching to the double horn. Stagliano continued to use an Alexander model, while Fred Fox was the first to change, in 1948, to the Conn 8D

---

[5] Of the many resources available on the web, we mention only the website *The Jazz Horn* (http://feinsteins.net/music/jazzhorn.html), which has information on many other performers, and the Wikipedia page dedicated to American jazz horn players: http://en.wikipedia.org/wiki/Category:American_jazz_horn_players.

[6] For more information on the horn in film music in the last thirty years, see Liu 2005. The dissertation contains an in-depth analysis of the use of the horn in movie soundtracks, starting from the success of *Star Wars* (1977), although it is not always a reliable resource when it comes to the history and esthetics of the instrument.

[7] The history of the Los Angeles hornists and the use of the instruments in that field are covered in Howard Hilliard's essay "*The History of the Horn Playing in Los Angeles*," and on the website http://howardhilliard.com/old/index.html, which contains further information, audio files, photographs, and more.

[8] Alfred Brain arrived in Los Angeles in 1923. A 1912 photograph shows him holding a single three-valve Courtois horn crooked in F.

in nickel silver. This horn, based on the Kruspe Horner model, had a wide, dark, and heavy sound, and was then becoming the standard in many American symphony orchestras (New York, Cleveland, and Philadelphia), playing a dramatic role in the change of sound preference for the instrument. This esthetic change came about not only through performances in concert halls, but also through the portentous means of diffusion that is the cinematic soundtrack (see online, "*Mission: Impossible*: Wagner tubas and the movies").

29

THE PRESENT-DAY HORN

An early radical mutation inevitably occurred with the adoption of the valves, whether they were used in the modern way or only for changing the key (as required on the omnitonic horn, for example), since in any event they changed the selection of crooks prescribed by the composer. A crucial, if surprising, change in esthetics in the Western tradition was from a sound concept that relied on tonal differences to one that, established in the last decades of the nineteenth century, aimed at a complete homogeneity of sound throughout the range (of the horn, of course, but of all other instruments as well). A further esthetic transformation occurred with the passage to the modern design of the double F/B-flat horn, at least when the preference for the higher section was definitively established.

In the second part of the twentieth century there were further changes in taste that had a considerable effect on the careers of instrumentalists, especially those in the orchestra. Until World War II, it was almost unthinkable that a horn player could be hired in an orchestra without training in the local performing style so that they could match the timbre of the entire group of their colleagues. In this regard, we simply remind readers of the differences in sound between a French horn player and a German or American one. A privileged witness of these esthetic divergences was Morley-Pegge (1973, 5) himself: He questions the survival of the Viennese horn, underlines the clear difference in sound of the ascending model in vogue in France, and remarks the choice of "first and third chair horn players" in favor of the single B-flat horn, with a valve for the *bouchés* notes or for the F harmonics.

A great many instrumentalists and distinguished teachers then began a march toward the performance style of what were—and still are in many cases—the leading orchestras at the international level, both because of their eminent musical tradition and their recordings (the Berlin Philharmonic, several renowned American orchestras, some London orchestras to a lesser extent, and of course the Vienna Philharmonic and the unique horn model in use there).

This led to a true globalization of sound, which—with the notable exception of the Viennese horn—was promoted by the availability of instruments on the international market that were easy to obtain at competitive prices. It also became easier to listen to orchestras and instrumentalists of other nations and traditions thanks to the increased diffusion and better quality of technological media (the radio at first, and then recordings on 78rpm discs, LPs, and, in recent times, CDs, DVDs, and other media). Today, the internet makes it even easier to obtain all kinds of digital media, so hornists can instantaneously compare excerpts or entire works, modern or historical recordings, and videos of concerts or lessons held all over the world (we need only mention the imposing quantity of material available on YouTube and Spotify).

Internationally distinguished soloists, instrumentalists, and orchestral ensembles can move around much more easily today, and if tours by the great orchestras were a real rarity at the beginning of the twentieth century, they are now a common custom, allowing for easier circulation and understanding of the different performance language of each group, since not all details can always be fully understood from a recording.

On the other hand, all these factors have led to the aforementioned uniformity of timbre and sound that can also be considered, as it is by authoritative voices, to be a serious loss of identity. In many cases, orchestras play Bach or Mozart with the same instruments and the same sound as they play Mahler, Debussy, Stravinsky, Rossini, and Verdi. This globalization of sound offers instrumentalists more job opportunities and facilitates their international circulation—once again to the detriment of variety, however.

The horn player of the third millennium is thus faced with the almost total disappearance of the difference in sounds by virtue of the codification of a single "jack of all trades" role that meets all the requirements that could be asked of a professional. This fact explains the great success of the triple horns or the use of two different instruments, a full double and a B-flat/F alto or E-flat descant, with mouthpieces of different sizes on hand to use for different repertoires.

Conductors, who exported feelings and esthetic notions, also played a central role in this change. Formerly, even the repertoire was more focused on local traditions, while today the choice is rather the result of market needs and monetary restrictions that sometimes greatly limit what works can be performed in a given season.

A new frontier is undoubtedly the revival of instruments and of earlier performance practices that have gained a considerable reputation in the most recent decades, encompassing music from the early baroque to the Romantic repertoire and even "historical" performances of compositions such as Stravinsky's *Sacre du Printemps*. We could consider this to be a return wave that would in turn suggest adopting different techniques depending on the repertoire performed. This is a decision that can only be made by an elite group of musicians, since in this case, not only are specific musical skills required, but also historical and esthetic knowledge, as well as the availability of as many instruments as the repertoires performed. It is a difficult but not impossible goal that relies on a better knowledge of the history and technology of the horn, as well as on that of its performance practice.

Conversely, similar considerations may apply to the innovative sound palette that composers of the most recent age have demanded from the horn—sounds that are unusual and at times decidedly surprising and futuristic.

BIBLIOGRAPHY

ABBREVIATIONS

AMZ	*Allgemeine Musikalische Zeitung*
BAMZ	*Berliner Allgemeine Musikalische Zeitung*
DDT	*Denkmäler deutscher Tonkunst*
DTB	*Denkmäler der Tonkunst in Bayern*
Grove 1980	*The New Grove Dictionary of Music and Musicians*, 1980
Grove 2001	*The New Grove Dictionary of Music and Musicians*, 2001 (also online)
GSJ	*The Galpin Society Journal*
HBSJ	*Historic Brass Society Journal*
IMSLP	International Music Score Library Project (online)
MGG1	*Musik in Geschichte und Gegenwart*, 1949–1986
MGG2	*Musik in Geschichte und Gegenwart*, 1994–2008 (online, 2016)
NBA	*Neue Bach Ausgabe*
NZfM	*Neue Zeitschrift für Musik*
RISM	Répertoire International des Sources Musicales
THC	*The Horn Call*
ZfI	*Zeitschrift für Instrumentenbau*

Abert 2007: Hermann Abert, *W.A. Mozart*, London, Yale University Press, 2007 (orig. German edition 1923–1924)

Adorni 1840: Giovanni Adorni, *Vita del conte Stefano Sanvitale*, Parma, Carmignani, 1840

Ágústsson 2017: Jóhannes Ágústsson, "Joseph Johann Adam of Lichtenstein, Patron of Vivaldi," *Studi Vivaldiani*, 17 (2017), 3–77

Ahrens 1986: Christian Ahrens, *Eine Erfindung und ihre Folgen. Blechblasinstrumente mit Ventilen*, Kassel, Bärenreiter, 1986 (English edition, *Valved Brass: The History of an Invention*, Hillsdale, NY, Pendragon Press, 2008)

Ahrens 2005: Christian Ahrens, "Horn", in *MGG2*

Ahrens 2006: Christian Ahrens, " '2 Clarini o 2 Corni da Caccia' – Zur Frage der Austauschbarkeit von Trompete und Horn in der Barockmusik," in *Jagd- und Waldhörner* 2006, pp. 135–153

Ahrens 2007: Christian Ahrens, "Metallic Mutes used in the 18th Century," *GSJ*, 60 (2007), 220–223

Ahrens 2008: Christian Ahrens, "Further Information concerning Metallic Mutes for the French Horns," *GSJ*, 61 (2008), 322–323

Ahrens 2009: Christian Ahrens, *"Zu Gotha ist eine gute Kapelle ..." Aus dem Innenleben einer thüringischen Hofkapelle des 18. Jahrhundert*, Stuttgart, Steiner, 2009

Ahrens 2014: Christian Ahrens, " '. . . tubis sylvestribus vulgo Jägerhorn'. Frühe Quellen zur Verwendung von Waldhörner im Stift Kremsmünster," *Musicologica Austriaca*, 31/32 (2012/13), 83–94

Ahrens 2015: Christian Ahrens, *Die Weimarer Hofkapelle 1683–1851*, Sinzig, Studio Verlag, 2015

Ahrens 2023: Christian Ahrens, "Corni da caccia (Waldhörner) at the Electoral Court of Saxony," in *Musica a corte* 2023, pp. 1–22

Ahrens–Klinke 1998: Christian Ahrens & Gregor Klinke, *Musikinstrumentensammlung Hans und Hede Grumbt*, vol. 3: *Blechblasinstrumente*, Bochum, Ruhr-Universität & Stadt Bochum, [1998]

Albrecht 1999: Theodore Albrecht, "Elias (Eduard Constantin) Lewy and the First Performance of Beethoven's Ninth Symphony," *THC*, 29/3 (May 1999), 27–33, 85–94

Albrecht 2003: Theodore Albrecht, "Benedict Fuchs, Franz Eisen, and Michael Herbst: The Hornists in Beethoven's Eroica Symphony at its First Performances in Vienna, 1805–1809," *THC*, 34/1 (October 2003), 39–49

Albrecht 2006: Theodore Albrecht, "Beethoven's Brass Players: New Discoveries in Composer–Performer Relations," *HBSJ*, 18 (2006), 47–72

Allenbach 2015: Daniel Allenbach, "Frühen Ventilhornschulen in Frankreich," in *Romantic Brass* 2015, pp. 199–213

Allenbach 2016: Daniel Allenbach, "Französische Ventilhornschulen im 19. Jahrhundert," in *Romantic Brass* 2016, pp. 154–171

Altenburg 1795: Johann Ernst Altenburg, *Versuch einer Anleitung zur heroisch-musikalischen Trompeter- und Pauker-Kunst*, Halle, Hendel, 1795 (English edition trans. by Edward Tarr, Nashville, TN, The Brass Press, 1974; Italian edition trans. by Tranquillo Forza, Varese, Zecchini, 2007)

Altenburg 1910–1911: Wilhelm Altenburg, "Die Wagnertuben und ihre Einführung in die Militärmusik," *ZfI*, 31 (1910–1911), 1105–1107

Altenburg 1973: Detlef Altenburg, *Untersuchungen zur Geschichte der Trompete im Zeitalter der Clarinblaskunst*, 3 vols., Regensburg, Bosse, 1973

Althöfer 2000: Ulrich Althöfer, *Von Zinken, Serpenten und Giraffenklavieren*, Lübeck, Museum für Kunst und Kulturgeschichte, 2000

Altmann 1905: Wilhelm Altmann, *Richard Wagners Briefe nach Zeitfolge und Inhalt*, Leipzig, Breitkopf & Härtel, 1905

Andersch 1829: Johann Daniel Andersch, *Musikalisches Wörterbuch*, Berlin, Natorff, 1829

Anderson 1938: *The Letters of Mozart and his Family*, ed. by Emily Anderson, 3 vols., London, Macmillan & Co., 1938

Annuaire 1833: *Annuaire des artistes français, statistique des beaux-arts en France. 2e année–1833*, Paris, Guyot de Fère, 1833–1834

Antolini 1813: Francesco Antolini, *La retta maniera di scrivere per il clarinetto ed altri istromenti da fiato*, Milan, Buccinelli, 1813

Antolini – Bini 1988: Bianca Maria Antolini & Annalisa Bini, *Editori e librai musicali a Roma nella prima metà dell'Ottocento*, Rome, Torre d'Orfeo, 1988

Aringer 2006: Klaus Aringer, "Instrumentales Idiom und musikalische Physiognomie: Grundzüge der Verwendung von Hörnern in Werk Georg Philipp Telemanns," in *Jagd- und Waldhörner* 2006, pp. 119–134

Atrapart 1838: Jean-Louis-Constant Atrapart, "Méthode de cor," in *Manuel complet de musique (vocale et instrumentale), ou Encyclopédie musicale, 1836–1839*, ed. by Alexandre-Étienne Choron & Juste Adrien de La Fage, Paris, Roret et Schonenberger, 1838, pp. 1–31

Atti 1881: *Atti del congresso dei musicisti italiani riunito in Milano dal 16 al 22 giugno 1881*, Milan, Ricordi, 1881

Bachaumont 1777: Louis Petit de Bachaumont, *Mémoires secrets pour servir à l'histoire de la République des Lettres en France*, vols. 2 and 3, London, Adamson, 1777

Bachmann-Geiser 2001: Brigitte Bachmann-Geiser, *Europäische Musikinstrumente im Bernischen Historischen Museum. Die Sammlung als Spiegel bernischer Musikkultur*, Bern, Bernisches Historisches Museum, 2001

Bacon 2000: Louise Bacon, "William Bull, Musical Instrument Maker (*ca.* 1650–1712): Working Methods and Instruments Analysis," in *Instruments pour demain. Conservation et restauration des instruments de musique*, conference proceedings (Limoges, June 15–16, 2000), Champs-sur-Marne, SFIIC, 2000, pp. 85–97

Bacon 2003: Alice Louise Bacon, *A Technical Study of the Alloy Compositions of "Brass" Wind Musical Instruments (1651–1867) Utilizing Non-Destructive X-Ray Fluorescence*, dissertation, Institute of Archeology, University College London, 2003

Bagans 1829: Karl Bagans, "Ueber die Trompete in ihrer heutigen Anwendbarkeit im Orchester," in *BAMZ*, 6 (1829), 337–341

Baines 1948: Anthony Baines, "James Talbot's Manuscript (Christ Church Library Music MS 1187), I. Wind Instruments," *GSJ*, 1 (1948), 9–26

Baines 1976: Anthony Baines, *Brass Instruments: Their History and Development*, London, Faber, 1976 (repr. Dover, 1993: the latter edition is referred to in this book)

Baines 1982: Anthony Baines, "The William Bull Horn," *GSJ*, 35 (1982), 157–158

Baker 1949: Charles H. Collins Baker & Muriel I. Baker, *The Life and Circumstances of James Brydges, First Duke of Chandos, Patron of the Liberal Arts*, Oxford, Clarendon Press, 1949

Balis 1986: Arnout Balis, *Rubens Hunting Scenes*, London & Oxford, Miller & Oxford University Press, 1986

Barclay 1992: Robert Barclay, *The Art of the Trumpet-Maker*, Oxford, Clarendon Press, 1992

Barnickel 1737: [Johann Christoph] Barnickel, *Kurzgefaßtes musicalisches Lexikon*, Chemnitz, Stössel, 1737

Bassompierre 1703: François de Bassompierre, *Mémoirs du Maréchal de Bassompierre contenant l'histoire de sa vie et de ce qui s'est fait et passé de plus remarquable à la cour de France pendant plusieurs années*, 4 vols., Cologne, Sambix, 1703 (1st ed. Cologne, Marteau, 1665/6)

Beakes 2007: Jennifer Beakes, *The Horn Parts in Handel's Operas and Oratorios and the Horn Players Who Performed in These Works*, DMA dissertation, City University of New York, 2007

Becker-Glauch 1951: Irmgard Becker-Glauch, *Die Bedeutung der Musik für die Dresdener Hoffeste bis in die Zeit Augusts des Starken*, Kassel, Bärenreiter, 1951

Behn 1912–1913: Friedrich Behn, "Die Musik im römischen Heere," *Mainzer Zeitschrift*, 7 (1912–1913), 36–47

Benade 1990: Arthur H. Benade, *Fundamentals of Musical Acustics*, 2nd rev. ed., New York, Dover, 1990

Benedikt 1923: Heinrich Benedikt, *Franz Anton Graf von Sporck (1662–1738). Zur Kultur der Barockzeit in Böhmen*, Vienna, Manz, 1923

Benedikt 1927: Heinrich Benedikt, *Das Königreich Neapel unter Kaiser Karl VI. Eine Darstellung auf Grund bisher unbekannter Dokumente aus den Österreichischen Archiven*, Vienna, Manz, 1927

Berdychová 2014: Tereza Berdychová (Žůrková), "Lesní rohy Michaela Leichamschneidera v českých sbírkách" (The horns of Michael Leichamschneider in Czech collections), *Hudební věda*, 51/1–2 (2014), 283–296

Berke–Flothuis 1999: *W.A. Mozart. Neue Ausgabe sämtlicher Werke, Serie 8, Kammermusik, Werkgruppe 21. Kritischer Bericht. Duos und Trios für Streicher und Bläser*, ed. By Dietrich Berke & Marius Flothuis, Kassel, Bärenreiter, 1999, pp. 25–30

Berlioz 1843–1844: Hector Berlioz, *Grand traité d'instrumentation et d'orchestration modernes*, Paris, Schonenberger, 1843–1844 (rev. German edition by Richard Strauss 1905; English edition, New York, Kalmus, 1948)

Berlioz 1844: Hector Berlioz, *Voyage musical en Allemagne et en Italie*, 2 vols., Paris, Labitte, 1844

Bernsdorf 1856: Eduard Bernsdorf, *Neues Universal-Lexikon der Tonkunst*, vol. 1, Dresden, Schaefer, 1856

Berthold–Fürstenau 1876: Theodor Berthold & Moritz Fürstenau, *Die Fabrikation musikalischer Instrumente und einzelner Bestandtheile derselben im Königlichen Sächsischen Vogtlande*, Leipzig, Breitkopf & Härtel, 1876

Biagi Ravenni 1986: Gabriella Biagi Ravenni, *Cantatas by Francesco Gasparini 1661–1727*, New York & London, Garland, 1986

Bierdimpfl 1883: K. A. [Karl August] Bierdimpfl, *Die Sammlung der Musikinstrumente des baierischen Nationalmuseums*, Munich, Straub, 1883

Bierey 1815: Gottlob Benedict Bierey, "Notizien: Neue Erfindung," *AMZ*, 17 (1815), cols. 309–310

Billiet 2016: Jeroen Billiet, "Belgium, France and the Horn in the Romantic Era: Tradition, Influences, Similarities and Particularities," in *Romantic Brass* 2016, pp. 328–339

Birsak 1976: Kurt Birsak, "Die 'Jagd-Waldhörner' im Salzburger Museum Carolino-Augusteum," *Salzburger Museum Carolino-Augusteum. Jahresschrift*, 22 (1976), 79–101

Blandford 1922: W. F. H. Blandford, "The French Horn in England," *Musical Times*, August 1, 1922, pp. 544–547

Blaut 1999: Stephan Blaut, "Die Jägerhörner in der Rüstkammer der Staatlichen Kunstsammlungen Dresden," *Musica Instrumentalis*, 2 (1999), 8–22

Bonanni 1722: Filippo Bonanni, *Gabinetto armonico pieno d'istromenti sonori*, Rome, Placho, 1722

Bouëssée 1979: Joël Bouëssée, *La trompe de chasse et Gaston de Marolles*, Paris, Société de vénerie & Fédération internationale des trompes de France, 1979

Brenet 1900: Michel Brenet, *Les concerts en France sous l'ancien régime*, Paris, Fischbacher, 1900

Brewer 2011: Charles E. Brewer, *The Instrumental Music of Schmeltzer, Biber, Muffat and Their Contemporaries*, London, Ashgate, 2011

Bridwell-Briner 2014: Kathryn Eileen Bridwell-Briner, *The Horn in America from Colonial Society to 1842: Performers, Instruments, and Repertoire*, DMA dissertation, University of North Carolina, Greensboro, 2014

Brisson 1899: Adolphe Brisson, "Le corniste Eugène Vivier et les souverains d'Europe," in *Portraits intimes*, 4th series, Paris, Colin, 1899, pp. 245–255

Brook 1975: Barry S. Brook, "The Symphonie Concertante: Its Musical and Sociological Bases," *International Review of the Aesthetics and Sociology of Music*, 6/1 (1975), 9–28 (republished in the same magazine, 25 (1994), 131–148)

Brownlow 1996: James Arthur Brownlow, *The Last Trumpet: A History of the English Slide Trumpet*, Stuyvesant, NY, Pedragon Press, 1996

Brüchle 1970, 1975, 1983: Bernhard Brüchle, *Horn Bibliographie*, Wilhelmshaven, Heinrichshofen, 1970; vol. 2, 1975; vol. 3, von Daniel Lienhard, 1983

Brüchle–Janetzky 1976: Bernhard Brüchle & Kurt Janetzky, *Kulturgeschichte des Horns. Ein Bildsachbuch: A Pictorial History of the Horn*, Tutzing, Schneider, 1976

Brüchle–Janetzky 1988: Bernhard Brüchle & Kurt Janetzky, *The Horn*, London, Batsford, 1988

Brummitt 2013: Eric Brummitt, "Antonio Tosoroni's Metodo per Il Corno a Tre Pistoni: Valve Horn Technique in Nineteenth-Century Italy," *THC*, 43/3 (May 2013), 60–62

Bryan 1975: Paul R. Bryan, "The Horn in the Works of Mozart and Haydn: Some Observations and Comparisons," *The Haydn Yearbook*, 9 (1975), 189–255

Bryan 2002: Paul R. Bryan, "Mozart's Use of Horns in Bb and the Question of Alto-Basso in the Eighteenth Century," *HBSJ*, 14 (2002), 165–192

Cagnoli 1987: Bruno Cagnoli, *Domenico Ceccarossi, principe dei cornisti*, Lanciano, Carabba, 1987

Caluori 2005: Nicholas Caluori, "Lorenzo Sansone (1881–1975)," *THC*, 35/2 (February 2005), 47–57

Cambridge Companion 1997: *The Cambridge Companion to Brass Instruments*, ed. by Trevor Herbert & John Wallace, Cambridge, Cambridge University Press, 1997

Cameron 1905: Ludovick Charles Cameron, *The Hunting Horn: What To Blow and How To Blow It*, London, Köhler & Son, [1905]

Camier 2009: Bernard Camier, "De Marseille à Saint-Domingue et Philadelphie: Victor Pelissier (Marseille 1756–New Jersey ? ca. 1820)," *Généalogie et Histoire de la Caraïbe*, 223 (March 2009), 5830–5831

Canal 1881: Pietro Canal, "Della musica in Mantova," *Memorie del Reale istituto veneto di scienze, lettere ed arti*, 21 (1881), 665–774 (repr. Bologna, Forni, 1977)

Carlone 1995: Mariagrazia Carlone, *Iconografia musicale nell'arte biellese, vercellese e valsesiana*, Rome, Torre d'Orfeo, 1995

Carré 1937: Henri Carré, *Jeux, sports et divertissements des rois de France*, Paris, Gallimard, 1937

Carse 1925: Adam Carse, *The History of Orchestration*, London, Kegan Paul & Trench, 1925, repr. New York, Dover, 1964

Carse 1939: Adam Carse, *Musical Wind Instruments*, London, Macmillan, 1939; repr. New York, Da Capo Press, 1965

Carter 2005: Stewart Carter, "Othon Vandenbroek on the Horn: One Author, Two Perspectives," in *Brass Music at the Cross Road of Europe*, ed. by Keith Polk, Utrecht, STIMU, 2005, pp. 97–109

Castellamonte 1674: Amedeo di Castellamonte, *La Venaria Reale Palazzo di piacere, e di Caccia Ideato dall'Altezza Reale di Carlo Emanuel II, Duca di Savoia, Re di Cipro etc. Disegnato et delineato dal Conte Amedeo di Castellamonte, L'Anno 1672*, Turin, Zappata 1674 [but 1679]

Castil-Blaze 1825: François Castil-Blaze, *Dictionnaire de musique moderne*, 2 vols., Paris, Lyre moderne, 1821; 2nd ed. 1825.

Castil-Blaze 1832: François Castil-Blaze, *Chapelle-Musique des Rois de France*, Paris, Paulin, 1832

Castil-Blaze 1838: François Castil-Blaze, "Paër," *Revue de Paris*, 10 (October 1838), 43–76

Castil-Blaze 1841: François Castil-Blaze, "Le Musicien. III," *La France Musicale*, 4/49 (December 5, 1841), 525–528

Castil-Blaze 1843: François Castil-Blaze, "Actéon, G. Paer, E. Vivier," *La France Musicale*, 6/20 (May 14, 1843), 163–164

Castil-Blaze 1855: François Castil-Blaze, *L'Académie impériale de musique*, 2 vols., Paris, Castil-Blaze, 1855

Castil-Blaze 1856: François Castil-Blaze, *L'Opéra italien*, Paris, Castil-Blaze, 1856

Cataldi 1985: Luigi Cataldi, "I rapporti di Vivaldi con il 'Teatro detto Il Comico' di Mantova," in *Informazioni e Studi Vivaldiani*, vol. 6, Milan, Ricordi, 1985, pp. 88–109

C. B. 1875: C. B. [Carl Billert], "Horn", in Mendel 1870–1879, vol. 5, 1875, pp. 289–303

Ceccarossi 1957: Domenico Ceccarossi, *Il corno, attraverso il suo sviluppo tecnico e coloristico*, Milan, Ricordi, 1957

Cellesi 1906: Luigia Cellesi, *Storia della più antica banda musicale senese*, Siena, Tip. Sordomuti, 1906.

Chase 1955: Gilbert Chase, *America's Music*, New York, McGraw-Hill Books, 1955 (2nd ed., 1966)

Chastenay 1896, 1897: [Victorine de Chastenay], *Mémoires de madame de Chastenay, 1771–1815*, ed. by Alphonse Roserot, 2 vols, Paris, Plon, vol. 1: 1896, vol. 2: 1897

Chaussier 1889: Henry Chaussier, *Notice explicative sur les noveaux instruments en Ut*, Paris, Dupont, 1889

Cheney 1998: *Recueil de pièces de viole en musique et en tablature, 1666: fac-similé du Ms M2.1.T2.17C. Case, Washington, Library of Congress*, ed. by Stuart Cheney, Geneva, Minkoff, 1998

Cheney 2008: Stuart Cheney, "A Newly Discovered Source of French Hunting Horn Signals, ca. 1666," *HBSJ*, 20 (2008), 23–36

Chiappori 1825: Giuseppe Chiappori, *Terza continuazione della serie cronologica delle rappresentazioni drammatico pantomimiche poste sulle scene dei principali teatri di Milano dal giorno 26 dicembre 1820 al giorno 30 giugno 1824 divisa in tre parti*, Milan, Silvestri, 1825

Chirico 2014: Teresa Chirico, "The Dawn of the Hunting Horn in Rome and in Italy: A Historic Overview of the First Half of the Seventeen Hundreds, New Findings on the Use of the corni da caccia in Early Eighteenth-Century Roman Orchestras," *Recercare*, 26 (2014), 109–123

Chladni 1821: Ernst Florens Friedrich Chladni, "Nachrichten von einigen (theils wirklichen, theils vielleich nur angeblichen) neueren Erfindungen und Verbesserungen musikalischer Instrumente," *AMZ*, 23 (1821), cols. 393–398

Choron–Fayolle 1811: Alexandre Etienne Choron & François Joseph Marie Fayolle, *Dictionnaire historique des musiciens, artistes et amateurs, morts ou vivans, qui se sont illustres en une partie quelconque de la musique et des arts qui y sont relatifs*, vol. 2, Paris, Valade-Lenormant, 1811

Choron–Lafage 1838: Alexandre Etienne Choron & J. Adrien de Lafage, *Nouveau manuel complet de musique vocale et instrumentale, ou Encyclopédie musicale*, 3 vols., Paris, Roret, 1836–1839

Claretta 1877: Gaudenzio Claretta, *Adelaide di Savoia duchessa di Baviera e i suoi tempi*, Turin, Paravia, 1877

Clark 2001: Andrew Clark, "The Heyday of the Hand Horn and the Birth of the Valved Horn: A Study of Nineteenth-Century Horn Technique as Revealed in the Solo Works for Horn by Carl Czerny," *HBSJ*, 13 (2001), 118–127

Coar 1952: Birchard Coar, *A Critical Study of the Nineteenth Century Horn Virtuosi in France*, Illinois, Dekalb, 1952

Comettant 1860: Oscar Comettant, *Histoire d'un inventeur au XIXe siècle. Adolphe Sax, ses ouvrages et ses luttes*, Paris, Pagnerre, 1860

Conestabile 1851: Giancarlo Conestabile, *Vita di Niccolò Paganini da Genova*, Perugia, Bartelli, 1851

Conforzi 1994: Igino Conforzi, "Girolamo Fantini, 'Monarch of the Trumpet': New Light on His Works," *HBSJ*, 6 (1994), 32–60

Cools 2005: Jacques Cools, "A propos des cylindres droits ou pistons dits 'belges'," *Larigot*, 36 (October 2005), 12–20

Coon 1883: Oscar Coon, *Harmony and Instrumentation: The Principles of Harmony, with Practical Instruction in Arranging Music for Orchestras and Military Bands*, Cincinnati, OH, A. Squire, 1883

Cramer 1783: Carl Friedrich Cramer, "Nachrichten von Concerten in Hamburg," *Magazin der Musik*, December 21, 1783, pp. 1400–1401

Cucuel 1913: Georges Cucuel, *Études sur un orchestre au XVIII.me siècle: l'instrumentation chez les symphonistes de la Pouplinière, œuvres musicales de Gossec, Schencker et Gaspard Procksch*, Paris, Fischbacher, 1913

Dacci 1888: Giusto Dacci, *Cenni storici e statistici intorno alla Reale scuola di musica in Parma*, Parma, Battei, 1888

Dahlqvist 1991: Reine Dahlqvist, "Corno and Corno da Caccia: Horn Terminology, Horn Pitches, and High Horn Parts," *Basler Jahrbuch für historische Musikpraxis*, 15 (1991), 35–80.

Dahlqvist 1993a: Reine Dahlqvist, "Pitches of German, French, and English Trumpets in the 17th and 18th Centuries," *HBSJ*, 5 (1993), 29–41

Dahlqvist 1993b: Reine Dahlqvist, "Gottfried Reiche's Instrument: A Problem of Classification," *HBSJ*, 5 (1993), 174–191

Dahlqvist 1994: Reine Dahlqvist, "Die Einführung des Hornes in die Kunstmusik und Johann Beers Konzert für Horn und Posthorn," in *Kongressbericht Feldkirch/Vorarlberg 1992* (Alta Musica, 16), ed. by Wolfgang Suppan, Tutzing, Schneider, 1994, pp. 129–154

Dahlqvist 2006: Reine Dahlqvist, "Das Horn in Mitteldeutschland bis um 1720," in *Jagd- und Waldhörner* 2006, pp. 105–118

Dal segno al suono 2010: *Dal segno al suono. Il conservatorio di musica San Pietro a Majella. Repertorio del patrimonio storico-artistico e degli strumenti musicali*, ed. by Gemma Cautela, Luigi Sisto, & Lorella Starita, Naples, Arte-M, 2010

Dampierre 1738: Marc-Antoine de Dampierre, *Fanfares nouvelles pour deux cors de chasse*, Paris, de la Chevardiere, [1738]

Dampierre *ca.* 1775: Marc-Antoine de Dampierre, *Récueil de fanfares pour la chasse*, Paris, Le Clerc, *ca.* 1775

Dampierre 2001: Éric de Dampierre, "Dampierre, Marc-Antoine", in *Grove* 2001

Dart 1960: Thurston Dart, "Bach's 'Fiauti d'echo'," *Music and Letters*, 41 (1960), 331–341

Das Waldhorn 1983: *Das Waldhorn in der Geschichte und Gegenwart der Tschechischen Musik / The Horn in the Past and Present of Czech Music*, Prague, Tschechischen Musikgesellschaft, 1983

Dauprat 1816: Louis-François Dauprat, *Partition des trios, quatuors et sextuors pour cors en differens tons*, Paris, chez l'Auteur, 1816

Dauprat 1824: Louis-François Dauprat, *Méthode de cor alto et cor basse*, 3 vols., Paris, Zetter, 1824 (English trans. by Viola Roth, Bloomington, IN, Birdalone Music, 1994)

Dauprat 1828: Louis-François Dauprat, *Extrait d'un traité inédit du cor a pistons*, Paris, Schönenberger, 1828

Dauprat 1857: Louis-François Dauprat, *Le professeur de musique*, Paris, Quinzard, 1857

Dauverné 1857: François George Auguste Dauverné, *Méthode pour la trompette*, Paris, Brandus Dufour, 1857 (facs. Paris, I.M.D., 1991)

Day 1891: C. R. Day, *A Descriptive Catalogue of the Musical Instruments Recently Exhibited at the Royal Military Exhibition, London, 1890*, London, Eyre & Spottiswoode, 1891

DDT 1905: Friedrich Wilhelm Zachow, *Gesammelte Werke*, ed. by Max Seiffert, Leipzig, 1905 (*DDT*, 21/22)

De Adam 1966: Salimbene De Adam, *Cronica*, ed. by Giuseppe Scalia, Bari, Laterza, 1966

Dean 1997: Roger Thorton Dean, "Jazz, Improvisation and Brass," in *Cambridge Companion* 1997, pp. 217–235

De l'Aulnaye 1816: "D. L." [De l'Aulnaye], "Gluck," in *Biographie universelle ancienne et moderne*, vol. 17, Paris, Michaud frères, 1816, pp. 517–522

Delpriori 2007–2008: Luca Delpriori, *L'influenza della corte napoleonica sulla scrittura cornistica del primo '800*, disserttation, Conservatorio di Cesena, 2007–2008

De Luynes 1735–1758: Charles-Philippe d'Albert de Luynes, *Mémoires du duc de Luynes sur la cour de Louis XV (1735–1758)*, vol. 15: *(1756–57)*, ed. by L. Dussieux & E. Soulié, Paris, Didot, 1864

Dempf–Seraphinoff 2016: Linda Dempf & Richard Seraphinoff, *Guide to the Solo Horn Repertoire*, Bloomington & Indianapolis, Indiana University Press, 2016

Dent 1905: Edward J. Dent, *Alessandro Scarlatti*, London, Arnold, 1905

Description 1834: Description des machines et procédés spécifiés dans les brevets d'invention de perfectionnement et d'importation, Paris, Huzard, 1834, Tome XXXIX

Deutsch 1978: Otto Erich Deutsch, *Schubert: Thematic Catalogue of all His Works*, London, Dent & Sons, 1951 (new ed. *Franz Schubert. Thematisches Verzeichnis seiner Werke in chronologischer Folge*, Kassel, Bärenreiter, 1978)

Dictionnaire 1689: Nouveau dictionnaire françois-allemand et allemand-françois à l'usage de deux nations, vol. 2, 4th ed., Strasbourg, König, 1689

Dlabacž 1815: Gottfried Johann Dlabacž, *Allgemeines historisches Künstler-Lexikon für Böhmen und zum Theil auch für Mähren und Schlesien*, 3 vols., Prague, Haase, 1815

Döbel 1746: Heinrich Wilhelm Döbel, *Eröffnete Jäger-Practica oder der wohlgeübte und erfahrene Jäger*, Leipzig, Hensius, 1746

Dodworth 1853: Allen Dodworth, *Brass Band School*, New York, Dodworth & Co., 1853

Domnich 1807: Heinrich Domnich, *Méthode de premier et de second cor*, Paris, Conservatoire, 1807

D'Origny 1788: Antoine d'Origny, *Annales du Théâtre Italien depuis son origine jusqu'à ce jour*, 3 vols., Paris, Veuve Duchesne, 1788

Drechsel 1927–1928: F. [Friedrich] A. [August] Drechsel, "Neue Nachrichten über die Erfinder der Inventionen und Ventile an Blasinstrumenten," *ZfI*, 48 (1927–1928), 634–635

Ducrest 1828: [Georgette Ducrest], *Mémoires sur l'imperatrice Joséphine, ses contemporains, la cour de Navarre et de la Malmaison*, Paris, Ladvocat, 1828

Du Fouilloux 1561: Jacques Du Fouilloux, *La Vénerie*, Poitiers, Marnefz et Bouchetz frères, 1561

Dufourcq–Benoît 1969: Norbert Dufourcq & Marcelle Benoît, "Documents du Minutier Central. Musiciens français du XVIIIᵉ siècle," *Recherches sur la musique française classique*, 9 (1969), 216–238

Dumoulin 2006: Géry Dumoulin, "The Cornet and Other Brass Instruments in French Patents of the First Half of the Nineteenth Century," *GSJ*, 59 (2006), 77–100

Dumoulin 2007: Géry Dumoulin, *Sax et le cornet: le cornet à pistons dans la production d'Adolphe Sax, 1814–1894*, conference proceedings "Paris: un laboratoire d'idées, facture et répertoire des cuivres entre 1840 et 1930" (Paris – Cité de la Musique, June 29–July 1, 2007), 233–286 (http://www.citedelamusique.fr/pdf/insti/recherche/colloques_factures/sax.pdf)

Dunoyer 1868: Dunoyer de Noirmont, *Histoire de la chasse en France*, 3 vols., Paris, Bouchard-Huzard, 1867 (vol. 1); 1868 (vols. 2, 3)

Dupâquier 1969: Jacques Dupâquier, "Essai de cartographie historique: le peuplement du Bassin parisien en 1711," *Annales. Économies, Sociétés, Civilisations*, 24/4 (1969), 976–998

Dürr 2005: Alfred Dürr, *The Cantatas of J.S. Bach*, Oxford, Oxford University Press, 2005 (orig. German edition, 1992)

Duvernoy 1799: Frédéric Nicolas Duvernoy, *Méthode pour le Cor*, Paris, Conservatoire, 1799

D'Yauville 1788: [Jacques Le Fournier] D'Yauville, *Traité de vénerie*, Paris, Imprimerie Royale, 1788

Ebitz 1986: David Ebitz, "The Oliphant: Its Function and Meaning in a Courtly Society," *Houston German Studies*, 6 (1986), 123–141

Ebner 1996: Hermann Ebner, *Die Hornisten bei Haydn am Hofe Esterházy*, Vienna, WWV Verlag, 1996

Egger 2006: Rainer Egger, "Corno bzw. Tromba da caccia," in *Jagd- und Waldhörner 2006*, pp. 361–372

Eichborn 1897: Hermann Ludwig Eichborn, *Die Dämpfung beim Horn oder die musikalische Natur des Horns: eine akustisch-praktische Studie*, Leipzig, Breitkopf & Härtel, 1897

Eichborn 1899: Hermann Ludwig Eichborn, "Ein neues Doppelhorn," *ZfI*, 20/3–4 (1899–1900), 63–65; 97–99

Eisel 1738: Johann Philipp Eisel, *Musicus autodidaktos oder der sich selbst informirende Musicus, bestehend sowohl in vocal- als üblicher Instrumental-Musique, welcher über 24 Sorten . . .*, Erfurt, Funcken, 1738.

Eitner 1900–1905: Robert Eitner, *Biographisch-bibliographisches Quellen-Lexicon der Musiker und Musikgelehrten der christlicher Zeitrechnung bis zur Mitte des neunzehnten Jahrhunderts*, 11 vols., Leipzig, Breitkopf & Härtel, 1900–1905

Eldredge 2002: Niles Eldredge, "A Brief History of Piston-Valved Cornets," *HBSJ*, 14 (2002), 337–390

Eliason 1970: Robert E. Eliason, "Early American Valves for Brass Instruments," *GSJ*, 23 (1970), 86–96

Encyclopediana 1791: *Encyclopediana ou Dictionnaire encyclopédique des ana*, ed. by Jacques Lacombe, Paris, Panckoucke, 1791

Encyclopédie méthodique 1785: *Encyclopédie méthodique des Arts et métiers mécaniques*, vol. 4: *Art du faiseur d'instrumens de musique, et lutherie*, ed. by J. Lacombe, Paris, Panckoucke, 1785

Encyclopédie méthodique 1791: *Encyclopedie Méthodique. Musique*, vol. 1, ed. by Framery et Ginguené, Paris, Panckoucke, 1791

Eppelsheim 1961: Jürgen Eppelsheim, *Das Orchester in der Werken Jean-Baptiste Lullys*, Tutzing, Schneider, 1961

Ericson 1997: John Ericson, "Heinrich Stoelzel and Early Valved Horn Technique," *HBSJ*, 9 (1997), 65–82

Ericson 1998: John Ericson, "The Double Horn and Its Invention in 1897," *THC*, 28/2 (February 1998), 31–33

Fanelli 1997: Jean Grundy Fanelli, "German Wind Players in and around Florence at the Turn of the Eighteenth Century," in *Relazioni Musicali tra Italia e Germania nell'età Barocca*, conference proceedings VI° Convegno internazionale sulla musica italiana nei secoli XVII–XVIII, July 11–13, 1995, A.M.I.S., Como, 1997, pp. 433–445

Faulkner 1971: Robert R. Faulkner, *Hollywood Studio Musicians: Their Work and Careers*, Chicago, Aldine Atherton, 1971

Ferrari 1993: Pierluigi Ferrari, "Una collezione di strumenti musicali verso la fine del Cinquecento. Lo 'studio di musica' di Luigi Balbi," *Liuteria Musica e Cultura*, 1993, 15–21

Fétis 1827: François-Joseph Fétis, "Cors à pistons. Exposition des produits de l'industrie. Instrumens de cuivre," *Revue Musicale*, 1/2 (1827; print. 1828), 153–162

Fétis 1837: François-Joseph Fétis, *Manuel des compositeurs, directeurs de musique, chef d'orchestre et de musique militaire*, Paris, Brandus, 1837

Fétis 1854: François-Joseph Fétis, "Le cor simple et le cor à pistons," *Revue et Gazette musicale de Paris*, 21/40 (1854), 317–319

Fétis 1860–1868: François-Joseph Fétis, *Biographie universelle des musiciens et bibliographie générale de la musique*, 8 vols., 2nd ed., Paris, Didot, 1860–1868

Fétis 1868: François-Joseph Fétis, "Classe X. Instruments de musique", in *Exposition universelle de Paris en 1867: documents et rapports*, Brussels, Guyot, 1868, pp. 471–560

Findeizen 1928–1929: Nikolai Findeizen, *History of Music in Russia from Antiquity to 1800*, ed. by Miloš Velimirović and Claudia R. Jensen, 2 vols., Bloomington and Indianapolis, Indiana University Press, 2008 (orig. edition in Russian, 1928–1929)

Fitzpatrick 1970: Horace Fitzpatrick, *The Horn and Horn-Playing: And the Austro-Bohemian Tradition from 1680–1830*, London, Oxford University Press, 1970

Fitzpatrick 1976: Horace Fitzpatrick, "Ein Huthorn von Adam Buchshwinder mit einem Mundstück aus der Barockzeit," *Salzburger Museum Carolino Augusteum Jahrschrift*, 22 (1976), 61–65

Flachs 1994: Werner Flachs, *Das Jagdhorn: seine Geschichte von der Steinzeit bis zur Gegenwart*, Zug, Kalt-Zehnder, 1994

Fleming 1719, 1724: Hans Friedrich von Fleming, *Der volkommene teutsche Jäger*, 2 vols., Leipzig, Martini, 1719 (vol. 1); 1724 (vol. 2)

Fletcher–Rossing 1998: Neville H. Fletcher & Thomas Rossing, *The Physics of Musical Instruments*, 2nd ed., New York, Spring Verlag, 1998

Font 1882: Louis Font y Mirapeix, *Breve reseña histórica sobre el origen y el progresos de la trompa*, Ms. Madrid, E-Mc 1-15185, October 24, 1882

Forkel 1782: Johann Nepomuk Forkel, *Musikalischer Almanach für Deutschland auf das Jahr 1782*, Leipzig, Schwickert, 1782

Forsyth 1914: Cecil Forsyth, *Orchestration*, London, Macmillan and Co., 1914

Francoeur 1772: Louis J. Francoeur, *Diapason général de tous les instruments à vent*, Paris, Chez Des Lauriers M. de Papiers, 1772

Franz 1881: Oscar Franz, *Preisgekrönte grosse theoretisch-praktische Waldhorn-Schule für den systematischen Unterricht vom ersten Anfang bis zur höchsten Vollendung*, Dresden, Seeling, 1881

Franz 1884–1885: Oscar Franz, "Die neuen Musik-Instrumente Richard Wagner's," *ZfI*, 5 (1884–1885), 46

Freeman 2009: Daniel E. Freeman, *Josef Mysliveček "Il Boemo," the Man and His Music*, Sterling Heights, MI, Harmonie Park Press, 2009

Freemanová 2006: Michaela Freemanová, "Horns and Horn Makers in Bohemia and Moravia in the Eighteenth and Nineteenth Centuries," in *Jagd- und Waldhörner* 2006, pp. 215–226

Frew–Myers 2003: Catherine Frew & Arnold Myers, "Sir Samuel Hellier's 'Musicall Instruments'," *GSJ*, 56 (2003), 6–26

Friesenhagen 2010: Andreas Friesenhagen, "Haydns Sinfonien: Besetzungsprobleme und Aufführungstraditionen," *Studia Musicologica* (Haydn 2009: A Bicentenary Conference, Part I), 51/1–2 (March 2010), 127–140

Fröhlich 1811: Joseph Fröhlich, *Vollständige theoretisch-pracktische Musikschule*, Bonn, Simrock, Part III, n.d. [1811]; (repr. separately, 1813; repr. in *Systematischer Unterricht in der vorzüglichsten Orchester-Instrumenten*, part 2: *Horn-Schule*, Würzburg, Bauer, 1829, pp. 184–226)

Fröhlich 1834: Joseph Fröhlich, "Horn," in J. S. Ersch & I. G. Gruber, *Allgemeine Encyklopädie der Wissenschaften und Künste*, Part II, vol. 11, Leipzig, Brockhaus, 1834, pp. 4–11

Furetière 1690: Antoine Furetière, *Dictionnaire universel contenant généralement tous les mots françois tant vieux que modernes et les termes de toutes les sciences et des arts*, 3 vols., La Haye, Leers, 1690

Fürstenau 1861, 1862: Moritz Fürstenau, *Zur Geschichte der Musik und des Theaters am Hofe zu Dresden*, 2 vols., Dresden, Kuntze, 1861, 1862 (repr. Leipzig, Peters, 1971)

Gallavotti 2009: Elia Gallavotti, *Giornale di notizie risguardanti Santarcangelo di Romagna 1700–1905*, ed. by S. Beretta, Cesena, Il Ponte Vecchio, 2009

Gamucci 1877: Baldassarre Gamucci, "Relazione della Commissione Accademica," in *Atti dell'Accademia del R. Istituto Musicale di Firenze*, xv, Firenze, Civelli, 1877

Gantzland 1711: Christian Gantzland, *De buccinatoribus eorumque iure / vom Recht der Trompeter*, Jena, Müller, 1711 (see Wildvogel 1753)

Garigue *ca.* 1888: Henri Jean Garigue, *Grande Méthode de cor en fa à deux et à trois pistons*, Paris, Millereau, *ca.* 1888

Garsault 1761: François Alexandre Garsault, *Notionaire, ou mémorial raisonné*, Paris, Desprez, 1761

Gassner 1838: Ferdinand Simon Gassner, *Partiturkenntnis: ein Leitfaden zum Selbstunterricht für angehende Tonsetzer*, vol. 1, Kalsruhe, Groos, 1838

Gathy 1835: August Gathy, *Musikalisches Conversations-Lexikon*, Hamburg, Neimeyer, 1835

Gerber 1790, 1792: Ernst Ludwig Gerber, *Historisch-Biographisches Lexicon der Tonkünstler, welches Nachrichten von dem Leben und Werken musikalischer Schriftsteller, berühmter Componisten, Sänger, Meister auf Instrumenten, Dilettanten, Orgel- und Instrumentenmacher, enthält*, Leipzig, Breitkopf, 1790 (vol. 1); 1792 (vol. 2)

Gerber 1812, 1813, 1814: Ernst Ludwig Gerber, *Neues historisch-biographisches Lexikon der Tonkünstler, welches Nachrichten von dem Leben und den Werken musikalischer Schriftsteller, berühmter Komponisten, Sänger, Meister auf Instrumenten, kunstvoller Dilettanten, Musikverleger, auch Orgel- und Instrumentenmacher, älterer und neuerer Zeit, aus allen Nationen enthält*, Leipzig, Kühnel, 1812 (vols. 1–2); 1813 (vol. 3); 1814 (vol. 4)

Gervasoni 1800: Carlo Gervasoni, *La scuola della musica in tre parti divisa*, Piacenza, Orcesi, 1800 (facs. Bologna, Forni, 1969)

Gervasoni 1812: Carlo Gervasoni, *Nuova teoria di musica ricavata dall'odierna pratica*, Parma, Blanchon, 1812

Gétreau 2006: Florence Gétreau, "The Horn in Seventeenth and Eighteenth Century France: Iconography Related to Performances and Musical Works," in *Jagd- und Waldhörner* 2006, pp. 43–76

Gétreau 2009: Florence Gétreau, "Les faiseurs d'instruments du roi," in *Le prince et la musique. Les passions musicales de Louis XIV*, ed. by Jean Duron, Wavre, Mardaga, 2009, pp. 179–210

Gétreau 2023: Florence Gétreau, "Les peintures de Jan Miel (1659–1661) dans la Sala di Diana à la Venaria Reale: contexte, modèle(s), impact," in *Musica a corte* 2023, pp. 225–253

Gevaert 1863: François-Auguste Gevaert, *Traité Général d'instrumentation*, Paris, Katto, 1863

Gevaert 1885: François-Auguste Gevaert, *Nouveau traité d'instrumentation*, Paris & Brussels, Lemoine & Fils, 1885

Gevaert 1890: François-Auguste Gevaert, *Cours méthodique d'orchestration*, Paris & Brussels, Lemoine & Cie, 1890

Giannini 2014: Tula Giannini, "The Raoux Family of Master Horn Makers in France: New Documents and Perspectives," *Journal of the American Musical Instrument Society*, 40 (2014), 112–162

Giazotto 1973: Remo Giazotto, *Antonio Vivaldi, catalogo delle opere a cura di Agostino Girard, discografia a cura di Luigi Bellingardi*, Turin, ERI, 1973

Giegling 1987: Franz Giegling (ed.), *Neue Mozart-Ausgabe, Serie V: Konzerte. Werkgruppe 14: Konzerte für ein oder mehrere Streich-, Blas- und Zupfinstrumente und Orchester*, vol. 5: *Hornkonzerte*. Kassel, Bärenreiter-Verlag, 1987.

Gleich 1853: Ferdinand Gleich, *Handbuch der modernen Instrumentirung für Orchester und Militairmusikcorps*, Leipzig, Kahat, 1853

Glüxam 2006: Dagmar Glüxam, "Die Bläserensembles in der Wiener Oper zwischen ca. 1700 und 1740," in *Zur Geschichte und Aufführungspraxis der Harmoniemusik* (Michaelstein Konferenzberichte, 71), ed. by von Boje E. Hans Schmuhl & Ute Omonsky, Augsburg & Michaelstein, Wißner, 2006, pp. 53–68

Goldschmidt 1901: Hugo Goldschmidt, *Studien zur Geschichte der italienischer Oper*, vol. 1, Leipzig, Breitkopf & Härtel, 1901

Goli 1834: Antonio Goli, *Vita di Bonifazio Asioli*, Milan, Ricordi, 1834

Gossec 1829: François-Joseph Gossec, "Notice sur l'introduction des cors, des clarinettes et des trombones dans les orchestres français," *Revue Musicale*, 5 (1829), 217–223

Gounod *ca.* 1839: Charles Gounod, *Méthode de cor à pistons*, Paris, Colombier, [*ca.* 1839]

Gregory 1961: Robin Gregory, *The Horn: A Comprehensive Guide to the Modern Instrument and its Music*, London, Faber and Faber, 1961 (2nd ed. 1969)

Grenot 2016: Cyrille Grenot, "La facture instrumentale des cuivres dans la seconde moitié du XIXe siècle en France," in *Romantic Brass* 2016, pp. 11–102

Gross 1730: Johann Heinrich Gross, *Kurtzer doch gründlicher Begriff der edlen Jägerey*, Nordhausen, Gross, 1730

Grove 2014: *The Grove Dictionary of Musical Instruments*, 2nd ed., Oxford, Oxford University Press, 2014

Grünsteudel 2013: Günther Grünsteudel, " 'Les hobois et les cors sont l'ame de l'orguestre . . .', part 2: Die Hornisten der Wallersteiner Hofkapelle," *Rosetti-Forum*, 14 (2013), 4–24

Gutmann 1982: Veronika Gutmann, *Mit Pauken und Trompeten. Die Sammlung historischer Blechblasinstrumente und Trommeln von Pfarrer Dr. h.c. Wilhelm Bernoulli (1904–1980)*, Basel, Historisches Museum, 1982

Haas 2012: Frithjof Haas, *Hermann Levi: From Brahms to Wagner*, Lanham, MD, Scarecrow Press, 2012

Hachenberg 1992: Karl F. Hachenberg, "Brass in Central European Instrument-Making from the 16th through the 18th Centuries," *HBSJ*, 4 (1992), 229–252

Hachenberg 2006: Karl F. Hachenberg, "Der Werkstoff Messing im Musikinstrumentenbau vom 16. bis zum Ende des 18. Jahrhundert," in *Jagd- und Waldhörner* 2006, pp. 433–448

Hachenberg–Ullwer 2013: Karl F. Hachenberg & Hellmut Ullwer, *Messing nach dem Galmeiverfahren: Drei Handschriften des 18. Jahrhunderts experimentell erläutert*, Hamburg, Disserta Verlag, 2013

Hall 1845: Samuel C. Hall, *The Baronial Halls, Picturesque Edifices, and Ancient Churches of England*, vol. 1, London, Chapman & Hall, 1845 (repr. London, Willis and Sotheran, 1858)

Halle 1764: Johann Samuel Halle, *Werkstäte der heutigen Künste oder die neue Kunsthistorie*, vol. 3, Halle, Brandenburg & Leipzig, 1764

Haller 1970: Klaus Haller, *Partituranordnung und musikalischer Satz*, Tutzing, Schneider, 1970

Hampel–Punto *ca.* 1794: [Anton J.] Hampel & [Giovanni] Punto, *Seule et vraie méthode pour apprendre facilment les eléments des Primier et Second Cors (. . .) Composée par Hampl et perfectionnée par Punto, son elève*, Paris, Naderman, *ca.* 1794

Hanslick 1869: Eduard Hanslick, *Geschichte des Concertwesens in Wien*, Vienna, Braunmüller, 1869

Haumuller 1844: Haumuller (Hanmüller, J. A.), Méthode élementaire de Cor à pistons, Paris, Schonenberger, 1844

Haupt 1960: Helga Haupt, "Wiener Instrumentenbauer von 1791 bis 1815," *Studien zur Musikwissenschaft*, 24 (1960), 120–184.

Haupt 1983: Herbert Haupt, "Kulturgeschichtliche Regesten aus den geheimen Kammerzahlamtsabrechnungen Kaiser Josephs I. (1705–1711)," *Mitteilungen des Österreichischen Staatsarchivs*, 36 (1983), 329–373

Hauptmann 1851: Moritz Hauptmann, "Vorwort des Herausgebers," in *Johann Sebastian Bach's Kirchencantaten*, vol. 1, Leipzig, Breitkopf & Härtel, 1851, pp. xv–xx

Haydn 1965: *Joseph Haydn. Gesammelte Briefe und Aufzeichnungen*, ed. H. C. Robbins Landon and Dénes Bartha, Kassel, Bärenreiter, 1965

Haynes 2002: Bruce Haynes, *A History of Performing Pitch: The Story of A*, Lanham, MD, Scarecrow Press, 2002

Heartz 1987–1988: Daniel Heartz, "Leutgeb and the 1762 Horn Concertos of Joseph and Johann Michael Haydn," *Mozart-Jahrbuch* (1987–1988), 59–64

Heide 1991: Geert Jan van der Heide, "Brass Instrument Metalworking Techniques: The Bronze Age to the Industrial Revolution," *HBSJ*, 3 (1991), 122–150

Heinitz 1929: Wilhelm Heinitz, *Instrumentenkunde*, Potsdam, Athenaion, 1929 (repr. 1934)

Heintze 1978: James R. Heintze, "Alexander Malcolm: Musician, Clergyman, and Schoolmaster," Maryland Historical Magazine, 73 (1978), 226–235

Heinzl 1976: Brigitte Heinzl, "Die Zinn- und Goldschmiedesammlung der kunsthistorischen Abteilung des OÖ. Landesmuseums," *Jahrbuch des Oberösterreichischen Musealvereines – Gesellschaft für Landeskunde*, 121/1 (1976), 233–250

Heise–Gelloz 2013: Birgit Heise & Thierry Gelloz, *Musikinstrumente für Richard Wagner. Ergänzende Anmerkungen zum Katalog "Goldene Klänge im mystischen Grund,"* n.d. [2013] (https://mfm.uni-leipzig.de/dt/media/PDF/Musikinstr_f_R_Wagner.pdf)

Hell 1971: Helmut Hell, *Die neapolitanische Opernsinfonie in der ersten Hälfte des 18. Jahrhunderts*, Tutzing, Schneider, 1971

Heller 1997: Karl Heller, *Antonio Vivaldi, the Red Priest of Venice*, trans. and ed. by David Marinelli, Portland, OR, Amadeus Press, 1997 (orig. German edition, Leipzig, Reclam, 1991)

Hermann 1782: Benedikt Franz Hermann, *Abriß der physikalischen Beschaffenheit der Oesterreichschen Staaten*, Vienna, s.d.t., 1782

Heyde 1982: Herbert Heyde, *Hörner und Zinken (Musikinstrumenten-Museum Leipzig, Katalog, 5)*, Leipzig, VEB Deutscher Verlag, 1982

Heyde 1985: Herbert Heyde, *Trompeten, Posaunen, Tuben*, Wiesbaden, Breitkopf & Härtel, 1985

Heyde 1986: Herbert Heyde, *Musikinstrumentenbau 15.–19. Jahrhundert. Kunst – Handwerk – Entwurf*, Leipzig & Wiesbaden, VEB Deutscher Verlag für Musik & Breitkopf & Härtel, 1986

Heyde 1987a: Herbert Heyde, *Das Ventilblasinstrument*, Leipzig & Wiesbaden, VEB Deutscher Verlag für Musik & Breitkopf & Härtel, 1987

Heyde 1987b: Herbert Heyde, "Blasinstrumente und Bläser der Dresdner Hofkapelle in der Zeit des Fux-Schülers Johann Dismas Zelenka (1710–1745)," in *Johann Joseph Fux und die barocke Bläsertradition*, ed. by von Bernhard Habla, Tutzing, Schneider, 1987, pp. 39–65

Heyde 1987c: Herbert Heyde, "Das Instrument von Gottfried Reiche," *Beiträge zur Bachforschung*, 36 (1987), 96–109

Heyde 1994: Herbert Heyde, *Musikinstrumentenbau in Preußen*, Tutzing, Schneider, 1994

Hiebert 1992: Hiebert Thomas, "Virtuosity, Experimentation, and Innovation in Horn Writing from Early 18th-Century Dresden," *HBSJ*, 4 (1992), 112–159

Hiebert 1996: Thomas Hiebert, "Old and New Roles for the Horn in J.F. Fasch's Hunt Concerto," *THC*, 8 (1996), 15–28

Hiebert 2006: Thomas Hiebert, "Extraordinary Horn Writing in the *Egerton Manuscript Collection*: A Contribution to the History of the Horn in Mid-Eighteenth Century England," in *Jagd- und Waldhörner* 2006, pp. 239–246

Hilfiger 1993: John Jay Hilfiger, "Who Composed 'Haydn's Second Horn Concerto'?," *THC*, 5 (1993), 1–6

Hiller 2000: Albert Hiller, *Das grosse Buch vom Posthorn*, 2nd ed., Wilhelmshaven, Noetzel, 2000

Hinrichs 1796: Johann C. Hinrichs, *Entstehung, Fortgang und jetzige Beschaffenheit der russischen Jagdmusik*, St. Petersburg, Schnoor, 1796

Hofer 2006: Achim Hofer, "Geburtsmomente der Harmoniemusik. Beispiele – Perspektiven," in *Zur Geschichte und Aufführungspraxis der Harmoniemusik* (Michaelstein Konferenzberichte, 71), ed. by von Boje E. Hans Schmuhl & Ute Omonsky, Augsburg &Michaelstein, Wißner, 2006, pp. 37–52

Hoffmann 1830: Carl Julius Adolph Hoffmann, *Die Tonkünstler Schlesiens. Ein Beitrag zur Kunstgeschichte Schlesiens vom Jahre 960 bis 1830*, Breslau, Aderholz, 1830

Hofmann 1893: Richard Hofmann, *Praktische Instrumentationslehre*, 7 vols., Leipzig, Dörffling & Franke, 1893 (*Practical Instrumentation*, trans. by Robin H. Legge, London & New York, Augener & Schirmer, 1897)

Holman 2010: Peter Holman, *Life after Death: The Viola da Gamba in Britain from Purcell to Dolmetsch*, Woodbridge, Boydell, 2010

Hopfner 2002: Rudolf Hopfner, "Leichamschneider (Leichnamschneider), Familie," *Oesterreichisches Musiklexikon online* (http://www.musiklexikon.ac.at/ml)

Hübner 2006: Ulrich Hübner, "Das Horn auf dem Porträt von Frédéric Duvernoy," in *Jagd- und Waldhörner* 2006, pp. 77–90

Hübner 2016: Ulrich Hübner, "Das Cor Chaussier. Ein Praxisbericht," in *Romantic Brass* 2016, pp. 363–376

Humphries 2000: John Humphries, *The Early Horn: A Practical Guide*, Cambridge, Cambridge University Press, 2000

Humphries 2021: John Humphries, "'This French-Horn Gentleman . . .' Giovanni Punto in London," *HBSJ*, 33 (2021), 15–34

Humphries 2023: John Humphries, "The Various Uses of the Horn beyond the Concert Room in 18th Century Britain: Hunting, Water Parties, Pleasure Gardens, the Military, Mischief and Merrymaking," in *Musica a Corte* 2023, pp. 107–126

Israël 1876: Carl Israël, *Frankfurter Concert-Chronik von 1713–1780*, Frankfurt a.M., Verein für Geschichte und Alterthumskunde, 1876

Jablonski 1721: Johann Theodor Jablonski, *Allgemeines Lexicon der Künste und Wissenschaften*, Leipzig, Fritschen, 1721

Jagd- und Waldhörner 2006: *Jagd- und Waldhörner. Geschichte und musikalische Nutzung* (Musikinstrumentenbau-Symposium Michaelstein, 25), ed. by Boje E. Hans Schmuhl & Monika Lustig, Augsburg, Wissner, 2006

Jahn 1882: Otto Jahn, *Life of Mozart*, 3 vols., London, Novello & Ewer, 1882

Janowka 1701: Thomas Balthasar Janowka, *Clavis ad thesaurum magnae artis musicae*, Vetero-Pragae, Labaun, 1701 (repr. Amsterdam, Knuf, 1973)

Kade 1893: Otto Kade, *Die Musikalien-sammlung des Grossherzoglich Mecklenburg-Schweriner Fürstenhauses*, 2 vols., Schwerin, Sandmeyer, 1893

Kalkbrenner 1882: A. [August] Kalkbrenner, *Wilhelm Wieprecht. Sein Leben und Wirken*, Berlin, Prager, 1882

Kalmus 1937: Ludwig Kalmus, *Weltgeschichte der Post*, Vienna, Göth, 1937

Karstädt 1964: Georg Karstädt, *Laßt lustig die Hörner erschallen!*, Berlin, Parey, 1964

Kastner 1837: Georges Kastner, *Traité général d'instrumentation*, Paris, Philipp, 1837

Kastner 1844: Georges Kastner, *Méthode elémentaire pour le Cor*, Paris, Troupenas, [1844] (Italian translation as *Metodo elementare per corno*, Milan, F. Lucca, [1845])

Kastner 1848: Georges Kastner, *Manuel général de musique militaire à l'usage des armées françaises*, Paris, Didot frères, 1848

Kastner 1854: Georges Kastner, "Revue critique. Méthode de cor à trois pistons ou cylindres par M. Urbin," *Revue et gazette musicale de Paris*, 21/29 (1854), 232–233

Kearns 1986: Andrew K. Kearns, *The Eighteenth-Century Horn Concertos in the Thurn and Taxis Court Library in Regensburg*, dissertation, University of Illinois at Urbana-Champaign, 1986

Keeß 1824: Stephan von Keeß, *Darstellung des Fabriks- und Gewerbswesens in seinem gegenwärtigen Zustande*, vol. 2, ex. ed., Vienna, Mörschner & Jasper, 1824

Keeß 1830: Stephan von Keeß, *Systematische Darstellung der neuesten Fortschritte in den Gewerben und Manufacturen*, vol. 2, Vienna, Gerold, 1830

Kellner 1956: Altman Kellner, *Musikgeschichte des Stiftes Kremsmünster*, Kassel & Basel, Bärenreiter, 1956

Kenyon 2005: Beryl Kenyon de Pascual, "Brass Instruments and Instrumentalists in the Spanish Royal Chapel from the Late Seventeenth to Mid-Eighteenth Centuries," in *Brass Music at the Cross Roads of Europe: The Low Countries and Contexts of Brass Musicians from the Renaissance into the Nineteenth Century*, Utrecht, STIMU, 2005

Klaus 2000: Sabine K. Klaus, "Outstanding Trumpets, Trombones, and Horns in the Instrument Collection of the Historical Museum, Basel," *HBSJ*, 12 (2000), 1–22

Klaus 2006: Sabine K. Klaus, "Horn oder Trompete? Ein Instrument von Johann Carl Kodisch, Nürnberg 1684," in *Jagd- und Waldhörner* 2006, pp. 155–176

Klaus 2012: Sabine K. Klaus, *Trumpets and Other High Brass*, vol. 1: *Instruments of the Single Harmonic Series*, Vermillion, SD, National Music Museum, 2012

Kleefeld 1900: Wilhelm Kleefeld, "Das Orchester der Hamburger Oper, 1678–1738," *Sammelbände der Internationalen Musikgesellschaft*, 1/2 (1900), 219–289

Kling 1865: Henry Kling, *Horn-Schule. Méthode pour le cor (simple et chromatique)*, Leipzig & Berlin, Breitkopf & Härtel, n.d. [Geneva, 1865]

Kling 1882: Henry Kling, *Populäre Instrumentationslehre*, Hanover, Oertel, 1882 (English translation as *Modern Orchestration and Instrumentation*, enlarged ed., New York, Fischer, 1905)

Kling 1908: Henry Kling, "Giovanni Punto, célèbre corniste," *Bulletin français de la S.I.M.*, 4/10 (1908), 1066–1082

Kling 1911: Henry Kling, "Le cor de chasse," *Rivista Musicale Italiana*, 28 (1911), 95–136

Kloss–Anderson 1997: Marilyn Bone Kloss & Mark J. Anderson, "Horn Design by Tuckwell," *THC*, 27/3 (May 1997), 41–44

Koch 1802: Heinrich Christoph Koch, *Musikalisches Lexikon*, Frankfurt a.M., Hermann, 1802

Koch 1980: Hans Oscar Koch, *Sonderformen der Blasinstrumente in der deutschen Musik vom spaten 17. bis zur Mitte des 18. Jahrhunderts*, Ph.D. dissertation, Ruprecht-Karl-Universität zu Heidelberg, 1980

Köchel 1869: Ludwig von Köchel, *Die kaiserliche Hof-Musikkapelle in Wien von 1543 bis 1867 nach urkundlichen Forschungen*, Vienna, Hölder, 1869.

Kolman 1985: Barry H. Kolman, *The Origins of American Wind Music and General Instrumental Tutors*, D.A. dissertation, University of Northern Colorado, 1985

Kolman 2018: Barry Araújo Kolman, *American Wind Music: Its Origin and the Instrumental Tutors*, Newcastle upon Tyne, Cambridge Scholars Publishing, 2018

Kolneder 1970: Walter Kolneder, *Antonio Vivaldi: His Life and Work*, London, Faber & Faber, 1970

Körner 1969: Friedrich Körner, "Ein Horn von Michael Nagel in Graz," *Historisches Jahrbuch der Stadt Graz*, 2 (1969), 87–96

Kroll 2014: Mark Kroll, *Ignaz Moscheles and the Changing World of Musical Europe*, Woodbridge, Boydell Press, 2014

Kuhnau 1700: Johann Kuhnau, *Der musikalische Quacksalber*, Dresden, Miethen & Zimmermann, 1700

La Borde 1780: Jean-Benjamin de La Borde, *Essai sur la musique ancienne et moderne*, 4 vols., Paris, Pierres, 1780

Laborde 1877, 1880: Léon Laborde, *Les comptes des bâtiments du roi (1528–1571) suivis de documents inédits sur les châteaux royaux et les beaux-arts au 16e siècle, recueillis et mis en ordre*, Paris, Baur, 1877 (vol. 1); 1880 (vol. 2)

Laloy 1908: Louis Laloy, *Rameau*, Paris, Félix. Alcan, 1908 (3th ed. 1919)

La musica 2001: *La musica e i suoi strumenti. La collezione granducale del Conservatorio Cherubini*, ed. by Franca Falletti, Renato Meucci, & Gabriele Rossi Rognoni, Florence, Giunti, 2001

Langey 1890: Otto Langey, *Newly Revised Tutor for French Horn*, 2nd ed., New York, Fisher, 1890

Laubhold 2009: Lars E. Laubhold, *Magie der Macht. Eine quellenkritische Studie zu Johann Ernst Altenburgs "Versuch einer Anleitung zur heroisch-musikalischen Trompeter- und Pauker-Kunst" (Halle 1795)*, Würzburg, Königshausen & Neumann, 2009

La Via 1995: Stefano La Via, "Il cardinale Ottoboni e la musica: nuovi documenti (1700–1740), nuove letture e ipotesi," in *Intorno a Locatelli*, ed. by Albert Dunning, Lucca, LIM, 1995, pp. 319–526

Lesure 1968: François Lesure, *Music and Art in Society*, Pittsburgh, Pennsylvania State University Press, 1968

Lichtenthal 1826: Pietro Lichtenthal, *Diʒionario e bibliografia della musica*, 2 vols., Milan, Fontana, 1826

Limouzin 1888: Charles Limouzin, *Eugène Vivier. La vie et les aventures d'un corniste. 1817–1852*, Paris, Marpon & Flammarion, 1888

Lindner 1898: Josef Lindner, "Hie F-Horn, hie B-Horn, was ist recht?," *Deutsche Musiker-Zeitung. Organ für die Interessen der Musiker und des musikalischen Verkehrs*, 29/34 (1898), in Pizka 1986, pp. 279–286

Lionnet 1996: Jean Lionnet, "Les événements musicaux de la légation du cardinal Flavio Chigi en France, été 1664," *Studi Musicali*, 25 (1996), 127–153

Lipowski 1811: Felix Joseph Lipowsky, *Baierisches Musik Lexicon*, Munich, Giel, 1811

Litzmann 1913: Berthold Litzmann, *Clara Schumann, an Artist's Life*, trans. by Grace E. Hadow, 2 vols., London, Macmillan, 1913

Liu 2005: Yi-Hsin Cindy Liu, *The Examination of the Appearance and Use of the French Horn in Film Scores from 1977 to 2004*, D.M.A. dissertation, University of Cincinnati, 2005

Lustig 2006: Monika Lustig, "Jagd- un Waldhörner in niedersächsischen Museen," in *Jagd- und Waldhörner* 2006, pp. 295–327

MacCracken 1990: Thomas G. MacCracken, "Further Observations on Bach's Use of the Horn: A Reply to Bertil H. van Boer Jr.," *THC*, 2 (1990), 97–104

Mahillon 1893, 1909, 1900, 1912: Victor-Charles Mahillon, *Catalogue descriptif et analytique du Musée instrumental . . . Bruxelles*, 2nd ed., Gand, Hoste, 1893 (vol. 1), 1909 (vol. 2), 1900 (vol. 3), 1912 (vol. 4)

Mahillon 1907: Victor-Charles Mahillon, *Instruments à vent*, vol. 2: *Le cor, son histoire, sa théorie, sa construction*, Brussels, Mahillon & Co., [1907]

Majer 1732: Joseph Friedrich Bernhard Caspar Majer, *Museum musicum*, Hall, Majer, 1732 (facs. Kassel, Bärenreiter, 1954)

Maniguet 2015: Thierry Maniguet, "La dynastie des Raoux, facteurs de 'cors de chasse' du XVIIe au XVIIIe siècle," *Musique Image Instruments*, 15 (2015), 227–247

Marcaletti 2023: Livio Marcaletti, "Hunting Horns and Venatorial Scenes in Viennese Baroque Opera," in *Musica a corte* 2023, pp. 23–38

Maricourt 1627: René de Maricourt, *Traité de la Chasse du Lièvre et du Chevreuil*, Ms., 1627 (F-Pn) (published as *Traicté et abrégé de la chasse du lièvre et du chevreuil, dédié au roy Louis tresiesme*, Paris, Bouchard-Huzard, 1858)

Marolles 1930: Gaston de Marolles, *Notice historique sur la trompe de chasse*, in Boursier de la Roche, *Les plus belles fanfares de chasse*, Paris, Nourrit, 1930, pp. 35–67

Martini 1883: Angelo Martini, *Manuale di metrologia, ossia misure, pesi e monete in uso attualmente e anticamente presso tutti i popoli*, Turin, Loescher, 1883

Martz 2003: Richard J. Martz, "Reversed Chirality in Horns, or Is Left Right? The Horn, on the Other Hand," *HBSJ*, 15 (2003), 173–232

Marx 1847: Adolf Bernhard Marx, *Lehre von der musikalischen Komposition, praktisch theoretisch*, vol. 4, Leipzig, Breitkopf & Härtel, 1847

Marx 1988: Josef Marx, "An Introduction to Mozart's 12 Duos for Two French Horns (K.487)," *THC*, 29/1 (October 1988), 49–65 (orig. German edition, 1947)

Mattheson 1713: Johann Mattheson, *Das neu-eröffnete Orchestre*, Thum, Schuller, 1713

Mattheson 1723: Johann Mattheson, *Critica musica*, vol. 1, Hamburg, author, 1723

Mattheson 1737: Johann Mattheson, *Kern melodischer Wissenschafft*, Hamburg, Herold, 1737

Maunder 1998: Richard Maunder, "Viennese Wind-Instrument Makers, 1700–1800," *GSJ*, 51 (1998), 170–191

Maury 2016: Claude Maury, "Les cors omnitoniques," in *Romantic Brass* 2016, pp. 103–153

May 1905: Florence May, *The Life of Brahms*, London, Reeves, 1905

Mc Corkle 1984: Margit L. Mc Corkle, *Johannes Brahms. Thematisch-Bibliographisches Werkverzeichnis*, Munich, Henle, 1984

Mc Credie 1964: Andrew D. Mc Credie, *Instrumentarium and Instrumentation in the North German Baroque Opera*, dissertation, Universität Hamburg, 1964

Meer 1979: John Henry van der Meer, *Verzeichnis der Europäischen Musikinstrumente im Germanischen Nationalmuseum Nürnberg*, Wilhelmshaven, Heinrichshofen, 1979

Meer 1993: John Henry van der Meer, *Strumenti musicali europei del Museo Civico Medievale di Bologna*, Bologna, Nuova Alfa Editoriale, 1993

Meifred 1829a: Joseph Emile Meifred, *Première étude raisonnée dans tous les tons majeurs pour le cor à pistons précédée d'un tableau synonimique de toute l'étendue de son échelle par demi tons*, Paris, Heu, 1829

Meifred 1829b: Joseph Emile Meifred, *De l'eténdue, de l'emploi et des ressources du cor en général et des corps de rechange en particulier*, Paris, Richault, 1829

Meifred 1835: Joseph Emile Meifred, "Du cor a pistons," in *Encyclopedie Pittoresque de la Musique*, vol. 1, ed. by Adolphe Ledhuy & Henri Bertini, Paris, Delloye, 1835, xxxiii livraison, pp. 125–126, and following insert, pp. 1–4

Meifred 1840: Joseph Emile Meifred, *Méthode pour le cor chromatique ou à pistons*, Paris, Richault, 1840 (repr. Paris, Richault, 1849)

Meifred 1851: Joseph Emile Meifred, *Notice sur la fabrication des instruments de musique en cuivre en général et de celle du cor chromatique en particulier*, Paris, De Soye, 1851

Melton 2008: William Melton, *The Wagner Tuba: A History*, Aachen, Ebenos, 2008

Mendel 1870–1879: Hermann Mendel, *Musikalisches Conversations-Lexikon*, 11 vols., Berlin, Oppenheim, 1870–1879

Ménestrier 1669: Claude-François Ménestrier, *Traité des tournois, joustes, carrousels et autres spectacles publics*, Lyons, Muguet, 1669

Ménestrier 1681: Claude-François Ménestrier, *Des représentations en musique anciennes et modernes*, Paris, Guignard, 1681

Ménestrier 1682: Claude-François Ménestrier, *Des ballets anciens et modernes selon les règles du theatre*, Paris, Guignard, 1682

Mengal 1835, ca. 1840: Jean-Baptiste Mengal, *Méthode de cor suivi du doigté du cornet à pistons*, Paris, Meissonnier, [1835]; repr. as *Méthode de cor et cor à pistons suivie du doigté du cornet à trois pistons*, Paris, Meissonnier, [ca. 1840] (unique copy known: I-Mc)

Menke 1934: Werner Menke, *Die Geschichte der Bach- und Handeltrompete / History of the Trumpet of Bach and Handel*, London, Reeves, 1934 (English only: London, Reeves, 1960; repr. Nashville, TN, Brass Press, 1985)

Mersenne 1637: Marin Mersenne, *Harmonie universelle*, vol. 2, Paris, Ballard, 1637

Meucci 1989: Renato Meucci, "Roman Military Instruments and the Lituus," *GSJ*, 42 (1989), 85–97

Meucci 1994: Renato Meucci, "The Pelitti Firm: Makers of Brass Instruments in Nineteenth-Century Milan," *HBSJ*, 6 (1994), 304–333

Meucci 1998: Renato Meucci, "I timpani e gli strumenti a percussione nell'Ottocento italiano," *Studi Verdiani*, 13 (1998), 184–254 (English edition, trans. by Mike Quinn, as *The Timpani and Percussion Instruments in 19th-Century Italy*, [Lugano], 2011)

Meucci 2006: Renato Meucci, "Social and Political Perspectives in the Early History of the Horn," in *Jagd- und Waldhörner* 2006, pp. 15–28

Meucci 2010: Renato Meucci, "Strumenti e strumentisti nella Milano di metà Settecento," in *Antonio Brioschi e il nuovo stile musicale del Settecento lombardo*, international conference proceedings ed. by Davide Daolmi & Cesare Fertonani, Milan, Led, 2010, pp. 137–150

Meucci 2021: Renato Meucci, "Spontini's Letter to the Paris Académie (1840) on Blühmel's Priority in the Invention of Valves for Brass Instruments," *HBSJ*, 33 (2021), 1–14

Meucci 2023: Renato Meucci, "On the Early History of the Horn in Turin, Versailles, and Nuremberg, with Some Remarks on Differences in Brass Manufacture," in *Musica a corte* 2023, pp. 177–192

Meucci–Ghirardini 2019: Renato Meucci & Cristina Ghirardini, "Bizzarrie di strumenti musicali," in *Musique Images Instruments. Mélanges en l'honneur de Florence Gétreau*, ed. by Yves Balmer, Alban Framboisier, Fabien Guilloux, & Catherine Massip, Turnhout, Brepols, 2019, pp. 391–414

Meucci–Rocchetti 2001: Renato Meucci & Gabriele Rocchetti, "Horn", in *Grove* 2001

Meyer 1956: Ernst Hermann Meyer, "Die Bedeutung der Instrumentalmusik am Fürstbischöflichen Hofe zu Olomouc (Olmütz) in Kroměříž (Kremsier)," *Die Musikforschung*, 11/4 (1956), 388–411

Michel 1975: Paul Michel, "Hof- und Feldtrompeter in Thüringen. Ein Beitrag zur Sozialgeschichte des Musikers," in *Festschrift Walter Senn*, ed. by Erich Egg & Ewald Fässler, Munich &Salzburg, Katzbichler, 1975, pp. 135–141

Millgrove 1797: Benjamin Millgrove, "Improvement of the French-Horn," *Monthly Magazine*, 4 (1797), 341

Mitroulia–Myers 2008: Eugenia Mitroulia & Arnold Myers, "Adolphe Sax: Visionary or Plagiarist?," *HBSJ*, 20 (2008), 93–141

Mitroulia–Demoulin–Eldredge 2008: Eugenia Mitroulia, Géry Dumoulin, & Niles Eldredge, "On the Early History of the Périnet Valve," *GSJ*, 61 (2008), 217–229

Montagu 1763: Mary Wortley Montagu, *Letters of the Right Honourable Lady Mary Wortley Montague*, vol. 1, London, 1763

Montagu 1986: Jeremy Montagu, "On the Skill of the Viennese Brass Instrument Makers: A Tribute," *FoMRHIQ*, 43/722 (1986), 124–126

Morin 1708: Jean-Baptiste Morin, *La chasse du cerf (1708)*, Paris, Ballard, 1709

Morley-Pegge 1973: Reginald Morley-Pegge, *The French Horn: Some Notes on the Evolution of the Instrument and of its Technique*, London, Benn, 1960 (2nd ed., London, Benn, 1973).

Mürner 2016: Martin Mürner, "Meifred und die Einführung des Ventilhorns in Frankreich," in *Romantic Brass* 2016, pp. 223–233

Murray 1986: Sterling E. Murray, "The Double Horn Concerto: A Specialty of the Oettingen-Wallerstein Court," The Journal of Musicology, 4/4 (Autumn 1985–Autumn 1986), 507–534

Murray 2014: Sterling E. Murray, *The Career of an Eighteenth-Century Kapellmeister: The Life and Music of Antonio Rosetti*, Rochester, NY, University of Rochester Press, 2014

Museo 1997: *Museo degli Strumenti Musicali*, ed. by Andrea Gatti, Milan, Electa, 1997

Musica a corte 2023: *Il corno da caccia. Musica a corte tra Piemonte ed Europa (secc. XVI-XIX)*, ed. by Renato Meucci, Florence, Olschki, 2023

Myers 1997: Arnold Myers, "Design, Technology and Manifacture since 1800," in *Cambridge Companion* 1997, pp. 115–130

Myers 2002: Arnold Myers, "Brasswind Innovation and Output of Boosey & Co. in the Blaikley Era," *HBSJ*, 14 (2002), 391–423

Myers 2006: Arnold Myers, "The Internal Evolution of the French Horn and the Trompe," in *Jagd- und Waldhörner* 2006, pp. 373–390

Nettl 1921–1922: Paul Nettl, "Weltliche Musik des Stiftes Osseg im 17. Jahrhundert," *Zeitschrift für Musikwissenschaft*, 4 (1921–1922), 351–357

Nettl 1953: Paul Nettl, "Franz Anton Graf von Sporcks Beziehungen zur Musik," *Die Musikforschung*, 6 (1953), 324–335

Neumann–Schulze 1963: Werner Neumann & Hans-Joachim Schulze, *Bach-Dokumente*, vol. 1: *Schriftstücke von der Hand Johann Sebastian Bachs*, Kassel, Bärenreiter, 1963

Nickel 1971: Ekkehard Nickel, *Der Holzblasinstrumentenbau in der freien Reichsstadt Nürnberg*, Munich, Katzbichler, 1971

Niemistö 2009: Paul Niemistö, *The Johann Friedrich Anderst Brass Music Instrument Collection at Kuopio Cultural History Museum*, Kuopio, Cultural History Museum, 2009

Noack 1967: Elisabeth Noack, *Musikgeschichte Darmstadts vom Mittelalter bis zur Goethezeit*, Mainz, Schott, 1967

Nocerino 2009a: Francesco Nocerino, "Artigianato musicale a Napoli nel Settecento. Gli strumenti, le botteghe, i costruttori," in *Napoli La Città Cantante. Laboratorio del Museo per la Musica*, Milan, Mondadori-Electa, 2009, pp. 43–49

Nocerino 2009b: Francesco Nocerino, "Gli strumenti musicali a Napoli nel secolo XVIII," in *Storia della musica e dello spettacolo a Napoli. Il Settecento* ed. by Francesco Cotticelli & Paologiovanni Maione, Naples, Pietà dei Turchini, 2009, pp. 773–804

Noe 2011: Alfred Noe, *Die italienische Literatur in Österreich*, vol. 1: *Von den Anfangen bis 1797*, Vienna, Cologne, & Weimar, Böhlau, 2011

Nösselt 1980: Hans-Joachim Nösselt, *Ein ältest Orchester 1530–1980. 450 Jahre Bayerisches Hof- und Staatsorchester*, Munich, Bruckmann, 1980

Odling–Girodo 1999–2000: Francesca Odling & Lorenzo Girodo, "Documenti sulla costruzione degli strumenti a fiato a Torino fra il XVII e XVIII secolo," *Liuteria Musica e Cultura* (1999–2000), 25–42; abridged reprint in *Musica a corte 2023*, pp. 257–267

Oldman 1961: C. [Cecil] B. [Bernard] Oldman, "Mozart's Scena for Tenducci," *Music & Letters*, 42/1 (1961), 44–52

Onerati 1994–1995: Alessandro Onerati, *Strumenti a fiato nella vita musicale fiorentina dell'Ottocento*, dissertation, Università degli studi di Urbino, 1994–1995

Osborne 2007: Richard Osborne, *Rossini: His Life and Works*, 2nd ed., Oxford, Oxford University Press, 2007

Owens 1995: Samantha Kim Owens, *The Württemberg Hofkapelle c. 1680/1721*, dissertation, Wellington (NZ), Victoria University, 1995

Passadore 2007: Francesco Passadore, *Catalogo tematico delle composizioni di Giuseppe Torelli (1658–1709)*, Padua, Solisti Veneti, 2007

Paul 1976: Ernst Paul, "Das Horn als Signalinstrument einst und heute," *Salzburger Museum Carolino-Augusteum. Jahresschrift*, 22 (1976), 37–60

Pearn–Gardner-Thorpe 2005: John Pearn & Christopher Gardner-Thorpe, "Tubular Branches, Additaments, Holes and Ventages: William Close (1775–1813), Lake District Apothecary and Surgeon; and His Invention of Polyphonian Trumpets and French Horns," *GSJ*, 58 (2005), 38–45

Pedrell 1897: Felipe Pedrell, *Diccionario biográfico y bibliográfico de músicos y escritores de música españoles, portugueses e hispano americanos antiguos y modernos*, Barcelona, Berdós y Feliu, 1897

Pierre 1890: Constant Pierre, *La facture instrumentale à l'Exposition universelle de 1889*, Paris, Librairie de l'art indépendant, 1890 (online ed.: Paris, CNRS, 2011 (https://www.nakala.fr/nakala/data/11280/5c06ef8c))

Pierre 1893: Constant Pierre, *Les facteurs d'instruments de musique. Les luthiers et la facture instrumentale. Précis historique*, Paris, Sagot, 1893

Pierre 2000: Constant Pierre, *Histoire du Concert Spirituel, 1725–1790*, 2nd ed., Paris, Société française de musicologie & Heugel et Cie., 2000

Piersig 1927: Fritz Piersig, *Die Einführung des Hornes in die Kunstmusik und seine Verwendung bis zum Tode Joh. Seb. Bachs: ein Beitrag zur Geschichte der Instrumentation*, Halle, Niemeyer, 1927

Pisarowitz 1970: Karl Maria Pisarowitz, "Mozarts Schnorrer Leutgeb; dessen Primärbiographie," *Mitteilungen der Internationalen Stiftung Mozarteum*, 8/3–4 (1970), 21–26

Pizka 1986: Hans Pizka, *Hornisten-Lexikon / Dictionary for Hornists*, Kirchheim bei Munich, Pizka, 1986

Pohl 1871: Carl Ferdinand Pohl, *Denkschrift aus Anlass des hundertjähringen Bestehens der Tonkünstler-Societät*, Vienna, Gerold's Sohn, 1871

Pontecoulant 1861: Louis-Adolphe de Pontécoulant, *Organographie, essai sur la facture instrumentale, art, industrie et commerce*, 2 vols., Paris, Castel, 1861

Porfiryeva–Stepanov 1998: Anna L. Porfiryeva & Alexander A. Stepanov, "Kyoò'bel' (Kölbel), Ferdinand," in *Musical St Petersburg: Musical-Encyclopedic Dictionary*, vol. 2, ed. by A. L. Porfiryeva, St. Petersburg, Compozitor, 1998, pp. 52–55

Praetorius 1619–1620: Michael Praetorius, *Syntagma musicum*, vol. 2: *Theatrum instrumentorum seu Sciagraphia*, Wolfenbüttel, Holwein, 1619, (Plates), 1620

Proksch 2011: Bryan Proksch, "The Context of the Tromba in F in J.S. Bach's Second Brandenburg Concerto, BWV 1047," *HBSJ*, 23 (2011), 43–66

Prota-Giurleo 1952: Ulisse Prota-Giurleo, "Breve storia del teatro di corte e della musica a Napoli nei secoli XVII e XVIII," in Felice de Filippis, *Il Teatro di Corte nel Palazzo reale di Napoli*, Naples, L'Arte tipografica, 1952, pp. 19–125

Prout 1877: Ebenezer Prout, *Instrumentation*, London, Novello & Co., 1877 (Italian translation as *Strumentazione*, ed. by Vittorio Ricci, Milan, Hoepli, 1892)

Prout 1898: Ebenezer Prout, *The Orchestra*, vol. 1, London, Augener & Co., 1898

Prunières 1911: Henry Prunières, "La musique de la chambre et de l'Ecurie sous le règne de François Ier, 1516–1547," *L'année musicale*, 1 (1911), 215–251

Prunières 1914: Henry Prunières, *Le ballet de cour en France avant Benserade et Lully suivi du Ballet de la délivrance de Renaud*, Paris, Laurens, 1914

Quoika 1956: Rudolf Quoika, *Die Musik der Deutschen in Böhmen und Mähren*, Berlin, Merseburger, 1956

Raccolta 1823: *Raccolta degli atti del governo e delle disposizioni generali emanate dalle diverse autorità*, vol. 2, Milan, Imp. Regia Stamperia, 1823

Radiciotti 1927: Giuseppe Radiciotti, *Giacchino Rossini. Vita documentata, opere, ed influenza su l'arte*, vol. 1, Tivoli, Chicca, 1927

Rädlein 1711: Johann Rädlein, *Europäischer Sprach-Schatz [. . .] oder Wörter-Buch der vornehmsten Sprachen in Europa*, 3 vols., Leipzig, Braun, 1711

Rapports 1855: *Exposition universelle de 1855. Rapports du jury mixte international*, vol. 2, Paris, Imprimerie Imperiale, 1856

Rasmussen 1961–1962: Mary Rasmussen, "The Manuscript Katalog Wenster Litteratur I/1–17b (Universitetsbiblioteket, Lund): A Contribution to the History of the Baroque Horn Concerto," *Brass Quarterly*, 5 (1961–1962), 135–152

Registers 1906: *The Registers of Saint Paul's Church, Covent Garden, London*, vol. 2: *Christenings, 1752–1837*, ed. by William H. Hurt, London, Hughes & Clarke, 1906

Regli 1860: Francesco Regli, *Dizionario biografico dei più celebri poèti ed artisti melodrammatici, tragici e comici, maestri, concertisti, coreografi, mimi, ballerini, scenografi, giornalisti, impresarii, ecc. ecc. che fiorirono in Italia dal 1800 al 1860*, Turin, Dalmazzo, 1860

Reichardt 1896: Johann Friedrich Reichardt, *Un hiver à Paris sous le Consulat (1802–1803) d'après les lettres de J.-F. Reichardt*, ed. by A. Laquiante, Paris, Plon & Nourrit et Cie, 1896

Ribock 1784: Justus Johannes Heinrich Ribock, "Beytrag zur Geschichte des Waldhorns," *Magazin der Musik*, 2 (July 9, 1784), 8–10

Richter 1909–1910: P. E. Richter, "Eine zweiventilige Trompete aus dem Jahre 1806 und die Wiener Instrumentenmacher Kerner," *ZfI*, 30 (1909–1910), 36–38

Rieche–Wenke 2006: Christiane Rieche & Wolfgang Wenke, "Jagd- und Waldhörner in mitteldeutschen Museen: Überblick zu den Erfassungsergebnissen und Objektliste," in *Jagd- und Waldhörner* 2006, pp. 329–360

Rimsky-Korsakov 1922: Nikolay Rimsky-Korsakov, *Principles of Orchestration*, 2 vols., posthumously completed by Maximilian Steinberg, Berlin, Editions Russes de musique, 1922

Robbins Landon 1955: Howard Chandler Robbins Landon, *The Symphonies of Joseph Haydn*, London, Universal Edition & Rockliff, 1955

Robbins Landon 1999: Howard Chandler Robbins Landon, *Horns in High C: A Memoir of Musical Discoveries and Adventures*, London, Thames & Hudson, 1999

Rocchetti 1990: Gabriele Rocchetti, "Benedetto Bergonzi, cornista, compositore e inventore cremonese," *Recercare*, 2 (1990), 151–171

Rocchetti 2006: Gabriele Rocchetti, "The Development of Horn Writing in Italy during the Eighteenth Century," in *Jagd- und Waldhörner* 2006, pp. 267–283

Rocchetti 2007: Gabriele Rocchetti, "A Window on the Horn in Early Nineteenth-Century Italy: The 'Brevi Cenni' of Giovanni Simone Mayr," *HBSJ*, 19 (2007), 25–70 (English translation from the Italian edition: Bergamo, Mariani e Monti, 2000)

Rocchetti 2023a: Gabriele Rocchetti, "'Corno vel Clarino': corni o trombe, ovvero 'corni alla maniera di trombe'," in *Musica a corte* 2023, pp. 39–57

Rocchetti 2023b: Gabriele Rocchetti, "'Al fragor dei corni audaci': la musica di Vivaldi per corno", *Recercare*, 35 (2023), 175–215

Rocchetti–Rossi-Rognoni 1998: Gabriele Rocchetti & Gabriele Rossi-Rognoni, "Gli strumenti musicali premiati dall'Istituto Lombardo di Scienze, Lettere ed Arti nell'Ottocento," in *Liuteria Musica e Cultura*, Lucca & Cremona, LIM, 1998, pp. 3–17

Rode 1860: Theodor Rode, "Zur Geschichte des Horns oder Waldhorns," *Neue Berliner Musik-Zeitung*, 14 (1860), 241–243, 249–252

Roeser *ca.* 1764: Valentin Roeser, *Essai d'instruction à l'usage de ceux qui composent pour la clarinette et le cor*, Paris, Mercier, *ca.* 1764

Rogan 1996: William Rogan, "Stopped Notes on the Horn: Some Estethetic Considerations," *HBSJ*, 8 (1996), 53–68

Rolf 1995: Marie Rolf, "A New Manuscript Source for Mozart's Rondo in E-flat for Horn, K.371," *THC*, 25/3 (May 1995), 23–27

Rollinson 1886: Thomas H. Rollinson, *Treatise on Harmony, Counterpoint, Instrumentation and Orchestration*, Philadelphia, Pepper, 1886

Romantic Brass 2015: *Romantic Brass. Ein Blick zurück ins 19. Jahrhundert*, ed. by Claudio Bacciagaluppi, Martin Skamletz, & Daniel Allenbach, Schliengen, Argus, 2015

Romantic Brass 2016: *Romantic Brass. Französische Hornpraxis und historisch informierter Blechblasinstrumentenbau*, ed. by Daniel Allenbach, Adrian von Steiger, & Martin Skamletz, Schliengen, Argus, 2016

Romero 1864: Antonio Romero y Andía, *Memoria sobre los instrumentos de Música*, Madrid, Imprenta Nacional, 1864

Romero 1871: Antonio Romero y Andía, *Método de trompa de pistones o cilindros con nociones de la mano*, Madrid, Romero, 1871

Rooney 2008: Kimberly D. Rooney, *Compositional Trends in Solo Horn Works by Horn Performers (1970–2005): A Survey and Catalog*, D.M.A. dissertation, University of Cincinnati, 2008

Rossmann 1886: Louis Rossmann, *Horn-Schule*, Augsburg, Böhm & Sohn, 1886

Rühlmann 1851: Julius Rühlmann, "Über Messinginstrumente mit Ventilen," *NZfM*, 28/34 (1851), S. 248–251, 270–272, 280–282; *NZfM*, 28/35 (1851), S. 9–11, 49–52

Rühlmann 1870–1873: Julius Rühlmann, "Das Waldhorn," *NZfM*, 37/66 (1870), S. 293–295, 301–303, 309–311, 317–320, 325–327; *NZfM*, 39/68 (1872), S. 399–401, 411–414, 422–423, 431–433, 483–485, 496–498; *NZfM*, 40/69 (1873), S. 255–257, 265–266, 277–279, 285–287

Sachs 1908: Curt Sachs, "Bachs 'Tromba da tirarsi'," *Bach-Jarhbuch*, 5 (1908), 141–143

Sachs 1940: Curt Sachs, *The History of Musical Instruments*, New York, Norton, 1940

Sadie 2006: Stanley Sadie, *Mozart: The Early Years 1756–1781*, Oxford, Oxford University Press, 2006

Saenger 1907: Gustav Saenger, "A New Double French Horn," *The Metronome*, 13/1 (January 1907), 12

Sainsbury 1824: John Sainsbury, *Dictionary of Musicians*, London, Sainsbury & Co., 1824

Salnove 1655: Robert de Salnove, *La vénerie royale, divisée en IV parties*, Paris, Antoine de Sommaville, 1655

Saloman 1978: Ora Frishberg Saloman, "Victor Pelissier, Composer in Federal New York and Philadelphia," The Pennsylvania Magazine of History and Biography, 102/1 (January 1978), 93–102

Sansone 1975: Lawrence Sansone Jr., "In Memoriam Lorenzo Sansone," *THC*, 6/1 (November 1975), 17–19

Santoro 1995: Elia Santoro, *I teatri di Cremona: Nazari, Concordia, Ponchielli: cronologia degli spettacoli rappresentati al Nazari 1747–1799*, ed. by Roberto Fiorentini & Laura Pietrantoni, Cremona, Turris, 1995

Sartori 1990–1994: Claudio Sartori, *I libretti italiani a stampa dalle origini al 1800. Catalogo analitico con 16 indici*, Cuneo, Bertola & Locatelli, 1990–1994

Scharnberg 1978: William Scharnberg, "The Manuscript Katalog Wenster Litteratur I/1–17b," *THC*, 8/2 (May 1978), 79–83

Schering 1921: Arnold Schering, "Die Leipziger Ratsmusik von 1650 bis 1775," *Archiv für Musikwissenschaft*, 3 (1921), 17–53

Schering 1926: Arnold Schering, *Musikgeschichte Leipzigs*, vol. 2: *Vom 1650 bis 1723*, Leipzig, Kistner & Siegel, 1926

Schiedermair 1914: Ludwig Schiedermair, *Die Briefe W. A. Mozarts und seiner Familie: Erste kritische Gesamtausgabe*, 5 vols., Munich, Georg Müller, 1914.

Schilling 1835–1838: Gustav Schilling (ed.), *Encyclopädie der gesammten musikalischen Wissenschaften, oder Universal-Lexicon der Tonkunst*, 6 vols., Stuttgart, Köhler, 1835–1838 (vol. suppl. 1842; 2nd ed. 1840–1842).

Schlesinger 1910: Kathleen Schlesinger, "Horn," in *Encyclopedia Britannica*, vol. 13, 11th ed., New York, Britannica, 1910, pp. 697–706

Schlosser 1920: Julius von Schlosser, *Die Sammlung alter Musikinstrumente*, Vienna, A. Schroll & Co., 1920

Schmid 2015: Manfred Hermann Schmid, "Richard Wagner und das Münchner Hoforchester," in *Richard Wagner in München*, ed. by von Sebastian Bolz & Hartmut Schick, Munich, Allitera Verlag, 2015, pp. 117–148

Schmidt 1933: Gustav Friederich Schmidt, *Die frühdeutsche Oper und die musikdramatische Kunst Georg Kaspar Schürmanns*, 2 vols., Regensburg, Bosse, 1933

Schneider 1817: Friedrich Schneider, "Wichtige Verbesserung des Waldhorns," *AMZ*, 19 (1817), cols. 814–816.

Schneider 1834: Wilhelm Schneider, *Historich- technische Beschreibung der musicalischen Instrumente*, Neisse & Leipzig, Hennings, 1834

Schreiber 1938: Ottmar Schreiber, *Orchester und Orchesterpraxis in Deutschland zwischen 1780 und 1850*, Berlin, Triltsch & Huther, 1938 (facs. Hildesheim, Olms, 1978)

Schubart 1806: Christian Friedrich Daniel Schubart, *Ideen zu einer Ästhetik der Tonkunst*, Vienna, Degen, 1806

Schuller 1992: Gunther Schuller, *Horn Technique*, 2nd ed., Oxford, Oxford University Press, 1992

Schumann 1982: Robert Schumann, *Tagebücher*, vol. 3: *Haushaltbücher*, part 2: *1847–1856*, ed. by Gerd Nauhaus, Basel & Frankfurt a.M., Stroemfeld/Roter Stern, 1982

Schweikert 1990: Norman Schweikert, "In Memoriam: Pellegrino Lecce (1896–1989)," *THC*, 20/2 (1990), 82–85

Scott–Chick–Myers 2019: Anneke Scott, John Chick, & Arnold Myers, "The 'Cor Solo': History and Characteristics", *HBSJ*, 31 (2019), pp. 119–133

Sehnal 1978: Jiří Sehnal, "Die Musikkapelle des Olmützer Erzbischofs Anton Theodor Colloredo-Waldsee 1777–1811," *Das Haydn Jahrbuch*, 10 (1978), 132–150

Sehnal 1983: Jiří Sehnal, "Anfänge des Waldhorns in Mähren," in *Das Waldhorn* 1983, pp. 33–38

Sehnal 2008: Jiří Sehnal, *Pavel Vejvanovský and the Kroměříž Music Collection*, Olomouc, Palacký University, 2008

Serré de Rieux 1734: Jean Serré de Rieux, *Les dons des enfans de Latone: la musique et la chasse du cerf*, Paris, Prault, Desaint, & Guerin, 1734

Shackleton 1987: Nicholas Shackleton, "The Earliest Basset Horns," *GSJ*, 40 (1987), 2–23

Shaw 1932: Georges Bernard Shaw, *Music in London, 1890–94*, 3 vols., London, Constable, 1932

Slevogt 1711: Johann Philipp Slevogt, *Programma [. . .] lectioni auspicali Christiani Ganzlandi summorum in utroque iure honorum candidati clarissimi praemissum*, Ienae, Gollner, 1711

Smith 1980: Nicholas E. Smith, *The Horn Mute: An Acoustical and Historical Study*, dissertation University of Rochester, New York, 1980

Smith 2003: Jack H. Smith, "David James Who? Some Notes on David James Blaikley," *GSJ*, 56 (2003), 217–223

Smith 2005: Patrick Gregory Smith, *Julius Watkins and the Evolution of the Jazz French Horn Genre*, dissertation, University of Florida, 2005

Smithers 1971: Don L. Smithers, "The Hapsburg Imperial *Trompeter* and *Heerpaucker* Privileges of 1653," *GSJ*, 24 (1971), 84–95

Snedeker 1994: Jeffrey L. Snedeker, "The Early Valved Horn and Its Proponent in Paris, 1826–1840," *THC*, 6 (1994), 6–17

Snedeker 1997: Jeffrey L. Snedeker, "The Horn in Early America," in *Perspectives in Brass Scholarship: Proceedings of the International Historic Brass Symposium, Amherst, 1995*, New York, Pendragon Press, 1997, pp. 151–170

Snedeker 2006: Jeffrey L. Snedeker, "Hand and Valve: Joseph Emile Meifred's *Méthode pour le cor chromatique ou à pistons* and Early Valved Horn Performance and Pedagogy in Nineteenth Century France," in *Jagd- un Waldhörner* 2006, pp. 91–103

Snedeker 2021: Jeffrey L. Snedeker, *Horn Teaching at the Paris Conservatoire, 1792 to 1903: The Transition from Natural Horn to Valved Horn*, London & New York, Routledge, 2021

Snyder 2007: Kerala J. Snyder, *Dieterich Buxtehude, Organist in Lübeck*, rev. ed., Rochester, NY, University of Rochester Press, 2007

Solerti 1904: Angelo Solerti, *Gli albori del melodramma*, Milan, Palermo, & Naples, Sandron, [1904]

Sonneck 1907: Oscar George Theodore Sonneck, *Early Concert-Life in America (1731–1800)*, Leipzig, Breitkopf & Härtel, 1907

Soury 2018: Thomas Soury, "Rameau et le cor sonneur," in *La trompe de chasse ad libitum*, Paris, Montbel, 2018, pp. 63–82

Spohr 1865: *Louis Spohr's Autobiography: Translated from German*, London, Longman & Green, 1865

Stählin 1770: Jakob von Stählin, "Nachrichten von der Musik in Russland," in Johann Joseph Haigold, *Beylagen zum neuveränderten Russland*, vol. 2, Riga & Leipzig, Hartknoch, 1770

Starzer 1998: Helene Starzer, "Herkunft und Jugendzeit des Komponisten Joseph Starzer," *Studien zur Musikwissenschaft*, 46 (1998), 77–94

Storck 1907: Karl Storck, *The Letters of Robert Schumann*, London, Murray, 1907

Stradner 1986: Gerhard Stradner, *Musikinstrumente in Grazer Sammlungen (Grazer öffentliche Sammlungen)*, Vienna, Österreichischen Akademie der Wissenschaften, 1986

Strauchen 2000: Elizabeth Bradley Strauchen, *Giovanni Puzzi: His Life and Work. A View of Horn Playing and Musical Life in England from 1817 into the Victorian Era (c. 1855)*, dissertation, Oxford University, 2000

Strauchen-Scherer 2006: Elizabeth Bradley Strauchen-Scherer, " 'Nomen est omen': The 'French Horn' in England during the Nineteenth and First Half of the Twentieth Century," in *Jagd- und Waldhörner* 2006, pp. 247–265

Sundelin 1828a: Augustin Sundelin, *Die Instrumentierung für das Orchester, oder Nachweisungen über alle bei demselben gebräuchliche Instrumente*, Berlin, Wagenführ, 1828

Sundelin 1828b: Augustin Sundelin, *Die Instrumentierung für sämtliche Militär-Musik-Chöre, oder Nachweisungen über alle bei denselben gebräuchliche Instrumente*, Berlin, Wagenführ, 1828

Sutherland Edwards 1895: H. [Henry] Sutherland Edwards, "Eugène Vivier," *The Musical Times*, February 1, 1895, pp. 87–89

Szórádová 2006: Eva Szórádová, "Zur Geschichte des Waldhorns in der Slowakei," in *Jagd- und Waldhörner* 2006, pp. 227–238

Tableau 1759: *Tableau de Paris pour l'année mil sept cent cinquante-neuf*, Paris, Herissant, 1759

Talbot 1993: Michael Talbot, *Vivaldi*, 2nd ed., London, Dent, 1993

Tamboer–van Vilsteren 2006: Annemies Tamboer & Vincent van Vilsteren, "Celtic Bugle, Roman Lituus, or Medieval Ban Horn?," in *Studien zur Musikarchäologie*, vol. 5: *Musikarchäologie in Kontext*, ed. by von Ellen Hickmann, Arnd Adje Both, & Ricardo Eichmann, Rahden, Leidorf, 2006, pp. 221–236

Täntzer 1689: Johann Täntzer, *Der Dianen hohe und niedere Jagtgeheimnüß*, vol. 3, Copenhagen, Erythropilus, 1689

Tarr 1986: Edward Tarr, "The Coiled Hunting Instrument by J. W. Haas in Bad Säckingen," *Brass Bulletin*, 54/2 (1986), 8–22

Tarr 2001: Edward Tarr, "Further Mandate against the Unauthorized Playing of Trumpets (Dresden, 1736): Introduction and Translation," *HBSJ*, 13 (2001), 67–89

Tarr 2004: Edward Tarr, *East Meets West: The Russian Trumpet Tradition from the Time of Peter the Great to the October Revolution* (Historical Brass Society Series, 4), Pendragon Press, Nashville, 2004

Terry 1932: Charles Sanford Terry, *Bach's Orchestra*, 1932 (repr. London, Oxford University Press, 1972)

Teulon Lardic 2011: Sabine Teulon Lardic, "Adolphe Adam et l'Allemagne: allers et retours Paris–Berlin autour de l'opéra-ballet *Die Hamadryaden* (1840)," in *Art lyrique et transferts culturels 1800–1850*, Venice, 2011

Thomas 1966: Günter Thomas, *Friedrich Wilhelm Zachow* (Kölner Beiträge zur Musikforschung, 38), Regensburg, Bosse, 1966

Thompson 1989: Brian Ernest Thompson, "A History of the Early Sources of Mozart Horn Concertos K. 412/514, K. 417, K. 447, and K. 495," *THC*, 1 (1989), 2–19

Tiella–Primon 1990: Marco Tiella & Luca Primon, *Strumenti musicali dell'Istituto della Pietà di Venezia*, Venice, Delchi, 1990

Toffetti 2004: Marina Toffetti, *Gli Ardemanio e la musica in Santa Maria della Scala di Milano nella prima metà del Seicento*, Lucca, LIM, 2004

Tosoroni 1846: Antonio Tosoroni, *Metodo per il corno a tre pistoni secondo gli ultimi perfezionamenti di questo strumento*, Florence, Milan, & Berni, F. Lucca, 1846

Tosoroni 1850: Antonio Tosoroni, *Trattato pratico di strumentazione*, Milan, Lucca, 1850 [but 1851]

Tozzi 1978: Lorenzo Tozzi, "I musicisti per il balletto," in *Duecento anni alla Scala*, Milan, Electa, 1978

Tuckwell 1983: Barry Tuckwell, *Horn*, London, Macdonald & Co., 1983

Tyson 1987–1988: Alan Tyson, "Mozart's Horn Concertos, New Dating and the Identification of Handwriting," *Mozart-Jahrbuch* (1987–1988), 121–137

Utley–Klaus 2003: Joe R. Utley & Sabine Klaus, "The 'Catholic' Fingering – First Valve Semitone: Reversed Valve Order in Brass Instruments and Related Valve Constructions," *HBSJ*, 15 (2003), 73–161

Vaast 2015: Corinne Vaast, "Une dynastie de chaudronniers, facteurs de trompe ordinaires du Roi (1611–1737)," in *Les fastes de la trompe, actes du colloque (2013)*, ed. by Jean-Pierre Chaline & Jean-Michel Leniaud, Paris, Tallandier, 2015, pp. 57–83

Vaast 2023: Corinne Vaast, "Carlin (?–1781) et les Blanvalet (1691–début XIXe siècle). Facteurs à la cour aux trajectoires exceptionnelles," in *Musica a corte* 2023, pp. 127–143

van Aerde 1914: Raymond van Aerde, "Les Tuerlinckx. Facteurs d'instruments de musique à Malines XVIIIe et XIXe siècles," *Mémoires de la section d'Archéologie et des sous-sections de l'Histoire d'art et de la musicologie*, 3 (1914), 311–338

van Boer 2000: Bertil H. van Boer, " 'Laßt lustig die Hörner erschallen': Resolutions to Two Problems in Horn Performance Practice of the Late Eighteenth Century," *HBSJ*, 12 (2000), 113–160

Vandenbroek ca. 1797: Othon-Joseph Vandenbroek, *Méthode nouvelle et raisonée pour apprendre à donner du cor*, Paris, Nadermann, *ca.* 1797

Vandenbroek after 1797: Othon-Joseph Vandenbroek, *Suite de la Méthode ou Manière d'enseigner à donner du cor suivie de plusieurs duo d'une difficulté gradu[ée]*, Ms., after 1797 (F-Pn)

Vandenbroek after 1803: Othon-Joseph Vandenbroek, *Traité général de tous les instruments à vent à l'usage des Compositeurs*, Paris, Boyer, after 1803

Verdú 2000: Josep Antoni Alberola Verdú, *Introducció i ús de la trompa a les capelles musicals valencianes*, Benaguasil, Consolat de Mar, 2000

Vernooy 1987: Alfons Vernooy, *J.S. Bach Complete Horn Repertoire*, 3 vols., Monteaux, Musica Rara, 1987

Virdung 1511: Sebastian Virdung, *Musica getutscht*, Basel, Michael Furter, 1511

Vitali 1995: Carlo Vitali, "I nove 'principi di altezza' corrispondenti di Vivaldi e la dedica enigmatica del Concerto RV 754. Alla ricerca dell'indirizzario perduto," in *Informazioni e studi vivaldiani*, Milan, Ricordi, 1995, pp. 59–90

Volek 1983: Tomislav Volek, "Die Mannsfeldschen und die Thunschen Hornisten," in *Das Waldhorn* 1983, pp. 44–46

Voss 1981: Egon Voss, " 'Etwas ganz curioses, glaub ich'. Schumanns Konzertstück für vier Hörner und Orchester F-Dur op. 86," *Schweizerische Musikzeitung* 121 (1981), 169–175

Walther 1732: Johann Gottfried Walther, *Musikalisches Lexicon*, Leipzig, Deer, 1732

Waterhouse 1993: William Waterhouse, *The New Langwill Index*, London, Bingham, 1993

Webb 1996: John Webb, "Mahillon's Wagner Tubas," *GSJ*, 49 (1996), 207–212

Weber 1812: Gottfried Weber, "Wesentliche Verbesserung des Horns," *AMZ*, 14 (1812), cols. 759–764

Weber 1816: Gottfried Weber, "Bassposaune," *AMZ*, 18 (1816), cols. 749–753

Weber 1835: Gottfried Weber, "Ueber Ventilhorn und Ventitrompete mit drei Ventilen," *Cäcilia*, 17 (1835), 72–105

Wegeler–Ries 1906: Franz Gerhard Wegeler & Ferdinand Ries, *Biographische Notizen über Ludwig van Beethoven*, with additions by von Alfred Christlieb Kalischer, Berlin & Leipzig, Schuster & Loeffler, 1906

Weigel 1698: Christoph Weigel, *Abbildung der Gemein-nützlichen Haupt-Stände*, Regensburg, Weigel, 1698

Werckmeister 1691: Andreas Werckmeister, *Der Edlen Music-Kunst Würde, Gebrauch und Mißbrauch*, Franckfurt & Leipzig, Calvisius, 1691 (ed. by Pieter Bakker, Schraard (NL), Stichting Kunst en Wetenschap, 2008)

Werner 1911: Arno Werner, *Städtische und fürstliche Musikpflege in Weissenfels bis zum Ende des 18. Jahrhunderts*, Leipzig, Breitkopf & Härtel, 1911

Westernhagen 1973: Curt von Westernhagen, *Die Entstehung des "Ring"*, Zürich, Atlantis, 1973

Whitaker 1907: Tina Whitaker, *Sicily and England: Political and Social Reminiscences 1848–1870*, London, Constable & Co., 1907

Wicquefort 1682: Abraham von Wicquefort, *L'ambassadeur, oder Staatsbotschaffer und dessen hohe Fonctions und Staatsverrichtungen*, Frankfurt a.M., Knochen, 1682

Wieprecht 1845a: Wilhelm Wieprecht, "Der Instrumentenmacher Sax in Paris als Erfinder," *Berliner Musikalische Zeitung*, 2/29 (1845), [3–4]

Wieprecht 1845b: Wilhelm Wieprecht, "Das natürliche Waldhorn und Eugène Vivier," *Berliner Musikalische Zeitung*, 2/50 (1845) [1–2]

Wignall 1995: Harrison James Wignall (alias Harrison Slater), *Mozart and the First "Mitridate"*, *Guglielmo d'Ettore*, Ph.D. dissertation, Brandeis University, 1995

Wildvogel 1753: Christian Wildvogel, *Tractatio iuridica de buccinatoribus eorumque iure / vom Recht der Trompeter*, Halae Magdeburgicae [Halle], Hendel, 1753 (see Gantzland 1711)

Wills 1997: Simon Wills, "Brass in the Modern Orchestra," in *Cambridge Companion* 1997, pp. 157–176

Winch 1746: Christopher Winch (attrib), *The compleat Tutor for the French Horn containing the best and easiest instructions for learners to obtain a Proficiency after a perfect new method by Mr Winch and other eminent Masters*, London, Simpson, 1746 (2nd ed., London, Thompson, 1756)

Wirth *ca.* 1876: Adam Wirth, *Méthode pratique de Cor*, Frankfurt a/M., Offenbach a/M.-André, *ca.* 1876

Withwell 1983: David Whitwell, *The Wind Band and Wind Ensemble*, 9 vols., California, WINDS, 1983

Woodbury 1844: Isaak Baker Woodbury, *The Elements of Musical Composition and Thorough-Bass: Together with Rules for Arranging Music for the Full Orchestra and Military Bands*, Boston, Keith, 1844

Zedler 1745, 1747: Johann Heinrich Zedler, *Grosses vollständiges Universal-Lexikon aller Wissenschafften und Künste*, Halle & Leipzig, vol. 45, cols. 1106–1131 ("Trompeter"); vol. 52, col. 1366 ("Waldhorn")

Ziegler 1823: Anton Ziegler, *Addressen-Buch von Tonkünstlern*, Vienna, Strauss, 1823

Zohn 2008: Steven Zohn, *Music for a Mixed Taste: Style, Genre, and Meaning in Telemann's Instrumental Works*, Oxford, Oxford University Press, 2008

Žůrková 2015: Tereza Žůrková, *Výroba nátrubkových dechových nástrojů v Českých zemích v 18. a 19. století se zaměřením na lesní rohy* (Production of brass wind instruments in the Czech lands in the 18th and 19th centuries, with a focus on the horns), D.M.A. dissertation, University of Brno, 2015

Žůrková 2023: Tereza Žůrková, "La musica da caccia nei paesi boemi del Sei e Settecento," in *Musica a corte* 2023, pp. 59–74

Online sources

https://www.hornsociety.org/
https://www.french-horn.net/index.php
https://www.historicbrass.org/
http://horniconography.com/
https://www.rjmartz.com/horns/
https://www.hornmatters.com/about/john-ericson/
https://www.wagner-tuba.com/
http://musicsack.com/SearchTheMusicSack.cfm
https://www.horn-u-copia.net/
http://www.linfoulk.org/
http://www.phys.unsw.edu.au/jw/brassacoustics.html

INDEX

Adam, A. C., 234, 235, 245
Adams, N., 252, 300, 302
Agrell, J., 333, 334
Agujari, L., 164
Ahrens, C., 141
Albano, G., 67
Albert, Mr., horn player, 305
Alberti, D., 66
Albrecht, T., 192fn6
Alexander Company, 208, 308fn1, 310, 314, 315, 318, 319, 326, 330
Alinovi, G., 240
Allenbach, D., 270
Alun, F., 332
Alzira, Spain, 95
Amati Company, 316
Amorschall, 212
Amram, D., 334
Anderst, J. F., 241
animal horn
    Hifthorn, 45, 100
    metal imitation, 16
Antwerp
    Vleeshuis Museum, 11
Apostel, H. E., 332
Apparuti, A., 292
Arnold, M., 332
Artôt, J. D., 288
Asioli, B., 270
Atrapart, J. L. C. A., 187
Augustus, duke of Saxony-Gotha-Altenburg, 234
Augustus Frederick, Prince of England, 209

Bach, J. S., 59, 78, 81, 326, *see also case study online*
Bachaumont, L. P. de, 159
Bachmann, horn player, 121
Bacon, T., 334

Bad Säckingen, Germany
    Trompetenmuseum, 15
Badia, C. A., 56
Bagans, K., 267
Baillioni, G., 104
Baines, A., 309
Balen, E. van, 14
Barboteau, G., 332
Bärenreiter Company, 269
Barillon, J. J., 236
Barr, maker, 135
Barsanti, F., 103
Bartolini, F., 295
Basel
    Historisches Museum, 32, 45, 56, 145
    Musikinstrumentenmuseum, 216
Basler, P., 332
basset horn, 214
Bassompierre, F. de, 20
Baumann, H., 332
Baumgart, D. W., 50, 51
Bay, R., 293
Beck, J., 64fn7
Beecham, T., 320
Beer, J. (Ursinus), 47, 48
Beethoven, L. van, 194
    changing the esthetic of the horn, 192
    Ninth Symphony, 4th horn solo, 192
    see also case study online
Behn, F., 4fn1
Belke, F. A., 267
Bellini, F., 293
Belloli, 174, 195, 197
Belloli, A., 178
Belloli, G., 199, 293
Belloli, L., 178, 190, 195, 197, 205, 218, 273
Bellonci, C., 151
Bendinelli, C., 16
Benedict "of the cornetta," 5

Bergonzi, B., 218
Berlin
    Berliner Philharmonisches Orchester, 320
    Musikinstrumentenmuseum, 31, 45
    Opera House, 245
    Prussian Ministry of Commerce, 248
    State Archives, 228
Berlioz, H., 268, 306
    prescription of hand horns, 269
Bernardi, C., 240
Berner, F. W.
    early music for valve horn, 266
Bertin, S., 76fn19
Bertini, H., 284
Besson, G. A., 251
Biener, J. C., 64
Bierey, G. B., 228, 231
Billert, C., 279
Birmingham
    University Library, 109
Birnkraut, J. J., 106
Birsak, K., 49
Blaikley, D. J., 311, 320
Blanchet, L. G.
    portrait of Rodolphe (?), 162
Bliesener, horn player, 266
Blühmel, F., 227, 236, 260, 299
    early experiments, 229, 241
    inventor of tubular valves, 232
    patent request, 229
    rotary valves, 248
    Spontini's report on, 235
Blumenstengel, J. M., 105, 106
Blusenn, horn player, 267
Bochum
    Musikinstrumentensammlung Grumbt, 141
Böck, I. and A., 169, 172, 176, 178, 180
Bode, F., 266
Boel, P., 10
Boësset, J. B., 39
Boïeldieu, F. A., 169
Boismortier, J. B. de, 102
Bologna
    Museo della Musica, 238, 254
    Teatro Comunale, 240
Bonanni, F., 68
Bondioli, F. A. and G. M., 64
Bonnart, N., 26
Bonnart, R., 24
Bononcini, G., 67
Boosey Company, 311, 320
    Sotone production line, 311
Borsdorf, F. A., 207fn25, 208, 291
Boudewyns, A. F., 24

Boxberg, C. L., 57
Boyer, P., 160fn27
Bracelli, G. B., 10
Brahms, J.
    natural horn predilection, 307
    see also case study online
Brain, A., 291, 319
Brain, A. E., 292, 335
Brain, D., 208, 292, 319, 323
Breitkopf Company, 96
Brémond, F., 276, 286
Bretschneider, D., 19
Britten, B., 292, 323
Brizzi, L., 273
Brohn, W. E., 71fn16
Brown, T., 329
Bruckner, A., see case study online
Brun, J., 175, 178
Brussels
    Conservatoire, 288, 289
    Musée d'Instruments de Musique, 317
Bryant (O'Brien), C., 204
bucina, 3
bugle horn, 216, 218, 222
Buhl, D., 236
Bujanovski, V., 332
Bull, W., 61
Busby, T. R., 291
Busch & Dodworth Company, 254
Butti, F., 308fn1

Cabaza, M., 106
Caldara, A., 67
Callcott, J., 221
Cambefort, J. de, 39
Cambini, G., 190
Camerata Cornello, Italy
    place of origin of Thurn und Taxis
        family, 16
Campra, A., 103
Canti, A., 296
Capelle, horn player, 102
Caresana, C., 39
Carl August, Grand duke of Weimar, 228
Carlin (J.-C. Manne), 69
Carrogis (Carmontelle), L., 162
Carse, A., 103
Castil-Blaze, 133, 134, 138
Catherine II, Empress of Russia, 213
Cauwelaert, F. van, 248
Cavalli, F., 38
Cave, J., 333
Cazzani, G. B., 297, 315, 317, 320
Ceccarossi, D., 315, 322, 332

Červený, F., 248
Červený, V. F., 265, 287
Chancey, V., 334
Charles IV, king of Spain, 209
Charles VI, Emperor, 43, 63
Charles IX, king of France, 40
Charles Emmanuel I, duke of Savoy, 38
Charles Emmanuel II, duke of Savoy, 22, 44
Charles, Mr., *see* Vernsberg, C.
Charleston, SC
　St. Cecilia Society, 209
Chase, G., 210
Chastenay, V. de, 188
Chaussier, H., 276, 287
Chelard, I., 268
Chemnitzer, E., 316
Cherubini, L., 133, 138
　Chant sur la Mort de Joseph Haydn, 189
　Médée, horn solo, 172
Chicago, IL
　Symphony Orchestra, 314, 315
Chicos, J. A., 106
Chicos, J. J., 106
Chicos, J. M., 106
Chigi, F., Cardinal, 24
China, Mr., horn player, 82
Chladni, E. F. F., 254
Choron, A. E., 174, 178
Christian, duke of Sachsen-Weissenfels, 58, 63
Christine of France, duchess of Savoy, 24
Cimarosa, D., 195
Cipriani Potter, P., 207
Clagget, C., 215
　chromatic trumpet and French horn, 215
Claremont, CA
　Pomona College, 326
clarino, 81, 184
　dismissal, 182
　register of, 49, 82, 96
　style, 81, 82, 100, 158, 171, 177, 195
　technique, 96, 99, 100, 134, 173
　writing, 82
Clark, J., 334
Clarke, K., 334
Clevenger, D., 334
Close, W., 216
Cognengo di Castellamonte, A., 22
coiled *trompe*, 8
　Ardemanio collection in Milan, 9
　inventory of Florence Court, 9
　miniature, from Ambras Castle, 11fn3
　surviving items, 11
　in Turin, 9
　from Villedieu-les-poêles, 12

Coin, A., 139
Colin, P. L., 187
Colombi, M., 240
Coltrane, J., 334
Compardelle, E., 10
Conn Company, 335
Conn, C. G., 303
Copenhagen
　Musikhistorisk Museum, 31
　National Museum, 5
　Statens Museum for Kunst, 33
cor solo, 285
　by L. J. Raoux, 153
　by Tuerlinckx, 155
　distinctive features, 153
　first mention, 153
　valve horn substitute, 254
　with box valves, 258
Corbett, W., 61
Cormery, J. F., 145
cornu, 3
Corradini (Coradigni), F., 105
Corrette, M., 101
Corselli, F., 105
Cotelle le jeune, J., 25
Couesnon Company, 285, 311
Courtois Company, 251
Courtois frère, 196, 235
Coypel, A., 77
Cremona
　Teatro della Concordia, 205
Crétien, 12, 29, 30, 52, 69, 102
Crétien, C., 69, 124fn9
Crétien, J., 30
Crétien, J. II, 30
Crétien, Jac. I, 20fn2, 30
Crétien, N., 70fn14
Crétien, R. I, 30
crooks, 53, 88, 89, 95
　additamentis seu steclis, 94
　"double," 92
　earliest set (?by Werner), 94
　early evidence, 94
　fork, 119, 141, 142fn3, 148
　full sets, 120, 135, 159
　high and low on valve horns, 282
　on hunting horns, 89
　increasing number, 94
　in low A, 201
　in low A-flat, 202
　low pitches in Italy, 199
　master and couplers, 119, 135, 136
　pictured by Praetorius, 32
　replaced by valves, 203

shanks, 53, 89, 91, 92
slide, 119, 120, 142, 143, 144, 145, 147, 148, 149, 155
Spanish (*tudeles*), 95
substituted by transposition, 153
terminal, 89, 91, 94, 95, 119, 135, 137, 146, 155
for three-size horns, 89, 90, 91, 94
trombone-like, 222
tuning bits, 149
tuning slide, 120, 148
Turin, Vicco, 95
for Viennese model, 244
curée, 20, 22, 24, 58, 89
Curlando, G. B., 45, 55

Dacci, G., 240
Dahlqvist, R., 47
Dall'Asta, L., 238, 240, 251
Dalvimare, M. P., 187, 188
Dampierre, M. A. de, 70, 76
fanfares by, 76
Danzi, F., 173
D'Aula, C. A., 67
Daun, W. P. von, 65
Dauprat, L. F., 110, 133, 146, 153, 158, 163, 178, 181, 184, 190, 191, 199, 205, 210, 232, 236, 259, 262, 269, 294
Dauverné, F. G. A., 233
David, G., 33, 163
Davis, M., 334
De Angelis, E., 196
De Luigi, G., 240
de Marez Oyens, T., 332
De Marolles, G., 30
De Prins Company, 316
Debussy, C., 334
Decker, J., 326
Dehmal, A., 283
DeRosa, V., 335
Deshays, A., 263, 302
Destouches, A. C., 77
Devienne, F.
Les Visitandines, horn solo, 169
Devémy, J., 318fn23
Dickhut, C., 222
Distin, H., 303
Ditters von Dittersdorf, C., 165
Dlabacž, G. J., 168
Dodworth, A., 300
Domnich, F., 100
Domnich, H., 66, 123, 133, 144, 159, 187, 191, 210
Donizetti, G., 195, 202, 203

Don Pasquale, 200
Dörfeldt, A., 241
Dornaus, C., 176
Dornaus, J. P. and P., 176
double horns
alto/descant, 326
compensating, 308, 310, 315
full, 308
new techniques, 331
Drayton, M., 5
Dresden, 64, 81, 84, 85, 87, 94, 99, 121, 123, 124
Court chapel, 83
Kunstsammlungen, 11
Dröschel, C., 12, 18
Du Fouilloux, J., 7
Dukas, P.
Villanelle, 276
Duke of Aumont, 94fn8, 120
Dummuscheit, A., 317
Duni, E., 159
Dupont, J. B., 220
Duport, J. L., 162
Durante, F., 86
Duvernoy, F., 133, 153, 178, 186, 187, 188, 190, 268

early signals
Du Fouilloux, 8, 20
Mersenne, 20
monotonic, 6
Philidor, 73, 76
Recueil des pièces, 20, 41, 76
Ebert (Hébert), horn player, 90, 102
Eder, A., 100
Edinburgh
Musical Instrument Museum, 55, 72, 204
Edouard, horn player, 102
Egerton, A. S., 103
Ehe, F., 31, 32
Ehe, J. L., 32
Eichborn, H., 297, 309
Eichentopf, J. H., 56
Eliason, R. E., 300
Elisabeth Christine, Empress, 63, 65
Ernest Frederick III, duke of Saxe-Hildburghausen, 165
Ernst, horn player, 102
Evans, G., 333, 334

Fahrbach, J., 283
falsetto, 84, 126, 128, 134, 184, 252
Fantini, G., 84
Ferber, A., 53, 92
Ferdinand Maria, Elector of Bavaria, 44

Fétis, F. J., 257, 288
Fiala, J., 173
Fick, J. P., 48
Fideler, W., 64
Finke Company, 328
Fischer, C., 314
Fischer, J. A., 64, 81, 82, 96, 99
Fischer, J. C., 97
Fiske, I., 303
Florence
    Galleria dell'Accademia, 137, 148
    Teatro della Pergola, 294
Font y Mirapeix, L.
    manuscript by, 298
Fontana, C., 320
Fontanellato, near Parma
    Scuola di musica strumentale, 205, 238
Forkel, J. N., 144
Förster, C. H., 96, 97, 98, 99
Forsyth, C., 320
Fouquières, J., 10
Fox, F., 335
Francis I, king of France, 5, 40
Francoeur, L. J., 127
Franz, O., 281, 282, 291, 332
Frederick Augustus I "The Strong," Elector of
    Saxony, 56, 63, 124
Frederick Augustus II, Elector of Saxony, 17,
    99
Frederick William I, king of Prussia, 63
Frederick William III, king of Prussia, 227
Freiberg, G., 322
Frilloux, S., 30
Fritsch, C., 100
Fritsch, J., 100
Fröhlich, J., 86, 191, 274
Frontori, L., 275
Fulda, M., 34
Fyt, J., 10

Gabler, J. C., 230
Gallas, J. W. von, 67
Gallay, J. F., 153, 163, 178, 192, 332
Gallehus, Denmark
    golden horns, 5
Galliani, A., 166
Galliard, J. E., 62
Galuppi, B., 213
Gamucci, B.
    on mixture of natural and valve horns, 280
Gandini, A., 292
Ganspöck (Gänsporck), J. C. and M., 45, 64, 78
Gantzland, C., 16, 29, 32, 33
Garat, P. G., 169

Garay, R., 106
Gasparini, F., 61, 105
Gatti, L., 163, 195
Gautrot Company, 252, 285, 286
Gautrot Companyy, 299
Gayer (Geier), J., 46
Gehra/Gehring, J. M. (?), 98, 159
Gellhorn, L. E., Count of Blansko, 46
Gerber, E. L., 59, 91, 94, 110, 121, 123,
    140, 141, 142, 144, 147, 153, 168, 176, 213,
    214
Gerhard, chief miner, 231
Gervasoni, C., 132fn21, 184fn1
Gevaert, F. A., 279, 280
    on Wagner's instrumentation, 280
Geyer, C., 315
Geyer, H., 17
Gijsbrechts, C., 33
Gillespie, D., 334
Glaseman, horn player, 267
Gleich, F., 275
Glière, R., 322
Gluck, C. W., 110
Goodale, E., 210
Goring, E., 222
Gossec, F. J., 102, 103
Gotha
    account books of the Court, 78
    Court orchestra, 144
    Werner's horns, 144
Göttingen, 145
Goudot jeune, 252
Gounod, C., 269, 270
Graas, J., 333
Grandi, G.; 64
Graun, C. H. (?), 96, 97, 98
Green, J., 107, 210
Greer, L., 332
Gregory Smith, P., 333
Griebel, horn player, 267fn5
Griessling & Schlott, 260, 261, 299
Grinwolt (Grünwald). J. G., 102
Grove, G. Sir, 254
Gugel (Gugl), J. and H., 176
Guignon, J. P., 102
Gumpert, E., 308
Gumpert, F., 305, 308, 312, 326

Haas, E. J. C., 32
Haas, J. W., 17, 32
Haas, W. W., 17, 31, 32
Haas family, 56
Hachr, G. A., 64
Haensel, F., 213

Halary, A., 251, 252, 262, 263, 264, 269fn8, 270, 271, 294
Halary, J., Jr., 284
Halévy, J. F., 268, 278
half-moon horn, 25, 39, 52
    from Villedieu-les-poêles, 12
Halle, J. S., 35
Haltenhof, J. G., 119, 141, 142, 144, 145
    inventor of slide crooks, 145
    successors, 145
Hamers, M., 9
Hampel, A., 63, 98, 99, 119, 120, 121, 123, 124, 125, 126, 146, 168
Hampel, J. M., 121
Hanau
    working place of Haltenhof, 141
hand horn, 148
    bell dimensions, 184
cor alto, 184
    cor basse, 184
    cor du milieu, or cor mixte, 184, 187
    criticisms to genre mixte, 186
    Dauprat's method, 191
    discovery, 125
    dismissal, 306
    early handbooks, 172
    early use, 119, 121, 123, 124, 125, 127
    embouchure, 184
    first-period technique, 171
    introduced in France by Rodolphe, 159
    introduced in Italy by Paer, 162
    invention of, 120, 121, 123, 124, 126, 127
    lasting preference in France, 200, 276, 286
    lasting preference in Great Britain, 289
    Punto's and Domnich's style, compared with Dauprat's, 191
    range of first and second horn, 184
    register of first and second horn, 182
    technical development, 175
    transposition, 189
    widespread adoption, 182
    see also stopped notes
Handel, G. F., 62, 82, 83, 101, 103, 326, see also case study online
Hanover
    Historisches Museum, 52
Harburg, Bavaria, 100
    Wallerstein Castle, 93
Hartosch, J., 64
Harty, H. Sir, 320
Hasse, J. A., 66, 81, 83, 209
Haudek, C., 99, 121, 124
Haumuller (Hanmüller, J. A.), 269, 298

Haydn, F. J., 101, 139, 165, 178, 216, 326, see also case study online
Haydn, M., 165, 173
Hein, A., 232
Heinichen, J. D., 69, 81, 82, 85, 99
Heller, B., 332
Hellier, S., 104, 135
Henriette Adelaide of Savoy, 44
Herbst, M., 194
Hernandez, M., 298
Heyde, H., 228, 229, 230, 248, 309
Hiebert, T., 103
Hill, D., 332, 334
Hindemith, P., 322, 323
Hoffmann, horn player, 64
Hoffmann, J. G., 96, 97
Hoffmann, M., 96
Hofmann, L., 165
Hofmaster, J. C., 95, 135, 136, 204
Hogarth, G., 290
Holliger, H., 332
Holyoke, S., 210
hooped trompes, 45
    admission in the orchestra, 76
    alternative to trompette, 76
    circular trumpet, 26, 31, 32, 84
    by Crétien, 30
    by Dröschel/Nagel, 12, 18
    early scores, 46, 47
    with larger loop, 25
    in Munich, 44
    manufacture in Turin, 24
    olicorni, 44
    trombae breves (?), 45, 47
    trompas de caza, 105
    unusual wraps, 33
    Venaria model, 22, 24
    in Versailles, 24, 25
    see also Trompe de chasse; Waldhörner
Horner, A., 312, 318
Hosa brothers, 176
Hoss, W., 335
Hotteterre family, 53
Houasse, M.-A., 105
Hoyer, B., 305
Hradisko, Moravia
    monastery, 57, 59, 93
Hübner, U., 152, 156, 258
Hyde, A., 320

Indianapolis
    Symphony Orchestra, 333
Inventionshorn, 123, 140
    à l'anglaise, 145, 147

with all slide crooks, 147, 148, 149, 155, 156
cor à coulisse, 155
cor d'invention, 155
by Cormery, 145
different meanings, 147, 151
early design by Werner, 146
by Gabler & Krause, 145fn9
by Haltenhof, 145
from Hanau and Vienna, 145
by J. Kerner, 151
Maschinenhorn, 152fn16
with terminal and slide crooks, 155
with terminal crooks and tuning slide, 155, 156
three-size model, 93, 148, 149
Isouard, N., 190

Jacob, G., 323
Jacob, G. W., 59, 89
Jägerhörner, 9
Austrian for *Waldhörner*, 92
James Brydges, duke of Chandos, 62
Janárčeková, V., 332
João V, King of Portugal, 106
Johann Georg II, Elector of Saxony, 45
Johnsen, H. P., 98
Jommelli, N., 124, 158, 199
Joseph, J., 100
Joséphine de Beauharnais, empress of France, 91fn2

Kail, J., 243, 262, 270
Kalison Company, 324, 326
Kalkbrenner, A., 260
Kalliwoda, J. W., 276
Kastner, J. G., 260, 269, 284
on valve horn's crooks, 282
Keen, J., 107
Keeß, S. von, 147, 148
Keisser, R., 57
Kellner, G., 204
Kenn, J. J., 133, 170
Kenton, S., 333
Kerner, A., Jr., 147, 150
workmanship, 151
Kerner, A., Sr., 92, 119, 146, 147, 148, 150, 152
counterfeit (?), 152
full set of slide crooks, 148
full set of terminal crooks and tuning slide, 150
wide bell, 149
Kerner, Ad., 178
Kerner, I., 150
Kerner, J., 139, 150, 152
counterfeit (?), 152

Kersten, J. G., 254
Key, T., 204, 222, 290
keyed horns
anonymous, (?) Bohemian, 216
by Bergonzi, 218
by Schugt, 216
by Weidinger, 216
Kirchner, J. C., 71
Klaus, S., 282
Klemm & Bro. Company, 300
Kling, H., 169
on valve horn's crooks, 282
Klingenberg, F. G., 57, 58
Knechtel, J. G., 98, 99, 121
Knopf, K. A., 316
Knüttel, J., 64fn7
Koch, H. O., 59
Koch, M., 50, 51, 55
F-horn model, 93
Kodisch, J. C., 31, 45
Kölbel, F., 212, 215
Konvička, M., 80
Koppfasack, horn player, 267
Kopprasch, G., 271
Korn, P. F., 145
Kraus, J. M., 139
Kremsmünster, 59, 88
Abbey, 92
Kreutzer, C., 194
Kreutzer, R., 169
Krol, B., 332, 334
Kroměříž, Moravia
Sonata da caccia, 46
Krommer, F., 194
Kruspe Company, 312, 314, 336
1930 price-list, 314
Kruspe, E., 308, 310
Kruspe, F., 308
Kuopio, Finland
Cultural History Museum, 241

La Doue, T. B. de, 77
Labbaye Company, 251, 285, 319
Labbaye, J. C., 213, 221, 251, 258, 259, 284, 299
Labbaye, J. C., Jr., 38
Lachner, F., 194
Lafage, J. A., 174, 178
Lainate, near Milan
villa Visconti, 104
Lalande, M. R. de, 77
Lamberg, Count of Upper Austria, 62
Lang, F., 173
Láng, I., 332
Langey, O., 303

INDEX

Lathrop Allen, J., 303
Lažanský, count of Manětín, 80
Lázaro, G., 95
Le Brun, C., 33
Le Brun, maker, 55, 69, 71
Leander, T., L. H., V. T., 203
Lecce, P., 314
Leclaire, J. M., 157
Leclerc, S., 33
Ledhuy, A., 284
Legros, J., 160
Lehmann, C., 316
Leichamschneider, 53, 59, 92, 93, 94
    F-horn model, 93
Leichamschneider, J., 55, 62, 93
Leichamschneider, M., 55, 56, 88, 92, 93
Leipzig
    Stadtpfeifer, 81
Lenss, H., 266
    early music for valve horn, 267
Leopold Ignaz, prince of Dietrichstein, 46
Lesueur, J. F., 188
Leutgeb, J., 164, 165, 166, 167, 168, 172
Lewy brothers, 245
Lewy, J. R., 267, 269, 290
Lichtenthal, P.
    description of Pini's horn, 239
Lidl, J., 316
Lindner, J., 304
Lisbon
    Real Seminário da Patriarcal, 107
lituus, 3, 59
Livet, or Olivet, horn player, 20
Lolli, A., 159
London, 82
    BBC Symphony Orchestra, 319, 320
    Concert of Antient Music, 207
    Covent Garden Opera Orchestra, 204
    Great Exhibition, 1851, 222
    Horniman Museum, 62, 208
    International Exposition, 1862, 297
    King's Theater, 207
    Lyceum Theater, 207
    Philharmonic Orchestra, 320
    Philharmonic Society, 203, 207
    Royal Academy of Music, 208
    Royal Military Exhibition, 1891, 149
Lopez, M., 78
Lorber, J. C., 45, 78
Lorenz, M., 167
Lotti, A., 61, 66, 69, 77, 81, 85, 99
Louis, Dauphin of France, 72
Louis XI, king of France, 40
Louis XIII, king of France, 20, 40

Louis XIV, king of France, 42
Louis Augustus, prince of Pless, 227, 229, 231
Louis Musical Instrument Co. Ltd., 317
Louis Philippe, duke of Orleans, 72
Lovecký Ohrada, Bohemia
    hunting castle, 142fn3
Lübeck
    Museum für Kunst und Kulturgeschichte, 149
Ludging, clarinet player, 267
Lully, J. B., 39, 40, 41
Lumpe, J. W., 64
Lund
    University Library, Wenster Manuscript, 96, 97, 99

Madrid
    Prado Museum, 14
    Real Capilla, 297
    Real Conservatorio, 297, 299
    Sociedad de Conciertos, 298
    Teatro Nacional, 298
Magnasco, S., 10
Mahillon Company, 288, 317
Mahillon, C., 252
Mahler, G., *see case study online*
Mahler, J. P., 64
Majer, J. F., 89
Makeroth, H., 107
Manchester
    Hallé Orchestra, 320
Maniguet, T., 169
Mannheim
    performance tradition, 101
Mantua, 101
    Accademia Virgiliana, 166
manufacture (modern), 324, 325
manufacture (old), 35
    14th- and 15th-cent. in Siena, 6
    bell, 35, 50, 51, 182
    brass sheets, 34, 35
    calamine, 33
    gusset, 50, 51
    metal quality, 34
    slide crooks, 156
    tube bending, 6, 36, 150
    yellow copper, 33
Mareš, J. A., 214
Margaret Yolande of Savoy, 22, 44
Maria Anna of Austria, Queen of Portugal, 106
Maria Barbara, Queen of Spain, 106
Maria Josepha of Austria, 99

Mariani, G., 321
Marie Louise, Duchess of Parma, 238, 239, 267
Markneukirchen
  Musikinstrumentenmuseum, 248
Marschner, H., 193
Martin, J. B., 26
Martini, G. B., 86fn6
Martz, R. J., 219, 273, 287, 309, 310, 316
Matiegka, J., 63
Mattheson, J., 50, 54, 55, 62, 87, 91
Maximilian I, emperor, 16
Maximilian Emanuel II, Elector of Bavaria, 44, 45, 78
Maxwell Davies, P., 332
Mayr, J. S., 138, 153, 181, 190, 195, 222
Mayrhofer, A. and M., 214
Meer, J. H. van der, 238
Méhul, E. N., 133, 138, 190
Meifred, J. E., 135, 163, 232, 245, 251, 259, 262, 267, 268, 269, 275, 283, 294, 299
Melchiorri, F. detto "Gesuit," 238
Mendelssohn-Bartholdy, F., 194, 279
  natural horn, 279
  two natural and two valve horns, 279
Mengal, J. B., 134, 163, 252, 270
Menzel, U., 238
Merck, L. H., 289
Merewether, R., 330
Mersenne, M., 15, 31, 38
  fanfare playing, 19
Messiaen, O., 332
Michault, J. E., 210
Miel, J., 22, 24
Milan
  Conservatory, 197, 240
  Istituto Lombardo di Scienze, Lettere e Arti, 240
  Museo del Castello Sforzesco, 32, 56
  Music Conference 1881, 297
  Teatro alla Scala, 198
  Teatro della Canobbiana, 240
  Teatro Re, 240
Milhaud, D., 334
Millereau Company, 285, 299
Millgrove, B., 181
Mingus, C., 334
Modena
  Museo Civico, 292
Monk, T., 334
Montéclair, M. P. de, 77
Mordaxt, Baron von, 17
Morin, J. B., 76
Moritz, J. G., 250

Moritzburg
  hunting castle, 70
Morley-Pegge, R., 337
Moscheles, I., 207
Mouret, J. J., 77
Mozart, L., 100, 101, 166, 167, 175
Mozart, W. A., 137, 139, 161, 164, 188, 326
  borrowing from Mysliveček's *Demetrio*, 164, 166
  Leutgeb derision, 167
  Mitridate, horn solo, 163
  twelve duets, 177
  see also case study online
Mozer, horn player, 79
Müller, C. A., 245, 255, 265
Munich, 45
  Bayerisches Nationalmuseum, 56
  Court, 44, 45, 78
  Dr. Kaim's Orchestra, 305
mutes, 124, 178
  for Beethoven's Rondino, 178
  of Böck brothers, 176
  by Brun, 178
  Comma device, 182
  corni sordini, 124
  by Crétien, 124fn9
  deprecated by Dauprat, 181
  description by Fröhlich, 179
  Haltenhof horn, 1761, 141
  by Hampel, 123, 124
  by Kerner, 178
  for oboes, 123
  purchased in Sondershausen, 124
  by Raoux, 178
  in Telemann's music, 124
  in Vivaldi's music, 124
Mysliveček, J., 125, 164, 166, 195
  Bellerofonte, horn solo, 195
  Demetrio, horn solo, 164

Nadermann, F. J., 187
Nagel, J., 173
Nagel, M., 12, 18
Naples
  beginning of horn playing tradition, 61
  hand horn inception, 195
  importing Viennese musical customs, 65
Napoleon, Emperor, 187
Nappi, E., 174
natural horns
  12-foot F size, 55
  14-foot D size, 54
  16-foot C size, 77
  bell upwards, 133

Concerthörner, 148
with demountable bell, 62
in different keys, 90, 94
dismissal, 284, 291, 297, 299
doubled by a second pair, 137
English, 135
lasting preference in Great Britain, 292
modern music for, 286, 332
Parforcehorn, 54
played in pairs, 56
"Polyphonian," 216
reintroduced in training, 297
in silver, 148, 153
with terminal crooks, 155
vented horn, 329
water key, 216
see also Inventionshorn
Nemetz, A., 243, 269, 270
Nessmann, C. F., 216
New York
Metropolitan Museum, 248
Metropolitan Opera House, 314
Niemistö, P., 241
Nigoline, Italy
Palazzo Torri, 89
Nithard, composer, 267
Nitra, Slovakia
Piarist monastery, 94
Noguera, S., 106
notation
by Philidor, 73
changes due to valve horn adoption, 284
classical, 48
French treble clef, 40, 46, 73
in tablature, 46
modern, for F horn, 318
Neapolitan, 86
octave above (Saxon), 77
sign +, 269
Nuremberg, 17, 29, 30, 32, 51, 52, 60
Germanisches Nationalmuseum, 56
Nüztel, Captain, 60

Oberschleißheim, Bavaria
Lustheim Castle, 55
Oettingen-Wallerstein, House of, 100, 172, 175
oliphant, 5
omnitonic horns
natural, 219
with valve system, 286, 299
omnitonic horns, *Amorschall*, 213
Ondratscheck, J., 64
Ossegg, Bohemia
monastery, 59

Ostermayer, R., 266
Otto, F., 63
Oudry, J. B., 70
Oxford
Bate Collection, 204

Pace, C., 252, 289
Paer M., 162
Paer, F., 162, 195, 205, 206
Paer, G., 162, 163, 164, 172, 197, 198
Paersch, F. F., 207fn25, 291
Paglia, brothers, 197
Paglia, F., 205, 238
Paine, T. D.
cords driving the mechanism, 249
rotary valves, 302
Paisiello, G., 187, 189
Pallavicino, F., 44
Palsa, J., 153, 172, 173, 175
Pangratz, horn player, 64
Paoli, F., 295
Pappé, A., 307fn1
Paquis, A. V., 307fn1
Paradís, M., 105
Parforcehorn, 71
Parforce-jagd, 78
Paris, 42, 45
Académie des Beaux-Arts, 234
Concert de Mrs. les amateurs, 161
Concert Spirituel, 159, 166
Conservatoire, 133, 135, 184, 210
Exhibition, 1827, 284
Exhibition, 1867, 288
Musée d'arts et métiers, 145
Musée de la musique, 10, 11, 32, 142
Opéra, 159
Opéra Comique, 138
prince Conti's orchestra, 159
Royal Chapel, 160
Société des Concerts, 267
Théâtre Italien, 200, 205, 206
Parma
Ducal orchestra, 198
Imperial Theater, 205
Reale Concerto da Camera, 157, 205
Teatro Ducale, 157
Patiño, C., 105
Paxman Company, 330
Pelissier, V., 210
Pelitti Company, 293, 297
Pelitti, G., Sr., 287
Pelitti, G., Jr., 296
Pelting, horn player, 143
Penderecki, K., 332

Penna, L., 106
Pepper, J. W., 303
Pepusch, G., 79
Pepusch, J. C., 62, 107
Percival, T., 216, 222, 252, 289
Pergolesi, G. B., 83
Périnet, E. F., 250
Perry, Mr., horn player, 290
Péterlard, P. le Jeune, 160
Peterson, O., 334
Petri, B. A., 83
Petrides, J. and P., 176, 203, 205, 207, 209
Pettex-Muffat Company, 73
Pfaffe, horn player, 266
Pfaffe, multi-instrumentalist judged
    by Bach, 81
Philidor family, 53
Philidor, A. D. (aîné), 39, 56, 73
Philidor, P. D., 56, 74
Pike, T., 209
Pimlott Oates, J., 251
Pini, L., 197, 243, 263
    early music for valve horn, 267
    performances with his valve horn, 240
    rotary valves, 238, 248
    valve slide invention, 251
    see also Dall'Asta, L.
Pisendel, J. G., 69
pitch
    Cammerton and Chorton, 53
Pittsburgh
    Symphony Orchestra, 312
Plaffer, horn player, 267
Platt, H., 204, 290
Plazzeriani (Placeriano), Ba., 167
Plazzeriani (Placeriano), Bi., 167
Pokorny, F. X., 101, 171, 175
Polekh, V., 322
post-horn, 16
    animal horn, 16
    corno da posta, 85
    golden, 17
    manufacture, 29
    pictured by Weigel, 17
    Ristori's score, 83fn4
    size, 18
    Ursinus' score, 47
Poulenc, F., 323
Pouplinière, A. J. J. le Riche de, 102
Prades, J., 61
Praetorius, M., 9, 17, 32, 84, 88
Prague
    National Music Museum, 102
Prandel, J. M., 59

Prince of Liechtenstein, 121
Produktive Genossenschaft Company, 283
Proechel, S., 210
Prout, E., 291
Provers, I., 162
Prussian Jäger Guards, 261fn4
Punto, G., 121, 123, 124, 129, 153, 163, 168, 172,
    178, 191
    multiple sounds, 169
Puzzi, G., 153, 197, 198, 205, 267, 290
Puzzi22, major contributor to IMSLP, 270
Pyle, R., 326

Quantz, J. J., 96, 97, 98
Quinault, J. B. M., 77

Racines, Italy
    Museum of Hunting, 89
Radius French horn, 221
Rädlein, J., 78
Rae, J., 204, 290
Raich, J. M., 64
Rameau, J. P., 103
Rampone & Cazzani Company, 315
Ranuccio II Farnese, duke of Parma, 22
Raoux, 69, 169, 207, 291, 293, 311, 319
    constructive features, 285
    two horns in Munich, 29fn3
Raoux, L. J., 153, 169, 178, 208
    Dauprat's horn by, 153
Raoux, M. A., 208, 270
Raoux–Labbaye Company, 208
Ravel, M., 286
Rdt, C. (pen name), alias Reissiger (?),
    274, 277
Rebel, J.-F. père, 103
Rebky, Mr., horn player, 305
Reicha, A., 190
Reicha, J., 173
Reiche, G., 16, 81
Reichel, L. G., 63
Reinecke, C., 304
Reinert (Reinhardt), C., 144
Reinert (Reinhardt), C. (?), 98
Reinhardt, B., 332
Reinold, B., 56
Reissiger, C. G., see online
Reiter, J. and F. X., 305
Rejoy, M., 298
Reppe, A., 95
Respighi, O., 319
Ribock, J. J. H., 140, 141, 142, 144
Ricci, V., 291fn9, 297
Richter, master smith, 230

Ricordi Company, 293
Riedl, J. F., 240, 243, 262, 263, 270, 293, 294, 299
  early rotary valves, 249
  price-list, 256
Riepl, J., 101
Ries, F., 194
Ristori, G. A., 61, 82, 83, 123
Rivet, M., 252
Rode, P., 169
Rode, T., 234
Rodenbostel, G. H., 135
Rodolfi, G., *see* Rodolphe, J. J.
Rodolphe, J. J., 95, 128, 136, 157, 162, 163
Roeser, V., 127
Roland, at Roncesvalles, 5
Rolla, A., 198
Röllig, J. G. (?), 98
Röllig, P., 43
Rombouts, T., 9
Rome, 38, 124
  early introduction of the horn, 67
  Museo degli Strumenti Musicali, 315
  Teatro Apollo, 295
  Trajan's column, 4
Romero y Andía, A., 297
  handbook, 298
Römhild, J. T., 78
Rosetti (Rösler), F. A., 171, 172, 173
Rossi, M., 38
Rossi, W., 63
Rossini G.
  challenging use of natural horn, 196
Rossini, G., 195, 196
  Aureliano in Palmira, horn solo, 200
  five duets, 177
  Matilde di Shabran, horn solo, 195
Roth, C., 254
Roth, F., 297
Rühlmann, J., 264
  on valve systems, 281
Russian horns, 214

Sacristá, M., 298
Saenger, G., 309
St. Francis, 5
St. Hubert, 43
St. Petersburg
  Museum of Theater and Music, 241
Salimbene of Parma, 5
Salzburg
  Museum Carolino-Augusteum, 32, 62
Samm, F. A., 64, 81, 99
Sandbach, W., 204
Sandhas, W., 150fn15

Sansone, L., 319, 335
Sanvitale, S., Count, 205
Sarti, G., 222
Sassaigne, F. F. M., 251
Sattler, C. F., 241, 243, 254
Saumur, France
  Church of Notre-Dame de Nantilly, 6
Saurle, M., 137, 156, 248, 254
  price-list, 155, 255
Sax, A., 250, 252, 260, 264, 265, 285, 289, 299
  compensating valve slide, 290
Sax, C., 221, 288
Sax, C. J., 252
Scarlatti, A., 61, 65, 68, 124
Scarlatti, D., 106
Scelsi, G., 332
Schamal, W., 249
Schediwy, F., 326
Scheffler, A., 106
Scheinhardt, C. S., 57
Schifer, composer, 102
Schindler, J. A. and A., 83, 99
Schlott, B. M., 257
Schmeltzer, J. H., 46, 47
Schmid, E., 325, 329, 330
Schmidt, C. F., 308fn1, 314
Schmidt, J. G., 149
Schmitz, H., 302
Schneider, F., 228
Schneider, G. A.
  early music for valve horn, 266
Schnitzer, A., 16
Schoeck, O., 322
Schoenaers, H., 285
Schöller, P., 120
Schön, horn player, 162
Schott Company, 246, 255
  price list, 155
Schubart, C. F. D., 60
Schubert, F., 194, 278
  Fünf Duette, 177
  horn writing, 193
  see also case study online
Schugt, Mr., inventor, 216, 218
Schuller, G., 333, 334
Schumann, R., 278, *see also case study online*
Schunke, A., 266, 267, 274
Schunke, C., 257
Schunke, J. and C., 266
Schürmann, G. C., 63
Schuster, F. W., 232, 257, 258, 262
Scott, R., 335

Selmer Company, 285, 311
Senlis, France
    Musée de la Vénerie, 30
Seraphinoff, R., 329
Shaw, A., 333
Shaw, L., 334
Shaw, W., 216
Shilkloper, A., 334
Sieber, J. G., 79, 128
Simonis, F., 238
Smeykal, H., 62
Smith & Sons, J., 204
Snedeker, J., 270, 333, 334
spiral horns, 13
    à plusieurs tours (Mersenne), 15
    Ballet de la délivrance, 1617, 15
    cors tortillez, 14fn3
    dismission, 14fn3
    engravings by W. Hollar, 14
    by Fayta, 13
    by Haas, 1688, 15
    Jägertrommet (Praetorius), 13
    Jeger-horn (Virdung), 13
    made in Dresden, a.1668
    in Mantua, 1486, 13
    by Pfeifer, 1697, 15
    pictured by Brughel, 14
    pictured by Rubens, 14
    pictured by van Balen, 14
    sculpured illustration in Versailles, 33
    by Springer, 15
Spohr, L., 194, 215, 293
Spontini, G., 188, 189, 233, 260, 262, 299
    on early valves, 234
Sporck, F. A. von, 42, 46, 56, 62, 63, 78, 140
Springer, V., 15
Stagliano, J., 335
Stählin, J. von, 212
Stamitz, C. P., 101, 173
Stará Voda, Silesia
    Piarist seminary, now destroyed, 80
Starck, H., 31, 45
Stare Křečany, Bohemia
    parish church inventory, 94
Starzer, K., 92, 137, 146
Steffani, A., 47
Steidle, P., 328
Steinmetz (Staimetz, Slamitz), F., 102
Steinmetz, G. F., 31, 45
Stich, J. V., *see* Punto, G.
Stockholm
    Scenkonst Museet, 145fn9
    Statens Musiksamlingar, 139
Stölzel, G. H., 69, 78

Stölzel, H., 227, 235, 236, 257, 260, 272
    about valve horn adoption, 233
    autographed letter, 1819, 228
    his music for valve horn, 266
    instrument maker, 228, 233
    inventor of box valves, 232
    patent request, 228, 229
stopped notes, 129, 132, 133, 134, 171, 172
    the sign +, 269, 306
    on valve horns, 264, 268, 284
    with mute, 179
    see also online "The Concerto by Gehra/
        Gehring"
Störl, J. G. C., 58
Stotherd, Mr., horn player, 210
Strauss, F., 305, 333
Strauss, J., Sr., 245
Strauss, R.
    on high B-flat horns, 306,
    see also case study online
Stravinsky, I., 334, 339
Strengel, J., 64
Stuttgart
    Jommelli's orchestra, 158
Suardi, M. & F., 95
Sundelin, A., 233
Süßmayr, F. X., 167fn41, 168
Sweda (Svída), W., 43
Syryyneck (Širineck), horn player, 102

taille d'amour, 213
Talbot, J., 54, 61
Tassis, F. de, 16
Taylor, M., 334
Tchaikovsky, P. I., *see case study online*
Teixeira, A., 106
Telemann, G. P., 78, 81, 124, *see also case
    study online*
Téniers, D. "le jeune," 33
terminology
    difference between *cor* and *trompe*,
        13fn1
    early, 112
    old ambiguity of the names "horns" and
        "trumpets," 33
    for valve and natural horn distinction, 277
Teyber, A., 173
Thévet, L., 311
Thibouville-Lamy Company, 291, 311
Thornhill, C., 333
Thun, J. J. von, 124, 168
Thurn und Taxis, family, 16
Thürrschmidt, C., 147, 173, 175, 176
Tiedt, O., 308fn1, 316

Todd, R., 334
Tognini, R., 199
Tommasini, F., 5
Torelli, G., 60
Tornauer, R., 304
Torri, P., 78
Tosoroni, A., 293, 320
    changing over to the valve horn, 294
    playing technique, 294
    treatise on orchestration, 294
    unique valve horn model, 294
Tossi, G., 64
Traetta, T., 124, 157
transposition
    cor mixte, 186
    criticism by Dauprat, 153
    criticism by Mayr, 155
    criticism by Prout, 291
    forced by Schuster's valve system, 258
    with high-pitched horns, 304
    lowest keys, 203
    in orchestral practice, 153
    for timbric homogeneity, 189
Trial, J. C., 128
triple horns
    Alexander, full, 330
    Paxman, compensating, 330
    Schmid, with E-flat descant, 330
trompe de chasse, 44, 61, 69
    à la dauphine, 72
    Orleans model, 72
    tayauté, 75
    see also coiled *trompe*; half-moon horn
trumpeters' privileges
    Mandaten, 15, 29
    transgressions, 15
    University of Jena, 16
    Weimar court, 16
trumpets
    circular, 28
    Inventionstrompete, 16fn7
    keyed, 216
    in post-horn shape, 17
    spiral, 13, 17, *see also* spiral horns
tuba, 3
Tuckwell, B., 326
Tuerlinckx, 288
    price list, 149, 153, 155
Tugend (virtue and bravery), 43
Türrschmidt family, 176
Türrschmidt, C., 153, 172, 178
Türrschmidt, J., 100
Tyson, A., 167fn41
Tzschimmer, G., 45

Uhlmann, L., 244, 281, 299
    and Italian market, 295
    price-list, 256
Ursinus, A. F., 48, 96
Utley, J. R., 282

Vachon, P., 162
valve horns
    with all slide crooks, 156
    with all terminal crooks, 156
    bassocorno by Anderst, 241
    chromatisches Waldhorn, 233, 243
    compensation system, 285
    cor sauterelle, 276, 285
    criticisms, 274
    early announcement, 228
    early composition, 234
    early handbooks, 269
    exceptionally used in France, 201
    French made, 234, 291
    Halevy, *La Juive*, 268
    high-pitched, 261fn4, 304
    an Italian judgement, 1844, 293
    at the Paris Conservatoire, 275
    by Pini and Dall'Asta, 238
    played badly in France, 288
    prompt acceptance by wind bands, 233,
        261fn4, 273
    right-handed, 273
    with two valves, 252
    unique Italian model, 294
    Viennese, with rotary valves, 283
valve slides, 251, 302
    compensating, 290
    by Halary, 263
    with long tenons, 282
    Maschinenhorn, 152fn16
    master slide, 119
    by Pini and Dall'Asta, 238
    two semitone slides of different rench,
        254
    on Viennese model, 244
valves
    "butterfly," 241
    Berliner Pumpen, 250, 260, 261, 264
    box, 229, 232, 257, 258, 261, 262
    "catholic," or Bavarian, 282
    clock spring action, 265
    cords driving the mechanism, 249
    crooks' substitutes, 269, 276, 286
    crooks' substitutes, 259, 263
    early set of three, 230, 241, 243, 255
    indipendent pistons, 289
    Klinkendruckwerk, 246

Neumainₓer Maschine, 246, 248, 265
Périnet, 250, 264, 303, 314
permutation system, 302
"pistons" in French, 262
plaques mobiles, 264
prototype (?) of Viennese type, 243
rotary, 232, 238, 240, 248, 261, 263, 264,
    265, 302
soupapes ou clapets, 264
spiral spring action, 262
Stölzel's model by Anderst, 243
système belge, 248
third ascending, 264, 265, 284
Tonwechselmaschine, 265
tubular, 229, 232, 233, 261, 264
two-tones, 252, 254
valvules ou clapets, 263
Viennese, 243, 244, 265, 283
van Cauwelaert, 288
Van Engelen Company, 288
van Loo, L. M., 106
Vandenbroek, O. J., 129, 177, 187
Varner, T., 334
Vaughan Williams, R., 292
Vecchietti, V., 295
Vegetius, F. R., 4
Vejvanovský, P., 47, 96
    Sonata da caccia con un cornu, 46
Venaria Reale, Turin, 22, 24, 26, 89
Venice, 68, 84
    Istituto della Pietà, 139
Verdi, G., *see case study online*
Vermillion
    National Music Museum, Utley Coll., 31
Vernier, J. A., 162
Vernon, Normandy
    working place of the Crétien family,
        12, 30
Vernsberg, C., 103
Versailles
    deer hunting, 24, 42
    visit of von Sporck, 42
Vibert, horn player, 102
Vicco family, 22
Vicco, C. G., 95
Vicco, C. P., 24
Vidal, L., 210
Vienna, 17, 82, 93, 94, 101, 119, 146
    Burgtheater, 165
    Imperial Music Academy, 240
    Philharmonic Orchestra, 200, 244, 283, 328
    Technisches Museum, 56
Vigevano, Italy
    Castle, 6

Villedieu-les-poêles, Normandy, 29
    famous foundries, 12
Vinci, L., 85
Visconti, M., 104
Vivaldi, A., 69, 81, 83, 85, 100, 101, 105, 124,
    139, *see also case study online*
Vivier, E., 268
Vlatković, R., 332
von Bülow, H., 304
Vuillermoz, L. and E., 311

Wagner tuba, *see online*
Wagner, R., *see case study online*
    preface to *Tristan und Isolde*, 306
    sign +, 269
    two valve and two natural horns,
        280
Waldhörner, 43, 50, 51, 58, 78, 92
    in chamber pitch, 53
    cornu sylvestre, 29
    franƶösische, 31, 45, 46
    instead of trumpets, 78
    or *litui*, 59, 94
    played like trumpets, 29
    in small ensemble, 57, 58
    of Viennese make, 94
Walsh, J., 109
Warrensburg, MO
    Don Essig Collection, 302
Warwick Castle, 5
Watkins, J., 333
Webb, J., 329
Weber, C. M. von, 169, 204
    advocating for the valve horn, 234
    evocative use of the horn, 193
Weber, G., 216, 222
Wecker, J. G., 95
Weidinger, A., 216
Weigel, J. C., 17, 29, 36, 51, 58
Weill, K., 334
Weiß, S., 82
Wellesley, A., duke of Wellington, 207
Wentzely, F. X., 59
Werckmeister, A., 80
Werner, J., 119, 123, 144, 146, 147
    earliest set of crooks (by him?), 94
    slide crooks' (?) inventor, 144
Wieprecht, W., 229, 232, 235, 250, 260
Wiesbach, F., 123
Wiesczeck (Vischek), maker, 43
Wilderer, H. von, 57
Wildvogel, C., 16
Wiley, K., 334
Woodbury, I. B., 299

INDEX

Wortley Montagu, M., 63
Wunderlich, R., 315

Zachow, F. W., 57, 89
Zdar nad Sázavou, Moravia
  monastery, 80
Zeddelmayer, J. T., 63

Zedler, J. H., 16
Zeitz, Saxony
  local band, 1715, 58
Zelenka, J. D., 81, 82, 101, 124
Ziwný brothers, 176
Zobel, E., 332
Zwierzina, F., 173, 175